SOCIAL LIFE
AND
SOCIAL KNOWLEDGE

The Jean Piaget Symposium Series
Series Editor:
Ellin Scholnick
University of Maryland

Available from LEA/Taylor and Francis

Overton, W.F. (Ed.): The Relationship Between Social and Cognitive Development.

Liben, L.S. (Ed): Piaget and the Foundations of Knowledge

Scholnick, E.K. (Ed): New Trends in Conceptual Representations: Challenges to Piaget's Theory?

Niemark, E.D., DeLisi, R. & Newman, J.L. (Eds.): Moderators of Competence.

Bearison, D.J. & Zimiles, H. (Eds.): Thought and Emotion: Developmental Perspectives.

Liben, L.S. (Ed.): Development and Learning: Conflict or Congruence?

Forman, G. & Pufall, P.B. (Eds.): Constructivism in the Computer Age.

Overton, W.F. (Ed.): Reasoning, Necessity, and Logic: Developmental Perspectives.

Keating, D.P. & Rosen, H. (Eds.): Constructivist Perspectives on Developmental Psychopathology and Atypical Development.

Carey, S. & Gelman, R. (Eds.): The Epigenesis of Mind: Essays on Biology and Cognition.

Beilin, H. & Pufall, P. (Eds.): Piaget's Theory: Prospects and Possibilities.

Wozniak, R.H. & Fisher, K.W. (Eds.): Development in Context: Acting and Thinking in Specific Environments.

Overton, W.F. & Palermo, D.S. (Eds.): The Nature and Ontogenesis of Meaning.

Noam, G.G. & Fischer, K.W. (Eds.): Development and Vulnerability in Close Relationships.

Reed, E.S., Turiel, E. & Brown, T. (Eds.): Values and Knowledge.

Amsel, E. & Renninger, K.A. (Eds.): Change and Development: Issues of Theory, Method, and Application.

Langer, J. & Killen, M. (Eds.): Piaget, Evolution, and Development.

Scholnick, E., Nelson, K., Gelman, S.A. & Miller, P.H. (Eds.): Conceptual Development: Piaget's Legacy.

Nucci, L.P., Saxe, G.B. & Turiel, E. (Eds.): Culture, Thought, and Development.

Amsel, E. & Byrnes, J.P. (Eds.): Language, Literacy, and Cognitive Development: The Development and Consequences of Symbolic Communication.

Brown, T. & Smith, L. (Eds.): Reductionism and the Development of Knowledge.

Lightfoot, C., LaLonde, C. & Chandler, M. (Eds.): Changing Conceptions of Psychological Life.

Parker, J., Langer, J., & Milbrath, C. (Eds.): Biology and Knowledge Revisited: From Neurogenesis to Psychogenesis.

Goncu, A., & Gaskins, S. (Eds.): Play and Development: Evolutionary, Sociocultural, and Functional Perspectives.

Overton, W., Mueller, U., & Newman., J. (Eds.): Developmental Perspectives on Embodiment and Consciousness.

Wainryb, C., Turiel, E., & Smetana, J. (Eds.): Social Development, Social Inequalities, and Social Justice.

Muller, U., Carpendale, J., Budwig, N., Sokol, B. (Eds.): Social Life and Social Knowledge: Toward a Process Account of Development.

SOCIAL LIFE
AND
SOCIAL KNOWLEDGE

Toward a Process Account of Development

Edited by

Ulrich Müller
Jeremy I. M. Carpendale
Nancy Budwig
Bryan Sokol

Lawrence Erlbaum Associates
Taylor & Francis Group

New York   London

Lawrence Erlbaum Associates
Taylor & Francis Group
270 Madison Avenue
New York, NY 10016

Lawrence Erlbaum Associates
Taylor & Francis Group
2 Park Square
Milton Park, Abingdon
Oxon OX14 4RN

Printed in the United States of America on acid-free paper
10 9 8 7 6 5 4 3 2

International Standard Book Number-13: 978-0-8058-6068-9 (Hardcover)

Library of Congress Cataloging-in-Publication Data

Social life and social knowledge : toward a process account of development / editors,
    Ulrich Müller ... [et al.].
        p. cm. -- (The Jean Piaget symposium series ; 37)
    Includes bibliographical references and index.
    ISBN-13: 978-0-8058-6068-9 (alk. paper) 1. Socialization. 2. Cognition and culture.
    3. Social psychology. I. Müller, Ulrich, 1944-

HM686.S63 2008
303.3'2--dc22   2007030267

Visit the Taylor & Francis Web site at
http://www.taylorandfrancis.com

and the LEA and Routledge Web site at
http://www.routledge.com

Contents

Contributors

Michael Bamberg—Clark University, Department of Psychology, Worcester, Massachusetts, USA

Tanya Behne—Max Planck Institute for Evolutionary Anthropology, Leipzig, Germany

Maximilian B. Bibok—Simon Fraser University, Department of Psychology, Burnaby, British Columbia, Canada

Mark H. Bickhard—Lehigh University, Department of Psychology, East Bethlehem, Pennsylvania, USA

Nancy Budwig—Clark University, Department of Psychology, Worcester, Massachusetts, USA

Jeremy I. M. Carpendale—Simon Fraser University, Department of Psychology, Burnaby, British Columbia, Canada

Malinda Carpenter—Max Planck Institute for Evolutionary Anthropology, Leipzig, Germany

Judy Dunn—King's College London, Institute of Psychiatry, London, UK

Gerard Duveen—Social and Developmental Psychology, University of Cambridge, Cambridge, UK

Maria Gräfenhain—Max Planck Institute for Evolutionary Anthropology, Leipzig, Germany

Christopher R. Hallpike—Gloucestershire, UK

Jessica Hobson—Tavistock Clinic and University College London, Developmental Psychopathology Research Unit, London, UK

Peter Hobson—Tavistock Clinic and University College London, Developmental Psychopathology Research Unit, London, UK

Charlie Lewis—Lancaster University, Psychology Department, Lancaster, UK

Kristin Liebal—Max Planck Institute for Evolutionary Anthropology, Leipzig, Germany

Ulf Liszkowski—Max Planck Institute for Evolutionary Anthropology, Leipzig, Germany

Jack Martin—Simon Fraser University, Faculty of Education, Burnaby, British Columbia, Canada

Henrike Moll—Max Planck Institute for Evolutionary Anthropology, Leipzig, Germany

Ulrich Müller—University of Victoria, Department of Psychology, Victoria, British Columbia, Canada

Charis Psaltis—University of Cyprus, Department of Psychology, Nicosia, Cyprus

Hannes Rakoczy—Max Planck Institute for Evolutionary Anthropology, Leipzig, Germany

Vasu Reddy—University of Portsmouth, Department of Psychology, King Henry Building, Portsmouth, UK

Bryan Sokol—St. Louis University, Department of Psychology, St. Louis, Missouri, USA

Michael Tomasello—Max Planck Institute for Evolutionary Anthropology, Leipzig, Germany.

Elliot Turiel—University of California, Berkeley, Graduate School of Education, Berkeley, California, USA

Felix Warneken—Max Planck Institute for Evolutionary Anthropology, Leipzig, Germany

Emily Wyman—Max Planck Institute for Evolutionary Anthropology, Leipzig, Germany

Preface

Human life is essentially social life. Describing and explaining the role of social interaction in development is thus an important task. Even though there is general agreement that social interaction plays an important role in development, there is considerable controversy regarding the nature and type of interactions that promote development. Furthermore, researchers also differ in terms of the general conceptual framework they use to conceive of and explain the relations between the individual and the social group. The present volume addresses these issues by examining the links between the development of forms of social life and the development of human forms of thought.

This volume is based on the 35th Annual Symposium of the Jean Piaget Society for the Study of Knowledge and Development, entitled, "Social Life and Social Knowledge," which met in Vancouver, British Columbia, Canada, June 2005. The authors contributing chapters to this book systematically explore the ways in which social interaction affects development in general, and social development, social cognition, and moral development in particular. The book is unique in that it systematically addresses the complex ways in which social interaction affects development, and it transcends narrow disciplinary boundaries by integrating approaches and insights from a variety of different disciplines, including developmental psychology, psychopathology, philosophy, anthropology, sociology, evolutionary biology, and primatology. By bringing together leading researchers from different disciplines, the book comprehensively addresses the following conceptual questions that are central to understanding human life and development. First, to what extent, if any, is the human form of social life reducible to its biological processes? Second, what are the psychological abilities that are constitutive of the specifically human form of social life? Third, what are the processes by means of which, and the contexts within which, these psychological abilities develop? Fourth, how should we conceptualize the links between social life and the development of thought—how do individuals and society contribute to these processes?

Given the recent interest in the question of how social interaction influences development, this book addresses a timely issue that should appeal to developmental psychologists in a variety of research areas, including (but not limited to) social cognition, social development, developmental psychopathology, and cognitive development. This book would also be of interest for psychologists, philosophers, primatologists, anthropologists, biologists, sociologists, and educational psychologists who are looking for up-to-date perspectives on both theoretical and empirical views on this topic. The volume is also suitable for upper-level undergraduate and graduate courses on social development, as well as seminars that focus on the intersection between social cognition, development, and culture.

We thank the Jean Piaget Society for the Study of Knowledge and Development for supporting the 2005 conference on which this volume is based. In particular, we thank the JPS board and President at the time, Elliot Turiel, and especially Eric Amsel, Michael Chandler, Chris Lalonde, Cynthia Lightfoot, Ashley Maynard, and Cecilia Wainryb for their sustained efforts in helping us make the conference a reality. The local organizing committee kept details organized so participants could focus on scholarly ideas. Thanks are also due to Ellin Kofsky Scholnick for her skill as series editor for the Jean Piaget Society symposium series. We want to close the preface by dedicating this volume to Lawrence Erlbaum who has provided tremendous guidance and generous support to the Jean Piaget Society over many years. Larry's openness to innovation and rigorous interdisciplinary study has fostered the lively exchange of ideas that has led to a better understanding of the development of knowledge. This book series forms part of his legacy, and we dedicate our volume to him as a small thank you for the many years of friendship and wisdom he has shared with society members.

ULRICH MÜLLER
JEREMY CARPENDALE
NANCY BUDWIG
BRYAN SOKOL

1

Developmental Relations between Forms of Social Interaction and Forms of Thought

An Introduction

Ulrich Müller, Jeremy I. M. Carpendale, Nancy Budwig, and Bryan Sokol

Human life is social life. "As soon as one observes phenomena that are specifically human, one enters the realm of the social. Man's specific humanity and his sociality are inextricably intertwined. *Homo sapiens* is always, and in the same measure, *homo socius*" (Berger & Luckmann, 1966, p. 49). The social nature of human life is attested by the unfortunate cases of "wild" children who grow up under conditions of extreme social isolation. From these sobering "natural experiments," it is clear that human development is intimately connected with the patterns of social life in which individuals are embedded. Even though philosophers have expended considerable efforts in creating thought-experiments that explore the logical possibility of isolated individuals (wolf-children, Robinson Crusoes) acquiring language and following social rules and norms, "all the evidence goes to show...their psychological impossibility.... Since actual cases of articulate Crusoes have not come up, we have not had to decide what to say about them" (Stevenson, 1993, p. 447).

But then, in a way, every creature is social, if simply for reasons of procreation. Thus, the question arises of what distinguishes the human form of social life from those of other species. The attempt to characterize the specifically human form of social life in turn raises a number of interrelated questions. First, to what extent, if any, is the human form of social life reducible to its biological constituents or constrained by biological adaptations unique to human beings? Second, what are the psychological abilities that are constitutive of the specifically human form of social life? Third, what are the processes by means of which, and the contexts within which, these psychological abilities develop? Fourth, how should we conceptualize the links between social life and the development of thought— how do individuals and society contribute to these processes? These questions, among others, are addressed in the chapters of this volume, from different theoretical angles, using different methodological approaches. In this introduction, we elaborate on the theoretical relevance of these questions for theories of social development, and we will use them as an organizing device to contextualize the contributions to this volume.

BIOLOGY AND SOCIAL LIFE

Any genuinely psychological contribution to the explanation of human social life rests on the irreducibility of social life to biological processes. This idea, of course, is not new and can be seen in the early work of such influential scholars as Lev Vygotsky (1934/1986), John Dewey (1925/1958), George Herbert Mead (1934), and James Mark Baldwin (1911). Baldwin's work, in particular, articulates a number of themes that are cornerstones of the sociogenetic view of human development (Valsiner & Van der Veer, 1988, 2000). The sociogenetic view can be characterized by two assumptions: (1) *"all human cognition is social in nature,"* and (2) *"the social nature of human cognition emerges in the process of internalization of external social experiences by individuals in the process of socialization"* (Valsiner & Van der Veer, 1988, p. 118; emphasis in original). However, these assumptions raise many issues about the nature of this process and the conceptualization of internalization (see Susswein, Bibok, & Carpendale, in press, on the issue of internalization).

With respect to the relation between human life and biology, Baldwin held that there must be a particular psychological relation or mental bond between humans for a human society to exist, and that to reduce this mental bond to biological conditions would miss what is specific to human society (Baldwin, 1911, p. 31). In his book on the individual and society, Baldwin (1911) distinguished between three different modes of social or collective life: the instinctive, the spontaneous, and the reflective. In the instinctive mode, social interactions are stereotypical, fixed, and not progressive. "We may say, then, that such instinctive actions, however psychological their results may appear to be, *are in their modus operandi biological reactions.* They can be explained only on the biological principles of selection and inheritance" (Baldwin, 1911, p. 38; emphasis in original). For Baldwin, these constrained forms of interaction restrict the emergence of any authentic social experience. They are not, as Baldwin claims, "in any true sense social. They appear to show external solidarity, but this does not require any degree of psychic community" (Baldwin, 1911, p. 39).

In the spontaneous mode, social interaction is based on behavior learned through experience. The learning is characterized as trial-and-error learning, "persistent imitation, gradual selection of happy hits in the direction of better accommodation and adjustment" (Baldwin, 1911, p. 41). These acquired modes of collective action illustrate social transmission rather than physical heredity, and require that the individual is plastic in the sense of being "relatively free from the compulsion of inherited instinct" (Baldwin, 1911, p. 42). Even though social interactions in the spontaneous mode are based on psychological processes, they are limited by their conservative link to collective pressures: "The individual grows into the tradition of the group.... The individual does not go by this method beyond what the group has already acquired; his learning is limited to tradition. All individuals of the group *learn the same things*; and what they learn is the body of useful actions already established in the collective life of the group" (Baldwin, 1911, p. 43; emphasis in original).

Finally, the reflective mode involves intentional and voluntary cooperation among individuals in the pursuit of intelligent ends. It is only the reflective mode of cooperation that "constitutes a group that may properly be called 'social'" (Baldwin, 1911, p. 46). The modes of action and thought characteristic of the reflective mode are social novelties, and they make it possible for individuals to be critical of and go beyond established conventions and traditions. The reflective mode "unifies the individual and society, and establishes solidarity on the higher plane of common intelligence and joint volitions" (Baldwin, 1911, p. 49).

Baldwin (1911, p. 35) believed that these different modes of social life are genetically related and represent "a progressive development in actual social association and organization, as advance is made in the scale of animal life." In addition, Baldwin linked these different modes of social life to "the evolution of mind" (Baldwin, 1911, p. 35). With successive development, external social relations established through instinct or habit are (re-)constructed by internally motivated, intentional, and voluntary relations. These latter forms of social life cannot be explained on the basis of purely biological principles; rather, they represent a qualitative novelty.

Baldwin's proposal presupposes that new forms of social life emerge that are not reducible to biological processes. This raises the question as to the conditions that make the emergence of new forms of life possible. At the most general level, one may ask for the metaphysical framework within which emergence is possible because emergence "is a difficult and sometimes contentious issue" (Bickhard, 2003, p. 105). To characterize phenomena as emergent, it is necessary that these phenomena are not just epiphenomenal but have causal consequences at lower levels of organization: "we should find downward causation from emergent phenomena" (Bickhard, 2003, p. 107).

In chapter 2, Bickhard argues that explaining the emergence of the individual as a social person is only possible within a theoretical framework of process metaphysics. The framework of substance metaphysics, by contrast, forecloses the possibility of the emergence of a social person. Process metaphysics is based on the general assumption that entities are in a continuous state of flux and progressive change, or becoming, which is constitutive of their being (Fetz, 1988). Piaget's genetic epistemology, for example, is based on these assumptions of process metaphysics because, according to Piaget, life is essentially self-organization, and "the very nature of life is constantly to overtake itself" (Piaget, 1967/1971, p. 362; see Chapman, 1992).

After demonstrating that a process metaphysical framework avoids several problems encountered by a substance theoretical framework, Bickhard lays out, within a process metaphysics, how the organism's interactions with the world allows for the construction of increasingly complex levels of functioning that result in the specifically human level of social reality. Each ontological emergence provides opportunities for new interactions, which, in turn, result in new realities and, thus, new opportunities for interaction. As Bickhard shows, a process metaphysical framework has numerous implications for the conceptualization of representation, language, social reality, culture, and values. Social reality and social persons are not independent but constitutive of each other, and language, in particular, is the major social institution creating and transforming that reality. Culture, within this framework, represents the sedimentation of social constructions (i.e., the historic aspect of social realities), and it constrains and provides opportunities for (but does not shape) the ontogenetic construction of persons.

WHAT ABILITY IS SPECIFIC TO HUMAN SOCIALITY?

In order to delineate human social life from other (animal) forms of social life, Baldwin referred to a mental bond that makes possible the intentional cooperation among individuals characteristic of the specifically human form of social life. Baldwin's idea has been further elaborated by George Herbert Mead (1934), who suggested that it is the ability to take the perspective of another person toward the self that distinguishes the human form of social life from animal social life. By taking the perspective of the other toward myself, my actions become mediated through the other, as, reciprocally, the actions of the other are mediated through me.

Following Mead, psychologists and philosophers have argued that the ability to take a perspective on oneself is the foundation of language, thinking, and personhood. The reciprocity of perspectives, as Plessner (1983a, p. 332) suggests, is the foundation on which language is built: "when I am speaking, I am as another, exchangeable with the other because I am steeped into the reciprocity of perspectives already built into the structure of language" (our translation). In a similar vein, Tomasello (1999) suggests that the use of language is based on the reciprocity of perspectives, or what he calls role-reversal learning. Role-reversal learning is a prerequisite for the understanding of a symbol in a conventionally appropriate way; in order to understand vocal utterances as symbols the child must realize that the other person makes a vocal utterance in order to direct the child's attention toward some third entity (Tomasello, 1999, p. 103). In addition, the use of vocal utterances as conventional symbols (i.e., spoken language) requires that "the child must learn to use a symbol toward the adult in the same way the adult used it toward her" (Tomasello, 1999, p. 105). Hobson (2002/2004), in turn, argues that the ability to take the perspective of another person onto herself enables the child to begin "to *think* in terms of her own and others' perspectives.… Through others, she gains a vantage-point from which to relate to her own attitudes and actions" (p. 106; emphasis in original). The reciprocity of perspectives constitutes person-hood by distancing the relation of a human being to the world. In this manner, the reciprocity of perspectives makes possible self-reference (i.e., reflexivity) and the notion of an inner mental life (interiority). As a result of the reciprocity of perspectives, "the human being conceives of herself as a person, which means, according to Kant, that she can, as the only living creature, say 'me' to herself" (Plessner, 1983b, p. 330, our translation).

The idea that personhood is intimately related to perspective taking is taken up by Jack Martin in chapter 3. Martin understands persons as *embodied selves and agents (both rational and moral) with social and psychological identities, and rights and duties, who care about and can understand something of their existence and circumstances"* (p. 49, emphasis in original). Similar to Bickhard, and consistent with a process metaphysical framework, Martin suggests that our biological constitution is a necessary but not a sufficient condition for the emer-gence of persons. Martin grounds personhood in social interactions and practices. In particular, drawing on Mead, Martin suggests that through the participation in joint social interactions (such as social games) children learn to "differenti-ate, integrate and coordinate the different perspectives associated with different phases in such interactions" (p. 57). Because the perspectives of others are often directed toward the child him- or herself, the child, by reacting to these perspec-tives, essentially becomes aware of his own perspective and develops a reflec-tive form of self-understanding. Reflexive self-understanding, in turn, is a core process in the emergence of personhood. Thus, perspective taking is constitutive of personhood, and persons have a social ontology. Martin concludes that "our personhood issues from our active participation in interpersonal interactions and sociocultural practices, and the perspectives that such active participation makes available to us" (p. 60).

Contemporary research on the social abilities of other species has further clarified the structure of the social bond that underlies human culture. The aim of chapter 4 by Behne and colleagues is to identify, from a comparative perspective, the ontogenetic roots that enable the uniquely human abilities for cultural learning and creation. Behne and colleagues summarize their systematic line of research that compares the social abilities of human infants and great apes. Specifically, the chapter reviews infants' and chimpanzees' understanding of intentional action and perception, shared attention abilities, communication, collaboration, and pre-tence. Based on their findings, Behne and colleagues distinguish between two different ontogenetic pathways, with each pathway reflecting a distinct biological adaptation. The first pathway, which is shared among the great apes (and possibly all primates), concerns the understanding of intentional action and perception. The second pathway is constituted by the uniquely human motivation to share psychological states with others and is evident in the dyadic exchanges between infants and their caregivers. In human ontogeny, the two pathways intersect with the emergence of triadic interaction at the end of the first year of life, and infants start to share with other people attention to outside objects, as manifest in joint attention, collaborative co-operation, and symbolic communication. Chimpanzees lack the ability to share intentionality with another individual in collaborative actions, but this ability emerges in human infants in the second year of life. Returning to the theme of reciprocity developed above, shared intentionality requires the reciprocity of perspectives because both individuals engaged in collaborative action must take the attitude of the other individual toward their own actions.

Behne and colleagues then raise the question as to how these two strands of ontogeny come together for cultural learning and cultural creation. They suggest that human infants differ from great apes in that they have a stronger motivation to share psychological states and engage in shared activities. Thus, in contrast to their earlier view (Tomasello, 1999), Behne and colleagues highlight that both social-cognitive (the understanding of perception and intentional action) and emotional-motivational (motivation to share psychological states) are important in explaining the uniquely human abilities for cultural learning.

Complementing this comparative line of research, Peter Hobson and Jessica Meyer in chapter 5 also address the question of what makes human forms of social cognition unique, as well as how human culture and language are possible, by comparing typically developing children with children with autism. As is commonly known, children with autism display extreme social deficits, despite being raised in caring and responsive environments. For Hobson and Meyer, characterizing the atypical social relations of individuals with autism not only helps to explain the core features of the disorder, but also the socially constitutive nature of thought in typically developing children. They argue that social relations require that one understands the other as a source of subjective orientation. The development of this understanding is not a process in the course of which infants learn to gradually infuse bodies with minds, but rather a process in which they acquire an understanding of how people who are differently endowed in bodily terms have their own separate perspectives and selves in relation to a common world. "This requires that we characterize preconceptual, affectively charged, relational foundations for self-concepts, and provide an account of how the infant moves from *experiencing* to *understanding* person–world psychological relations" (p. 106, emphasis in original). Central and specific to the human form of life is the ability to identify with the attitudes of another person. "The critical feature of this particular kind of interpersonal connectedness and communicative exchange is that one person's experience encompasses that of another in such a way that the other's attitude is assumed *in part*, without loss of 'otherness' in what is identified-with" (pp. 108, emphasis in original). Hobson and Meyer's own research shows that children with autism have impairments in intersubjective engagement. Hobson and Meyer argue that children with autism lack the ability to identify with the bodily attitude of another person. In typical development, identification leads to the objectification of the self as a holder of person-centered attitudes; that is, identification leads to an awareness of perspectives and prepares the stage for language and thinking.

PROCESSES, CONTEXTS, AND THE DEVELOPMENT OF SPECIFIC HUMAN SOCIAL ABILITIES

Identifying abilities that make the human form of social life possible is only the first step; the second step—which is, in some way, addressed in all contributions to this volume—is to describe the processes that lead to the emergence of these abilities and to explicate how these abilities are transformed in the course of development. Different processes have been suggested to account for the unique human social abilities. These accounts differ in terms of the basic assumptions guiding them, how much they attribute to innate biological endowment, and the particular process that is referred to explain the development of human social abilities.

One key difference between various accounts of social abilities is whether they assume that the infant is separate from the other—"children begin as individuals and then become social" (Hobson, 2002, p. 259)—or forms a relational matrix with the other (interpersonal sphere is primary). Hobson (2002, p. 259) termed the former account the "joining-together" account, and the latter the "differentiating-out account." According to the joining-together account, the major task of the infant is to become engaged with other people; emphasis is placed on the matching of states and experiences that lead to the inference that the other person is "like me" (analogical argument; see Meltzoff, 2007). "The joining-together account says that the baby perceives bodies and then infers the existence of minds…and that children begin with their own thoughts, and then learn to communicate with others" (Hobson, 2002, p. 258). By contrast, the differentiating-out account argues that children derive thoughts and feelings and concepts of body and mind from something composite, person-centered modes of relatedness: "The differentiating-out approach says that children begin with an ability to communicate with others, and through communication they distil out thoughts-for-themselves" (Hobson, 2002, p. 258).

The joining-together account is deeply rooted in a Cartesian framework that assumes (1) the perception of other persons consists in the perception of physical bodies, and (2) the isolated ego is the primary datum of experience, and experience of other persons is derived from the experience of the ego (Müller, Carpendale, Bibok, & Racine, 2006). In contemporary theorizing, these assumptions can be seen at work in the idea that infants and children take a theoretical stance toward understanding another person because they have no direct access toward the other person's mental life (Gallagher, 2004). For example, according to theory theory (Gopnik & Meltzoff, 1997), the infant is a little scientist who holds and tests theories that "involve abstract theoretical entities, with coherent causal relations among them" (Gopnik & Meltzoff, 1997, p. 41). This position implies that all kinds of knowledge—"even apparently 'ordinary' kinds of knowledge, like our knowledge that this is a jar and that is a table" (Gopnik & Meltzoff, 1997, p. 44)—are considered to be theoretical knowledge, based on "the application of everyday theories" (Gopnik & Meltzoff, 1997, p. 44). In addition, infants are said to behave like scientists in that they make predictions, produce interpretations, and give abstract, coherent, and causal explanations (Gopnik & Meltzoff, 1997, pp. 36–38).

Although a contemplative, "theoretical" attitude is certainly important in more advanced levels of cognitive functioning, from a developmental perspective it seems implausible to imagine that it characterizes the starting point of social understanding. Rather, proponents of a more relationally oriented differentiating-out approach argue that the concrete experience of the attitude of the other person in affectively charged relationships grounds the development of social understanding. Social development takes place against the "background of sharing" (Hobson, 2002, p. 259). This point is forcefully made by Vasudevi Reddy in chapter 6. Central to Reddy's approach is the distinction between different types of social relationships that ground not only perspective taking (and personhood) but awareness of all aspects of the world. In contradistinction to a third-person ("I–it") approach, she adopts, drawing on Buber (1923/1937), a second-person ("I–thou") approach to highlight the importance of direct experience of otherness for the development of self- and other-awareness: "In an I–Thou engagement with an 'other' we *experience* the other in a way that is not available in more reflective, detached I-It relations" (p. 124, emphasis in original). Second- and third-person relationships differ in a number of ways. In second-person relationships, the other is concretely experienced in his or her affective and bodily presence in mutual engagement; individuals adopt a personal attitude and recognize each other as persons. Furthermore, compared to third-person relationships these second-person relationships are emotionally more intense and open. Being addressed by another person as "You" is vital for existing as a self: "It is when I as an individual am noticed by someone who talks to me as a person, who addresses me as a You, who recognizes me as an individual consciousness, that I begin to exist as a Self" (p. 131).

The emphasis on second-person relationships counters the assumption of the Cartesian epistemological framework that we have only indirect access to another person's mind. A second-person approach to social development assumes that the other is directly experienced. Reddy takes the awareness of attention as an example to illustrate the primacy of second person relations and their significance for awareness of other minds. She argues that the awareness of another person requires that the infant must experience being perceived by another person. Based on a review of empirical research, Reddy suggests that there is evidence that infants from very early on are aware of the gaze of the other. Reddy sketches a developmental sequence of self-awareness according to which infants gradually expand the objects to which another person's attention can be directed (self-body, actions, distal objects). According to Reddy, children with autism have problems with I–Thou relations, specifically, with the emotional significance of I–Thou relations.

The argument that infants develop a more reflective level of social understanding from practical, embodied interactions with other people is developed further in chapter 7 by Bibok, Carpendale, and Lewis. Bibok and colleagues critically examine the currently dominant representational theory of mind framework, particularly the assumption that knowledge is attained when one holds a mental representation that matches with a true state of affairs in the world. They argue that this assumption is fundamentally flawed, and that social understanding cannot be attained in the manner proposed by this framework. As an alternative, Bibok and colleagues suggest that social understanding is based on action and develops as the child interacts with his or her social environment. Within the action-based approach, social understanding is conceptualized as social skill. Social skills are practical and person-directed abilities that children gradually develop in particular types of situations and social contexts. Knowledge is embodied in skills as interactive potential or know-how. In infancy, social skills develop as infants respond to the social behaviors of their parents. Infants and parents share the same human resources so "infants inevitably come to construct social skills which are reciprocal to those of their parents" (p. 157).

Language is essential in the transition from a practical to a reflective level of social understanding. Based on the social skills developed in infancy, language, in turn, provides opportunities for the development of more complex forms of social skills. In the process of learning how to use words that pertain to practical skills, children begin to become reflectively aware and conceptualize these skills: "The development of conceptual knowledge via language allows children self-reflectively to contemplate and understand at a new level what was previously a practical and nonverbal form of knowledge" (pp. 161–162). Bibok, Carpendale, and Lewis discuss implications of their action-based approach for the conceptualization of internalization and nonhuman social intelligence.

The chapters by Hobson and Meyer as well as Reddy suggest that affectively charged, intimate I–you relationships are particularly important for social development in early infancy. In chapter 8, Judy Dunn draws our attention to the links between toddlers' and preschoolers' social relationships and their developing social understanding. She points out that during the period between 18 months and 3 years children show great development in their understanding of what others are thinking and feeling, and demonstrate "increasingly effective powers of teasing, deceiving, joking and comforting," as well as consolidation in "their skills of conciliation, of companionship in shared fantasy play" (p. 171). This early social competence contrasts with their comparatively disappointing performance on standard tests of false belief understanding. This discrepancy directs our attention to a number of factors but particularly to young children's emotionally significant personal relationships. What Dunn draws from this is that children are motivated to understand others in their close personal relationships, and the development of social understanding is based on communication within such relationships. Young children are embedded in emotionally saturated personal relationships, and their early social understanding is manifest as they try to "get things done" in these relationships: teasing, managing conflict, cooperating in shared pretence where it is crucial to understand what the other person is thinking or planning, anticipating what a sibling is doing to gain parental attention. According to Dunn, children acquire and exercise their social understanding in the pursuit of practical goals before they can use this understanding to reason about detached and decontextualized problems such as those presented in the experimental procedures of standard false belief tasks.

Examining individual differences in social development shows that factors such as cooperative play with older siblings, participation in talk about feelings and thoughts, disputes between mothers and siblings, secure attachment, parental education, and attitudes are all related to advanced understanding of beliefs (for reviews see Carpendale & Lewis, 2004, 2006). This evidence of links between social development and relationships raises the question of the causal direction involved. Dunn reviews evidence that early social understanding is related to later relationship quality in terms of factors such as smoother communication, more insight regarding friends' needs and feelings, increased moral sensitivity, and greater skill in resolving conflicts. Dunn also notes evidence for the opposite causal direction. For example, children in relationships characterized by secure attachment tend to be advanced in social development. Thus, there seem to be bidirectional relations between social development and relationships. Dunn suggests that further exploring the link between relationships and social development would involve examining questions such as how children's social understanding is related to particular relationships.

The role of interaction within different relationships for social-cognitive development is also addressed by Duveen and Psaltis (chapter 9) and Bamberg (chapter 10). However, whereas the previous chapters describe processes such as identification and participation at a large-scale level, these two chapters offer a more fine-grained description capturing the moment-to-moment processes that make up these more general levels. The analysis of the fine-grained, microgenetic process of negotiating relationships, identity, and power, and how these moment-to-moment negotiations influence social and cognitive development illuminates, contextualizes, and fills with life the large-scale processes underlying social development.

Duveen and Psaltis (chapter 9) examine, from a microgenetic perspective, the relations between social interaction and cognitive development, and illustrate the subtle process of negotiating cooperative and mutual relationships. Their approach is based on the idea, systematically developed by Doise and Mugny (1984), that sociocognitive conflict promotes cognitive development. Following Piaget (1932),

Duveen and Psaltis distinguish between asymmetrical social relationships (constraint), where individuals have unequal power, and symmetrical relationships (cooperation), where individuals have equal power. They argue that only the latter type of relationships allow for authentic forms of intellectual exchange. A central question in this work, however, is how best to capture the many dimensions of social relations on which symmetries and asymmetries may occur. Duveen and Psaltis examine this issue by presenting same sex and opposite sex pairs with problems requiring collaborative solutions and studying the consequences of interaction for cognitive development. Expecting to find power differentials between opposite sex pairs, their analysis more clearly shows the importance of the microgenetic structure and content of conversations for cognitive development apart from other influences of gender. Furthermore, Duveen and Psaltis demonstrate that different types of conversation have different consequences for cognitive development. In particular, they show that cognitive development is promoted in situations in which a balanced triadic structure of child-child-task is established. In such a balanced triadic structure each child actively participates in the process of structuring and solving the task, and different viewpoints are expressed and coordinated in such a way that each child is recognized as an active contributor to the solution. Thus, circumstances beneficial for cognitive development are those in which "children engage with their peer and the task as active agents, responsible for their own perspective and responsive to the perspective of the other. Participation in this sense is the cooperative moment at the heart of children's interactions" (p. 201).

In chapter 10, Michael Bamberg takes a process orientation to the development of identity within social interaction by examining particular situations in which identity is negotiated. He focuses on two aspects of identity, in particular: (1) the "identity dilemma" ("How it is possible to consider oneself as the same in the face of constant change?"), and (2) the "who-is-in-charge-dilemma" ("Does the person construct the social world or is the person constructed by the world?"). Unlike other, more sociologically driven accounts, Bamberg attempts to link the micro and the macro of our social world not by starting with preexisting societal forces that shape individuals from the outside, but instead by showing how such social structures are the "*products* or *outcomes* of individual actions in interaction" (p. 212, emphasis in original). To be clear, this does not mean that Bamberg takes an individualistic approach. Instead, he argues that it is from within situations of actual social engagement that a sense of self and other is constructed. In Piaget's terms, this approach rejects both collectivist and individualist accounts and posits, instead, a relational approach. If social interaction influences development, this influence must occur within particular situations of social engagement. Macro- and microsocial worlds are linked within concrete situations of social engagement in which individuals position themselves in relation to dominant discourses or "master narratives"—either aligned with or in opposition to them. In this way sociogenesis naturally implicates the microgenesis of social engagement within local situations.

Although identity tends to be considered a global characteristic that individuals carry with them through multiple situations across time, Bamberg's approach takes the opposite tack by emphasizing how identity is constructed within particular sequences of social engagement. More specifically, Bamberg takes an approach he characterizes as microethnography: a technique for analyzing the microgenesis of identity within brief moments of interaction. His chapter presents a microanalysis of a group of 10-year-old boys engaged in discussion in which they try out and negotiate identities. Bamberg analyzes the way in which the referential world is constructed in the process of interaction. This entails determining how the participants want to be understood making their sense of self manifest.

THE INDIVIDUAL AND SOCIETY

For Baldwin, as mentioned above, some of the distinctive characteristics of human social life are rooted in its generative potential that allows for the emergence of social novelties, social criticism, and opposition. Given such generativity, however, it is important to clarify the constraints that society places on the individual's acquisition of knowledge. According to the sociogenetic view, individuals acquire knowledge by internalizing social experiences in the process of socialization. One of the more problematic features of this view concerns the ambiguity associated with the process of internalization. On the one hand, internalization may refer to a passive process in which the individual simply absorbs external social experiences (transmission). On the other, internalization may refer to a process of active reconstruction and appropriation of external social experiences (transformation). Closely tied to the challenge of clarifying the ambiguous meaning of internalization are serious questions about the nature of rationality (i.e., whether "truth" is a matter of mere conventionality or is universalizable), culture and social context (i.e., whether they are understood as separate structures from individual interactions), human agency (whether individuals are "free" in any robust sense), and (perhaps more practically) the unit of analysis for conducting psychological research (i.e., whether a focus on the individual is appropriate or even possible). A constructivist approach such as Piaget's begins to engage some of these problems by highlighting the child's active role in the construction of knowledge.

Piaget was a staunch critic of the transmission model of internalization. For him, particularly, social transmission failed to explain why an individual may criticize collective beliefs in the name of human rights and truth, thereby contrasting "the universal to the collective, i.e., 'truth' to 'opinion'" (Piaget, 1977/1995, p. 185). Following this line of reasoning, a transmission model of internalization encounters two fundamental problems (see Duveen & Psaltis, this volume). First, it fails to account for social change and social opposition. Second, it leaves no room for the experience of normative autonomy. This latter point has been articulated by Boesch (1992): "Knowledge, thus, is not simply 'received', absorbed, but assimilated, thereby undergoing multiple processes of selection, transformation, and integration into individual systems of action" (p. 93).

In chapter 11, Hallpike applies this notion that social knowledge is a constructive process to a sociohistorical analysis of moral concepts. Drawing on the theories of moral development by Piaget and Kohlberg, Hallpike shows similarities in the historical and ontogenetic development of moral reasoning. He suggests that collective representations of what is right and wrong are not passively absorbed by individuals, but are appropriated in an active process of assimilation:

> Collective representations, like the game of marbles or parliamentary democracy, may have been produced by social collaboration, but they all have to be learned and handed on from one generation to the next by *individuals*, and because individuals can only transmit ideas as they each understand them, their cognitive capacities must have a fundamental influence on the collective representations that they learn, develop, and pass on to subsequent generations. (p. 230, emphasis in original)

Hallpike argues that moral rules develop with societal complexity, accounting for the general correlation between the historical and the psychological development of moral thinking. However, because moral rules cannot simply be transmitted but need to be reconstructed with each new generation, this correlation is not a direct product of growing social complexity by itself. Instead, the relationship is due to a dialectical process between social and psychological factors. The dialectic is played out in social institutions and their changes that, although created by human individuals, take on a life of their own. Individuals, in turn, deal with "living" social institutions by cognitively creating new collective representations. Hallpike presents two case studies that illustrate that less complex forms of moral thinking are associated with small-scale atomistic societies, and more complex forms of moral thinking are associated with larger, corporate societies.

Different ways of conceptualizing the influence of society and culture on autonomy and rationality are the focus of chapter 12 by Turiel. Drawing on classic psychoanalytic and behaviorist theories that deny individuals freedom and choice in the process of decision making, Turiel illustrates how many contemporary theories (despite some conceptual distance from these more classic accounts) make similar assumptions about individual autonomy, or lack thereof. For example, in recent social psychological approaches to decision making, rational consideration and choice are reduced to a series of heuristics, rules, biases, or emotional intuitions. In still other models, rational decision making is reduced to principles of maximizing self-benefits, making rationality little more than an economic strategy of weighing costs and benefits. All of these approaches neglect the variety of goals that individuals have or the diversity of their experiences. Most importantly, however, Turiel argues that these approaches fundamentally deny individuals any real sense of agency.

Turiel argues that decisions are not just the application of a rule or principle and further suggests that decision-making is not bounded in one domain. Rather, it involves coordination with domains such as morality, prudence, convention, and personal jurisdiction. Consistent with other research showing the diversity of considerations that individuals apply in moral decisions (e.g., Carpendale, 2000; Carpendale & Krebs, 1992, 1995; Krebs, Denton, Vermeulen, Carpendale, & Bush, 1991), Turiel demonstrates how decisions to act morally involve a complex coordination of domains. Counter, then, to Kohlberg who argued for a principle of consistency in the application of a unified global structure of moral thought, Turiel points to the many inconsistencies in individuals' reasoning and how these inconsistencies can be addressed by identifying distinct domains of thought. According to Turiel, development occurs in these domains and distinct social experiences are associated with different domains. Individuals distinguish different social domains and from an early age construct forms of reasoning within their interaction in these differing domains. Culture does not determine choices; individuals examine and critique cultural practices. Culture does not constrain individual's moral judgments, and, thus, according to Turiel, there is room for agency and the construction of new forms of thought.

CONCLUSION

The authors of the chapters in this volume grapple with an important set of questions concerning the links between forms of social life and the development of human forms of thought. The authors address different problems such as cognitive, social cognitive, moral, and identity development at various ages and take different approaches to these topics. Despite this diversity, a number of common themes run through the chapters:

First, even though the human infant is biologically preadapted to interact with others, the human form of social life is not reducible to biology but constitutes an emergent level of reality. Second, essential to the human form of social life and to personhood is the ability to take the perspective of another person. Third, this perspective-taking ability gradually emerges over the first two years of life, starting with the emotionally charged, face-to-face interactions between infant and caregiver ("I-Thou"), and, through increasing differentiation (e.g., by being moved into the attitude of the other, by violating expectations, and by comparison and contrast; Piaget, 1954; Royce 1894, 1895).

Fourth, different types of relationships, as well as language, are reciprocally linked to social skills. The quality of relationships affects social and cognitive development in infancy and childhood, but social and cognitive development, in turn, affect the types of relationships that are constructed. Similarly, language is learned in the context of embodied, practical interactions between the infant and other people, but the emergence of language—because it is a condition of reflective self-awareness—enables children to engage in more complex forms of social interaction and social-cognitive growth (Budwig, 2003; Carpendale & Lewis, 2006).

Fifth, and finally, larger social structures influence development, but do this through particular microcontexts of social engagement, and their influence depends on the individual's level of cognitive development. Rather than a case of simple transmission, the internalization of knowledge is an active process of transformation, thereby illustrating the constant interaction between the individual and society. Different forms of thought emerge within particular social (relationship) contexts, and, in turn, different relationships and social contexts depend on different forms of thought.

In conclusion, the chapters in this volume forcefully make the point that persons and human forms of thought are socially constituted. At the same time, the chapters address many conceptual problems that arise when thinking about the relation between social life and the individual, and offer unique solutions to these problems. The chapters converge on the conclusion that the relations between social interaction, social understanding, and thinking, between social interaction and language, and between individual and society are reciprocal and cannot be assimilated to unidirectional models of causality. In this manner, the chapters provide a conceptual framework for future research that aims at a better understanding of the processes in which we engage in creating the human form of life.

References

Baldwin, J. M. (1911). *The individual and society.* Boston: Durham Press.

Berger, P. L., & Luckmann, T. (1966). *The social construction of reality.* Garden City, NY: Doubleday.

Bickhard, M. H. (2003). The biological emergence of representation. In T. Brown & L. Smith (Eds.), *Reductionism and the development of knowledge* (pp. 105–131). Mahwah, NJ: Lawrence Erlbaum.

Boesch, E. E. (1992). Culture-individual-culture: The cycle of knowledge. In M. von Cranach, W. Doise, & G. Mugny (Eds.), *Social representation and the social bases of knowledge* (pp. 89–95). Lewiston, NY: Hogrefe & Huber.

Buber, M. (1937). *I and thou.* London: T. & T. Clark. (Original work published 1923)

Budwig, N. (2003). Context and the dynamic construal of meaning in early childhood. In C. Raeff & J. Benson (Eds.), *Social and cognitive development in the context of individual, social, and cultural processes* (pp. 103–130). London: Routledge.

Carpendale, J. I. M. (2000). Kohlberg and Piaget on stages and moral reasoning. *Developmental Review, 20,* 181–205.

Carpendale, J. I. M., & Krebs, D. L. (1992). Situational variation in moral judgment: In a stage or on a stage? *Journal of Youth and Adolescence, 21,* 203–224.

Carpendale, J. I. M., & Krebs, D. L. (1995). Variations in level of moral judgment as a function of type of dilemma and moral choice. *Journal of Personality, 63,* 289–313.

Carpendale, J. I. M., & Lewis, C. (2004). Constructing an understanding of mind: The development of children's social understanding within social interaction. *Behavioral and Brain Sciences, 27,* 79–151.

Carpendale, J. I. M., & Lewis, C. (2006). *How children develop social understanding.* Malden, MA: Blackwell.

Chapman, M. (1992). Equilibration and the dialectics of organization. In H. Beilin & P. Pufall (Eds.), *Piaget's theory: Prospects and possibilities* (pp. 39–59). Hillsdale, NJ: Lawrence Erlbaum.

Dewey, J. (1958). *Experience and nature.* New York: Dover. (Original work published 1925)

Doise, W., & Mugny, G. (1984). *The social development of the intellect*. Oxford: Pergamon.

Fetz, R. L. (1988). On the formation of ontological concepts: The relationship between the theories of Whitehead and Piaget. *Process Studies, 17,* 262–272.

Gallagher, S. (2004). Understanding interpersonal problems in autism: Interaction theory as an alternative to theory of mind. *Philosophy, Psychiatry, and Psychology, 11,* 199–217.

Gopnik, A., & Meltzoff, A. N. (1997). *Words, thoughts, and theories*. Cambridge, MA: MIT Press.

Hobson, R. P. (2004). *The cradle of thought*. Oxford: Oxford University Press. (Original work published 2002)

Krebs, D., Denton, K., Vermeulen, S., Carpendale, J., & Bush, J. (1991). The structural flexibility of moral judgment. *Journal of Personality and Social Psychology, 61,* 1012–1023.

Mead, G. H. (1934). *Mind, self and society*. Chicago: University of Chicago Press.

Meltzoff, A. W. (2007). "Like me": A foundation for social cognition. *Developmental Science, 10,* 126–134.

Müller, U., Carpendale, J. I. M., Bibok, M., & Racine, T. (2006). Subjectivity, Identification and Differentiation: Key issues in early social development. *Monographs of the Society for Research in Child Development, 71* (Serial No. 284), 167–179.

Piaget, J. (1932). *The moral judgement of the child*. London: Routledge & Kegan Paul.

Piaget, J. (1954). *The construction of reality* (M. Cook, Trans.). New York: Basic Books. (Original work published in 1937)

Piaget, J. (1971). *Biology and knowledge*. Chicago: University of Chicago Press. (Original work published in 1967)

Piaget J. (1995). *Sociological studies*. London: Routledge. (Original work published 1977)

Plessner, H. (1983a). Der Mensch als Lebewesen. In H. Plessner, *Gesammelte Schriften: Vol. 8: Conditio Humana* (pp. 314–327). Frankfurt: Suhrkamp. (Original work published in 1967)

Plessner, H. (1983b). Das Problem der Unmenschlichkeit. In H. Plessner, *Gesammelte Schriften: Vol.8. Conditio Humana* (pp. 328–337). Frankfurt: Suhrkamp. (Original work published in 1967)

Royce, J. (1894). The external world and the social consciousness. *Philosophical Review, 3,* 514–545.

Royce, J. (1895). Preliminary report on imitation. *Psychological Review, 2,* 217–235.

Stevenson, L. (1993). Why believe what people say? *Synthese, 94,* 429–451.

Susswein, N., Bibok, M. B., & Carpendale, J. I. M. (in press). Reconcepualizing internalization [Special issue]. *International Journal of Dialogical Science,*

Tomasello, M. (1999). *The cultural origins of human cognition*. Cambridge, MA: Harvard University Press.

Valsiner, J., & Van der Veer, R. (1988). On the social nature of human cognition: An analysis of the shared intellectual roots of George Herbert Mead and Lev Vygotsky. *Journal of the Theory of Social Behaviour, 18,* 117–136.

Valsiner, J., & Van der Veer, R. (2000). *The social mind: Construction of the idea*. New York: Cambridge University Press.

Vygotsky, L. (1986). *Thought and language*. Cambridge, MA: MIT Press. (Original work published 1934)

2

Are You Social?

The Ontological and Developmental Emergence of the Person

Mark H. Bickhard

In what way does human sociality differ from that of ants or bees? The sociality of social insects is an emergent at the level of the nest or hive, an emergent of the organization of interactions among the *biological* organisms: Each individual insect remains as a biological being no matter how complex the social organization. There is a sense in which that is the case for humans, but human sociality also involves an additional social ontological emergence for each individual. This is the *developmental* emergence of the *social person*. Modeling how this occurs, and accounting for how it could possibly occur, will be the foci of this chapter.

Accounting for how ontological emergence is possible *at all* takes us into issues of philosophy and physics. Accounting for how the individual level social emergence of *persons* is possible in human beings, but not in insects, takes us into issues of mind and development. Modeling how this occurs in human beings takes us into issues of knowledge, values, and culture.

ONTOLOGICAL EMERGENCE

Parmenides argued that change could not occur, because for A to change into B would require that A cease to exist and B emerge out of nothingness. Since nothingness cannot exist, this turning into nothingness and emerging out of nothingness cannot occur—therefore change cannot occur (Campbell, 1992; Gill, 1989; Guthrie, 1965; McKirahan, 1994; Reale, 1987).

Problems with "nothing" may sound slightly archaic to contemporary ears, a century or so after Frege showed how to render such notions as "some," "all," and "none" as quantifiers rather than as concepts, but modern thought has had and still has its own related serious problems with that which does not exist and that which is false. For example, how could a representation encode something that doesn't exist? Or have an encoding relationship with a false state of affairs—and just what would a false state of affairs be?

Russell, for example, struggled for years with these and related problems early in the 20th century, as did Wittgenstein and many others. The problems seem less pressing now because we tend to think of such representations of non-existents and falsehoods as constructed out of component representations, and to assume that it is the *structure* of the representation that makes it represent a non-existent or makes it false. The component representations might themselves be composite, but ultimately there must be (in this view) some basic level of atomic representations out of which all others are constructed. Representation of nonexistents or falsehood is no more a solved problem for these base level representations than it was for Russell—or Parmenides.

In any case, the Greeks took these arguments quite seriously and devoted major effort to overcoming their counterintuitive consequences. In particular, Empedocles devised his system of the substances earth, air, fire, and water in response to Parmenides, and Democritus developed his notion of atoms in similar response. Earth, air, fire, and water did not change, thus satisfying the Parmenidean constraint, but manifest change in the world could nevertheless be accommodated as alterations in locations and mixtures of the basic substances. Similarly, atoms did not change, but apparent change could be accommodated as alterations in locations of the atoms.

Aristotle's versions of the earth, air, fire, and water metaphysics was much more sophisticated and subtle than that of Empedocles, but involved similar motivations to avoid the Parmenidean problems. Aristotle's metaphysical framework of substance and property (though not necessarily all of the Aristotelian details and sophistications) became the dominant metaphysics throughout most of Western history. Its legacy is with us still today.

Substance Metaphysics
In particular, a substance metaphysics carries with it several deep, usually implicit, commitments. First, substances were introduced precisely in order to avoid real metaphysical change. They do not change; they are inert. Stasis, therefore, is the explanatory default, and any purported change requires explanation.

Second, substances were introduced in order to avoid emergence. New substances cannot emerge, and substances cannot change into one another.[1] The term and explicit notion of emergence is relatively modern (Stephan, 1992), but the metaphysical concept was precluded by the basic metaphysics inherited from the Greeks.

Third, substances or atoms were actual and factual. They outlined a world of substance or atoms, and their configurations and properties. In particular, they did not involve properties of normativity, intentionality, or modality. A substance or atom metaphysics, therefore, assumes a fundamental split between the actual, factual world and the realm or realms of normativity, intentionality, and modality. In particular, it assumes a fundamental split between the physical realm and the realm of mentality. Implicitly, mind was dirempted from the rest of the world.

Three Metaphysical Options
A substance metaphysics, then, commits to there being two possible realms: that of the substantive (or atomistic) and factual and that of the normative, intentional, modal mind. Within this framework, there are only three coherent options.

The first is to assume two realms, one of substance and one of what is not included in that substantive realm—a realm of concepts, intentionality, normativity, and so on. Aristotle had a two-realm framework, with substance and form characterizing the two. Descartes famously, or infamously, posited two kinds of substances. Kant proposed a noumenal realm and a transcendental realm. And, most recently, analytic philosophy assumes a factual, atomistic realm of the sciences, and a normative, modal realm of language and philosophy (Rouse, 2002; Sacks, 1998).

A second option would be to attempt to account for everything in terms of a single "mindlike" realm. This yields various forms of idealism, such as that of Hegel, Green, or Bradley. Contemporary versions tend to be linguistic idealisms (Bickhard, 1987, 1995, 1998a).

The third option is to attempt to account for everything strictly (or as close as you can get) in terms of the factual, "scientific," physical realm. Hobbes and Hume (at least as he is most often interpreted) represent this approach. An important contemporary advocate is Quine. In eliminating the analytic philosophy distinction between the analytic (modal, normative) and the synthetic (factual), Quine rendered everything that he could in terms of the factual "scientific" realm, and this is the perspective that today dominates much philosophical thought and almost all work in psychology.[2]

What about Emergence?
It might seem, and has to some, that the mental and the nonmental realms could be integrated by some notion of emergence: perhaps normativity, intentionality, and so on are emergent phenomena, emergent within and from the natural, physical, biological, world. Such ideas have become somewhat more common over the last century or so, but it is not often realized that the basic metaphysical presuppositions within which we tend to think were historically introduced precisely to preclude such notions of emergence—and that they do a good job of precisely

that. Emergence may be a tempting notion, but it is not possible to consistently develop it within a substance or atomistic metaphysical framework.

Aspects of (parts of) this point concerning the apparent impossibility of emergence have been realized and argued. I will address two of them, one logical and the other metaphysical. The logical challenge derives from Hume, and the metaphysical challenge from Jaegwon Kim.

Hume   Hume (1739–1740/1978) argued that norms could not be derived from facts: "no 'ought' from 'is'". His argument is not, in fact, very fully developed, but it is standardly interpreted as being based on a conception of what is involved in validly introducing any new term into a deduction. In particular, any new terms must be defined on the basis of those initial factual terms. So, if the premises of the reasoning include only factual terms, then the conclusion can only (validly) contain factual terms. The central point is that any new terms in the conclusion could, in principle, always be eliminated in favor of the defining phrase or clause. Such back-translation through the definitions can continue until only the original terms in the premises remain, and, by assumption, those are strictly factual. Therefore, the conclusion(s), if valid, can be fully rendered in those original factual terms: the conclusions themselves can only be factual: No "ought" from "is."

The general form of this argument, however, is that you can only (validly) get rearrangements of whatever you begin with. The point, then, holds for any kind of novelty: a valid conclusion is restricted to arrangements of premise terms. There cannot be anything fundamentally new in the conclusion: there cannot be any metaphysical emergence.

In effect, Hume (partially) codified the split between fact and norm, substance and mind, and did so in a way that reached down to the level of the preclusion of emergence. Mixtures and rearrangements of substances and atoms are permitted, but nothing more.

If Hume's argument were sound, it would in itself preclude emergence, and, thus, preclude any emergent account of the normative. I will argue in a moment, however, that it is unsound. First, however, I turn to a metaphysical challenge to emergence from Kim.

Jaegwon Kim   In a series of sophisticated arguments, Kim (1989, 1990, 1991, 1992a, 1992b, 1993a, 1993b, 1997) has shown that, given a few reasonable assumptions, such as that the physical world is causally closed, any emergent phenomena or entity will be causally epiphenomenal. The basic core of the arguments is that causality is a property of whatever the fundamental particles of physics turn out to be, and that all phenomena more complex than single particle interactions are resultants of those basic interactions. There are no new causal powers, only the working out of the causal dance of the basic particles in whatever configuration they are in.

So, there may well be "new" resultant causal manifestations given "new" configurations, but there is still nothing more than the particle interactions that are causal themselves. Configuration or organization is just the stage setting for genuine particle causality. All potentially or supposedly emergent phenomena, therefore, are causally epiphenomenal: all the genuine metaphysical causality is resident in the basic particles, whatever they may be (Bickhard, 2000a, 2003/2004b; Kim, 1991).[3]

I have rendered Kim's argument in a way that makes especially clear its reliance on a particle metaphysics of the general substance or atom form. I will argue that avoiding Kim's argument requires transcending that metaphysics, and, conversely, that moving to a process metaphysics instead of a substance or atomistic metaphysics does in fact avoid Kim's argument.

Contra Hume Hume's argument precludes all emergence, not just normative emergence. But the argument is unsound: it rests on a false assumption, namely that the only valid form of definition is explicit, abbreviatory definition—definition of the kind that permits back-translation of the defined term into the defining terms.

The alternative form of definition is implicit definition, contrasted with the explicit form of definition that Hume assumes. Hume did not know about implicit definition, but it was introduced in a forceful (and controversial) way by Hilbert in his axiomatization of geometry around the advent of the 20th century (Kneale & Kneale, 1986).[4] Within formal contexts, such as Hilbert's geometry, the axioms are taken to implicitly define the class of interpretations of the terms in those axioms that would satisfy them. So an axiom with a form something like "Two Xs determine a Y" could be interpreted as two points determine a line, or two lines determine a point (their intersection, so long as points at infinity are accepted). The more general form of implicit definition is that of the implicit definition of the class that satisfies a set of conditions or constraints (Hale & Wright, 2000).

For my purposes, the important point about implicit definition is that it exists, and that it cannot be back-translated through. The Humean argument against the possibility of introducing terms that cannot be back-translationally rendered in terms available in the premises, therefore, is blocked. Hume's argument is based on the false assumption that abbreviatory definition, that *can* be back-translated through, is the only valid form of definition. His argument, therefore, is unsound, and the possibility is opened of new properties emerging that are more than just rearrangements of properties already available—and, perhaps, of *normative* properties emergent on the basis of nonnormative phenomena.[5]

Contra Kim Kim's arguments turn on a presupposition of a particle metaphysics—in particular, of some metaphysically basic level at which the bearers of causal power can participate in organization but that have no organization themselves. With this split between causal power and organization, the latter is delegitimated as a potential locus of causal power; thus, new causal power emergent in new organization is precluded.

The first point to make in rejoinder is that, if the world were constituted of only point particles, nothing would ever happen because the probability of two points ever striking each other would be zero. So, a pure point particle metaphysics is not possible.

The second point is that particles do not in fact exist. A particle metaphysics is false according to our best contemporary physics (Cao, 1999; Davies, 1984; Huggett, 2000; Saunders & Brown, 1991; Weinberg, 1977, 1995, 1996). What appear as particlelike phenomena are in fact wavelike processes, and the superficial particle character of the phenomena is a manifestation of the quantization of the processes. That is, the oscillatory processes are quantized in the sense of taking on only integer (or half integer) values. This is similar to the sense in which the number of wavelengths in a vibrating guitar string is quantized, and there are no more physical particles than there are guitar sound particles.

What does exist are quantum fields: processes with various quantization and conservation properties. For current purposes, the crucial property of quantum fields is that they are processes, and that processes inherently have organization. Furthermore, quantum field processes possess whatever causal powers they do possess in strong part *in virtue* of their organization. So quantum fields have both causal power and organization, unlike particles, and the organization cannot be delegitimated as a locus of causal power without eliminating all causality from the universe.

Everything, then, is process, and causality must be a property (or properties) of, among other things, organization of process on pain of eliminating causality altogether. The way is open, therefore, to the possibility that macroscale organizations of (quantum field) processes might ground novel, emergent causality. The way is open to the possibility of emergent, nonepiphenomenal, causal power.[6]

Emergence
Genuine ontological emergence, thus, is not precluded. A process metaphysics, which is forced by both metaphysical considerations ("nothing but point particles" cannot constitute a world) and contemporary physics. This undoes the substance and particle framework from Parmenides, Empedocles, Democritus, and so on, and legitimates at least the core intuition of Heraclitus.

The possibility of genuine emergence is rescued, but to this point this is only a possibility. Metaphysical assumptions that make *any* kind of emergence impossible have been cleared away, but the task of accounting for normative emergence, of accounting for the emergence of mental processes, phenomena, and properties more generally, remains.

NORMATIVE EMERGENCE

Adopting a process metaphysical framework involves corollary shifts in all three of the consequences mentioned earlier of a substance metaphysics. In particular, the barrier to an integrated account of normativity and mental phenomena is removed, because the barrier to genuine emergence is removed. Addressing the positive task of developing a model of normative emergence, however, involves consideration of the first consequence of a substance framework. In particular, within a substance framework, stasis is the default and change requires explanation; within a process framework, change is the default and stability requires explanation. Understanding normative emergence begins with consideration of how processes can be stable at all.

There are two basic forms of stable process, and there is an asymmetry between them that, so I argue, underlies the asymmetries of normativity. The first stable kind is that of energy well stabilities. These are organizations of (quantum field) processes that are stable because to disrupt them requires more energy than is ambiently available. So long as the impinging energy is below some crucial threshold, the organization of process will persist. An easy example is that of an atom: such an organization can be changed and disrupted, but to do so requires energy not available in, for example, normal terrestrial conditions. Such organizations can remain stable for cosmological lengths of time.

The second stable kind is that of organizations of processes that are far from thermodynamic equilibrium. Atoms, and energy well stabilities in general, can happily continue to exist in isolation and in thermodynamic equilibrium. Far from equilibrium systems, however, cannot be isolated because they must be maintained in their far from equilibrium conditions. If they are isolated, they go to equilibrium and cease to exist. An example would be a pan of water heated from below that has self-organized into Benard cells of boiling water. This example illustrates both that if the source of heat is removed, the system goes to equilibrium and ceases to exist—in particular, the Benard cells cease to exist—and it illustrates that far from equilibrium systems can manifest properties of self-organization, the cells in this case.

The asymmetry between energy-well stabilities that do not need to be maintained, and the stabilities of far from equilibrium systems, which must be maintained, is the basis for the emergence of normativity (Bickhard, 2003/2004b, in preparation). Note that far from equilibrium systems are necessarily open systems, exchanging and interacting with their environments; they cannot be isolated. If they were not in interaction with their environments, their far from equilibrium conditions could not be maintained and they would cease to exist.

Self-Maintenance and Recursive Self-Maintenance
The pan of water is dependent for its stability entirely on external sources of heat. It makes no contributions to its own stability. But some systems do make such contributions.

A candle flame, for example, helps to maintain several of the conditions for its own existence—it is in that sense *self-maintenant*. The flame maintains above combustion threshold temperature, it melts the wax so that it percolates up the wick, it vaporizes the wax so that it is available for burning, and, in standard circumstances, it induces convection which brings in fresh oxygen and gets rid of waste. The self-organized properties of the candle flame are essential to its own continued existence.

The candle flame does only one thing, it burns, with several crucial consequences. There are several ways in which it is self-maintenant, but they all follow from the burning. The flame cannot adopt differing activities in the service of self-maintenance in differing conditions, but some systems can.

Consider the bacterium that can swim and continue swimming if it is going up a sugar gradient, but will tumble if it finds itself going down a sugar gradient (D. T. Campbell, 1974, 1990). In this case, swimming contributes to self-maintenance under some conditions—for example, oriented toward higher sugar concentrations—but swimming is dysfunctional for self-maintenance under other conditions—for example, oriented toward lower sugar concentrations.[7] The bacterium can detect the difference in relevant conditions and trigger appropriate activity, swimming or tumbling, accordingly. The bacterium, then, can maintain its condition of being self-maintenant under varying conditions: it is *recursively self-maintenant*.

Representation

With recursive self-maintenance, we have the grounds for the emergence of primitive representation. I will outline this model of representational emergence with a focus first on the crucial normativity, truth value, then on what constitutes representational content in this model, and, finally, I will elaborate on some of the resources of the model for accounting for more complex forms of representation.

The Emergence of Representational Normativity: Truth Value   The selection of particular interactions, such as swimming, will at some times be *successful*, in the sense of contributing to the self-maintenance of the system, and at other times not. In triggering or selecting an interaction, then, the system is implicitly predicating that this environment is one that is appropriate for swimming.

That predication may be *true* (e.g., if the orientation is toward higher sugar concentrations), or *false* (e.g., if the orientation is toward higher saccharin concentrations): the bacterium can be fooled just as we can. This is the primitive emergence of representational truth value out of normative pragmatic success or failure.

The Emergence of Representational Content   The selection of particular interactions, for example, swimming, will contribute to the self-maintenance of the system only under certain conditions. In the case of swimming, there is such a contribution if the orientation is toward higher sugar concentrations, but there is not such a contribution if the orientation is toward higher concentrations of saccharin.

The predication that the current environment is appropriate for swimming, then, presupposes that the environment has one or more of the properties that support the success of that interaction, that support that predication. This is normative functional presupposition: it is presupposed in the assumption of the appropriateness of the interaction.

The presupposed conditions, in turn, may be true, in which case the predication will be true and the interaction will contribute to self-maintenance, or they may be false, in which case the predication will be false and the interaction will fail to contribute to self-maintenance. The presupposed conditions constitute the *content* of the predication.

This content is implicit, presupposed, not explicit. The bacterium knows nothing that is explicit about sugar or gradients. For some purposes, this implicitness makes no special difference, though in others this difference from standard assumptions in which content, if there is any, is explicit can be of fundamental importance (e.g., Bickhard, 2001; Bickhard & Terveen, 1995).

Representation as predication of interactive appropriateness is a primitive form of representation. It captures the essential normativity of truth value and of content, but it is far from familiar kinds of representations, such as of objects, and raises the question of whether such an interactive model is adequate to more complex forms of representation.

Resources for More Complex Representation   I argue that it is adequate to more complex representation, and will illustrate this point with a central example of the representation of small manipulable objects. First, however, I need to elaborate some on what resources are available in the interactive model for greater representational complexity.

If we move from bacteria to more complex organisms, such as a frog, three resources for representational complexity can be illustrated. First, unlike the discussion of the bacterium in which swimming or tumbling is directly triggered, the frog may have multiple potential interactions available at a given time. It might be able to flick its tongue in one direction and thereby eat a fly, perhaps another direction and thereby eat a worm, and perhaps jump in the water in order to avoid the hawk whose shadow just passed overhead. Selecting an actual interaction to engage in, then, cannot be for the frog a simple triggering as it might be for the bacterium. There must be some way in which the frog can indicate what interactions are currently available so that it can then select among those available. The indications of interactive potentialities must be distinct from the selection of interaction.

The selection of interaction is central to motivation, which I will not address in this chapter (Bickhard, 2000b, 2003, in preparation); for current purposes the most relevant aspect of this example is the indication of interactive potentialities without necessarily engaging in those interactions. Crucially, such indications involve similar implicit predications and presuppositional contents as the direct triggering of the interactions: an indication of an interactive potentiality is an implicit predication that this environment is appropriate for that kind of inter-action, and it presupposes that this environment satisfies the implicit content consisting of sufficient support for the interaction to make that interaction appro-priate—that this environment possesses (a sufficiency of) the implicitly pre-supposed properties. Indicating interactive potentiality, then, itself constitutes representational emergence.

A second point illustrated by this example is that such indications can branch in multiple "directions." More than one interactive potentiality can exist at a given time, in particular circumstances.

A third point can be derived from consideration of the status of *potential indications* of interactive potentiality when initial conditions for those potenti-alities are not currently present. If certain visual processes *were* to occur, for example, then the frog would set up an indication that it could flick its tongue in some new direction with the consequence of eating a fly in that direction. This conditional *readiness* to set up a tongue-flicking and eating indication is available in the frog even when nothing is detected in the required direction. The setting up is conditional on proper prior visual detection, and the conditional as a whole is present even if it is not activated in particular conditions. These conditionals have roughly the form of "'condition satisfied' yields 'indication set-up'."

Such conditional interactive potentialities can, in principle, iterate in the sense that the engagement in one interaction may create the conditions for the potentiality of some further interaction. And that further interaction might create the conditions for a still further interaction. In sufficiently complex organisms, such branching and iterating indications of interactive potentialities can form vast and complex webs of indications of interactive potentiality. Such webs consti-tute one of the primary resources of the interactive model for capturing complex representation.

Complex Representations   Consider now a small manipulable object, such as a child's toy block. The block offers multiple possible interactions, such as manipu-lations and visual scans, and they are all interrelated with each other. In particu-lar, any one of them indicates the potentiality for each of the others, in some cases with appropriate intermediate interactions. So, a particular visual scan of one side of the block indicates, among other things, the possibility of a visual scan of some other side of the block, so long as the proper manipulations are engaged in so as to bring that other side into view. In general, the possible interactions with the block form a subweb of the overall web of interaction potentialities in which every part of the subweb is reachable from every other part: it is internally com-pletely reachable.

Furthermore, this internally reachable subweb is invariant under a large and important class of other interactions and other processes in the world. The child can drop the block, leave it on the floor and go somewhere else, put it in the toy box, and so on, and the entire subweb remains available so long as appropriate intermediate interactions occur to bring it back into manipulable range (e.g., walking back into the room). The subweb is not invariant under all possibilities, however: crushing or burning the block destroys that particular organization of interaction potentialities.

Such an internally reachable, translational and locomotor invariant subweb constitutes the child's representation of a small manipulable object. More generally, this illustrates how indications of interaction potentialities can address more complex representational phenomena, such as of objects.

Another challenge to the interactive model of representation would concern abstract representations, such as numbers. It may be that interactive representation can account for the physical world that is available for interaction, but what world is it that is available for interaction for representing abstractions? Such challenges (including that for objects) cannot be met by addressing every possible case because they are unbounded, but, again, I can illustrate how this model can address abstractions, and will do so with the case of number.

A system interacting with its environment might well have a servomechanism that can be called on during other interactions that would control engaging in some particular interaction and encountering failure three times before giving up on that interaction and switching to something else—a "try X three times before giving up on X" subroutine. If there were a second level system interacting with the first level, in generally the same sense in which the first level interacts with the environment, then the second level could represent various properties of organization and process in the first level. In particular, it could represent the property of "ordinal three" instantiated in the heuristic subroutine mentioned. In this sense, the overall system could represent abstractions.

More generally, a system interacting with—thereby *knowing*—its environment will instantiate properties that may be useful to interact with and represent from a second level of knowing, and the second level, in turn, may itself have properties that could be interacted with and represented from a third level, and so on. These potential levels constitute an extremely rich resource for addressing cognitions about and representations of abstractions. Again, the interactive model does not encounter perplexity in addressing more complex representation.

Representation, Piaget, and Pragmatism
The model of object representation outlined above is basically Piaget's model translated into the interactive framework (Piaget, 1954). The model of representing number is also similar to Piaget's model, though with more fundamental changes, especially regarding the nature of the levels of potential cognition and representation (Bickhard & R. L. Campbell, 1989; R. L. Campbell & Bickhard, 1986).

The interactive model can borrow from Piaget in this manner because both models are action based, both models are within the general pragmatist framework in which action serves as the foundation and framework for understanding mental phenomena (Joas, 1993). This is in strong contrast with standard approaches which attempt to model representation in terms of some sort of result of the processing of perceptual inputs.

Alternative Models of Representation

There are, in fact, multiple candidate models of representation in the contemporary literature, but the pragmatist nature of the interactive model alone suffices to distinguish it from most of them. A detailed comparison would require very lengthy discussion, but I can illustrate some of advantages of the interactive approach with just a few points.

Indications of interactive potentialities are *anticipative*. They anticipate the general flow of interaction should the indicated interaction be engaged in. It is such anticipations that can be true or false. Anticipations are modal (interaction *possibilities*), normative (*true* or *false*), and intentional (about interactions with *this* environment). They contrast in all these respects, and more, with standard approaches to representation.

Standard approaches to representation assume that representation is some form of special correspondence between the mental representation and what is to be represented that constitutes an *encoding* of what is being represented. They assume that representation is fundamentally a matter of encoding; thus I call such approaches to representation instances of *encodingism*. They are descendents and variants of the Aristotelian metaphor for perception of the signet ring pressing its form into wax—they have a very long history. In contrast, it has been only a little over a century since Peirce introduced pragmatism's core notions (Joas, 1993; Mounce, 1997; Rosenthal, 1983).

Within the encodingist framework, the central issue concerning representation is what the crucial correspondence relationship is that constitutes a representational relationship. It is variously proposed to consist of a causal correspondence, an informational correspondence, a lawful correspondence, a correspondence of structural iso- or homomorphism, or a correspondence with the right evolutionary history (Cummins, 1996; Dretske, 1988; Fodor, 1975, 1987, 1990a, 1990b, 1991, 1998; Millikan, 1984, 1993; Newell, 1980; Vera & Simon, 1993; cf. Bickhard, 2003/2004b; Bickhard & Terveen, 1995; Levine & Bickhard, 1999). There are multiple problems with such approaches: I will mention three.

First, consider a causal or informational correspondence between some mental activity and a table being visually perceived. Whatever that special correspondence is supposed to be, there is also such a correspondence with the light on the surface of the retina, with the quantum activities in the surface of the table, with the table a minute ago (note that the light reflected from the table in the past, however short a time into the past it may have been, but the continuity from the light to the table continues through the temporality of the table itself), the table a year ago, the manufacture of the table, the creation of the materials out of which the table is constructed, and so on to the Big Bang. Which of these instances of the "special" correspondence is the representational one, and how does the organism "know" which one it is?

Another problem arises from considering how representational error could be modeled. If the special encoding correspondence between representation and represented exists, then the representation exists, and it is correct. If the special correspondence does not exist, then the representation does not exist. These are the only two possibilities, but there is a third possibility that must be modeled: the representation exists and is *in*correct. There have been major efforts in the last decades to account for the possibility of representational error, but without success.

An even stronger criterion is not even addressed in the standard literature: how can *system* or *organism detectable* representational error be accounted for? Attempts to model representational error do so (however unsuccessfully) from the perspective of an external observer of the organism and its environment: the property of error is assessed, if at all, only from this external perspective. How the organism could detect its own error is not addressed.

But if the organism cannot, however fallibly, detect its own error, then error guided behavior and error guided learning are not possible. It is clear that error guided behavior and error guided learning do occur, so any model that makes this impossible or cannot account for it is thereby refuted.

The anticipations of the interactive model, in contrast, account for representational error very simply; the actual interaction, should it be engaged, may or may not proceed as anticipated. If it does not, then the anticipation is in error, and the organism is in a position to functionally detect that error and respond accordingly. Neither error per se, nor system detectable error, are problematic in principle for the interactive approach.

DEVELOPMENTAL EMERGENCES

An action or interaction based approach to representation yields several further consequences. In particular, it forces a constructivism of learning and development—and, thereby, sets the stage for the possibility of developmental emergences, constructive emergences, within individual organisms.

Implications for Learning and Development

If the world presses itself into a passive mind, as does the signet ring into wax, or, in more modern terminology, in sensory transduction (press into wax at a moment in time) or induction (scratch into wax over some duration or number of instances), then we are led to passive models of both perception and learning. There is little for development to do within such a framework.

If, however, representation is emergent in systems for action and interaction, there is no temptation to assume that competent interactive systems can be pressed into a passive mind by the world. Instead, interaction systems must be constructed. A pragmatist orientation forces a constructivism. Furthermore, absent prescience, these constructions must be tried out and rejected or modified if they are not successful: A pragmatist orientation forces a variation and selection constructivism, an evolutionary epistemology (D. T. Campbell, 1974).[8]

Recursive and Metacursive Constructionism
In simple organisms, it is likely that all learning is construction from the same base. In more complex organisms, however, constructions are in the context of prior constructions, and make use of prior constructions both as components and as loci for further variations. In this case, construction is *recursive*: prior constructions constitute a primary resource for later construction.

In still more complex organisms, including human beings, the processes of construction are themselves constructed, and these processes are also recursive: a kind of *metarecursivity*. It is worth noting that Piaget's model is recursive—prior constructions are very much used as resources in later constructions—but it is not metarecursive—equilibration remains the central constructive process throughout development. It is also worth noting that, although it is clear that metarecursivity is common in humans, it is almost universally overlooked in developmental models.

One consequence of recursive constructivism is that it introduces a kind of *historicity* into constructive trajectories over time. Earlier constructions can make certain later constructions easier, or make them possible at all. Learning can get easier in a domain in which significant prior learning (construction) has occurred (R. L. Campbell & Bickhard, 1992a). Of course, in some cases, such prior construction can make later learning more *difficult*, if the recursive constructive resources are in some sense inappropriate for a later task.

Learning and Development   Within such a constructivism, the study of learning is the study of how such constructions occur and how they are influenced by experience (Bickhard, 1992a, 2003). The study of development focuses on the historicities of construction involved, the constraints and possibilities of constructive trajectories, lattices, and weaves (Bickhard, 1980).

Constraints on Development
Development is a class of phenomena that emerge in constructive learning. Prior constructions can have strong effects on later constructions—making some constructions much more likely and, perhaps, others less likely, than before—and the historicities introduced are of crucial importance.

There are important constraints on constructive development that are not of a standard causal nature. The historicities of prior constructions is one example: prior constructions make a difference for later constructions, but they do not *cause* that difference (certainly not in any sense of efficient cause). Instead, they enable various other constructive processes to do what would otherwise be difficult or impossible.

Another source of developmental constraint derives from the constructive processes themselves. Constructions that might be complex and difficult with some constructive processes might be much simpler with some other constructive processes. Processes of construction impose a topology of nearness and farness on the space of potential constructions: roughly, more constructive steps means more complex, which means "farther" in that constructive topology. Note that a *meta*recursive developmental constructivism, by introducing new constructive processes, can drastically alter the topology of developmental space. It can make some things "near" and easy that were previously extremely complex and distant. This is one view on the advantages of constructive, learning heuristics (Bickhard & R. L. Campbell, 1996; Bickhard & D. T. Campbell, 2003).

Another constraint on constructive development arises from the levels of potential representation, of potential "knowing," where knowing is modeled in terms of capabilities for interaction with that which is known.[9] In particular, it is not possible to construct an interactive system at some level N+1 if there is nothing already constructed at level N to be interacted with. Again, this is not a causal constraint. In fact, it is much stronger than a causal constraint—it is a metaphysical necessity: if the space of potential constructions has such a simply ordered structure, then it is logically impossible to skip a level in construction because there would be nothing at the skipped level to be interacted with. Psychology is not accustomed to considering such ontological or metaphysical constraints (R. L. Campbell & Bickhard, 1986, 1992; Bickhard & D. T. Campbell, 2003).

Developmental Emergences
In the standard form of computer models of the mind, "development" consists of storing lots of information. Development is in scare quotes here because, in such models, there is, as mentioned before, little for development to do. For such a computer, it is of no particular consequence what the information is about—in particular, whether it is about interactions with the physical world, some abstract world, or the social world. There is no meaningful construction, just more chunks, and therefore no basis for emergence.

If mind is an interactive system, however, then constructive development does occur, with all of its recursions, historicities, constraints, levels, trajectories, and so on. In this case, development constructs particular kinds of interactive systems, perhaps more than one kind in a particular individual. This yields the possibility that there might be important *emergent* kind(s) of interactive system constructed. I will argue that this is in fact the case, with a central ontological focus on the emergence of the social person.

THE EMERGENCE OF SOCIAL ONTOLOGY

There is a complex dialectic involved in the emergence of the social person. Social levels of process and organization—social realities—are themselves emergent, and social persons are developmentally emergent as participants in, and as constituting the emergence base for, that social level of ontology. Social reality and the reality of social persons are in a continuous generational dance upon which each are centrally dependent for their existence, and even for the very possibility of their existence. Social reality and social persons are in an ontological interdependence.

There is a third aspect of this evolutionary developmental emergence, and that is language, which is simultaneously a social institution for creating and transforming social realities and also a central aspect of the ontology of that social reality—and, therefore, of the social persons who coparticipatively constitute it. Language enables the unfolding of the full complexities of society and culture—and persons. Sociality, social persons, and language are three aspects of one evolutionary, developmental, social dynamic (kind of) process that involves emergences at multiple levels and with respect to multiple aspects.

Situation Conventions

Social reality emerges out of an epistemological perplexity that agents pose to one another. In particular, when interacting with stones and toy blocks, the interactive potentialities available are determinable to a large degree just on the basis of the initial perceptual encounter, but when *agents* are dealing with each other, the interactive potentialities that each affords to the other are largely hidden from perceptual access. Much of the interactive potentiality afforded by an agent is constituted or determined by internal representational and motivational processes that are not directly accessible and that can change over relatively short time spans.

Even worse (epistemologically speaking), the interactive potentialities afforded by an agent depend in part on that agent's interactive characterizations of other agents in the situation, but their interactive affordances, in turn, depend in part on their characterizations of the first agent—and this problematic is reciprocal amongst all participants in the situation. No agent can interactively characterize the situation containing other agents without at least partly characterizing properties of those other agents' characterizations of him- or herself.[10] Interactive construal of the situation depends on construal of others, which depends on others' construal of you.

This kind of situation poses what Schelling called a coordination problem (Schelling, 1963): There are in general multiple joint construals of the situation that social situation participants might be satisfied to have. The problem is to arrive at a mutual framework of interactive construals among the participants that is in fact "joint," that are mutually consistent. The problem is to arrive at a coordinated organization of mutual construals. Modified from Lewis (1969), I call any solution to this coordination problem a *situation convention*: a social convention about how to interactively construe the social situation.

Situation conventions constitute the basic emergence of social reality. They are, if they exist at all, an inherently social organization with novel properties that cannot be modeled in any simple aggregative manner from the participants in a social situation (Wimsatt, 1986, 1997).

A lecture situation, for example, is so because of the mutual assumptions among its participants that it is so. If the same people were involved, but they all were mutually to assume that the situation was a birthday party, then it would be a birthday party. Social realities are constituted in the commonalities of presumptions concerning those social realities. Furthermore, social realities are real in a very basic sense—violations of conventions can have consequences: realities can resist and surprise.

Nonrecurrent Situation Conventions and Institutionalized Conventions   There are two basic kinds of situation conventions that need to be distinguished here: those that can occur but likely never recur, and those that do, or at least can, recur over times, situations, and people.

Nonrecurrent situation conventions are illustrated by the commonality of readiness to interpret a pronoun in a conversation in the same way amongst all the participants to that conversation: the particulars of that situation constitute a coordination problem—the participants would like to arrive at the same interpretation—so the fact of a common interpretation, and the condition of being ready to so interpret, constitute a situation convention that is not likely to recur simply because the particulars of the conversation are not likely to recur.

Institutionalized conventions are those, such as driving on the right side of the road, which are capable of multiple reinvocations across times and people. Institutionalized conventions derive from conventionalized means by which they are invoked. Meeting another vehicle on a road automatically invokes the "driving on the right side" convention across multiple societies and cultures. Lectures similarly involve complex conventions across large numbers of people. Institutionalized conventions need not be institutionalized across entire societies: personal relationships are constituted by intricate conventions, some of which may be of wider scope, but many of which may be specific to this pair or group of people. Roles emerge as conventionally typified kinds of participation in conventionalized kinds of organizations of social interactions (Berger & Luckmann, 1966; Bickhard, 1980, in preparation).

It might seem to be a puzzle how nonrecurrent situation conventions can occur other than by chance. How could such a convention ever come into existence if there were no past history for it to be based on? The key to this puzzle is to recognize that conventionalized means of invoking conventions, characteristic of institutionalized conventions, such as insignia of rank or the bang of a gavel, are not simply triggers, but, instead, are context sensitive transformations of prior conventional understandings into new or more specific conventions. Someone banging a gavel has very different conventional consequences depending on the prior situation and the status of other participants: it is context sensitive in its consequences. In general, this constitutes a limited example of a broader phenomenon of conventionalized *transformations* of conventions—in this case, a transformation of the existence or lack of existence of a formal institutional mode of interaction.

If there were a conventionalized *system* for constructing conventional *transformations* of social *situation conventions*, such a system could well create situation conventions that had never occurred before and likely never would again, simply by deploying (constructed) transformations that might themselves be novel in situations that might well be novel, so that the situation convention as (momentary) outcome of the invoked transformation will also be novel and nonrecurrent.

Such a conventionalized tool for interacting with situation conventions would also be extremely useful: situation conventions can be powerful and important, and resources for interacting with them correspondingly valuable.

Language   If such a social resource is *productive* in the sense of being capable of producing an unbounded number and range of possible situation convention transformations, it is called a *language* (Bickhard, 1980, 1998b).[11] This, as for the rest of the model, is a model of the nature of language as an interaction system, a social institution for interacting with social realities. It has kinships with, though also fundamental differences from, Wittgenstein's toolbox (Bickhard, 1987), J. L. Austin's speech acts (Bickhard, 1980), functional and categorial grammars (Bickhard & R. L. Campbell, 1992), and so on. It is drastically different from common assumptions about language as an encoding of mental contents for transmission to be decoded in someone else's mind (Bickhard, 1980; Bickhard & Campbell, 1992). I cannot focus on language here—it is among the more complex phenomena to attempt to model—but this basic approach to language as a social interactive system will suffice for the basic discussion that follows. Note that language is not only a tool for interacting *with* social realities, the potentialities for further language interactions constitute a major portion of the ontology *of* those social realities.

Social and Cultural Persons

The developing child will be constructing the abilities to interact with his or her environments. These will be massively social, ranging from family, to other children, to school, to the wider society and culture. The interactive agent that is constructed in this developmental process, therefore, will be an agent that can coparticipatively constitute the society(ies) in which he or she has grown up.

This social participative and social constituting agent will be quite different in kind from the more basic biological infant, however much it is the case that the particular infant is inherently open to such social development. Here, biological ontogenesis supports sociopsychological ontogenesis, and something new is emergently constructed: a social person, an interactive agent that is significantly social in its own ontology.

Furthermore, because societies and cultures are themselves historistic, the kind of social person developed in one culture may be deeply different from that developed in another (e.g., Geertz, 1973, 1983). The social person is not only an emergent agent, he or she is also an ontological heir to the historicity of the society and culture in which and out of which that emergence occurs.

There are at least two senses in which this constructive emergence takes place. The first is the more intuitive, and is simply the basic organization of what the person knows how to do as a social participant. The second is at first puzzling: cultures generate persons with fundamentally different values concerning multiple domains and scales of importance, and including values concerning what is important and worthwhile in life. It is such values that make social persons from different cultures most fundamentally different as persons. The difference is not just in skills, but in what can and will be taken to be meaningful, what can even be seriously considered as an option. It could not be a serious option, for example, for me to consider becoming a mendicant Buddhist monk: the value organization and presuppositions about the world and life are simply too different.

But how can such value differences be constructed? They are not instrumental skills that can be practiced and adopted for appropriate instrumental tasks; they are more fundamental to the person than that. They cannot be construed as being pressed into an otherwise passive mind: that approach to modeling is ruled out for all learning and development. What cultures provide is not values that can be pressed into children, but, rather, values as options that the child can construct to organize his or her life, or values as presuppositions of ways of being that the child can construct (Bickhard, 2004a). These are options both in the sense that the society will provide models for what it is like to live those values—guides to what to construct—and in the sense (usually) that the society provides ways for persons in that society to actually live those values, locations, or positions, or statuses that relate to persons in those positions in ways that make living those values possible. It is difficult, for example, to be a mendicant monk if there is no institution in the society of supporting such monks with food and other resources.

Hermeneutic Ontology   Social persons are significantly social in their ontology, not just in their instrumental skills. Sociality, in turn, is significantly linguistic in its ontology: much of social reality is constituted in organizations of potential further language activity. Social persons, then, are also significantly linguistic in their ontology: much of who and what we are is constituted in language potentialities, including language about ourselves as social and linguistic beings.

In this way, the interactive model of social persons partially converges with the hermeneutic model of human ontology (Gadamer, 1975, 1976). Human beings are constituted in important ways by their language-framed self-interpretations.

But this is an emergent ontology, emergent within and with the support of the biological base. The ontology of persons is not *only* social and linguistic, not only cultural and historical. Furthermore, being biological human beings as well as social persons, the possibility is open that there are shared intrinsic interests and constraints that cross societies and cultures. I will not pursue this possibility here, but mention it because it potentially avoids the apparent cultural relativism of a fully hermeneutic human ontology: if we are completely constituted in our culture and its history, then there is no possibility of warranted judgment, moral judgment, for example, from within one culture about issues in another (Bickhard, in preparation; R. L. Campbell & Bickhard, 1986). In this view, there is no warranted judgment from Western culture, for example, that Aztec human sacrifice involves any moral violation. In contrast, the universal possibility of violating intrinsic, thus universal, interests and constraints provides a framework, however fallible and difficult to explore, for warranted judgments of cross-cultural scope.

Persons and Culture   Persons, then, are developmental emergents; they are social developmental emergents. Because the ontology of social reality is largely constituted in language potentialities, persons have a social, cultural, linguistic ontology. They are constituted in and of a social/cultural emergent level of reality. Human society and persons coconstitute each other, both developmentally and occurrently.

Culture is the historistic aspect of social realities. It is the historical sedimentation of past social evolution and social constructions. Among the most important aspects of social and cultural processes is that culture induces the developmental emergent "production" of persons who can and do coconstitute that culture. In this manner, culture creates its own emergence base by guiding the developmental emergence of its constituent persons.

Culture, then, is a realm of evolution with its own historicities, an ontology that is partially independent of the biological base. It is a kind of emergent historistic process that creates its own emergence base ongoingly through its historical development. In this respect, culture is a unique realm of evolution: there are partial parallels elsewhere in evolution, but nowhere that the emergence base for an evolutionary process is created ongoingly by that very evolutionary process.

And persons are ontologically part of that process.

THEORETICAL COMMITMENTS

The model outlined here is dependent for its coherence on strong theoretical assumptions. The possibility of any kind of ontologically real emergence requires a process metaphysics. Otherwise all causality remains with the fundamental particles, whatever physics ultimately tells us they are.[12] The possibility of human developmental emergence presupposes the interactive nature of what emerges. Otherwise, the world can just impress itself into a passive mind and there is no significant constructive development. And the possibility of the emergence of persons requires the coconstituting emergence of social reality, language, and person, all with their cultural historicities. Otherwise, social knowledge is just a set of skills and data encoded in the databanks of biological computers, no different in kind from nonsocial knowledge and data. Recognizing the social emergent nature of persons is forced by these underlying theoretical commitments, but it is also not coherently possible without them.

PHILOSOPHY OF SCIENCE COMMITMENTS

Exploring ontologies is not a common or familiar practice in contemporary psychology. We are still burdened by the naïve inductivism of the neo-Macheanism inherited from behaviorism, and issues of ontology and metaphysics are not, within this framework, considered to be scientific. But there are very good reasons to reject this heritage: the empiricist epistemology is bankrupt (e.g., operational definitions were proven to be inadequate in the 1930s); the inductivism is false and misleading (e.g., not even logical positivism maintained the naïve inductivism that psychology still works with); the positivistic rejection of metaphysical issues is ungrounded and self-contradictory (empiricist positivism is itself a metaphysical commitment, just one that insulates itself from examination by its rejection of "metaphysics"). In sum, psychology is burdened with a deeply wrong conception of what science is, and, therefore, of how good science should be pursued. By the standards of contemporary psychology, contemporary physics, for example, is very bad science (Bickhard, 1992b).

The metaphysical explorations in this chapter, then, not only involve theoretical commitments, they also involve commitments in the philosophy of science in general, and the philosophy of psychology in particular. Within an empiricist inductivism, these explorations have no place. But, then, within such a view of science, exploring the nature of quantum fields and gravity has no legitimate place either.

CONCLUSION

The ontology of persons is an issue which *should* have a central place in psychology. Pursuing it here presupposes a number of theoretical and philosophical commitments that are not yet common in the field. This exploration has looked at issues regarding emergence in general and especially normative emergence, constructive developmental emergence still more specifically, and the developmental emergence of social persons as constitutive participants in society and culture in particular. The conclusion?—

Whether or not you are social in the sense of sociable, you *are* social ontologically (at least in a major way).

Notes

1. Aristotle's substances could change—into each other—but he had a still more fundamental level that did not change, that did satisfy the Parmenidean constraints (Gill, 1989). The assumption of "no change" has dominated thought since then.
2. A few years ago I heard a major psychologist respond to a question about the normativity of representation with the response: "I'm not interested in that mystical stuff." From within a purely factual perspective on the world, normativity is outside of the ken: it is mystical, not scientific, not part of the world to be scientifically accounted for.
3. Kim's more recent work makes increasing room for emergent phenomena (1998, 2005), but does so by making room for configuration, or organization, as a legitimate locus of causal power—and this is precisely what I argue is required for legitimate models of emergence. It is not clear, however, how Kim's legitimation of organization is justified by Kim's arguments.
4. Hilbert was not the first to recognize implicit definition (Hilbert, 1971; Kneale & Kneale, 1986), but he put the notion in play in a major way among early analytic philosophy. Schlick, for example, attempted to make use of implicit definition in his early work (Coffa, 1991; Schlick, 1925/1985).

5. Mention should be made at this point of Beth's theorem, which has frequently been used as an excuse for ignoring implicit definition (Doyle, 1985). Beth's theorem proves that, under certain conditions, implicit and explicit definition are of equal power. Why pay attention to implicit definition then? This conclusion is in error in at least three ways: (1) even if implicit and explicit definition were in fact equal in all other ways, it remains the case that implicit definition cannot be back-translated through, and, thus, that Hume's argument is unsound; (2) the equivalence of power proven in Beth's theorem is an extensional equivalence only, and has no bearing on issues of meaning; and (3) Beth's theorem is proven in first order predicate logic with infinite models (Chang & Keisler, 1990), and, in all other combinations of logics and models (e.g., infinitary logics, fixed point logics, finite models, etc.), implicit definition has been found to be either equally as powerful as explicit definition or *more* powerful than explicit definition (Dawar, Hella, Kolaitis, 1995; Hella, Kolaitis, Luosto, 1994; Kolaitis, 1990). In no case is it less powerful: implicit definition cannot be ignored.

6. The standard more naïve conception of contemporary physics is that of particles that interact with each other via various fields: gravitational, electrical, and so on. This view fits poorly with contemporary physics, but it nevertheless has already conceded the basic point above: if fields are countenanced, then organization is legitimated as a potential locus of causal power because fields are causal and are so necessarily in part in virtue of their organization.

7. I will skip over and not address here the simplest form of normative emergence, that of biological normative function. The grounding intuition, however, is itself simple: contributions to the maintenance of a far from equilibrium system are functional for the continued existence of that system (Bickhard, 1993, 2000c, 2003, in preparation; Christensen & Bickhard, 2002).

8. Consistent with this point, Piaget's model is a constructivist model. Piaget, however, though he acknowledged "random" variation and selection, thought that such a process was too weak to account for all aspects of development, and posited an inherent "groping" as the central process. I argue that Piaget was in error in this reasoning (Bickhard, 1992c).

9. This is very much a psychological notion of knowing, and knowledge. Its relationships with the philosophical criteria of justified, true, belief are not simple (Bickhard, in preparation). But the philosophical notion is a "success" notion: it is not ascertainable with certainty by an organism, including a human, whether or not some potential knowledge is in fact knowledge in this philosophical sense.

10. This introduces interesting and at times important levels of epistemological and ontological reflexivities to social situations (Bickhard, 1980). I will not address these here.

11. In at least one sense, it can be misleading to characterize utterances as *transformations* of social situations: this usage is consistent with a notion that utterances somehow *encode* transformations similar to the sense in which a mathematical formula might encode a function. There are strong arguments, however, that language not only is not an encoding phenomenon, but that it cannot be (Bickhard, 1980, 1992a, in preparation; Bickhard & R. L. Campbell, 1992). A more careful rendering might be to say that an utterance evokes a transformation of the social situation in the course of the (ap)perception of the utterance (Bickhard, in preparation; Bickhard & R. L. Campbell, 1992), but this would require considerable further discussion to elaborate.

12. But, of course, physics has already gone beyond this.

References

Berger, P. L., &Luckmann, T. (1966). *The social construction of reality.* Garden City, NY: Doubleday.

Bickhard, M. H. (1980). *Cognition, convention, and communication.* New York: Praeger.

Bickhard, M. H. (1987). The social nature of the functional nature of language. In M. Hickmann (Ed.), *Social and functional approaches to language and thought* (pp. 39–65). New York: Academic.

Bickhard, M. H. (1992a). How does the environment affect the person? In L. T. Winegar, J. Valsiner (Eds.), *Children's development within social contexts: Metatheory and theory* (pp. 63–92). Hillsdale, NJ: Lawrence Erlbaum.

Bickhard, M. H. (1992b). Myths of science: Misconceptions of science in contemporary psychology. *Theory and Psychology, 2,* 321–337.

Bickhard, M. H. (1992c). Piaget on variation and selection models: Structuralism, logical necessity, and interactivism. In L. Smith (Ed.), *Jean Piaget: Critical assessments* (Vol 3, pp. 388–434). London: Routledge.

Bickhard, M. H. (1993). Representational content in humans and machines. *Journal of Experimental and Theoretical Artificial Intelligence, 5,* 285–333.

Bickhard, M. H. (1995). World mirroring versus world making: There's gotta be a better way. In L. Steffe & J. Gale (Eds.), *Constructivism in education* (pp. 229–267). Hillsdale, NJ: Lawrence Erlbaum.

Bickhard, M. H. (1998a). Constructivisms and relativisms: A shopper's guide. In M. R. Matthews (Ed.), *Constructivism in science education: A philosophical debate.* (pp. 99–112). Dordrecht: Kluwer Academic.

Bickhard, M. H. (1998b). Levels of representationality. *Journal of Experimental and Theoretical Artificial Intelligence, 10,* 179–215.

Bickhard, M. H. (2000a). Emergence. In P. B. Andersen, C. Emmeche, N. O. Finnemann, & P. V. Christiansen (Eds.), *Downward causation* (pp. 322–348). Aarhus, Denmark: University of Aarhus Press.

Bickhard, M. H. (2000b). Motivation and emotion: An interactive process model. In R. D. Ellis & N. Newton (Eds.), *The caldron of consciousness* (pp. 161–178). Amsterdam: J. Benjamins.

Bickhard, M. H. (2000c). Autonomy, function, and representation [Special issue]. *Communication and Cognition—Artificial Intelligence, 17,* 111–131. (Special issue on: The contribution of artificial life and the sciences of complexity to the understanding of autonomous systems. Guest Editors: A. Exteberria, A. Moreno, & J. Umerez)

Bickhard, M. H. (2001). Why children don't have to solve the frame problems: Cognitive representations are not encodings. *Developmental Review, 21,* 224–262.

Bickhard, M. H. (2003). An integration of motivation and cognition. In L Smith, C. Rogers, & P. Tomlinson (Eds.), *Monograph Series: Vol. 2. Development and motivation: Joint perspectives* (pp. 41–56). Leicester: British Psychological Society.

Bickhard, M. H. (2004a). The social ontology of persons. In J. I. M. Carpendale & U. Müller (Eds.), *Social interaction and the development of knowledge* (pp. 111–132). Mahwah, NJ: Lawrence Erlbaum.

Bickhard, M. H. (2004b). Process and emergence: Normative function and representation. *Axiomathes—An International Journal in Ontology and Cognitive Systems, 14,* 135–169. (Original work published 2003)

Bickhard, M. H. (in preparation). *The whole person: Toward a naturalism of persons—Contributions to an ontological psychology.*

Bickhard, M. H., & Campbell, D. T. (2003). Variations in variation and selection: The ubiquity of the variation-and-selective retention ratchet in emergent organizational complexity. *Foundations of Science, 8*, 215–282.

Bickhard, M. H., & Campbell, R. L. (1989). Interactivism and genetic epistemology. *Archives de Psychologie, 57*, 99–121.

Bickhard, M. H., & Campbell, R. L. (1992). Some foundational questions concerning language studies: With a focus on categorial grammars and model theoretic possible worlds semantics. *Journal of Pragmatics, 17*, 401–433.

Bickhard, M. H., & Campbell, R. L. (1996). Topologies of learning and development. *New Ideas in Psychology, 14*, 111–156.

Bickhard, M. H., & Terveen, L. (1995). *Foundational issues in artificial intelligence and cognitive science: Impasse and solution.* Amsterdam: Elsevier.

Campbell, D. T. (1974). Evolutionary epistemology. In P. A. Schilpp (Ed.), *The philosophy of Karl Popper* (pp. 413–463). LaSalle, IL: Open Court.

Campbell, D. T. (1990). Levels of organization, downward causation, and the selection-theory approach to evolutionary epistemology. In G. Greenberg & E. Tobach (Eds.), *Theories of the evolution of knowing* (pp. 1–17). Hillsdale, NJ: Lawrence Erlbaum.

Campbell, R. (1992). *Truth and historicity.* Oxford: Clarendon Press.

Campbell, R. L., & Bickhard, M. H. (1986). *Knowing levels and developmental stages: Contributions to human development.* Basel, Switzerland: Karger.

Campbell, R. L., & Bickhard, M. H. (1992). Types of constraints on development: An interactivist approach. *Developmental Review, 12*, 311–338.

Cao, T. Y. (1999). Introduction: Conceptual issues in quantum field theory. In T. Y. Cao (Ed.), *Conceptual foundations of quantum field theory* (pp. 1–27). Cambridge: Cambridge University Press.

Chang, C. C., & Keisler, H. J. (1990). *Model theory.* North Holland.

Christensen, W. D., & Bickhard, M. H. (2002). The process dynamics of normative function. *Monist, 85*, 3–28.

Coffa, J. A. (1991). *The semantic tradition from Kant to Carnap.* Cambridge: Cambridge University Press.

Cummins, R. (1996). *Representations, targets, and attitudes.* Cambridge, MA: MIT Press.

Davies, P. C. W. (1984). Particles do not exist. In S. M. Christensen (Ed.), *Quantum theory of gravity* (pp. 66–77). Bristol: Adam Hilger.

Dawar, A., Hella, L., & Kolaitis, P. G. (1995, July 10–11). Implicit definability and infinitary logic in finite model theory. *Proceedings of the 22nd International Colloquium on Automata, Languages, and Programming*, ICALP 95, Szeged, Hungary (pp. 621–635). New York: Springer-Verlag.

Doyle, J. (1985). Circumscription and implicit definability. *Journal of Automated Reasoning, 1*, 391–405.

Dretske, F. I. (1988). *Explaining behavior.* Cambridge, MA: MIT Press.

Fodor, J. A. (1975). *The language of thought.* New York: Crowell.

Fodor, J. A. (1987). *Psychosemantics.* Cambridge, MA: MIT Press.

Fodor, J. A. (1990a). *A theory of content.* Cambridge, MA: MIT Press.

Fodor, J. A. (1990b). Information and representation. In P. P. Hanson (Ed.), *Information, language, and cognition* (pp. 175–190). Vancouver: University of British Columbia Press.

Fodor, J. A. (1991). Replies. In B. Loewer & G. Rey (Eds.), *Meaning in mind: Fodor and his critics* (pp. 255–319). Oxford: Blackwell.

Fodor, J. A. (1998). *Concepts: Where cognitive science went wrong.* Oxford.

Gadamer, H.-G. (1975). *Truth and method*. New York: Continuum.

Gadamer, H.-G. (1976). *Philosophical hermeneutics*. Berkeley: University of California Press.

Geertz, C. (1973). *The interpretation of cultures*. New York: Basic Books.

Geertz, C. (1983). *Local knowledge*. New York: Basic Books.

Gill, M.-L. (1989). *Aristotle on substance*. Princeton, NJ: Princeton University Press.

Guthrie, W. K. C. (1965). *A history of Greek philosophy: Vol. 2. The Presocratic tradition from Parmenides to Democritus*. Cambridge: Cambridge University Press.

Hale, B., & Wright, C. (2000). Implicit definition and the a priori. In P. Boghossian & C. Peacocke (Eds.), *New essays on the a priori* (pp. 286–319). Oxford: Oxford University Press.

Hella, L., Kolaitis, P. G., & Luosto, K. (1994, July 4–7). How to define a linear order on finite Models. *Proceedings: Symposium on Logic in Computer Science, Paris, France*. Los Alamitos, CA: IEEE Computer Society Press.

Hilbert, D. (1971). *The foundations of geometry*. La Salle, IL: Open Court.

Huggett, N. (2000). Philosophical foundations of quantum field theory. *The British Journal for the Philosophy of Science, 51*(Suppl.), 617–637.

Hume, D. (1978). *A treatise of human nature* (L. A. Selby-Bigge, Index; P. H. Nidditch, Notes). Oxford: Oxford University Press. (Original work published 1739–1740)

Joas, H. (1993). American pragmatism and German thought: A history of misunderstandings. In H. Joas, *Pragmatism and social theory* (pp. 94–121). Chicago: University of Chicago Press.

Kim, J. (1989). The myth of nonreductive materialism. *Proceedings and Addresses of the American Philosophical Association, 63*, 31–47.

Kim, J. (1990). Supervenience as a philosophical concept. *Metaphilosophy, 21*, 1–27.

Kim, J. (1991). Epiphenomenal and supervenient causation. In D. M. Rosenthal (Ed.), *The nature of mind* (pp. 257–265). Oxford: Oxford University Press.

Kim, J. (1992a). "Downward causation" in emergentism and non-reductive physicalism. In A. Beckermann, H. Flohr, & J. Kim (Eds.), *Emergence or reduction?Essays on the prospects of nonreductive physicalism* (pp. 119–138). Berlin: Walter de Gruyter.

Kim, J. (1992b). Multiple realization and the metaphysics of reduction. *Philosophy and Phenomenological Research, 52*, 1–26.

Kim, J. (1993a). *Supervenience and mind*. Cambridge: Cambridge University Press.

Kim, J. (1993b). The non-reductivist's troubles with mental causation. In J. Heil & A. Mele (Eds.), *Mental causation* (pp. 189–210). Oxford: Oxford University Press.

Kim, J. (1997). What is the problem of mental causation? In M. L. D. Chiara, K. Doets, D. Mundici, & J. van Benthem (Eds.), *Structures and norms in science* (pp. 319–329). Dordrecht: Kluwer Academic.

Kim, J. (1998). *Mind in a physical world*. Cambridge, MA: MIT Press.

Kim, J. (2005). *Physicalism, or something near enough*. Princeton, NJ: Princeton University Press.

Kneale, W., & Kneale, M. (1986). *The development of logic*. Oxford: Clarendon.

Kolaitis, Ph. G. (1990). Implicit definability on finite structures and unambiguous computations. In *Proceedings of the fifth IEEE LICS* (pp. 168–180).

Levine, A., & Bickhard, M. H. (1999). Concepts: Where Fodor went wrong. *Philosophical Psychology, 12*, 5–23.

Lewis, D. K. (1969). *Convention*. Cambridge, MA: Harvard University Press.

McKirahan, R. D. (1994). *Philosophy before Socrates*. Indianapolis, IN: Hackett.

Millikan, R. G. (1984). *Language, thought, and other biological categories*. Cambridge, MA: MIT Press.

Millikan, R. G. (1993). *White queen psychology and other essays for Alice*. Cambridge, MA: MIT Press.

Mounce, H. O. (1997). *The two pragmatisms*. London: Routledge.

Newell, A. (1980). Physical symbol systems. *Cognitive Science, 4*, 135–183.

Piaget, J. (1954). *The construction of reality in the child*. New York: Basic Books.

Reale, G. (1987). *A history of ancient philosophy: Vol. 1. From the origins to Socrates*. Albany, NY: SUNY Press.

Rosenthal, S. B. (1983). Meaning as habit: Some systematic implications of Peirce's pragmatism. In E. Freeman (Ed.), *The relevance of Charles Peirce* (pp. 312–327). La Salle, IL: Monist.

Rouse, J. (2002). *How scientific practices matter: Reclaiming philosophical naturalism*. Chicago: University of Chicago Press.

Sacks, M. (1998). The subject, normative structure, and externalism. In A. Biletzki & A. Matar (Eds.), *The story of analytic philosophy* (pp. 88–107). New York: Routledge.

Saunders, S., & Brown, H. R. (1991). *The philosophy of vacuum*. Oxford: Clarendon.

Schelling, T. C. (1963). *The strategy of conflict*. New York: Oxford University Press.

Schlick, J. (1985). *General theory of knowledge*. La Salle, IL: Open Court. (Original work published 1925)

Stephan, A. (1992). Emergence—A systematic view on its historical facets. In A. Beckermann, H. Flohr, & J. Kim (Eds.), *Emergence or reduction? Essays on the prospects of nonreductive physicalism* (pp. 25–48). Berlin: Walter de Gruyter.

Vera, A. H., & Simon, H. A. (1993). Situated action: A symbolic interpretation. *Cognitive Science, 17*, 7–48.

Weinberg, S. (1977). The search for unity, notes for a history of Quantum Field Theory. *Daedalus, 106*, 17–35.

Weinberg, S. (1995). *The quantum theory of fields*: *Vol. 1. Foundations*. Cambridge: Cambridge University Press.

Weinberg, S. (1996). *The quantum theory of fields: Vol. 2. Modern applications*. Cambridge: Cambridge University Press.

Wimsatt, W. C. (1986). Forms of aggregativity. In A. Donogan, A. N. Perovich, & M. V. Wedin (Eds.), *Human nature and natural knowledge* (pp. 259–291). Dordrecht: Reidel.

Wimsatt, W. C. (1997). Aggregativity: Reductive heuristics for finding emergence. In L. Darden (Ed.), *PSA 1996 Part II , 64* [Suppl.], 372–384.

3

Perspectives and Persons
Ontological, Constitutive Possibilities

JACK MARTIN

In contemporary developmental psychology, perspective taking is understood as an important process or mechanism by which we come to know that others are people with minds of their own, intentional agents whose goals, strategies, commitments, and orientations bear both similarities to and differences from our own. Herein, I will argue that perspective taking is more than a powerful epistemic mechanism of this sort, that it also and more foundationally is ontologically constitutive of us as social, psychological persons and rational, moral agents. On this account, human persons are understood as interactive kinds (Hacking, 1999) who care about and react to the ways in which they are described and classified, and such uniquely human care and reactivity are consequences of our perspectivity. It is because we are able to occupy and take perspectives that we are persons at all. It is by means of perspective taking that we are constituted as selves and agents, and that we simultaneously also come to differentiate and understand others.

Now, to assert that persons are constituted perspectivally is a huge claim, one that requires a great deal of argument, demonstration, and discussion, to which I am able only to offer a modest beginning herein. Fortunately, however, I am not laboring alone, but am able to stand on the shoulders of several influential others who have made significant contributions to such a view of perspectives and persons. Consequently, in selectively recounting some of their positions, I am able to initiate a good deal of the argumentation and demonstration that my claim concerning the perspectival constitution of persons as selves and agents requires.

PERSPECTIVE TAKING, PERSPECTIVES, AND PERSONS: CONCEPTUAL ISSUES AND DEFINITIONS

Perspective Taking

In developmental psychology, perspectives typically enter into discussions of important aspects of personhood (such as selfhood, agency, and self-understanding) through theorizing and inquiry concerning perspective taking (sometimes equated with role taking, person perception, decentration, social cognition, and psychological mindedness). For the most part, conceptions of perspective taking in developmental psychology converge on the idea of perspective taking as a kind of guesswork by which individuals attempt to determine "the covert, psychological processes of other people...their abilities, knowledge, perceptions, attitudes, motives, [beliefs] and intentions with respect to this or that concrete situation" (Flavell, Botkin, Fry, Wright, & Jarvis, 1968, p. v). Such guesswork may be (1) explicit or implicit; (2) perceptual, conceptual/cognitive, or affective; (3) behaviorally linked or not; (4) related to one's self-understanding or not; and (5) involve differing degrees of coordination and organization of the perspectives considered. All of these variations depend not only on the conceptions and definitions held by different researchers and theorists, but also upon the kinds of tasks and procedures employed in relevant inquiries.

Explicit or Implicit

Studies of perspective taking typically require explicit verbal or written responses from children concerning how another thinks, feels, or is likely to act. However, some research infers perspective taking from children's naturally occurring nonverbal and verbal actions. For example, Light (1979) relaxes the explicitness of the guesswork involved by focusing on "how far the child takes account of other people's perceptions, expectations or emotions in his dealings with them" (p. xi), with such "accounting" often inferred from the actions and words of very young children. As developmental research on perspective taking has focused on increasingly young children (especially in more recent years), such inferencing has become a matter of considerable conjecture and debate (e.g., Carpendale & Lewis, 2004; Hobson, 2002; Tomasello, Carpenter, Call, Behne, & Moll, 2005).

Perceptual, Conceptual/Cognitive, or Affective

In consideration of possible differences in the extent to which perspective taking is understood as perceptual, conceptual/cognitive, or affective, Shantz (1975) has distinguished five categories of social inference that seem to be implicated to differing extents in developmental research on perspective taking. These include inferences about what another is seeing, feeling, thinking, or intending, and more generally what another is like. In many studies, perceptual, cognitive or conceptual, and affective modes of perspective taking have been positively associated with prosocial behavior (Underwood & Moore, 1982), perhaps suggesting a more holistic form of perspective taking that includes all of these modalities. Whether or not any such general form is an aggregated composite of more particular forms is not clear. Another possibility is that distinctions among perceptual, cognitive/ conceptual, and affective forms of perspective reflect the analytic theoretical predilections of psychologists more than the reality of human activity (Harré, 1998).

Action Linked or Not

Debate concerning the extent to which conceptions of perspective taking are linked to action or self-understanding is reflected in a comparison of views like those of Sarbin (1954) and Carpendale and Lewis (2004). Sarbin, despite emphasizing the social origins of role-taking in general, draws a clear distinction between any given instance of role-taking as a prelude to the possibility of action based on perspectival understanding, and actual role-enactment. On the other hand, Carpendale and Lewis (2004), following Chapman (1991, 1999), view social understanding of the kind involved in perspective taking as unfolding within actual social activity with others and to thus be inseparable from social interaction.

Related to Self-Understanding or Not

Yet another source of diversity in conceptions of perspective taking lies in the fact that some developmentalists link perspective taking directly to the development of self and self-understanding (e.g., Hobson, 2002; Selman, 1980), while others (e.g., Flavell, 1992), although not uninterested in self-development, tend to focus on the information processing and epistemic functions of perspective taking in a more instrumental navigation of life's challenges. As already suggested, one of the primary aims of this chapter is to promote a more radically ontological focus for scholarly inquiry into perspective taking and selfhood.

Coordination and Organization

Finally, for some theorists, perspective taking is not just a matter of inferring the psychological life of others, but of coordinating and organizing various perspectives of self and others in a way that enables progressively higher forms of self and other understanding and functioning. Such an emphasis on coordination and organization is clearly evident in the works of Werner (1948), Piaget (1926, 1928, 1976; Piaget & Inhelder, 1948/1963), and Selman (1980), amongst others. In fact, Selman (1980) defines social perspective taking as including:

> ...a developing understanding of how human points of view are related and coordinated with one another and not simply what social or psychological information may appear to be like from an alternative individual's perspectives as in the construct of role-taking. (p. 22)

Towards greater holism, interactivism, and ontological focus
With respect to differing conceptions of perspective taking that flow from variations in the kind of inferential processes assumed in determining another's perspective, Chandler (2001) has painted a rather bleak picture.

> …many have found it perfectly natural to mix the properly perceptual
> subject of visual perspective taking with just about anything else having
> to do with the situatedness of social roles, or the ineluctably subjective
> nature of the knowing process. From there it has proved to be only a
> short step to the common confusion of making a single conceptual piece
> out of the otherwise disparate matters of visual perspective taking, social
> role taking, narcissism, self-absorption, empathy, and a hundred other
> things having to do with the fact that knowing, like seeing, lends itself to
> being discussed in the language of coordinated perspectives. The result
> has been a whole dog's breakfast of seriously incommensurable bits and
> pieces of theory and practice that…prove to be indigestible. (p. 49)

Of course, Chandler (2001) is correct to point to the common conceptual
confusion of assuming that all instances labeled in a particular way are necessarily similar in more than their labeling. Nonetheless, perspective taking may
be a kind of holistic, relational phenomenon with aspects that coherently may
be seen to encompass many of the diverse properties and processes attributed to
it by developmental psychologists and others. However, I believe that the envi-
sioning of such a possibility requires a consideration of the ontological status of
perspectives themselves. It also requires a shift away from the kind of inferential
guesswork assumed in the majority of the developmental literature on perspective taking, and toward those routines and conventions of social interactivity that
envelop the developing child.

Perspectives
Two features are common to most conventional definitions and uses of the term
perspective when employed in its psychological sense to mean a mental view.
One of these is an activity of seeing or viewing. The other concerns the private
or mental character of this apparently perceptual activity. Both of these features
reflect the dualisms of appearance versus reality, and mental or psychological
versus social, often implying a limited, personal or biased access to those entities,
events, and situations on which our perspectives are fixed. Things may not be as
they seem to be, and one's own view may diverge from communally sanctioned
conventions. As expressed by Drummond of Hawthornden in 1711 (Oxford English Dictionary, 1989), "All, that we can set our eyes on in these intricate mazes of
life, is but vain perspective and deceiving shadows, appearing far otherwise afar
off, than when…gazed upon at a near distance." The metaphoric extension of the
fallible, perceptual gaze that is evident in Drummond's statement so consistently
has attended everyday use of the term that perspectives commonly and broadly
may be understood as orientations to situations. That perspectives change and

develop is also readily evident—"time and experience...alter all perspectives" (Adams, 1907/1995, p. 22). Moreover, such orientations apparently serve particular functions of assisting our understanding of, and action within, those worldly situations in which we find ourselves, even if they may occasionally yield poor dividends as explanatory or anticipatory vehicles.

So *perspectives may be understood as orientations to situations (including things and events within them) that function to interpret and facilitate action within them, with the understanding that such orientations are not fixed but dynamically unfolding as situations continuously emerge and are transformed.* Such a definition and conceptualization leave open questions of the explicit/ implicit, perceptual/conceptual, cognitive/affective, real/imaginary, private/public, or psychological/social status of perspectives. Theoretically, perspectives may range from the highly idiosyncratic and fantastical to the strictly conventional and concrete. They may be explicitly and deliberately conscious or tacitly emotive and unplanned. Nonetheless, it is clear that *perspectives are relations between human persons and their biophysical, sociocultural world*, and that *these relations anchor our being and knowing as psychological persons.* Not only does such a conceptualization of perspectives fit everyday uses of the term (with respect to the senses discussed here), it also applies equally well to standard applications of the term within developmental psychology and to those more ontologically oriented positions that also will be discussed shortly.

To take a perspective then may be understood as adopting an orientation to a particular situation, whether this is done knowingly or not. But, if this is the case, what comes of the assumption that permeates, both explicitly and implicitly, so much of the scholarly literature to the effect that perspective taking is a uniquely human capability that is possibly responsible for much human communicative and sociocultural accomplishment? For example, Hobson (2002) ends his book, *The Cradle of Thought* by stressing the centrality of perspective taking to the human condition:

> To understand that one has a subjective perspective is to open the door to a world of meanings...[to think] about other people as individuals with subjective perspectives of their own. At this point...the infant has been lifted out of the cradle of thought. Engagement with others has taught this soul to fly. (p. 274)

Nonetheless, there would seem to be little doubt that all living things orient in some way to their environments. If this is all that is meant by perspective taking, we are a long way from Hobson's image of humanity. Of course, adding the functional consequences of *interpretation and action* to the definition of perspectives (see above) possibly does much to restrict perspective taking, at least to the higher primates. Such restriction would seem to flow from most conventional senses of these terms, especially the reflective connotations of *interpretation*. The codicil that perspectives are relations between human beings and their world that anchor their being and knowing as psychological persons (see above), obviously entails the restriction of perspective taking to persons, but seems to do so in an unduly, and perhaps unnecessarily stipulative manner. On the other hand, it may be that such a move can be defended with recourse to a consideration of the conceptual status of persons. If perspective taking is to be understood as something unique to human persons, it clearly behooves us to consider what we mean by persons. Indeed, something similar might be said of all developmental studies: "To see human development aright one must already have an account of the product, the mature human being" (Harré, 2004, p. 241).

Persons

In the social sciences and humanities, mature human beings are understood as persons. Locke's (1693/1995) famous essay on human understanding initiated the modern history of the topic by arguing that mature human beings ought be understood in psychological terms. For Locke, this meant treating personhood as a kind of psychological continuity, held together across time by memory, and linked to the future through the imagination. Parfit (1984) and other analytic philosophers have used the notion of "person stage" to describe the momentary slices of time in the history of a person. A series of person stages is held to be psychologically continuous if later members of the series develop in characteristic ways from earlier members of the series. The psychological capabilities posited as mechanisms or processes supplying the necessary coherence have included not only memory and imagination, but reason, self-consciousness, reflection, and agency. In recent years, the idea of persons as active, reflective agents who care about their circumstances and act in self-regulated ways to improve them has been prominent in much psychological literature (e.g., Bandura, 1997; Carver & Scheier, 1998).

However, many 20th-century philosophers and psychologists also have criticized Lockean and neo-Lockean conceptions of the person as too exclusively *intrapersonal*, the problem being that they seem to presuppose exactly the kind of psychological continuity that they claim as a criterion. Continuity of whatever kind is on offer presumably must be experienced, and what is it that performs such experiencing if not a person? Continuity cannot both constitute and require personhood simultaneously, at least not in accepted, analytic systems of logic. In response to such concerns, various attempts have been made to broaden the conception of persons beyond intrapersonal processes promising psychological continuity. For example, Peter Strawson (1959) claimed that persons are jointly constituted as basic particulars of the human world by both physical and psychological properties. For Strawson, concepts like identity, singularity, and uniqueness require the embodiment of a human being as a thing amongst other things in a biophysical and sociocultural world.

Others, like Taylor (1989) and Harré (1998) have added historical, cultural, and moral requirements to the joint criteria of psychological continuity and embodiment. Taylor (1989) thus considers persons to be unique embodied beings, with a rich repertoire of psychological capabilities and distinctive histories, who are morally responsible for their actions. In somewhat similar vein, Harré (1998) defines persons as social and psychological, embodied beings with a sense of their own existence, history, beliefs, attributes, and place amongst similar others. Such extensions serve to distinguish human persons from merely biological beings of the species *Homo sapiens sapiens*, and make it difficult to envision a reduction of personhood to entirely physical and material properties and processes. By adding historical, moral, and sociocultural dimensions to the concept of person, they introduce significant elements of rationality, normativity, intentionality, and perspectivity to their makeup.

And yet, despite admitting sociocultural, historical, and moral criteria in the form of self-understanding and rational and moral agency, most philosophical and psychological conceptions of personhood also resist strong versions of sociocultural constructionism (e.g., Gergen, 1991) that would understand persons as constituted solely by and in historical, sociocultural terms. To reconcile biology and culture, most contemporary theorists of personhood understand persons as coconstituted phylogenetically at the intersection of biophysical evolution and sociocultural history (e.g., Donald, 2001; Emmeche, Køppe, & Stjernfelt, 2000; Tomasello, 1999). Moreover, much as Piaget (1928, 1963, 1977/1995) consistently claimed, it is human activity within the biophysical and sociocultural world that occasions personal development during ontogenesis. Indeed, the self-understanding and self-determination (agency) that are central to notions of persons in much psychology typically are understood as emergent products of embodied activity with others within organized sociocultural contexts (e.g., Bickhard, 2004; Martin, 2003, 2005a; Tomasello, 1999).

Consistent with the general, contemporary consensus just articulated, I understand persons to be *embodied selves and agents (both rational and moral) with social and psychological identities, and rights and duties, who care about and can understand something of their existence and circumstances.* The agentive selfhood, identity, and personal understanding assumed in this definition would clearly be impossible in the absence of biophysically evolved human bodies and brains (Donald, 2001; Tomasello, 1999). However, such core criteria of personhood also would be impossible without ongoing interactions with others within historically established sociocultural contexts and practices during ontogenesis. For it is only through interacting with other persons that we gradually come to orient to our life circumstances reflexively as persons capable of self-understanding and self-determination who care deeply about our existence, our selves, and others. Such orientation is itself a matter of perspective taking. It is for this reason that philosophers as different in their views as Buber and Dennett have defined persons in perspectival terms—as beings capable of distinguishing between the I–it relationships that hold between oneself and a mere object, and the I–Thou relations that pertain between oneself and another person (Buber, 1923/1970), or as beings capable of taking an intentional stance toward other persons, which means understanding their actions in terms of beliefs, desires, intentions, and so forth (i.e., perspectives) (Dennett, 1987).

It is through taking the perspectives of others, as nested within the social practices (especially relational and linguistic practices) of the larger society, that we come to interpret ourselves and act as persons. Moreover, this kind of personal development is not primarily an epistemic matter that consists in our coming to know about our selves and our world. Of course, it is that, but more primarily and importantly it is an ontological matter of our coming to be persons at all. At least that is the view that has been advanced in various ways by a number of past and contemporary scholars, whose views I now wish to consider, admittedly in a rather selective manner, before turning to possible implications of this central idea of *perspectival personhood.*

PERSPECTIVES AND PERSONS: A SELECTION
OF EXTANT FORMULATIONS

Traditionally, realist metaphysics in philosophy tends to grant reality status to entities and events if they do not depend on other things, but stand on their own and can be accessed objectively. In contrast, traditional idealist metaphysics holds that all entities and events consist of the ideas we have of them—that the appearances we experience are the very objects and happenings in question. Perspectivism arose in the 18th century as a response to such traditional metaphysical positions. Interestingly, from its very inception, perspectivism was closely associated with notions of selfhood and personhood. For example, Gustav Teichmüller, whose work probably exercised great influence on the philosophical reflections of Nietzsche (cf. Stack, 1999), held that the self available in one's immediate experience constituted, through its ongoing activity, the world as it affects the conceptions of any individual. At a metaphysical level, he held that each metaphysical system consisted of a perspective on a complex reality that contained partial truths.

Nietzsche
Nietzsche (1887/1967a, 1901/1967b) stressed the perspectival nature of all thinking, and consequently the provisional nature of all knowledge. For Nietzsche, entities, events, and values can have no absolute existence in themselves, apart from their relations to persons. Such relations are the only reality available to us, but if viewed through a multiplicity of perspectives, they are sufficient to secure warrantable knowledge in relation to differing sorts of interest and practice. In particular, syntheses of perspectives may be adjudicated according to the extent to which they function as life-preserving and life-promoting (cf. Tanner, 2000). For Nietzsche, the ideal that animates all ways of life is a will to become what you are by taking "over the task of creating oneself as a work of art" (Guignon, 2004, p. 131). If all that exists is perspectival, including one's self, then it is best to get on with the creative crafting of perspectives that might prove most functional in relation to other life-enhancing perspectives encountered and considered in the course of one's worldly activity. In this way, as emphasized by a later perspectival philosopher, Ortega y Gasset, "the self is not an entity separate from what sur-

rounds it; there is a dynamic interaction and interdependence of self and things. These and the self together constitute reality...every self has a unique perspective" (quoted in Garcia, 1999, p. 637).

G. H. Mead

Perhaps the most thoroughgoing philosophical perspectivism that has been developed to date was forged by American philosopher and social psychologist, George Herbert Mead. For Mead (1938, 1932/2002) reality is perspectival in that all phenomena (objects, events, selves, others, ideas, theories) emerge in the relation of persons and their contexts. For Mead, a perspective is an orientation to an environment that is associated with acting within that environment, actually or imaginatively. Perspectives emerge out of activity, especially joint social, interpersonal activity with others, and enable increasingly complex, differentiated, and abstracted forms of activity. They also provide the bases for selfhood. It is by taking perspectives that exist in the interpersonal and sociocultural world that, according to Mead, we come to exist as self-interpreting beings. An individual becomes "an object to himself by taking the attitudes of other individuals toward himself within an organized setting of social relationships" (Mead, 1934, p. 255). Through repeated and graduated participation in routine, everyday interactions with others (including play and games), children take different positions, roles, and perspectives within these conventional interactions. Such experience enables them not only to take different perspectives in interaction with others, but eventually to be able to occupy different perspectives simultaneously in a way that allows the child to be other to herself (Gillespie, 2005). She is then able to react to those very perspectives that now constitute her as an object or a "Me."

Importantly, for Mead, the activity of the self is conditioned by, but not determined by the social situations and processes within which it emerges developmentally. To become an object to itself, it is not enough for the self to take the perspectives of others and the broader society as experienced in one's own past and current history of interactivity. It also is necessary to react to the "Me" that appears in current action and imagination as a consequence of this past engagement with others. Consequently, Mead's self is constituted not only by a socially spawned, perspectival "Me," but also by an ongoing, immediate reaction to the "Me." This fleeting, agentive "I" reacts to the "Me" in the immediate moment of action, and (especially in novel and problematic situations) generates changes to the perspectival structure of the "Me," resulting in a reconstructed "Me" of the next moment to which an immediately future "I" will respond (Martin, 2005b, 2006). Such an ongoing, dynamic process of perspective taking and perspectival emergence constitutes our selfhood, and only can occur in the context of our interactions with others during ontogenesis. Mead's perspectival self marks a true joining of selfhood with perspective taking, and constitutes a major development in the history of perspectival personhood.

Another important contribution of Mead's perspectival theorizing is that unlike Drummond of Hawthornden (see above) and others who have emphasized the self-serving bias and deception that may attend personal perspectives, Mead maintains that perspectives are both real and correctable if too removed from relevant biophysical and sociocultural reality and practices. For example, orienting to ocean waves or chatty friends with imperious hauteur and commands that they cease and desist, are unlikely to function in the ways intended. For Mead (1932/2002) all perspectives are potentially objective, but it is only those that achieve adequate degrees of functionality and agreement within the real world that operate effectively as constraints and affordances for our worldly activity. For example, individuals typically entertain and experiment with a variety of perspectives in particular problem solving situations, but only a few of these achieve levels of utility and consensus that warrant their continued deployment and perhaps eventual conventionalization. Like Nietzsche's, Mead's perspectivism is a fallible realism capable of anchoring personal being and securing knowledge claims through a combination of warrants such as demonstrable utility, consensus, and conventionalization.

Bakhtin
Much in the same manner as Mead understood mind and selfhood to arise through taking the perspectives of others and society, and making them one's own by reacting to them, the early 20th-century Russian literary theorist, Mikhail Bakhtin, calls attention to the dialogical character of our ordinary experience. For Bakhtin (1981, 1986), individual thought consists of a dialogue with real and imagined interlocutors. We always first experience the world through a "We," before we come to experience it as an "I." "According to Bakhtin's dialogical conception of human existence, we are at the deepest level *polyphonic* points of intersection with a social world rather than *monophonic* centers of self-talk and will" (Guignon, 2004, p. 121; italics in the original). All of our dialogical encounters with others add to the complex of other and self perspectives through which we experience, understand, and act. Interactors in dialogical encounters always give something to each other. They are simultaneously caught up in both "I-for-the-other" and "other-for-me" perspectives (Bakhtin, 1993).

Bakhtin's dialogical conception of the self takes social interactions as foundational to our identity and personhood. For Bakhtin, as for Mead, our agency is wrapped up in our reactivity to those perspectives that we have taken from our social experiences with others that unfold within the larger sociocultural, linguistic process. It is by reacting with our emergent first-person perspectives to these second- and third-person perspectives that we come to exist as persons who care about our existence and entertain commitments and projects of self and other enhancement.

Baker
At least, this is the view of contemporary philosopher of mind and personhood, Lynne Rudder Baker (2000), who claims that a first-person perspective underlies all forms of self-consciousness that might conceivably stand as bases for agency

and personhood, and that such a first-person perspective is necessarily relational. According to Baker, there is no mysterious object that is oneself-as-oneself (i.e., no transcendental ego, no soul, no inner homunculus). The referent of "I" is the embodied person acting in the world. When a person refers to herself, what she refers to is no different from what someone who knows her refers to by using her proper name. What is different is that she can conceive of herself in a way that no one else can—from the "inside" so to speak—because she has a first-person perspective. Acquisition of a first-person perspective carries with it a genuine self-conception and self-consciousness. Only persons have such perspectives.

On Baker's account, human bodies predate the selves that they partially constitute. A person is a developmental accomplishment beyond bodily, biological development alone. In support of her assertions, Baker offers a formal argument for the relational nature of any first-person perspective. Her three premises are that (1) one can have a first-person perspective if and only if one can think of oneself as oneself; (2) one can think of oneself as oneself only if one has concepts that can apply to things different from oneself; and (3) one can have concepts that apply to things different from oneself only if one has had interactions with such things. From these premises, she concludes that if one has a first-person perspective, then one has had interactions with things different from oneself. The kinds of interactions Baker has in mind "are those in which the infant naturally develops various senses of 'self,' as described by developmental psychologists" (Baker, 2000, p. 96) "who routinely describe the acquisition of self-concepts in tandem with the acquisition of concepts of other things as different from oneself" (p. 66). Thus, for Baker, a first-person perspective is relational in that it would be impossible for a biological organism alone in the universe to develop a first-person perspective.

Hobson

Unlike Mead or Bakhtin, who speculate about more specific interactionist and narrative mechanisms by which first-person perspectives might flow from reacting to second- and third-person perspectives experienced and appropriated from interactions with other persons, Baker leaves the details of the developmental account required to the theoretical and empirical inquiries of developmental psychologists. Although many developmental psychologists have toiled productively in these fields (e.g., Carpendale & Lewis, 2004; Chandler, 2001; Flavell, 1992; Müller & Runions, 2003; Piaget & Inhelder, 1948/1963; Selman, 1980; Tomasello, 1999), Peter Hobson's (2002) thought is especially useful in furthering a perspectival ontology of persons during ontogenesis. The aim of Hobson's work is to "begin with the mental life of babies and to end up with a story of how thinking…emerges in the course of early development" (p. xiii). Hobson's account assumes a central role for perspective taking, in that "Thinking becomes possible because the child separates out one person's perspective from another's. More than this: thinking arises out of repeated experiences of *moving* from one psychological stance to another in relation to things and events" (p. 105). More specifically, according to Hobson (2002), the child

...first has to take a perspective on herself and her own attitudes. It is only by doing this, by taking a view on her own ways of construing the world, that she can begin to *think* in terms of her own and others' perspectives. This happens through a particular species of identification: the child identifies with others' attitudes towards the child's own attitudes and actions. Once more, the child is lifted out of her own stance and is drawn into adopting another perspective—this time a perspective on herself and what she is feeling and doing. She becomes self-aware through others.... The change comes about through the child grasping something—or rather a number of things. First, that there are such things as perspectives, and perspectives are what people have. Second, that she herself is a person with a perspective. It is a perspective that may differ from someone else's. Third, that she can choose to adopt the perspective of someone else. She can even do this while retaining her own perspective. She can hold in mind not just one but two perspectives at once.... It is for this reason that she becomes able to adjust her actions to the perspective of someone else.... It is for this reason that she can adopt a perspective towards her own actions and attitudes.... It is for this reason that, most wonderful of all, she can choose to apply new perspectives to things. When she does this with the kind of non-serious intent of which she has been capable for months, she is engaging in symbolic play. (pp. 106–107)

To make his thought more concretely accessible, Hobson (2002) employs a model consisting of a triangle of relations in which an infant relates to objects, persons, or events in the world; to herself as the other relates to her; and to the other's relation to the world (see Chapman, 1991, 1999 for a similar, although not identical, model of relations which he labeled "the epistemic triangle"). One of the theoretical purposes to which Hobson puts his relatedness triangle is to explain how the infant becomes able to understand that there is not just one perspective (i.e., her own) but two perspectives (e.g., her own and her mother's) involved in her interactions with another concerning some aspect of the world (e.g., an object such as a toy). "What we need to explain is how the child comes to *know* that her movement into this position of the other amounts to her taking up a new perspective" (Hobson, 2002, pp. 108–109). Hobson's answer, making use of his relatedness triangle, is to claim that through triangulation, a given object is experienced as in receipt of two different attitudes and meanings, and that

it is this that prompts the infant to separate out her own attitude from that of the other.... Through this experience of having both her own and her mother's attitudes to the same things, the infant learns something about things on the one hand and attitudes on the other. In reading her mother's reaction to a toy, the infant learns something about the toy; but at the same time, the toy tells her something about her mother. What it tells her is that her mother is different from herself, in a particular way. It tells her that her mother has an attitude to the toy that is separate from her own attitude to the same toy.... Events such as these are usually considered in terms of the infant finding out about the world through another person. Fair enough. But at the same time the child is learning about the nature of persons-with-minds through relating to a common world. (p. 109)

PRACTICES, PERSPECTIVES, AND PERSONS

I have attempted to articulate explicitly the relational ontology and developmental constitution of persons that emerge from the foregoing perspectival theorizing (Martin, 2005a). By combining this integrative theorizing with equally recent attempts to clarify exactly what a relational ontology of persons might entail (e.g., Slife, 2004) and with recent reformulations of Mead's perspectival theorizing (e.g., Gillespie, 2005, 2006; Martin, 2005b, 2006), it is possible to sketch an ontogenetic, developmental scenario. This is a scenario that nests personhood ontologically within first-, second-, and third-person perspectives as these are available in the interpersonal, societal, and cultural contexts in which human infants are embedded from birth and live out their lives. Such an account has much in common with the interactional approaches presented in the other chapters of the current volume. However, it is somewhat unique in its emphasis on the nature of perspective taking as an emergent developmental process. This is a process that itself follows a developmental trajectory, which moves from the occupation and exchange of different phases or positions in social interactions and sociocultural practices to the intentional and critical consideration of different practices and traditions of understanding and acting.

Relational Practices

As Slife (2004) reminds us, "practices are more pre-theoretical than theoretical, more concrete than abstract" (p. 157). Slife notes that, "practices are probably [our] most important form of...relating, because practices require a relationship not only with our surroundings but also with our prior actions and the actions of others" (p. 159). The coordination of relations that practices entail is captured nicely in the triadic models of relationality provided by Hobson (2002) and Chapman (1991, 1999). However, Slife (2004) does more than point to the epistemic consequences of our relational practices as persons in interaction with other persons, things, and occurrences in the social and physical world. More fundamentally, he asserts the central ontological implications of our ongoing embeddedness, from birth, in such practices. "[I]n their fundamental realness (in their practical and concrete realities) all things are ontologically related to their context and can qualitatively change as their contexts change.... All things...are concretely dependent upon, rather than independent of, their contexts" (Slife, 2004, p. 159).

A Relational Ontology of Persons

That such a relational ontology not only applies to our selves, but is the best way to conceive of selfhood and its development has been the thesis of my own onto-logical investigations of selfhood, agency, and personhood (Martin, 2003, 2005a; Martin & Sugarman, 1999; Martin, Sugarman, & Thompson, 2003).

> In ontogenesis, persons are developmentally emergent (both temporally and ontologically) from the practical activity of biological human beings in the physical and sociocultural world…. [Our] psychological personhood emerges both substantively and relationally. Infants actively explore their surroundings, observing and touching themselves, others, and things, and being observed and touched by others.… Caregivers and others interactwith developing infants [within] relational practices [that provide] forms and means of personhood and identity extant within particular societies and cultures. Psychological development proceeds as these…sociocultural, linguistic, and relational practices are employed as bases for language, and eventually for thought and reflection…. Over time, the individual's activity in the world is transformed from one of prereflection to one in which reflective, intentional agency emerges and fosters a self-understanding and personal identity linked to one's particular existence and personal history of activity. Such psychological continuity imbues an individual life with meaning and significance. Open to the life-world, the psychological person emerges as an embodied being with deliberative agency, self-understanding, and personal identity defined by commitments and concerns associated with her particular existence and activity in the world. (Martin, 2003, p. 96)

What I would like to do here is to focus more specifically on the ontologi-cal significance of perspective taking in the constitution of persons as selves and agents during ontogenesis. To do so, I turn initially to some recent reinterpreta-tions of the developmental theorizing of George Herbert Mead, my own included, which understand perspective taking as both embedded in and emergent from our concrete relational practices of interactivity with others.

The Ontological Significance of Perspective Taking

Both Gillespie (2005, 2006) and I (2005a, 2006) discuss the way in which Mead's social ontology of selfhood depends on the child's occupation of different social positions within routine social interactions and sociocultural practices (also see Müller & Runions, 2003). In effect, what our neo-Meadian accounts attempt to do is to clarify the exact manner in which Mead claimed that "We are in possession of selves just in so far as we can and do take the [perspectives] of others toward ourselves and respond to those [perspectives]" (Mead, 1932/2002, p. 194). Despite some minor differences in our accounts, the main idea is that as young children accumulate experience in different phases of conventional social interactions, they gradually are able to differentiate, integrate, and coordinate the different perspectives associated with different phases and positions in such interactions. In doing so, they are able to take different perspectives on themselves and to react to those perspectives —a process that enables them to develop self-understanding and first-person experience of themselves.

The child's repeated occupation of different social positions in conventional interactions with others eventually enables remembrance of these positions and the experience of them. Thus, for example, repeated experiences of receiving a rolling ball from another and rolling it back, or of taking the different roles of hider and seeker in games of hide-and-seek, allow the child to remember the different social positions of receiver and passer, or hider and seeker. It then becomes possible for the child to be in one social position while remembering and perhaps anticipating being in another. For example, the seeking child may recall a recent successful experience as a hider, and seek in that same place for her hiding playmate. In this way, the child is able effectively to occupy or take two or more perspectives simultaneously. Importantly, with this ability to enter simultaneously into different perspectives, the differentiation, integration, and coordination of perspectives discussed by developmental psychologists, together with increasingly abstract forms of remembrance and imagination, become possible.

With respect to the differentiation and development of the self, the child's experience and remembrance of different social positions and perspectives includes the reactions of others to her. It is these reactions of others that, according to Mead, provide an initial means of reacting to her self. Over time, and with increased social experience that includes the gradual mastery of a reflexive language, a greater and greater variety of reactive and reflexive possibilities becomes available. Importantly, the child's self-development is fueled by the child's reactivity not only to the reactions of particular others with whom she has interacted, but also to more abstracted and generalized others extracted from her broader experience of those social, cultural, and linguistic practices that subsume her overall social interactivity.

Equally importantly, the child's reactions to her self do not simply reflect the perspectives of others that she has experienced and recalled. The child also *reacts* to those perspectives and to salient features of her social situations. As her social experience and linguistic capabilities expand, additional resources for her self-development become available through her ongoing immersion in more diversified interactions that reflect broader sociocultural practices and perspectives of selfhood and personhood which she also can take up and react to. For example, the adolescent's reading of novels and viewing of films may provide narrative content that assists her to reorganize, elaborate, differentiate, and integrate perspectives and self-perspectives in ways that go well beyond her immediate, everyday experiences. Formal and informal educational experiences may themselves be interpreted as containing a wide variety of perspectives that hold significant possibilities for further self-development and realization.

SOME POSSIBILITIES FOR THE STUDY AND
PROMOTION OF PERSPECTIVE TAKING

Both Mead (1934) and Gillespie (2006) have suggested that children's games
are an excellent vehicle for the study of the development of perspective taking
and selfhood. For example, Gillespie (2006) points out that the game of hide-
and-seek is especially well suited to exploring Mead's theory. With two distinct
positions of hider and seeker that entail different action orientations, and with
a scripted position exchange following completion of each of its segments, this
game (common to many cultures) incorporates the principal elements in the foregoing neo-Meadian account. It requires that a participant, in order to succeed in
the game, must clearly differentiate the two social positions and the perspectives
their occupation entails, and also must integrate the two perspectives so that he
can "regulate activity within one social position with respect to the complementary position" (Gillespie, 2006, p. 91). The necessity of coordinating positions and
perspectives within any segment of the game, and across alternative segments
when formal social positions shift, provides clear practice in, and demonstration
of, simultaneously occupying/considering two complementary perspectives.

Moreover, as Gillespie (2006) points out, in many contemporary cultures,
there is a clear longitudinal, developmental sequence that connects the game of
hide-and-seek to obvious precursors such as "peek-a-boo," and successors, such
as treasure hunts and more abstracted narratives that revolve around hiding/seek-
ing and escaping/chasing (e.g., as evident in many cinematic and real-life dramas).
At more advanced levels, actual position exchange and occupation gives way to
vicariously engaged processes of narrative and personal imagination, elaboration, and coordination of the various perspectives involved. It is relatively easy
to imagine a variety of longitudinal, "naturalistic" studies of positional exchange
and perspective taking that might focus on games such as hide-and-seek, together
with their logically connected antecedents and consequents. Such games, perhaps with theoretically driven variations, also might be incorporated into active
interventions that might be offered to groups of children of different ages (and
with numerous variations in relevant factors such as the age and developmental
level of playing partners), and contrasted experimentally with control conditions
or alternative forms of facilitating perspective taking and self-development (e.g.,
interventions based on "theory of mind" accounts that are more didactic and less
relational, experiential).

More generally, early childhood and K-12 education provide many opportunities for the study of perspective taking and self-development. Indeed, several
prominent educators have suggested that the entire process of education might
best be understood in terms that relate directly to perspective taking. An example
is available in the writings of Philippe Meirieu (2005). Meirieu maintains that
school is a place where children learn to disengage from their own experiences,
situations, and preoccupations through ongoing interaction with other children
and the curriculum. "L'École doit aider l'enfant à renoncer à être au centre du

monde" (p. 68, "School must help the child to renounce being at the center of the world"). They learn that there are conventions and practices of correctness and truth that resist their own desires, and that they must participate in such practices and judge themselves and others accordingly. For Meirieu, a critical aspect of this escape from their immediate desires is learning to respect and consider other perspectives. "À l'École, on apprend à passer progressivement de son point de vue et de ses intérêts personnels à la recherche du bien commun" (p. 72, "At school, one learns to progress from one's own point of view and interests to communal projects"). Indeed, a major goal of education is to help children take and evaluate different perspectives in cooperation with others within problem situations. For Meirieu, such perspective taking is an indispensable ingredient in the development of students as persons and citizens.

Consequently, it should not be surprising to discover that schooling provides many excellent venues for the study and facilitation of perspective taking and personal development. Taking and evaluating different perspectives encountered in formal curricula and informal classroom activities is an important part of the educational process in any society, but is especially critical for the preparation of citizens in democratic societies. What the neo-Meadian account offered herein makes clear is that the self-development of persons and citizens is not primarily a matter of turning inwards to discover one's authentic self, or of carefully cultivating a positive self-image, self-concept, or repertoire of self-regulatory strategies. As possibly useful as any of these might be, they are of limited educational value unless they make contact with perspectives available in interpersonal and community activity, including those perspectives that constitute a representative sampling of what currently are considered to be our best theories and practices in subject areas as diverse as history, mathematics, biology, athletics, and the fine and performing arts. Developmental psychologists interested in the study and development of perspective taking and personhood might form many useful partnerships with educators at all levels.

CONCLUSION

The neo-Meadian account adopted herein holds that both perspectives and persons have a relational, processural ontology. Perspectives emerge during ontogenesis through the child's occupation of different social roles. The remembrance and anticipation of complementary social positions within frequently repeated sequences of interaction with others gradually permits the child to differentiate, integrate, and coordinate the various interpretive and action orientations (i.e., perspectives) that emerge out of his repeated experiences of position occupation and exchange. Because an important subset of such perspectives is directed at the child himself in various social positions, in taking these perspectives and reacting to them, the child effectively constructs his own self-understanding and first-person experience. In this way, every self has a social ontology, but one that is mediated through its own activities of perspective taking and reflexivity. Such initial self-development ushers in a gradual, lifelong process of personal development. This is a process within which we creatively take and integrate multiple perspectives available to us through our sociocultural, interpersonal experiences. Not only our selves, but other aspects of our personhood, such as our rational and moral agency and sociopsychological identity, have a similarly perspectival ontology. It is through our social experience and activity with others that we come to care about and understand our own existence as human persons with rights and responsibilities, limitations and possibilities, and a full range of emotions and concerns that define us as individuals in communion with others.

Some readers may object that the heavy reliance on processes of emergence in the account offered herein obscures and blurs certain distinctions that ought to be made clearly if the theory offered is to be relevant and useful (see Chandler, 2001 for legitimate concerns of this kind). I agree that it is important to draw clear distinctions between processes such as the occupation of social positions and the taking of perspectives. However, I think such distinctions only can be made when, for example, perspectives have emerged from social experience and remembrance of social positions. To draw such distinctions prematurely prevents the consideration of emergent possibilities in ontogenetic development. The danger here is that when such possibilities are unavailable, the only options remaining are to fall back into overly strong forms of innateness on the one hand or social determinism on the other.

By treating perspectives as real and constitutive of personhood, thinkers as diverse as Nietzsche, Mead, Bakhtin, and Baker have provided a theoretical framework within which developmental psychologists and educators might seek more specific processes and mechanisms of perspective taking and personal development. Unlike more cognitively oriented theories of human development that tend to privilege reflection and thought over activity and action, this kind of perspectival theorizing takes as primary our activity with others in sociocultural context. Our personhood issues from our active participation in interpersonal interactions and sociocultural practices, and the perspectives that such active participation makes available to us.

References

Adams, H. B. (1995). *The education of Henry Adams, an autobiography.* New York Penguin Classics. (Original work published 1907)

Baker, L. R. (2000). *Persons and bodies: A constitution view.* Cambridge: Cambridge University Press.

Bakhtin, M. (1981). *The dialogical imagination: Four essays by M. M. Bakhtin* (M. Holquist, Ed.; C. Emerson & M. Holquist, Trans.). Austin, TX: University of Texas Press.

Bakhtin, M. M. (1986). *Speech genres and other late essays* (C. Emerson & M. Holquist, Eds.; V. W. McGee, Trans.). Austin: University of Texas Press.

Bakhtin, M. M. (1993). *Toward a philosophy of the act* (M. Holquist, Ed.; V. Liapunov, Trans.). Austin: University of Texas Press.

Bandura, A. (1997). *Self-efficacy: The exercise of control.* New York: W. H. Freeman.

Bickhard, M. H. (2004). The social ontology of persons. In J. I. M. Carpendale & U. Müller (Eds.), *Social interaction and the development of knowledge* (pp. 111–132). Mahwah, NJ: Lawrence Erlbaum.

Buber, M. (1970). *I and thou* (W. Kaufmann, Trans.). New York: Scribner. (Original work published 1923)

Carpendale, J. I. M., & Lewis, C. (2004). Constructing an understanding of mind: The development of children's social understanding within social interaction. *Behavioral and Brain Sciences, 27,* 79–96.

Carver, C. S., & Scheier, M. F. (1998). *On the self-regulation of behavior.* New York: Cambridge University Press.

Chandler, M. (2001). Perspective taking in the aftermath of theory-theory and the collapse of the social role-taking literature. In A. Tryphon & J. Vonèche, J. (Eds.), *Working with Piaget: Essays in honour of Bärbel Inhelder* (pp. 39–63). Hove, UK: Psychology Press.

Chapman, M. (1991). The epistemic triangle: Operative and communicative components of cognitive development. In M. Chandler & M. Chapman (Eds.), *Criteria for competence: Controversies in the conceptualization and assessment of children's abilities* (pp. 209–228). Hillsdale, NJ: Lawrence Erlbaum.

Chapman, M. (1999). Constructivism and the problem of reality. *Journal of Applied Developmental Psychology, 20,* 31–43.

Dennett, D. C. (1987). *The intentional stance.* Cambridge, MA: MIT Press.

Donald, M. (2001). *A mind so rare: The evolution of human consciousness.* New York: Norton.

Emmeche, C., Køppe, S., & Stjernfelt, F. (2000). Levels, emergence, and three versions of downward causation. In P. B. Andersen, C. Emmeche, N. O. Finnemann, & P. V. Chrstiansen (Eds.), *Downward causation: Minds, bodies, and matter* (pp. 13–34). Aarhus, Denmark: Aarhus University Press.

Flavell, J. H. (1992). Piaget's theory: Perspectives on perspective taking. In H. Beilin & P. Pufall (Eds.), *Piaget's theory: Prospects and possibilities* (pp. 107–139). Hillsdale, NJ: Lawrence Erlbaum.

Flavell, J. H., Botkin, P. T., Fry, C. L., Wright, J. W., & Jarvis, P. E. (1968). *The development of role-taking and communication skills in children.* New York: Wiley.

Garcia, J. J. E. (1999). Ortega y Gasset, José. In R. Audi (Ed.), *The Cambridge dictionary of philosophy* (2nd ed., p. 637). Cambridge: Cambridge University Press.

Gergen, K. J. (1991). *The saturated self.* New York: Basic Books.

Gillespie, A. (2005). G. H. Mead: Theorist of the social act. *Journal for the Theory of Social Behaviour, 35,* 19–39.

Gillespie, A. (2006). Games and the development of perspective taking. *Human Development, 49,* 87–92.

Guignon, C. (2004). *On being authentic.* London: Routledge.

Hacking, I. (1999). *The social construction of what?* Cambridge, MA: Harvard University Press.

Harré, R. (1998). *The singular self: An introduction to the psychology of personhood.* London: Sage.

Harré, R. (2004). The social construction of persons. In C. Lightfoot, C. Lalonde, & M. Chandler (Eds.), *Changing conception of psychological life* (pp. 241–250). Mahwah, NJ: Lawrence Erlbaum

Hermans, H. J. M. (2002). The dialogical self as a society of mind: Introduction. *Theory & Psychology, 12,* 147–160.

Hobson, P. (2002). *The cradle of thought: Exploring the origins of thinking.* London: Macmillan.

Light, P. (1979). *The development of social sensitivity: A study of social aspects of role-taking in young children.* Cambridge: Cambridge University Press.

Locke, J. (1995). *An essay concerning human understanding.* Amherst, NY: Prometheus. (Original work published 1693)

Martin, J. (2003). Emergent persons. *New Ideas in Psychology, 21,* 85–99.

Martin, J. (2005a). Real perspectival selves. *Theory & Psychology, 15,* 207–224.

Martin, J. (2005b). Perspectival selves in interaction with others: Re-reading G. H. Mead's social psychology. *The Journal for the Theory of Social Behaviour, 35,* 231–253.

Martin, J. (2006). Re-interpreting internalization and agency through G. H. Mead's perspectival realism. *Human Development, 49,* 65–86.

Martin, J., & Sugarman, J. (1999). *The psychology of human possibility and constraint.* Albany, NY: SUNY Press.

Martin, J., Sugarman, J., & Thompson, J. (2003). *Psychology and the question of agency.* Albany, NY: SUNY Press.

Mead, G. H. (1934). *Mind, self, & society from the standpoint of a social behaviorist* (C. W. Morris, Ed.). Chicago: University of Chicago Press.

Mead, G. H. (1938). *The philosophy of the act* (C. W. Morris, Ed.). Chicago: University of Chicago Press.

Mead, G. H. (2002). *The philosophy of the present.* Amherst, NY: Prometheus. (Original work published 1932)

Meirieu, P. (2005). *Lettre à un jeune professeur.* ESF Editeur: Paris.

Müller, U., & Runions, K. (2003). The origins of understanding self and other: James Mark Baldwin's theory. *Developmental Review, 23,* 29–54.

Nietzsche, F. (1967a). *On the genealogy of morals* (W. Kaufmann & R. J. Hllingdale, Trans.). New York: Vintage. (Original published 1887)

Nietzsche, F. (1967b). *The will to power* (W. Kaufmann, Trans.). (Original work published 1901)

Oxford English Dictionary. (2nd ed.). (1989). Oxford: Oxford University Press. http://dictionary.oed.com.proxy.lib.sfu.ca/cgi/entry/00181778

Parfit, D. (1984). *Reasons and persons.* Oxford: Oxford University Press.

Piaget, J. (1926). *The language and thought of the child.* New York: Harcourt Brace Jovanovich.

Piaget, J. (1928). *Judgment and reasoning of the child.* New York: Harcourt Brace Jovanovich.

Piaget, J. (1963). *The child's conception of the world.* Paterson, NJ: Littlefield, Adams.

Piaget, J. (1976). *The grasp of consciousness: Action and concept in the young child.* Cambridge, MA: Harvard University Press.

Piaget, J. (1995). *Sociological studies.* London: Routledge. (Original work published 1977).

Piaget, J., & Inhelder, B. (1963). *The child's conception of space* (F. J. Langdon & J. L. Lunzer, Trans.). London: Routledge & Kegan Paul. (Original work published 1948).

Sarbin, T. (1954). Role theory. In G. Lindzey (Ed.), *Handbook of social psychology* (Vol. 1, pp. 223–258). Cambridge, MA: Addison-Wesley.

Selman, R. L. (1980). *The growth of interpersonal understanding.* New York: Academic Press.

Shantz, C. U. (1975). The development of social cognition. In E. Hetherington (Ed.), *Review of child development research* (Vol. 5, pp. 257–323). Chicago: University of Chicago Press.

Slife, B. (2004). Taking practice seriously: Toward a relational ontology. *Journal of Theoretical and Philosophical Psychology, 24,* 157–178.

Stack, G. J. (1999). Teichmüller, Gustav. In R. Audi (Ed.), *The Cambridge dictionary of philosophy* (2nd ed., p. 904). Cambridge: Cambridge University Press.

Strawson, P. F. (1959). *Individuals: An essay in descriptive metaphysics.* London: Routledge.

Tanner, M. (2000). *Nietzsche: A very short introduction.* Oxford: Oxford University Press.

Taylor, C. (1989). *Sources of the self: The making of the modern identity.* Harvard, MA: Harvard University Press.

Tomasello, M. (1999). *The cultural origins of cognition.* Cambridge, MA: Harvard University Press.

Tomasello, M., Carpenter, M., Call, J., Behne, T. & Moll, H. (2005). Understanding and sharing intentions: The origins of cultural cognition. *Behavioral and Brain Sciences, 28,* 675–735.

Underwood, B., & Moore, B. (1982). Perspective taking and altruism: A search for mediating variables. *Psychological Bulletin, 91,* 143–173.

Werner, H. (1948). *Comparative psychology of mental development.* New York: International Universities Press.

4

Cultural Learning and Cultural Creation

Tanya Behne, Malinda Carpenter, Maria Gräfenhain,
Kristin Liebal, Ulf Liszkowski, Henrike Moll,
Hannes Rakoczy, Michael Tomasello,
Felix Warneken, and Emily Wyman

Human children become cultural beings by learning to participate in the cultural activities and practices going on around them. Household pets grow up in the midst of these same cultural activities and practices, but they do not learn to participate in them in anything like the same way as human children. Even chimpanzees and bonobos raised in human homes and treated like human children still retain, for the most part, their species-typical social and cognitive skills without turning into cultural beings of the human kind. This difference suggests that humans are biologically adapted, in ways that other animal species are not, for becoming cultural beings by tuning in to what others around them are doing, and thereby learning from them. Moreover, on occasion, young children even create with others small-scale cultural activities and routines involving one or another form of collaboration, or even collaborative pretense. Such cultural creation would also seem to be unique to human beings, and of course cultural creation leads to ever new cultural environments in which human cognitive ontogeny takes place.

We may therefore identify two sets of human cultural skills responsible, as they work over historical and ontogenetic time, for humans' unique form of social organization: cultural learning and cultural creation. These enable humans, and only humans, to have cultures which accumulate complexities in both social practices and cognitive artifacts—creating ever new cultural niches within which developing children become mature cultural beings. Tomasello (1999b) proposed that underlying these cultural abilities was a uniquely human social-cognitive skill for understanding others as intentional agents who, like the self, attend to things and pursue goals in the environment.

The collective aspect of cultural evolution in this theory was, in an important sense, taken for granted. Uniquely human types of social engagement such as joint attention, collaborative cooperation, and symbolic communication were seen as simply emanating naturally from the understanding of others as intentional agents like the self. However, recent research with nonhuman primates suggests that the origins of these skills should not be taken for granted. That is, a number of different studies have found that great apes do understand important aspects of intentional action and perception; for example, chimpanzees recognize the difference between intended actions and accidental actions and they know what others can and cannot see, in the sense of the contents of their perception (see below for more details). But they do not engage in shared activities or in processes of cultural learning and creation the way that humans do from an early age.

There may still be some differences in the ways that human children and great apes understand intentional action and perception, especially in the understanding of the choices an actor makes in creating action plans and focusing attention (taking perspectives) on things (see below). Nevertheless, these new data have driven us to acknowledge what seems to be a clear fact: human infants and young children have special motivations and skills for engaging in shared activities that go beyond the understanding of others as intentional agents like the self. Infants look to others when interesting things happen, often just to share attention to them. Infants are motivated simply to point to things so that others will share interest in them. Infants are motivated to form shared goals and shared intentions with others in their joint activities with objects. Young children create with others pretend realities that exist only in their shared intentionality. These skills and motivations for sharing do not seem to be present in nonhuman primates to nearly the same degree, if at all (Tomasello & Carpenter, 2005). The important point in the current context is that humans' unique skills and motivations for sharing psychological states with others play a crucially important role for cultural learning and cultural creation: they lead infants and young children to tune into and learn from what others are doing, and to create with others the kinds of novel interactive routines and cultural practices that characterize specific families and cultures, which serve to create the cultural niche within which the next generation develops.

Tomasello, Carpenter, Call, Behne, and Moll (2005) therefore proposed that uniquely human cultural skills depend on two ontogenetic pathways, each reflecting a distinct biological adaptation. The first pathway concerns the understanding of intentional action and perception. Much of this pathway is shared among all primates, or at least among the great apes, although humans may go somewhat further along this path. The second pathway is a uniquely human motivation to share psychological states with others. This can be seen in infants' earliest social interactions, known as protoconversations, in which they exchange emotions with adults dyadically, seemingly only for the purpose of sharing. When infants begin to understand intentional action and perception as directed at outside goals and targets, near the end of the first year of life, these two strands of ontogeny come together in a new way of special relevance for cultural learning and creation. Specifically, the motivation to share now manifests itself as the sharing of intentions and attention triadically in acts of joint attention, collaborative cooperation, and symbolic communication.

In this chapter we review recent research from our laboratory relevant to this theoretical account. First, we review our research on infants' and young children's understanding of intentional action and perception. Second, we look at infants' and young children's ability to engage in shared activities, examining specifically skills of joint attention, communication, collaboration and pretense. The attempt is to elucidate the ontogenetic roots of the human forms of social interaction and communication that enable uniquely human forms of cultural learning and creation. Thus, in each section we also compare the research findings to what is known about the respective abilities of non-human apes, especially chimpanzees.

UNDERSTANDING INTENTIONAL ACTION AND PERCEPTION

Understanding Goals and Intentions

At some point in infancy young children come to perceive the bodily motions of other people as intentional actions. Determining precisely when this developmental transition occurs is of theoretical interest because it marks an important step in the development of young children's cultural skills. In this section, we review our recent research on the development of infants' understanding of others' intentional action, and we discuss how infants use this understanding in cultural learning. We also briefly review our research on understanding of others' intentional action in apes and show how their perhaps more limited understanding can explain differences in which aspects of others' behavior they reproduce in cultural learning situations.

In our view intentional action involves crucially: (1) a *goal* or mental representation of a desired end state; (2) an *intention* or plan of action the actor chooses and commits himself to in pursuit of that goal; and (3) the ability to perceive and monitor one's actions and the environment in order to know when the state of the environment matches the goal (Tomasello et al., 2005). We will focus on the first two of these components here (see the next section for research on the third component).

Development of Infants' Understanding of Others' Goals and Intentions

When studying nonverbal infants' understanding of others' goals, the methodological challenge is to find a way to separate the actor's goal from the result that he or she achieves. The clearest way to do this is to study infants' reactions to actions that are not immediately successful, because in this case infants must infer the actor's goal even though it is not achieved (and therefore not observed). The two main categories of unsuccessful actions are failed attempts (trying) and accidents. Previously, the only studies investigating infants' understanding of others' failed attempts and accidents used imitation as a response measure. These studies found that 14- and 15-month-old and older infants showed an understanding of successful versus unsuccessful and intentional versus accidental actions; that is, that they could determine whether the actor's goal matched the external result and respond appropriately (Carpenter, Akhtar, & Tomasello, 1998; Johnson, Booth, & O'Hearn, 2001; Meltzoff, 1995). Twelve-month-olds, however, did not show this understanding, suggesting that it emerged in the months shortly after the first birthday (Bellagamba & Tomasello, 1999).[1]

But imitation is a fairly demanding response measure, and so the question arises whether infants can demonstrate the same understanding in another task paradigm at a younger age. We thus developed a procedure to use infants' natural behavioral responses in a social interaction to test younger infants' understanding of others' failed attempts and accidents. Behne, Carpenter, Call, and Tomasello (2005) engaged infants in a game in which an adult gave them toys across a table. Interspersed were trials in which the adult held up a toy but did not give it over. In some cases this was because the adult was unwilling in various ways, and in other cases it was because she was unable in various ways, each of which involved failed attempts or accidents (e.g., she could not extract the toy from a container or she dropped it clumsily while attempting to give it to the infant). In reaction to these activities, 9-, 12-, and 18-month-olds, but not 6-month-olds, showed more signs of impatience (e.g., reaching, turning away) when the adult kept the toy for herself than when she was making a good faith effort to give it over. Infants thus were first able to infer the adult's goal, even when it did not match what actually happened, by age 9 (but not 6) months.

A further question is when infants begin to understand not just an actor's goal, but also her intention—her plan of action for achieving that goal, including the rational basis for this choice of plan. As yet, the only studies investigating this understanding have used imitation as a response measure. In a recent study from our laboratory (Schwier, van Maanen, Carpenter, & Tomasello, 2006), which was inspired by a similar study of slightly older infants by Gergely, Bekkering, and Király (2002), we found that 12-month-old infants could infer an adult demonstrator's intention and at some level determine why she chose the particular action she chose to accomplish her goal. For example, infants in our study watched the adult use a particular action to achieve some end—she put a toy dog into a house through the chimney. In one condition the adult had to use that action (because an alternate, more usual action was blocked—the house's door was locked), and in the other condition the adult freely chose to use that action (the door was wide open). Infants responded differently in the different conditions, copying the particular action demonstrated by the adult more often when the adult had freely chosen to perform that action than when she was forced by her circumstances to use it, suggesting that infants saw the adult's action in each case as chosen for some rational reason and thus worthy (or not) of being copied.

In summary, by 9 months of age infants do not just perceive others' surface bodily motions, but rather they go deeper and interpret others' actions as a function of their goal, seeing others as persisting past failed attempts and accidents to achieve their goals. By 12 months of age, infants in addition are beginning to understand others' intentions, including the rudiments of the way others make rational decisions in choosing action plans for accomplishing their goals in particular contexts.

Understanding Goals and Intentions in Cultural Learning   The extent to which infants know what others are trying to do (their goal) and why they are doing it the way they are doing it (their intention) affects how deeply they can participate in cultural learning. Knowing what others are trying to do (their goal) is important because it allows learners to filter out goal-irrelevant aspects of a demonstration; for example, accidental actions (Carpenter et al., 1998), and it focuses learners on relevant aspects of a demonstration. For instance, we have shown that 12-month-old infants, like older, preschool-aged children (Bekkering, Wohlschläger, & Gattis, 2000), interpret and reproduce the same adult actions differently depending on what they see as the adult's goal (Carpenter, Call, & Tomasello, 2005). More dramatically, in some cases knowing an adult's goal may enable children to succeed at a task at which they could not otherwise succeed. For example, Carpenter, Call, and Tomasello (2002) demonstrated to five groups of 2-year-old children how to pull out a pin and open a box. What differed across groups was what children experienced just prior to this demonstration, with some children receiving (nonverbal) information about the demonstrator's goal (i.e., what she intended to do with the box as she approached it) and some not. Children who knew before the demonstration that the demonstrator intended to open the box were later significantly better at opening the box themselves than children in each of several control conditions who received no prior information or only goal-irrelevant information. Interestingly, children who did not know what the demonstrator was about to do performed just as poorly as children who received no demonstration at all.

In addition to reading others' goals, the ability to read others' intentions (i.e., engage in rational imitation) tells learners how the demonstrator is achieving her goal and why she is doing it in this way. This is especially important in human cultural learning, when sometimes it is necessary to do things the way others do (for example, when learning the conventional use of artifacts or communicative symbols; see Gergely & Csibra, 2006; Tomasello, 1999b) and sometimes it is not. Once infants understand the rational dimensions of action and choice, they are better able to know when they should follow the adult and when this is not necessary, in which case they can simply pursue any means that they think is effective for themselves, as they did in the studies of Gergely et al. (2002) and Schwier et al. (2006). Being able to make this distinction is an important ability for 1-year-old infants as they begin to participate in earnest in the cultural activities around them.

Apes' Understanding of Goals and Intentions   There is now growing evidence that chimpanzees understand something about others' goals, even at the level of failed attempts and accidents. For example, Call, Hare, Carpenter, and Tomasello (2004) tested chimpanzees in a food-giving context that was similar to the toy context used by Behne et al. (2005) with human infants (see above). Similar to human 9-, 12-, and 18-month-olds, chimpanzees showed more impatience (e.g., gestured more and left the area earlier) when the human was unwilling than when he was unable—in which case they tended to wait patiently throughout his well-meaning but unsuccessful attempts. The chimpanzees apparently understood the behavior of the human in the unable conditions as persistent attempts (trying) to give them food.

In addition, three studies have tested chimpanzees' understanding of failed attempts in a social learning context, using Meltzoff's (1995) behavioral reenactment procedure in which participants are shown either a successful, completed action or an unsuccessful, uncompleted attempt and then given the chance to act on the object themselves. Two of the studies (Call, Carpenter, & Tomasello, 2005; Myowa-Yamakoshi & Matsuzawa, 2000) were compromised by high levels of performance in a baseline condition, but the third study (Tomasello & Carpenter, 2005) found that three young enculturated chimpanzees, like the 18-month-old children in Meltzoff's study, completed the action equally as often when they saw a failed attempt as when they saw the completed action, thus showing that they inferred what the demonstrator was trying to do—her goal— in the failed attempt condition.

Finally, Call and Tomasello (1998) tested apes' ability to distinguish intentional from accidental actions in a different paradigm. They trained subjects to associate a marker situated on top of one of three opaque buckets with the location of hidden food. On test trials a human then placed the marker on one of the buckets purposefully, but either before or after this he let the marker fall accidentally onto one of the other buckets. Apes as a group chose the bucket that had been marked in a purposeful manner. Tomasello and Carpenter (2005) have further shown that enculturated chimpanzees copy intentional actions more than accidental ones.

Apes thus show some understanding of others' failed attempts and accidents—their goals. However, there is as yet little evidence that apes understand others' intentions as rational choices of action plans. In a recent series of studies in our lab (Buttelmann, Carpenter, Call, & Tomasello, in press), we have presented apes with many different versions of Gergely and colleagues' (2002) study, using tasks that are more relevant to apes (involving using tools to retrieve food). The overall finding was that most apes do not respond differentially depending on whether the demonstrator was forced to use the action he used or freely chose to use that action. This is the case even for some enculturated chimpanzees (Tomasello & Carpenter, 2005).

If apes do understand something about others' goals but not their intentions, this could help explain the general finding that in social learning situations, unlike human children, apes typically copy the end result and not the particular actions the demonstrator used (see, e.g., Carpenter & Call, in press, for a review). If apes do not understand that the demonstrator chose to use those particular actions for some reason, then it is no surprise that they do not copy those actions.

Conclusions In summary, by their first birthday, human infants understand that others have both goals and intentions and in many cases are able to infer what those goals and intentions are. This enables infants to learn from others in special ways, filtering out goal-irrelevant aspects of demonstrations and completing failed attempts, and, of particular importance in learning cultural or conventional behaviors, knowing when it is necessary to copy the exact way a more experienced demonstrator did something. As we shall see below, understanding others' goals, and especially their intentions, will also enable infants to participate in collaborative interactions with other members of their culture. Apes may understand others' goals but currently there is no evidence that they understand others' intentions, which limits the types of cultural learning they can engage in and their ability to collaborate with others (see below).

Understanding Perception, Attention, and Knowledge
Research on infants' understanding of others has mostly focused on the understanding of goal-directed and intentional action. However, also important is infants' understanding of what other people perceive, attend to, and know. For example, when 9- to 12-month-olds begin to understand that actors strive for goals they must know also that the actor perceives and monitors her actions and pays attention to those parts of the environment which are relevant for her goal. So, what do infants understand about what others perceive, attend to, and know?

Understanding Perception Infants' understanding of perception has for the most part been investigated with the gaze following paradigm. There is fairly strong agreement that by the end of their first year of life, infants follow an adult's gaze reliably to an outside target (e.g., Carpenter, Nagell, & Tomasello, 1998; Corkum & Moore, 1995). But more than just following an adult's head direction, infants by around 14 months have been shown to understand some important aspects of the seeing process. This was tested with several modifications of the classic gaze following paradigm, in which the *adult*'s vision of the target was manipulated in various ways. The results show that 14-month-old infants understand that (1) an adult's eyes need to be open in order for her to see an object (e.g., Brooks & Meltzoff, 2002); (2) the eyes and not just the head need to be oriented toward the object (e.g., Caron, Butler, & Brooks, 2002); and (3) the adult's line of sight to the object needs to be unobstructed (e.g., Dunphy-Lelii & Wellman, 2004). In sum, these findings indicate that by 14 months of age, infants have an understanding of some necessary conditions for seeing. For even younger infants of 12 months of age, however, the results were ambiguous. For example, in a study by Caron, Kiel, Dayton, and Butler (2002), 12-month-olds did not understand that an adult could see an object through a window in a screen, but not through an opaque barrier. Similarly, in Brooks and Meltzoff's (2002) study, 12-month-olds did not know that an adult could not see when her eyes were covered by a blindfold. It is important to note, however, that these tasks may be particularly demanding, because infants were confronted with conflicting information, on the one hand the adult's behavior (turning her head in the direction of an interesting target) and on the other hand the obstruction of the adult's view.

In order to investigate more closely what infants understand about visual perception, we thus took a different approach (Moll & Tomasello, 2004). Unlike the existing variations of the gaze following paradigm, we blocked the *infant*'s and not the adult's view to a target by various kinds of barriers, to see whether infants of 12 to 18 months of age would follow an adult's gaze to these locations. We thus created a situation in which the infant did not have immediate perceptual access to the target. Instead, the target was located outside of the infant's immediate visual field, and she had to either crawl or walk some distance in order to be able to see what the adult saw. In each of two studies, we found that 12- and 18-month-old infants crawled or walked a short distance in order to look behind a barrier an adult was looking behind and thereby see what the adult was seeing. They did not do this in two control conditions in which a barrier was present but no one was looking behind it (the adult was looking across the room or in front of the barrier). This is strong evidence that infants in this age range understand that others see things and that they are motivated to see what others are seeing. These findings are perhaps not so surprising for 18-month-olds, as a number of studies using a variety of different methods all converge on this conclusion (Brooks & Meltzoff, 2002; Butler, Caron, & Brooks, 2000; Corkum & Moore, 1995; Moore & Corkum, 1998). They are more surprising for 12-month-olds because previously there were few studies showing that 12-month-olds have some understanding of seeing. The results also show that Butterworth (1995) underestimated 12- to 18-month-olds' gaze following skills. According to him, "babies' capacity for joint attention is limited by the boundaries of the visual field…it is as if the infant…fails to comprehend the possibility of a space outside the range of immediate visual experience" (Butterworth & Jarrett, 1991, p. 56). The current results demonstrate that, contra Butterworth, infants' gaze following is more than a mere geometric extrapolation of a line of sight within the immediate visual field. One-year-olds can move beyond their immediate visual field (Moll & Tomasello, 2004) and look behind themselves (Deák, Flom, & Pick, 2000) in order to see what another person is seeing.

Perspective Taking   However, gaze following tasks like these do not involve any perspective taking. All the infant needs to know is *that* there is something to be seen behind the barriers. Together with a curiosity about what that something is, this suffices to be successful in these tasks, which do not require the infant to take the adult's perspective and imagine or predict *what* the adult can or cannot see from her visual point of view.

Research on the development of understanding of visual perspectives has focused on toddlers and preschoolers (Flavell, 1992). The tasks which have been developed for these age groups cannot be easily used with infants, because they pose relatively high linguistic and other task demands on the children. For instance, in probably the best-known task for toddlers and preschoolers, children have to respond verbally to the question of what they themselves and an adult can see (Masangkay et al., 1974). Other tasks involve nonverbal production measures, in which the child is asked to place an object relative to a screen such that an adult's visual access to the object is blocked (e.g., Flavell, Shipstead, & Croft, 1978; McGuigan & Doherty, 2002). Children solve these tasks at 2½ years of age, but younger children have not been systematically tested with these measures.

We investigated younger children's abilities to take another person's visual perspective using a new procedure with 18- and 24-month-olds (Moll & Tomasello, 2006). The question was whether these young children would know which of two objects was not visible from the perspective of an adult because her vision of it was blocked by an occluder. In the experimental condition, the adult searched for a toy, whereas in the control condition, she just made a neutral request. The result was that the 24-month-olds, but not the 18-month-olds correctly handed the adult the toy the adult could not see significantly more often in the experimental than in the control condition. Thus, by 2 years of age, children knew what the adult could and could not see and how this was related to her searching behavior. In contrast to the gaze following studies, this perspective-taking study required children to demonstrate that they know precisely what the adult could and could not see at a specific moment—without being given the opportunity to determine this on the basis of superficial cues like line of regard. The main difference between an understanding of perspectives and gaze following is thus that the child must know and be able to specify the content of what the other person sees.

It thus seems that infants can follow gaze (even to unperceived spaces) much earlier than they demonstrate an understanding of visual perspectives. One reason for this might be that following another person's gaze direction is much simpler than determining her focus when the only information which helps disambiguate the focus is the perceptual availability of the objects to that person. But usually, adults engage with their infants in richer interactions, in which it becomes clearer what they are focused on. This is in line with the findings from some studies on understanding attention, which we will turn to now.

Understanding Attention and Knowledge   Thus far, we have looked at infants' understanding of perception, namely, the fact that perception is object-directed (gaze-following studies) and is always bound to a specific visual point of view (visual perspective-taking). However, when we pursue a goal in acting, we do not just perceive but also selectively attend to what we think is relevant for our action and the achievement of our goal. Attending, more than perceiving, thus involves a concentration or focus on a specific part or feature of what is perceptually present (e.g., Husserl, 2004; James, 1890). From the perspective of the outside observer, it might seem more difficult to know what a person is selectively focused on than to just determine what is in her line of regard. But there is reason to believe that infants actually do not find it harder to understand selective attention. That is, understanding attention can be seen as analogous to understanding intention: in both cases, the infant needs to know that an actor or perceiver chooses one means or aspect over another for a reason (either to enact or to attend to). And since 1-year-olds already show some understanding of this when interpreting others' intentional action (Gergely et al., 2002; Schwier et al., 2006; see above), it is possible that they also understand attention to the same extent, namely, that people make decisions for reasons, in both action and perception.

A study by Tomasello and Haberl (2003) shows that indeed by one year of age, infants understand selective attention. In their study, 12- and 18-month-olds played with an adult with two toys in turn. Before a third toy was brought out by an assistant, the adult left the room. During her absence, the infant played with the third toy together with the assistant. Finally, all three toys were held in front of the infant, at which point the adult returned to the room and exclaimed excitement followed by an unspecified request for the infant to give her a toy (without indicating by gazing or pointing which specific toy she was attending to). Infants of both ages selected the toy the adult was attending to because it was new for her. In order to solve this task, infants had to understand (1) what the adult knew and did not know in the sense of what she had and had not become acquainted with from previous experience, and (2) the link between novelty and attention: namely, that people often attend to unknown objects.

There is thus converging evidence that by 12 to 14 months of age, infants not only have some understanding of perceiving, including some necessary preconditions for seeing (e.g., Caron, Kiel, et al., 2002), but also can determine what others selectively attend to, even when this requires in addition an understanding of what the person knows and does not know by acquaintance. This has now been demonstrated not just with the selection paradigm described above, but also with a different interactive response measure (Moll, Koring, Carpenter, & Tomasello, 2006) and habituation measures (Onishi & Baillargeon, 2005).

Apes' Understanding of Perception and Attention   There is growing evidence that chimpanzees and other great apes understand some important aspects of others' visual perception (see Call & Tomasello, 2005, for a review). For example, they follow the gaze direction of both conspecifics and humans to external targets (e.g., Itakura, 1996; Povinelli & Eddy, 1996; Tomasello, Call, & Hare, 1998), they check back to the looker (and eventually quit looking) if nothing is there (Call,

Hare, & Tomasello 1998; Povinelli & Eddy, 1996; Tomasello, Hare, & Fogle-man 2001) and they even follow the gaze direction of humans to targets behind barriers (Tomasello, Hare, & Agnetta, 1998). Importantly, they also show some understanding of the relation between what others can see and what they will do (Hare, Call, Agnetta, & Tomasello, 2000; Hare, Call, & Tomasello 2001; Hare, Call, & Tomasello, 2006; Melis, Call, & Tomasello, 2006).

In contrast to the wealth of research on apes' understanding of visual perception, very little is known about apes' understanding of others' attention. In the one experimental study that did address this question the chimpanzees tested (i.e., three young human-raised chimpanzees) did not demonstrate an understanding of others' selective attention (Tomasello & Carpenter, 2005).

Conclusion

This series of studies showed that infants as young as 12 to 14 months have an understanding of some important aspects of others' intentional action and perception. In particular, the research suggests that infants this age already understand that others act and attend to things for a reason. That is, infants recognize that others act in the pursuit of goals and that they choose means to fulfill these goals given their circumstances or constraints. Similarly, they also show some understanding that others perceive and selectively attend to certain aspects of the environment.

Importantly, recent studies have demonstrated that chimpanzees, too, understand some aspects of intentional action and perception. In particular, the new findings suggest that they read others' behavior as goal-directed, distinguishing between intentional and unintentional actions. Furthermore, they also show an understanding of what others can and cannot see. There is little evidence, however, that nonhuman primates understand the choices that an actor makes in creating action plans and focusing attention. This may be one contributing factor in the differences seen between apes and humans in processes of cultural learning and creation. However, another more fundamental factor giving rise to these differences may be the motivation and ability to engage in shared activities, as will be discussed next.

ENGAGING IN SHARED ACTIVITIES: FROM JOINT ATTENTION TO JOINT PRETENSE

Humans' cultural skills do not only rely on understanding other persons' actions and perception. The development of cultural practices and skills over historical and ontogenetic time also requires the ability to engage with others in joint activities with shared goals and intentions (Tomasello et al., 2005). We here examine the proposal that the ability to participate in cultural learning and creation crucially depends on skills of shared intentionality that young children already begin to develop during infancy. Thus we will first look at infants' joint attentional skills and their role in social-cognitive development. Then, we will review our research on infants' and young children's ability to communicate with others, to cooperate with others, and to pretend with others. Finally, we will focus briefly on children with autism to examine whether the relative strengths and impairments of children with autism may be related to specific deficits with respect to their motivation and skill to engage in shared activities.

Joint Attention and Engagement

Infants in their first year of life interact with both their social and their physical environment. That is, a 6-month-old infant may interact dyadically with objects, grasping and manipulating them, or she may also interact dyadically with other people, expressing emotions back-and-forth in a turn-taking sequence. But at around 9 to 12 months of age a qualitatively new set of behaviors begins to emerge that are triadic in the sense that they involve a referential triangle of child, adult, and object/event to which they share attention. Infants now jointly engage and share attention with others to third entities or events, they follow others' focus of attention and they also actively direct others' attention using pointing gestures (see Carpenter et al. 1998, for details).

Importantly, these joint-attentional skills open up the possibility of participating in processes of cultural learning and creation. For example, a number of studies have demonstrated the role of joint attentional engagement for toddlers' language acquisition (see Tomasello, 1999b, for a review). The Vygotskian proposal we wish to examine here is that joint engagement with others also scaffolds young children's social cognitive development. Specifically, we address the hypothesis that joint engagement is a powerful way for very young infants to develop an understanding of other people, in particular to come to know what others have and have not experienced.

The Role of Joint Engagement in Understanding Attention and Knowledge   In some situations infants as young as 12 months are already able to determine what others are selectively attending to, based on the other person's previous experience (Tomasello & Haberl, 2003, see above). That is, when an adult showed excitement and then made an unspecified request for one of three toys, infants gave the adult the toy that was new to her, even though for the infants themselves all three toys were equally familiar. How do infants at this young age do this? In order to investigate how infants come to know what others attend to based on what they know, we conducted a series of studies using Tomasello and Haberl's basic procedure (2003). Specifically, we explored the conditions under which infants know which of several objects is unknown for an adult and thus catches her attention.

In the first study (Moll & Tomasello, 2007), infants observed an adult experience each of two objects (known objects) and then leave the room while infants played with a third object (unknown object: target) along with an assistant. The adult experienced the first two objects in one of three different ways. The first was a situation of joint engagement in which infant and adult played with the objects, looking at and manipulating them together (Joint Engagement condition). The second was a situation of individual engagement in which the infant observed the adult actively manipulating, inspecting, and reacting to the objects by herself (Individual Engagement condition). The third was a situation of onlooking in which the infant observed the adult simply watching as the infant played with the objects (Onlooking condition). We tested 14- and 18-month-olds in these three conditions, using as a dependent measure the object infants selected when the adult returned to the room and exclaimed excitement. The results showed that infants of both age groups knew which objects the adult knew in the Joint Engagement condition, only the 18-month-olds knew this in the Individual Engagement condition, and infants at neither age knew this in the Onlooking condition. These results suggest that infants are first able to determine what adults know on the basis of their direct, triadic engagements with them. Only a few months later, by 18 months, infants are less dependent on these joint engagement contexts, as is evidenced also by word learning studies (Baldwin, 1993; Floor & Akhtar, 2006).

To zero in on the joint engagement effect found for the younger infants, we conducted two follow-up studies with 14-month-olds (Moll, Carpenter, & Tomasello, in press) and looked more closely at (1) whether joint engagement also helps infants understand what others know from visual experience alone, which generally seems hard for them (as we know from the Onlooking condition, see above); and (2) whether it is sufficient for infants at this age to witness the adult interact with a third person around the objects in order to register her as being acquainted with them. The results showed that, as long as the adult reacted in joint engagement as she watched the infants playing with the objects (without manipulating them herself), infants recognized which objects were known for her. However, infants did not distinguish between the known and the unknown objects when they witnessed, from a third-person perspective, the adult jointly engage with another person around the known objects, in a situation similar to "overhearing" word-learning studies (Akhtar, 2005).

Conclusion   By 12 to 14 months of age, infants can determine what others selectively attend to, even when this requires in addition an understanding of what another person knows and does not know by acquaintance. The current studies show that this kind of social-cognitive ability develops inside joint engagement episodes, in which the focus of the partner somehow becomes especially transparent and is perhaps made mutually manifest (Eilan, 2005; Heal, 2005). This might be because in these contexts, infants form with their partner a shared focus or even a shared goal (Tomasello et al., 2005). In any case, just as joint engagement seems to help infants determine the referents for words (e.g., Dunham, Dunham, & Curwin, 1993; Tomasello & Farrar, 1986), and engage in more mature forms of play (Bigelow, MacLean, & Proctor, 2004), it also helps them very generally to monitor and understand what others attend to and know.

Communicating with Others

A hallmark of human cultural learning and creation is the ability to communicate using linguistic symbols. As sociopragmatic accounts of language acquisition have emphasized, acquiring the conventional use of linguistic symbols presupposes the ability to recognize the communicative intentions expressed by others, and this relies on infants' understanding of intentional action and their ability to participate in joint attentional scenes (Bruner, 1983; Tomasello, 1999b). Importantly, however, understanding communicative acts presents a special case of intentional and attentional understanding. One aspect that distinguishes communicative intentions from intentions *simpliciter* is that to understand your communicative intention, I must recognize your intention towards my attentional state (e.g., Tomasello, 1999b). Many analysts have pointed out that people read others' communicative intentions based on the assumption that the communicator directs the addressee's attention in ways that are relevant to their joint interaction or background (e.g., Sperber & Wilson 1986). The question here is whether infants already understand others' communicative acts in this way too.

Understanding Communicative Intentions   One-year-old infants reliably follow others' gaze direction and pointing gestures. However, this does not necessarily mean that they recognize others' communicative intentions. A better situation for assessing infant understanding of communicative intent is one in which the infant follows an adult gesture to an otherwise uninteresting target and, in addition, needs to recognize why the adult took the trouble to direct her attention to that target. Following Sperber and Wilson (1986), we must look for situations in which the infant asks herself: Why did the adult do this for me? Why is this object to which he is gesturing relevant to our interaction?

    One possible task with this structure is the so-called object choice task that has been employed with both human children and nonhuman primates (e.g., Povinelli, Reaux, Bierschwale, Allain, & Simon, 1997; Tomasello, Call, & Gluckman, 1997). In this task, an adult hides a reward in one of several opaque containers and then indicates the reward's location by giving a communicative cue; for example, pointing to the baited container. This research showed that children aged 2.5 and 3.0 years not only followed the adult's indication to one of the containers, but they also inferred that the hidden reward could be found there (as evidenced by their search behavior). The children treated each communicative attempt as an expression of the adult's intention to direct their attention in ways relevant to the current interaction/game. In contrast, in the same situation great apes did not infer the location of the hidden food. This was not because they cannot follow the direction of pointing or gazing (they can; see Call & Tomasello, 2005, for a review), but because they did not tune in to the adult's communicative intention and infer why he was directing their attention to this location. They did not understand that the gesture was made for their benefit, and so they did not seek or find the relevance of this act in this context.

Whereas the ability of human children aged 2.5 and 3 years has been demonstrated in a number of investigations, it was unclear whether younger children—at the age when language first begins to emerge—were also able to understand others' communicative intentions in this way. Thus, to address this issue, we engaged 1-year-olds in hiding-finding games, which were based on the object-choice task. In particular, we were interested in whether children this age can recognize the communicative intent behind nonlinguistic gestures (1) when infants were addressed directly, and (2) when they "overheard" communicative gestures directed at a third person.

First, we examined infants' understanding of communicative gestures when they were addressed directly. Thus, after an introduction to the hiding game, an adult hid a toy in one of two identical opaque containers and then, addressing the infant, indicated the toy's location by giving a communicative cue—either pointing or ostensive gazing toward the correct location. Children aged 14, 18, and 24 months participated in this game. At all three ages they reliably searched in the correct container, indicating that they were using the adult's communicative cues to find the hidden toy. A control study demonstrated that infants' successful search performance was not simply based on low-level gaze following mechanisms. That is, when the adult produced similar surface behavior as before, but without expressing communicative intent (e.g., looking absent-mindedly at the baited container), infants' search performance was at chance level (Behne, Carpenter, & Tomasello, 2005). Taken together these findings suggest that infants as young as 14 months are able to recognize the communicative relevance of ostensive behavior directed at them.

Second, we examined whether infants can also understand the communicative intent of ostensive behavior that is not directed at them but instead at a third person (i.e., when infants are "overhearing" others' communicative interactions). Therefore, the same hiding-finding game was set up as described above, but throughout the game the adult directed her communicative cues (pointing and ostensive gazing) at another adult, without addressing the infant. When searching for the hidden toy, 18-month-old infants (and to a certain extent 14-month-olds, too) reliably chose the correct container, indicating that they recognized the communicative relevance of the gestures that they were "overhearing" (Gräfenhain, Behne, Carpenter, & Tomasello, submitted).

Conclusion In contrast to the poor performance generally shown by nonhuman primates in this type of task (see Call, Agnetta, & Tomasello, 2000 for a review), human infants used others' communicative gestures to guide their search, both when being addressed directly and when "overhearing" gestures directed at others. Importantly, this required more than low-level gaze or point following abilities. For successful search performance infants needed to attend to the communicative cue, recognize its relevance, and identify its referent. Our findings suggest that infants as young as 14 months are able to recognize other persons' communicative intent within the frame of an ongoing activity. As discussed above, this ability is essential for the acquisition of language, as well as for other forms of cultural learning and shared cooperative activities.

Infant Pointing   One-year-olds not only respond to attempts by others to direct their attention, they also actively direct others' attention themselves using pointing gestures. Infant communicative pointing has been proposed to express two distinct performatives (e.g., Bates, Camaioni, & Volterra, 1975; see also Camaioni, 1993): protoimperatives are requests for objects and protodeclaratives are attempts to share attention and interest to objects or events. These gestures appear to be truly communicative acts—as evidenced by the fact that while gesturing infants often alternate gaze between the adult's face and the object, suggesting that they check whether the adult is following and responding to their gesture (Bates et al. 1975; see Franco & Butterworth, 1996, for an elaboration).

       However, some researchers have expressed skepticism that 12-month-olds produce declarative gestures to share attention and interest (Moore & Corkum, 1994) or that their declarative points are even communicative at all (Desrochers, Morissette & Ricard, 1995). For example, Moore and colleagues argued that early points typically identified as protodeclaratives were in reality aimed at gaining adult attention to the self, rather than sharing attention and interest with the other person (Moore & Corkum, 1994; Moore & D'Entremont 2001). To address this controversy, we conducted a series of detailed studies on infant pointing. Specifically, we investigated the following three questions: First, do infants intend to communicate when they point declaratively? Second, do infants want to direct others' attention specifically to what they point at? Third, what are the underlying motives for infant pointing?

       Declarative Pointing   To investigate infant declarative pointing we have used a paradigm in which pointing is elicited on a number of trials by interesting events, like puppets appearing or lights flashing from behind a large screen at a distance. On each trial, if the infant points, an experimenter responds consistently in one of several ways in different experimental groups. We then measure the infants' reactions to the experimenter's responses to determine which response satisfies infants' intent when pointing.

       In a first study, we tested four hypotheses about what 12-month-olds want when they point (Liszkowski, Carpenter, Henning, Striano, & Tomasello, 2004). To test Desrochers et al.'s (1995) hypothesis that infants point noncommunicatively for themselves, the experimenter neither attended to the infant nor to the indicated event in response to infants' points (Ignore condition). To test Moore and D'Entremont's (2001) hypothesis that infants do not want to direct or share attention and just want to obtain attention to themselves, the experimenter never looked at the event and instead attended to the infant's face and emoted positively to the infant (Face condition). To test the hypothesis that infants only want to direct attention and nothing else, the experimenter only attended to the event

(Event condition). And to test our hypothesis that infants want to share attention and interest, the experimenter responded to the infant's point by alternating gaze between the event and the infant, emoting positively to the infant about the event (Joint Attention condition).

The main findings were that infants pointed communicatively to share attention and interest with the experimenter about the event. Infants preferred the Joint Attention condition and pointed significantly more across trials in that condition compared to each of the other three conditions. When the experimenter attended only to the infant but never to the event and emoted positively (Face condition), infants repeated their pointing within trials to that event significantly more often than in the Joint Attention condition, in an apparent attempt to direct the experimenter's attention to it. Thus, contrary to the account of Moore and D'Entremont (2001), infants wanted to direct the experimenter's attention to an event. However, when the experimenter only attended to the event and did not look and comment back to the infant (Event condition), infants also repeated their pointing within trials and, in addition, looked significantly more often to the experimenter than in any other condition. Just directing attention without sharing was thus not satisfactory either. Instead, infants expected some sort of a comment from the experimenter, indicative of sharing interest in the event that both attended to. In other words, when infants' communicative intent was not satisfied infants persisted with repeated pointing within trials and, across trials gave up pointing for the experimenter. It was only in the Joint Attention condition that infants' intent was satisfied as revealed by their continued pointing across trials and lack of repeated pointing within trials.

In a second study (Liszkowski, Carpenter, & Tomasello, 2007), we followed up on these results and investigated to what extent infant pointing already involves two main components of linguistic speech acts: reference and attitude (Searle, 1969). Using the same general paradigm as in the previous study, the experimenter either understood infants' referent and attended to what they pointed at, or he misunderstood the infants' referent and instead attended to a barrier which obstructed his line of sight to infants' referent. In addition, we manipulated whether the experimenter emoted positively, showing interest, or neutrally, showing disinterest, controlling the attitude expression about a referent. The main findings were that 12-month-olds preferred the condition in which both referent and attitude were shared (Joint Attention), pointing on significantly more trials in that condition than in each of the other three. When the experimenter emoted positively but misunderstood the infants' referent (Misunderstanding condition), infants were not satisfied and repeated pointing within trials significantly more often than in the Joint Attention condition, apparently to redirect the adult's attention to the correct referent. When the experimenter attended to the referent but was not interested in it (Uninterested condition), infants pointed overall on significantly less trials, and, in contrast to the misunderstanding condition, they did not repeat their pointing within a trial—not simply requesting positive emotions imperatively.

These two studies demonstrate that 12-month-olds point with the intent to communicate and want to direct others' attention specifically to what they point at. Pointing in this situation is motivated by sharing an attitude about the referent with a communicative partner. In sum, findings show that infant pointing is a joint communicative act, to comment on and point out something for the other person, and to share attitudes about it with the other person. Infants' declarative pointing is thus not motivated egocentrically to obtain something for the self. Instead, it is motivated by sharing and aligning self and other in some way.

Informative Pointing   Interestingly, adults also point for other reasons than sharing interest. For example, adults also point to the lost keys that someone is looking for, helping her find them by providing necessary information. The motive of such informative pointing is different from that of declarative pointing. In informative pointing the providing of information is not to engage mutually about the referent but instead mainly to benefit the other person. The pointing is more about the recipient's relation to the referent than the sender's, to help her find an object. Helping is an important feature of human shared cooperative activities (Bratman, 1992) but has previously not been investigated in infants this young.

In a third study (Liszkowski, Carpenter, Striano, & Tomasello, 2006), we therefore investigated whether 12-month-olds also point like adults to help others find what they are looking for by informing them of something they do not know. We designed a search paradigm, in which the experimenter first repeatedly demonstrated an action with one of two objects. Both objects then disappeared in various ways (e.g., they fell down or somebody put them away) and E then began searching. Findings were that infants pointed at the object E needed to continue her action significantly more often than at the other simultaneously misplaced object, and without requestive accompaniments like whining, reaching, or repeated pointing, apparently to inform E of its location. This study thus showed that infants point to provide information for others, which requires the cognitive ability to detect what information is relevant for an adult. In addition, it revealed for the first time in infants this young the presence of a prosocial motive of helping others freely and without direct benefit for the self.

Conclusion   It has been proposed that declarative pointing at 12 months is not communicative (Desrochers et al., 1995) or that it only serves to obtain attention to the self egocentrically, without any social-cognitive understanding of others' attentional states (Moore & D'Entremont, 2001). Our studies on infant pointing do not support such lean views. Instead, we have presented evidence that 12-month-olds point communicatively with the goal of directing others' attentional states, and do so with cooperative, prosocial motives such as sharing interest in things and helping by providing information for others.

Further studies in our laboratory are investigating when infants point at things others are already attending to, when infants point out what is new to others, how infants refer to absent referents, whether infants know that the addressee has to be able to see their pointing, and what role caregivers' pointing and infants' cognitive development play in the emergence of pointing. All findings converge on a new view of infant pointing as a prelinguistic, fully communicative act which involves both reference and attitude, prosocial motives like sharing and helping, and a social-cognitive understanding of others' psychological experiences (see Liszkowski, 2005; 2006, for an overview).

Interestingly, there is no evidence of any of this in the gestures of nonhuman primates. That is, there is no evidence that nonhuman apes produce declarative gestures or that they freely provide information for others that is not related to their own needs (Tomasello, 2006; Tomasello & Carpenter, 2005). Thus, infants' declarative and informative pointing seems to be a uniquely human form of communication, reflective of their motivation and social-cognitive skills to engage in shared activities.

Cooperating with Others

Social behaviors such as helping and cooperation are interesting both cognitively and motivationally: In order to successfully help another person with a problem, the helper must understand the other's unachieved goal and possess the altruistic motivation to act on behalf of the other. Such altruistic motivations are rare evolutionarily: In fact, several researchers have claimed that only humans act altruistically towards nonkin—in contrast to other primates who strive only after their own best benefit (Alexander, 1987; Fehr & Fischbacher, 2003), regardless of the benefits or costs for others (Jensen, Hare, Call, & Tomasello, 2006; Silk et al., 2005).

Whereas for helping, understanding the other's individual goal might be sufficient, cooperative activities are based upon the formation of a shared goal, including the motivation to mutually support each other's actions to reach that goal (Bratman 1992; Tomasello et al., 2005). Cooperative activities are thus another test case for the proposal that humans—and maybe only humans—engage in social interactions which are characterized by shared intentionality.

To investigate the phylogenetic and ontogenetic roots of these behaviors, we conducted a series of comparative studies. Here, we present two studies in which human children and chimpanzees were tested on a similar set of helping and cooperation tasks. Such comparisons are intriguing because they may enable us to distinguish behaviors which were present already in our common phylogenetic ancestor from aspects which are unique to the human lineage.

Helping in Young Children and Chimpanzees   A number of studies have demonstrated that young children show concern for others in distress—as a kind of emotional helping (see Eisenberg & Fabes, 1998, for an overview). Also, as Liszkowski et al. (2006) have shown (see above), 1-year-old infants help others by informing them about the location of an object they are looking for. However, no experimental studies have systematically assessed young children's instrumental helping—providing help to people who are faced with a problem and are unable to solve it on their own.

We thus designed a study aimed at investigating such instances of instrumental helping in young children at 18 months of age (Warneken & Tomasello, 2006). To do so, we developed 10 situations in which an experimenter was performing a specific action, but suddenly encountered a problem and needed assistance from the child to achieve his goal. It turned out that children performed spontaneous, unrewarded helping behaviors in diverse situations: For example, they helped the adult retrieve an out-of-reach object like a pen he had accidentally dropped on the floor and was unsuccessfully reaching for; they completed his stacking of books after his failed attempt to do this; or they opened the door of a cabinet when his hands were full. Importantly, the children did not perform these actions in control conditions in which no help was necessary (e.g., when he had thrown the pen on the floor on purpose), showing that their behavior depended upon the other's goal.

Interestingly, when we gave the same 10 (slightly varied tasks) to three human-raised chimpanzees (aged 36 to 54 months), they also helped in one type of situation: They helped a human caregiver by handing her objects she was unsuccessfully reaching for, but they did not help in the other kinds of situations (e.g. completing an action, opening a door for the other). The findings indicated that the chimpanzees were able to understand goal-directed action, at least when the goal was easy to discern, as in situations where a person is reaching for an object. Moreover, they demonstrated the altruistic motivation to instrumentally help the other, questioning the assumption that altruism is unique to humans. Ongoing research in our laboratory is attempting to clarify (1) whether this is restricted to the close relationship between the nursery-raised chimpanzees and their caregiver, and (2) whether it extends beyond this context, which may resemble an imperative request for handing over objects.

Taken together, these results show that young children seem to have a natural tendency to help others in a variety of ways—even when the other person is a stranger and children receive no benefit for helping. Furthermore, it appears that the common ancestor of chimpanzees and humans already possessed rudimentary forms of skills and motivations to help others.

Cooperative Activities in Young Children and Chimpanzees   We then may ask whether the same is true for activities that are based upon a shared goal. Engaging in cooperative activities with a shared goal is a crucial achievement in human ontogeny as it enables partners to reach goals which lie beyond the means of an individual, forming the basis for cultural creation. At what age do young children begin to engage in such activities by successfully coordinating their own actions with those of a partner to work towards a shared goal? Are chimpanzees motivated and able to engage in such activities as well?

To investigate these questions, Warneken, Chen, and Tomasello (2006) tested children at 18 and 24 months of age on four different cooperation tasks and compared their performance with that of the same three human-raised chimpanzees mentioned above. The rationale of all these tasks was that they could not be performed successfully by one person alone but required the joint activity of two people. Two of these tasks were cooperative games (such as a "trampoline" in which two people had to hold a large piece of cloth and make a toy bounce on it) and two others were cooperative problem solving tasks (e.g., two people had to perform complementary roles, such as one person holding a container open so that the other person could retrieve an object from inside). Children at both ages were able to successfully cooperate with an adult partner in most of both types of tasks (games and problem solving). In addition, we found that children at 24 months were coordinating their actions with the partner more skillfully than children at 18 months. For example, the older children would position themselves in the correct location more quickly and adjust their actions to their partner temporally by holding the container open until the other had completed his action. The most interesting findings were obtained when the adult partner interrupted his participation at a predetermined moment (see Ross & Lollis, 1983, who first devised this method): Children of both age groups frequently communicated to the partner in an attempt to request his cooperation. All children produced at least one such communicative attempt: They frequently used gestural communication, such as pointing to the apparatus or placing the apparatus in front of the partner, and at 24 months they often accompanied this with verbalizations. This at least shows that the children understood their own and their partner's action as interconnected parts of a joint activity. Moreover, this can also be taken as evidence that the children were trying to redirect their partner toward a shared goal, perhaps insisting on the commitment to support each other's actions in a cooperative activity.

When the three human-raised chimpanzees (aged 33 to 51 months) interacted with a human caregiver in the same tasks, they were able to solve a problem-solving task such as lifting a door so that the partner could retrieve a piece of food from inside (see also Melis, Hare, & Tomasello, 2006). In contrast, they showed no interest in co-operating in the social games, such as the trampoline game which had no other goal beyond doing something together. Most importantly, they never once attempted to reengage their partner when she refrained from cooperating—even in the problem-solving task in which they were able to successfully coordinate their action. The chimpanzees instead tried to solve the task alone, or else disengaged from the task completely, suggesting that they had not formed a shared goal with the other.

Human beings appear to be especially adapted for cooperative activities. Our chimpanzees—even though raised in a human environment—did not develop similar skills, at least with regard to forming shared goals with others. These findings therefore provide evidence for a uniquely human form of cooperative activity involving shared intentionality, which emerges in the second year of life.

Pretending with Others
Young children from the second half of their second year not only engage with others in shared cooperative activities of instrumental and playful kinds—they also enter into the collective space of fictional worlds in pretend play. This type of play is a uniquely human phenomenon (Gomez & Martin-Andrade, 2005). Part of the reason this is so, we think, is not so much that other species lack imagination, but that pretending is a form of social cooperative activity that is acquired by means of cultural learning, and is founded on an ability to participate in collective intentionality, both of which are absent in other species.

Cultural Learning of Pretense   The debate about the origins of pretending in ontogeny has been shaped by two contrasting approaches: Piaget's rather individualistic account and Vygotskian culturalism. According to Piaget (1945/1962), the child first creates pretend play autonomously, through individual rather than social processes and through interactions with the environment rather than with people. In contrast, the Vygotskian Soviet school has considered play as essentially situated in specific social and cultural contexts (El'Konin, 1966). In other words, whereas Piaget thought children invent their toys individually first, the Vygotskian tradition claims toys become toys initially in the same way that tools become tools—by cultural learning. In line with the Vygotskian tradition (see also Tomasello 1999a, 1999b; Tomasello, Kruger, & Ratner, 1993), we hypothesized that in fact pretend play is acquired as are other action forms, namely by cultural imitative learning. We pursued this claim in a set of studies on children's acquisition of pretense (Rakoczy, Tomasello, & Striano, 2005). The design was intended to simulate what might be called the cultural ontogeny of artifacts: young children's first encounters with hitherto unknown and (for them) functionless objects and their subsequent learning of how to use those objects as either tools or toys. Young children (18 and 24 months old) were first shown a series of novel objects. An adult then demonstrated instrumental actions on some and pretense actions on others. In a second phase the infants were then given the objects and could act with them several times themselves. The results were as follows: (1) Children imitated both kinds of actions in similar ways, with the same object as the demonstrator (though imitation rates were lower in absolute terms for pretense acts, and 18-month-olds were almost at floor in imitating pretense); (2) children produced few creative pretense acts (but many creative instrumental acts); and (3) during pretense acts children showed significantly more frequent and stronger forms of social behavior, namely gazing (and in one study smiling) at the adult. These results thus suggest that children in their second year begin to imitate pretense actions with objects in ways similar to their imitation of simpler kinds of actions. They also suggest that early pretense is only minimally creative and is an essentially social activity, in which creativity and solitary forms develop later. Tools become tools for children in similar ways as toys become toys—through picking up the intentional and cultural affordances and functions of objects by observing adults' actions with these objects.

However, pretend play, we think, is not acquired on the basis of blind mimicry, but instead is understood by young children as a meaningful, nonserious activity. This understanding of pretending as just another, albeit special kind of intentional activity enables children to imitatively acquire pretend play action forms, and to enter into shared cooperative pretense. Shared pretense, in fact, can be considered one of the earliest areas in which children enter into collective intentionality: Not only does the child observe others perform individual pretense acts of the form "I pretend X" and then performs such an individual "I pretend X" act as well; also, the child joins into shared cooperative "We pretend X" acts together with others. More specifically, this involves a mutual commitment to act together within the game as indicated by the production of actions that respect the implications of each other's pretend stipulations. For instance, if you pretend to "pour" water, I can pretend to "drink" it and must be careful not to "spill" it (see Rakoczy & Tomasello, in press, for details of this idea).

This view of pretend play, however, is a rich one, and it stands in contrast to a prominent view of early pretense understanding in the recent theory of mind literature. This is the so-called "behaving-as-if" construal (e.g., Lillard, 1993, 1998; Nichols & Stich, 2000; Perner, Baker, & Hutton, 1994). The basic claim of the "behaving-as-if" theory is that young children up to the age of 4 to 5 years do not yet understand the intentional structure of pretending, but merely have a very superficial understanding of pretending as a somehow deviant type of behavior ("behaving-as-if"), without grasping that pretending is intentionally and nonseriously acting-as-if.

Understanding Pretense Intentions In another set of studies, we set out to pit our claim and the "behaving-as-if" theory against each other (Rakoczy, Tomasello, & Striano, 2004; Rakoczy & Tomasello, in press). The logic of the studies was straightforward: children's imitative and inferential responses to two kinds of as-if-behaviors—pretending and trying—were compared. Two- and 3-year-old children were shown pairs of superficially analogous incomplete as-if-behaviors with objects: pretending to do an action and unsuccessfully trying to do the same action; for example, to pour from a (closed) container into a cup. In both cases the actor made pouring movements with a novel container over a cup, but without actually pouring. In one case, he marked the activity with signs of playfulness and sound effects as pretending to pour, and in the other case he marked it with signs of surprise and frustration as if trying to really pour. Importantly, the container really did contain water and thus could really be used to pour. In the first study the situation was set up as an imitation game. After the actor's demonstration children were given the object and could perform actions with it themselves. Three-year-olds (and to a weaker degree 2-year-olds) very clearly showed that they understood pretending and trying as such: after trying models, they performed the complete action themselves (e.g., actually poured the water) or tried to really perform it, often commenting on their failure (e.g. "I cannot do it either"). But after pretense models, they instead pretended themselves without appearing to care about the real effects of their acts (e.g., whether there was water coming out of the container).

In another study, children were presented with some of the same demonstration pairs, but not in a strict imitation game. Rather, the pragmatics of the situation were set up to encourage more creative inferential responses. In this study we found that when the 2- and 3-year-olds saw an actor try to pour, they themselves then really did the action or tried to, but did so using different means. For example, they used a tool to open the container first. When the actor had pretended to pour, in contrast, children themselves pretended to drink and to give a Teddy bear a drink. Thus, children showed a rich understanding of the intentional structures of pretending and trying as different forms of behaving-as-if: They grasped that in trying to pour, the actor wanted to perform the action properly and intended to make the proposition "there is water coming out of this container" true by bringing it about. They also understood that, in pretending to pour, the actor was acting intentionally but nonseriously as if pouring and as if the proposition "there is water coming out of this container" was true. Accordingly, these two kinds of behaviors license very different inferences that children grasped: in the trying case, other means should be used when one wants to perform the same action, but now successfully. In the pretense case, perceiving the other person's pretending as such (e.g., pretending to pour into a cup) licenses joining in a shared pretense scenario ("We pretend that there is water in the cup now").

In summary, these results suggest that young children by 2 years of age imitatively acquire pretend play from others, understand the basic intentional structure of pretending, and, based on this understanding, join in inferentially structured joint pretense founded upon a collective intention of the form "We pretend...."

Talking about Pretending   Note that in the studies reported so far, children's understanding of others' pretending and their ability to join into pretense were investigated as indicated in their systematic and inferential actions. In another study (Rakoczy, Tomasello, & Striano, in press), we directly compared this understanding in action to children's explicit understanding in words—the first study in the area of pretense comprehension to look at different levels of understanding with one and the same task. The same action demonstrations as in the "pretending-trying" studies were presented to children at 3, 4, and 6 years of age, and children were asked whether the character pretended to perform an action (e.g., drink) or tried to perform this action. This explicit verbal task proved rather difficult for children up to the age of 6. That is, there was a huge décalage between implicit understanding as expressed in children's systematic, appropriate, and inferential responses at 2 years, and explicit understanding as expressed in words at 6 years.

How is such a huge décalage to be explained? Again, in line with the Vygotskian tradition and recent cultural learning approach (Tomasello 1999a, 1999b), the idea is that of a dialectical development: Children's social understanding enables them to enter into shared activities, to learn culturally (i.e., imitatively and collaboratively), and to acquire social practices, particularly language and discourse. Participation in specific explicit forms of discourse in turn enables new levels of reflective understanding, social and otherwise (Tomasello, 1999a). In the specific case of pretense understanding, specific pretense discourse of the form "We pretend to X" and "We pretend that p," and so forth, should thus be crucial in developing a later explicit understanding of pretending (as measured in our verbal "pretending-trying" tasks and in many other verbal pretense understanding tasks). Support for this central role of explicit pretense discourse comes from a recent training study we conducted (Rakoczy et al., in press). Two groups of 3.5-year-old children received intensive experience with diverse pretense activities (and were compared with a control group that received functional play experience). For the Explicit Group, the pretense experience was accompanied by explicit discourse making use of "pretend that" (e.g. "I'm pretending that this stone is an apple, but really it is a stone") and "pretend to" (e.g. "She is pretending to give him an apple") constructions. In the Implicit Group, in contrast, the pretense scenarios were talked about implicitly, making use of specific implicit pretense discourse markers (e.g., "This is my apple" in a funny voice). In the posttest, only the Explicit Group showed improvement on pretense–reality distinction tests, in which children had to verbally state what an actor had pretended about an object and contrast this with what the object really was (Flavell, Flavell, & Greene, 1987), and tests in which children had to tell verbally whether someone had pretended or tried to do an action. Explicit discourse about pretending and the pretend identities of objects thus turned out to be crucial in the development of reflective understanding of pretense.

Conclusion Pretend play is a form of collective intentionality, involving the joint creation of and respect for status functions. These are functions which only exist because they are collectively assigned to objects and which are expressed in the formula "X counts as Y in context C": "This piece of paper counts as money in our currency area" or "This piece of wood counts as the queen in chess" are the standard examples (Searle, 1995). The collective nonliteral treatment of objects in pretend play, we argue, can be seen as the ontogenetic cradle of such status function creation which is at the heart of uniquely human institutional reality: "This (wooden block) counts as an apple in our pretense game" (Walton, 1990).

Since, according to our studies, young children from the age of 2 years participate in pretend play as a prominent form of collective intentionality, the question remains of exactly how much they understand about status functions. Two very basic characteristics of status function assignment are the following (Searle, 1995). First, status functions are context-relative: Only in context C does X count as a Y, but not in other contexts. For example, a piece of wood counts as a queen in chess but not in other board games. Second, status functions carry normative force: "X counts as Y in context C" implies that X ought to be treated as a Y in context C and ought not to be treated in other ways. For example, a dollar bill ought to be treated as money and not only as a piece of paper in the relevant currency area, and a queen in chess should be treated as having certain powers and not only as a piece of wood.

Such qualities as normativity and context-relativity are what Vygotsky observed in pretend play when he proposed that "Whenever there is an imaginary situation in play, there are rules" (1934/1978, p. 95). In our current research we are investigating children's understanding of these aspects of collective status function creation. In a recent study, for example, we found evidence that young 3-year-olds have a nascent understanding that one object can simultaneously count as different objects in different pretense contexts (Wyman, Rakoczy, & Tomasello, in preparation). Regarding the normative dimension of status function creation, in a pilot study we found that 3-year-olds actively protested against pretense acts by a play partner that were normatively inappropriate given the joint status function assignment (i.e., not treating the X as a Y in the relevant context) (Rakoczy, unpublished data).

In sum, children from 2 years of age participate in joint pretending, a form of collective intentionality which involves the joint assignment of status functions. As status functions are the conceptual building blocks of institutional reality, children's joint games of make-believe can be considered an ontogenetic cradle for entering into institutional reality.

Children with Autism

Autism is a neurodevelopmental disorder that is characterized by qualitative impairments in social interaction and in communication. Several theoretical proposals have been put forward, attempting to explain the pattern of abilities and difficulties shown by children with autism, among them the proposal that the core feature of autism is a problem in "theory of mind" understanding (e.g., for reviews, Baron-Cohen, 2000; Frith, 1997). Importantly, recent research suggests that children with autism do show some understanding of other people, in particular with respect to some aspects of intentional action (Aldridge, Stone, Sweeney, & Bower, 2000; Carpenter, Pennington, & Rogers, 2001) and perception (Leekam, Baron-Cohen, Perrett, Milders, & Brown, 1997). Thus, the question arises whether the relative strengths and impairments of children with autism may instead be accounted for by specific deficits related to their motivation and ability to engage in joint activities with shared goals (see also Hobson, 2002). In order to assess this proposal we briefly review the ability of children with autism with respect to engagement in the shared activities discussed above, that is, joint engagement, communication, pretend play, and cooperation.

First, deficits with regard to joint attention are so pervasive in children with autism that they actually represent diagnostic criteria (DSM-IV; American Psychiatric Association, 1994). Children with autism show very little coordinated joint engagement and they rarely initiate joint attention with others by declaratively pointing to or showing objects (e.g., Baron-Cohen, 1989; Charman et al., 1997). They also rarely respond to others' bids for joint attention (Leekam et al., 1997). Second, linguistic communication and the use of symbols is another problem area for children with autism, and their impaired ability to signal non-comprehension and make appropriate repairs to their own linguistic messages to help others are well documented—suggesting that their communication is not fully collaborative (Loveland, McEvoy, & Tunali, 1990; Sabbagh, 1999). Third, with regard to pretend play, deficits in this domain are so characteristic for young children with autism that this, too, is considered a diagnostic criterion.

Less is known, however, about the cooperative abilities of children with autism. It has been reported that children with autism engage in relatively little cooperative play with peers (Lord, 1984), but interacting with peers may be more demanding than engaging in cooperative activities with an adult, who may initially scaffold the interaction. Therefore, we explored the performance of children with autism in interactions with an adult, looking at both their helping behavior and their engagement in cooperative activities.

To study helping, Liebal, Colombi, Rogers, Warneken, and Tomasello (submitted) presented young children with autism and matched children with other developmental delays with four tasks involving an adult unsuccessfully reaching for an object, similar to the tasks Warneken and Tomasello (2006) used to elicit helping behaviors. We found that children with autism tended to help less frequently than children with other developmental delays when the adult unsuccessfully reached for an object.

To investigate cooperation, Liebal et al. (submitted) adapted a study by Warneken et al. (2006) and presented the same children who participated in the helping study with tasks that encouraged them to cooperate with an adult partner in either problem-solving tasks or social games. We found that children with autism were less likely to cooperate with an adult partner and less coordinated in their actions. This was especially the case for the social games in which the goal was not to retrieve an object (as in the problem-solving tasks) but "simply" to play the game with another person, like in the trampoline task where the only goal was to jointly bounce the block for the fun of it. During interruption periods in which the adult stopped interacting, children with autism showed fewer partner-oriented behaviors like waiting or redirecting the partner to the task, and they made fewer communicative attempts that involved eye contact than did children with other developmental delays. In sum, these findings support the proposal that children with autism show characteristic impairments with respect to their motivation and ability to engage in social interactions that involve a form of shared intentionality.

SHARED INTENTIONALITY

Together these empirical findings provide broad support for the theoretical proposals of Tomasello et al. (2005). They suggested that we should think of the development of human social-cognition as comprising two ontogenetic strands: (1) the understanding of intentional action and perception, and (2) the ability to understand and participate in social interactions involving one or another form of shared intentionality.

   The first strand of human social-cognitive ontogeny is the general primate (or perhaps only ape) understanding of intentional action. Based on the data reviewed here, as well as other data on primate cognition, we may propose that all apes, including humans, understand individual intentional action in terms of the pursuit of goals, as well as the basics of visual perception. There have been a number of proposals to the effect that this skill is a hard-wired and modular part of the human perceptual system. Just as humans automatically see certain perceptual sequences as causal (Leslie, 1984; Michotte, 1963), they automatically see certain actions performed by animate agents as goal-directed. Gergely and Csibra (2003), for example, have proposed that human infants possess an action interpretation system that perceives humanlike action as teleologically directed to a goal from the second half of the first year of life; independently developing is a reference interpretation system concerned with following gaze and the like (Csibra, 2003). Baron-Cohen (1995) proposes something similar, with two early developing innate modules involving the perceiving of goals and eye gaze direction. Soon after the first birthday an independent "shared attention mechanism" emerges, taking outputs from the two earlier modules as inputs.

   Although our view shares some features with these views, there are two important differences. First, we do not see infants' understanding of goals/intentions and perception/attention as blocked off from one another in a modular fashion. Indeed, much recent evidence on infant social-cognitive development suggests that in attempting to understand what others are doing and why they are doing it, infants comprehend intentional action and perception as an integrated system (i.e., as a kind of control system). They display such an integrated understanding from 9 months of age when they know that an actor pursues goals persistently (until he perceives that the world matches his goal) and also when they engage with other persons triadically around external objects—where they must infer people's perceptions from their goals and their goals from their perceptions. In general, we do not see how an observer can understand goal-directed action (much less rational action) without understanding a perceiving organism who monitors the world for signs of success, failure, obstacles, and so forth.

   Second, we believe that to understand the origins of a human cognitive skill we must go beyond simply labeling it as "innate." Indeed, although we concur that understanding actions as goal-directed is a biological adaptation, this says nothing about the ontogenetic process. It is very unlikely, in our view, that a human or ape kept in social isolation for the first year of life would suddenly understand others as goal-directed or intentional agents on its initial encounter with them; presumably the developmental pathway for understanding intentional action depends on species-typical social interactions early in ontogeny. This does not necessarily mean, however, any specific experiences. Thus, Kaye (1982) proposes that to understand intentions infants must themselves be treated by adults as intentional, in the sense that adults interpret their actions in adultlike terms and provide various types of feedback to this effect. The problem with this more specific hypothesis is that there seems to be fairly wide cultural variation in how infants are treated by adults—with adults in some cultures not really treating infants as fully intentional—and, by all accounts, all children in all cultures develop an understanding of others as intentional agents.

The second strand of human social-cognitive development is the sharing strand. Theorists such as Trevarthen (1979), Stern (1985), Bräten (2000), and especially Hobson (2002), have elaborated the interpersonal and emotional dimensions of early human ontogeny in great detail. We mostly agree with their accounts, but we find that they do not give sufficient attention to the other, intention-reading, line of social-cognitive development. Our proposal is that the uniquely human aspects of social cognition emerge only as uniquely human social motivations interact with an emerging, primate-general understanding of animate and goal-directed action, which then transforms the general ape line of understanding intentional action into the modern human line of shared intentionality.

Although the precise nature of this interaction is not entirely clear, our general view is that infants begin to understand particular kinds of intentional and mental states in others only after they have experienced them first in their own activity and then used their own experience to simulate that of others (Tomasello 1999b; see Sommerville & Woodward, 2005, for experimental evidence supporting this view). However, contrary to our previous view, we do not think that simple "identification with others" is a sufficient basis for the simulation process—certainly not if we mean bodily identification. There is now evidence that neonatal chimpanzees engage in the same kind of facial mimicking as human infants (Myowa 1996; Myowa-Yamakoshi, Tomonaga, Tanaka, & Matsusawa, 2004), and even some species of birds are good at copying actions (e.g., Zentall 1996). And so we would speculate at this point that more deeply psychological levels of identification with others—of a kind sufficient to enable individuals to simulate the intentional and mental states of others in an analogy with their own—depends crucially on the skills and motivations for interpersonal and emotional dyadic sharing characteristic of human infants and their caregivers (Hobson, 2002; this volume).

Again one can imagine that a species-typical social environment, involving human-typical social interactions with other persons, is required for the emergence of the sharing motivation and its related skills of social engagement. But again some theorists have proposed that some kinds of specific experiences are necessary. For instance, Stern (1985) proposes that parents must "mirror" back to infants their own emotions or behaviors and Gergely (2003) posits an especially important role for certain kinds of social contingencies in terms of timing. But again it is not clear that children in all cultures receive such experiences, or that children who are deprived of them end up unable to share psychological states with others. And so the ontogenetic process for sharing emotions and intentions with others may be fairly robust in the face of different particular human social environments.

Our proposal for the early developmental pathway characteristic of human social cognition is thus that it is the synergistic product of the general ape line of understanding intentional action, unfolding from 9 to 14 months (based on earlier recognition of object-directed actions; see Woodward, 1998), and the modern human motivation to share psychological states with others, present from very early in human ontogeny. There is almost no research establishing a solid relationship between any kind of particular social experience infants might have and individual differences in the unfolding of this developmental pathway. In the absence of such studies, we might tentatively conclude that this is a very robust, heavily canalized ontogenetic pathway in humans that (in the absence of neuro-biological disorders) emerges in all "normal" human environments.

What results from this developmental process, early in the second year of life, is the ability to engage in a number of different kinds of collaborative interactions involving shared intentionality. As a part of this, there also emerges a new form of cognitive representation, what Tomasello et al. (2005) called dialogic cognitive representations in which each participant conceives the collaboration holistically, with both roles in a single representational format (see also Fernyhough, 1996). Although we have no concrete evidence for where these novel forms of cognitive representation come from, our supposition is that they are Vygotskian internaliza-tions of these special collaborative activities. These representations then enable children's participation in cultural (mediated) practices such as linguistic com-munication and other forms of symbolic interaction. Dialogic cognitive represen-tations thus include and go beyond theoretical constructs such as "identification with others" (Hobson, 1993; Tomasello, 1999b), the "like me" stance (Meltzoff & Gopnik, 1993), and "self-other equivalence" (Barresi & Moore, 1996), which may be ontogenetic forerunners. That is to say, they capture the fact that the child both knows that she is in some sense equivalent to others—actors can substitute for one another in acts of imitation and role reversal—but at the same time she is different from others. Dialogic cognitive representations thus have built into them the functional equivalence (though not identity) of different participants in activi-ties, one of whom may be the self, but they have additional aspects (e.g., intentions about the other's intentions) deriving from the motivation to share psychological states with others.

In any case, our research efforts will continue to be aimed at answering ques-tions focused on the process by which human beings have evolved the skills and motivations to create and participate in the cultural activities and practices that constitute human societies.

Note

1. Other studies of younger infants that used looking time measures (e.g., Woodward, 1998) did not test infants' understanding of failed attempts and accidents, so, in our view, they do not provide clear evidence of understanding of others' goals.

References

Akhtar, N. (2005). The robustness of learning through overhearing. *Developmental Science, 8,* 199–209.

Aldridge, M., Stone, K., Sweeney, M., & Bower, T. (2000). Preverbal children with autism understand the intentions of others. *Developmental Science, 3,* 294–301.

Alexander, R. D. (1987). *The biology of moral systems.* Hawthorne, NY: Aldine de Gruyter.

American Psychiatric Association. (1994). *Diagnostic and statistical manual of mental disorders* (4th ed.). Washington, D.C.: Author.

Baldwin, D. A. (1993). Infants' ability to consult the speaker for clues to word reference. *Journal of Child Language, 20,* 395–418.

Baron-Cohen, S. (1989). Perceptual role taking and protodeclarative pointing in autism. *British Journal of Developmental Psychology, 7,* 113–128.

Baron-Cohen, S. (1995). *Mindblindness: An essay on autism and theory of mind.* Cambridge, MA: MIT Press.

Baron-Cohen, S. (2000). Theory of mind and autism: A fifteen year review. In S. Baron-Cohen, H. Tager-Flusberg, & D. J. Cohen (Eds.), *Understanding other minds—Perspectives from developmental cognitive neuroscience* (2nd ed., pp. 3–20). Oxford: Oxford University Press.

Barresi, J., & Moore, C. (1996). Intentional relations and social understanding. *Behavioral and Brain Sciences, 19,* 107–154.

Bates, E., Camaioni, L., & Volterra, V. (1975). The acquisition of performatives prior to speech. *Merrill-Palmer Quarterly, 21,* 205–224.

Behne, T., Carpenter, M., Call, J., & Tomasello, M. (2005). Unwilling versus unable: Infants' understanding of intentional action. *Developmental Psychology, 41,* 328–337.

Behne, T., Carpenter, M., & Tomasello, M. (2005). One-year-olds comprehend the communicative intentions behind gestures in a hiding game. *Developmental Science, 8,* 492–499.

Bekkering, H., Wohlschläger, A., & Gattis, M. (2000). Imitation of gestures in children is goal-directed. *The Quarterly Journal of Experimental Psychology A: Human Experimental Psychology, 53A,* 153–164.

Bellagamba, F., & Tomasello, M. (1999). Re-enacting intended acts: Comparing 12- and 18-month-olds. *Infant Behavior & Development, 22,* 277–282.

Bigelow, A. E., MacLean, K., & Proctor, J. (2004). The role of joint attention in the development of infants' play with objects. *Developmental Science, 7,* 518–526.

Bråten, S. (2000). *Modellmakt og altersentriske spedbarn. Essays on dialogue in infant and adult.* Bergen: Sigma.

Bratman, M. E. (1992). Shared cooperative activity. *Philosophical Review, 101,* 327–341.

Brooks, R., & Meltzoff, A. N. (2002). The importance of eyes: How infants interpret adult looking behavior. *Developmental Psychology, 38,* 958–966.

Bruner, J. (1983). *Child's talk.* New York: Norton.

Butler, S. C., Caron, A. J., & Brooks, R. (2000). Infant understanding of the referential nature of looking. *Journal of Cognition and Development, 4,* 359–377.

Buttelmann, D., Carpenter, M., Call, J., & Tomaseelo, M. (in press). Rational tool use and tool choice in human infants and great apes. *Child Development.*

Butterworth, G., (1995). Origins of mind in perception and action. In C. Moore & P. J. Dunham (Eds.), *Joint attention: Its origins and role in development* (pp. 29–40). Hillsdale, NJ: Lawrence Erlbaum.

Butterworth, G., & Jarrett, N. (1991). What minds have in common is space: Spatial mechanisms serving joint visual attention in infancy. *British Journal of Developmental Psychology, 9,* 55–72.

Call, J., Agnetta, B., & Tomasello, M. (2000). Cues the chimpanzees do and do not use to find hidden objects. *Animal Cognition, 3,* 23–34.

Call, J., Carpenter, M., & Tomasello, M. (2005). Copying results and copying actions in the process of social learning: Chimpanzees (*Pan troglodytes*) and human children (*Homo sapiens*). *Animal Cognition, 8,* 151–163.

Call, J., Hare, B., Carpenter, M., & Tomasello, M. (2004). "Unwilling" versus "unable": Chimpanzees' understanding of human intentions. *Developmental Science, 7,* 488–498.

Call, J., Hare, B., & Tomasello, M. (1998). Chimpanzee gaze following in an object-choice task. *Animal Cognition, 1,* 89–99.

Call, J., & Tomasello, M. (1998). Distinguishing intentional from accidental actions in orangutans (*Pongo pygmaeus*), chimpanzees (*Pan troglodytes*) and human children (*Homo sapiens*). *Journal of Comparative Psychology, 112,* 192–206.

Call, J., & Tomasello, M. (2005). What do chimpanzees know about seeing revisited: An explanation of the third kind. In N. Eilan, C. Hoerl, T. McCormack, & J. Roessler (Eds.), *Joint attention: Communication and other minds: Issues in philosophy and psychology* (pp. 45–64). New York: Clarendon Press/Oxford University Press.

Camaoni, L. (1993). The development of intentional communication: A re-analysis. In J. Nadel & L. Camaoni (Eds.), *New perspectives in early communicative development* (pp. 82–96). London: Routledge.

Caron, A. J., Butler, S. C., & Brooks, R. (2002). Gaze following at 12 and 14 months: Do the eyes matter? *British Journal of Developmental Psychology, 20,* 225–239.

Caron, A. J., Kiel, E. J., Dayton, M., & Butler, S. C. (2002). Comprehension of the referential intent of looking and pointing between 12 and 15 months. *Journal of Cognition & Development, 3,* 445–464.

Carpenter, M., Akhtar, N., & Tomasello, M. (1998). Fourteen- to 18-month-old infants differentially imitate intentional and accidental actions. *Infant Behavior and Development, 21,* 315–330.

Carpenter, M., & Call, J. (in press). Comparing the imitative skills of children and nonhuman apes. *Primatologie.*

Carpenter, M., Call, J., & Tomasello, M. (2002). Understanding "prior intentions" enables 2-year-olds to imitatively learn a complex task. *Child Development, 73,* 1431–1441.

Carpenter, M., Call, J., & Tomasello, M. (2005). Twelve- and 18-month-olds copy actions in terms of goals. *Developmental Science, 8,* F13–F20.

Carpenter, M., Nagell, K., & Tomasello, M. (1998). Social cognition, joint attention, and communicative competence from 9 to 15 months of age. *Monographs of the Society for Research in Child Development, 63* (4, Serial No. 255).

Carpenter, M., Pennington, B. F., & Rogers, S. J. (2001). Understanding of others' intentions in children with autism and children with developmental delays. *Journal of Autism and Developmental Disorders, 31,* 589–599.

Charman, T., Swettenham, J., Baron-Cohen, S., Cox, A., Baird, G., & Drew, A. (1997). Infants with autism: An investigation of empathy, pretend play, joint attention, and imitation. *Developmental Psychology, 33,* 781–789.

Corkum, V., & Moore, C. (1995). Development of joint visual attention in infants. In C. Moore & P. J. Dunham (Eds.), *Joint attention: Its origins and role in development* (pp. 61–83). Hillsdale, NJ: Erlbaum.

Corkum, V., & Moore, C. (1998). The origins of joint visual attention in infants. *Developmental Psychology, 34,* 28–38.

Csibra, G. (2003). Teleological and referential understanding of action in infancy. *Philosophical Transactions of the Royal Society of London Series B-Biological Sciences, 358,* 447–458.

Deak, G. O., Flom, R. A., & Pick, A. D. (2000). Effects of gesture and target on 12- and 18-month-olds' joint visual attention to objects in front of or behind them. *Developmental Psychology, 36,* 511–523.

Desrochers, S., Morissette, P., & Ricard, M. (1995). Two perspectives on pointing in infancy. In C. Moore & P. Dunham (Eds.), *Joint attention: Its origins and role in development* (pp. 85–101). Hillsdale, NJ: Lawrence Erlbaum.

Dunham, P. J., Dunham, F., & Curwin, A. (1993). Joint-attentional states and lexical acquisition at 18 months. *Developmental Psychology, 29,* 827–831.

Dunphy-Lelii, S., & Wellman, H. M. (2004). Infants' understanding of occlusion of others' line-of-sight: Implications for an emerging theory of mind. *European Journal of Developmental Psychology, 1,* 49–66.

Eilan, N. (2005). Joint attention, communication, and mind. In N. Eilan, C. Hoerl, T. McCormack, & J. Roessler (Eds.), *Joint attention: Communication and other minds: Issues in philosophy and psychology* (pp. 1–33). New York: Clarendon Press/Oxford University Press.

Eisenberg, N., & Fabes, R. A. (1998). Prosocial development. In W. Damon & N. Eisenberg (Eds.), *Handbook of child psychology: Vol. 3. Social, emotional, and personality development* (5th ed., pp. 701–778). Hoboken, NY: John Wiley.

El'Konin, D. B. (1966). Symbolics and its function in the play of children. *Soviet Education, 8,* 35–41.

Fehr, E., & Fischbacher, U. (2003). The nature of human altruism. *Nature, 425,* 785–791.

Fernyhough, C. (1996). The dialogic mind: A dialogic approach to the higher mental functions. *New Ideas in Psychology, 14,* 47–62.

Flavell, J. H. (1992). Perspectives on perspective-taking. In H. Beilin & P. B. Pufall (Eds.), *Piaget's theory: Prospects and possibilities: The Jean Piaget symposium series* (pp. 107–139). Hillsdale, NJ: Erlbaum.

Flavell, J. H., Flavell, E. R., & Green, F. L. (1987). Young children's knowledge about the apparent-real and the pretend-real distinctions. *Developmental Psychology, 23,* 816–822.

Flavell, J. H., Shipstead, S. G., & Croft, K. (1978). Young children's knowledge about visual perception: Hiding objects from others. *Child Development, 49,* 1208–1211.

Floor P., & Akhtar, N. (2006). Can 18-month-old infants learn words by listening in on conversations? *Infancy, 9,* 327–339.

Franco, F., & Butterworth, G. (1996). Pointing and social awareness: Declaring and requesting in the second year. *Journal of Child Language, 23,* 307–336.

Frith, U. (1997). The neurocognitive basis of autism. *Trends in Cognitive Sciences, 1,* 73–77.

Gergely, G. (2003). What should a robot learn from an infant? Mechanisms of action, interpretation and observational learning in infancy. *Connection Science, 15,* 191–209.

Gergely, G., Bekkering, H., & Király, I. (2002). Rational imitation in preverbal infants. *Nature, 415,* 755.

Gergely, G., & Csibra, G. (2003). Teleological reasoning in infancy: The naive theory of rational action. *Trends in Cognitive Sciences, 7,* 287–292.

Gergely, G., & Csibra, G. (in press). Sylvia's recipe: Human culture, imitation, and peda-gogy. In N. Enfield & S. Levinson (Eds.), *The roots of human sociality: Culture, cognition, and interaction.* Oxford: Berg.

Gomez, J. C., & Martin-Andrade, B. (2005). Fantasy play in animals. In A. Pellegrini & P. K. Smith (Eds.), *The nature of play: Great apes and humans* (pp. 139–171). New York: Guilford.

Gräfenhain, M., Behne, T., Carpenter, M., & Tomasello, M. (submitted). One-year-olds' understanding of nonverbally expressed communicative intentions directed to a third person.

Hare, B., Call, J., Agnetta, B., & Tomasello, M. (2000). Chimpanzees know what conspe-cifics do and do not see. *Animal Behavior, 59,* 771–785.

Hare, B., Call, J., & Tomasello, M. (2001). Do chimpanzees know what conspecifics know? *Animal Behavior, 61,* 139–151.

Hare, B., Call, J., & Tomasello, M. (2006). Chimpanzees deceive a human by hiding. *Cognition, 101,* 495–514.

Heal, J. (2005). Joint attention and understanding the mind. In N. Eilan, C. Hoerl, T. McCormack, & J. Roessler (Eds.), *Joint attention: Communication and other minds: Issues in philosophy and psychology* (pp. 34–44). New York: Clarendon Press/Oxford University Press.

Hobson, P. (1993). *Autism and the development of mind.* Hillsdale, NJ: Lawrence Erlbaum.

Hobson, R. P. (2002). *The cradle of thought.* Basingstoke, UK: Macmillan Education.

Husserl, E. (2004). Wahrnehmung und Aufmerksamkeit. Texte aus dem Nachlass (1893–1912). In T. Vongehr & R. Giuliani (Vol. Eds.), *Husserliana: Gesammelte Werke* (Vol. 38, pp.). Hamburg: Springer.

Itakura, S. (1996). An exploratory study of gaze monitoring in nonhuman primates. *Japa-nese Psychological Research, 38,* 174–180.

James, W. (1890). *The principles of psychology.* New York: Holt.

Jensen, K., Hare, B., Call, J., & Tomasello, M. (2006). What's in it for me? Self-regard precludes altruism and spite in chimpanzees. *Proceedings of the Royal Society B: Biological Sciences, 273,* 1013–1021.

Johnson, S. C., Booth, A., & O'Hearn, K. (2001). Inferring the goals of a nonhuman agent. *Cognitive Development, 16,* 637–656.

Kaye, K. (1982). *The mental and social life of babies: How parents create persons.* Chi-cago: University of Chicago Press.

Leekam, S., Baron-Cohen, S., Perrett, D., Milders, M., & Brown, S. (1997). Eye-direction detection: A dissociation between geometric and joint attention skills in autism. *British Journal of Developmental Psychology, 15,* 77–95.

Leslie, A. M. (1984). Spatiotemporal continuity and the perception of causality in infants. *Perception, 13,* 287–305.

Liebal, K., Colombi, C., Rogers, S., Warneken, F., & Tomasello, M. (submitted). Helping and cooperation in children with autism. *Journal of Autism and Developmental Disorders.*

Lillard, A. S. (1993). Young children's conceptualization of pretense: Action or mental representational state? *Child Development, 64,* 372–386.

Lillard, A. S. (1998). Wanting to be it: Children's understanding of intentions underlying pretense. *Child Development, 69,* 981–993.

Liszkowski, U. (2005). Human twelve-month-olds point cooperatively to share interest with and provide information for a communicative partner. *Gesture, 5,* 135–154.

Liszkowski, U. (2006). Infant pointing at twelve months: Communicative goals, motives, and social-cognitive abilities: In N. Enfield & S. Levinson (Eds.), *The roots of human sociality: Culture, cognition, and interaction.* Oxford: Berg.

Liszkowski, U., Carpenter, M., Henning, A., Striano, T., & Tomasello, M. (2004). Twelve-month-olds point to share attention and interest. *Developmental Science, 7,* 297–307.

Liszkowski, U., Carpenter, M., & Tomasello, M. (2007). Reference and attitude in infant pointing. *Journal of Child Language, 34,* 1–20.

Liszkowski, U., Carpenter, M., Striano, T., & Tomasello, M. (2006). Twelve- and 18-month-olds point to provide information for others. *Journal of Cognition and Development, 7,* 173–187.

Lord, C. (1984). The development of peer relations in children with autism. In F. Morrison, C. Lord, & D. Keating (Eds.), *Advances in applied developmental psychology* (pp. 165–229). New York: Academic Press.

Loveland, K. A., McEvoy, R. E., & Tunali, B. (1990). Narrative story telling in autism and Down's syndrome. *British Journal of Developmental Psychology, 8,* 9–23.

Masangkay, Z. S., McCluskey, K., McIntyre, C. W., Sims-Knight, J., Vaughn, B. E., & Flavell, J. H. (1974). The early development of inferences about the visual percepts of others. *Child Development, 45,* 357–366.

McGuigan, N., & Doherty, M. J. (2002). The relation between hiding skill and judgment of eye direction in preschool children. *Developmental Psychology, 38,* 418–427.

Melis, A. P., Call, J., & Tomasello, M. (in press). Chimpanzees conceal visual and auditory information from others. *Journal of Comparative Psychology.*

Melis, A. P., Hare, B., & Tomasello, M. (2006). Chimpanzees recruit the best collaborators. *Science, 311,* 1297–1300.

Meltzoff, A. (1995). Understanding the intentions of others: Re-enactment of intended acts by 18-month-old children. *Developmental Psychology, 31,* 1–16.

Meltzoff, A. N., & Gopnik, A. (1993). The role of imitation in understanding persons and developing a theory of mind. In S. Baron-Cohen, H. Tager-Flusberg, & D. J. Cohen (Eds.), *Understanding other minds: Perspectives from autism* (pp. 335–366). New York: Oxford.

Michotte, A. (1963). *The perception of causality.* London: Methuen.

Moll, H., Carpenter, M., & Tomasello, M. (in press). Fourteen-month-olds know what others experience only in joint engagement with them. *Developmental Science.*

Moll, H., Koring, C., Carpenter, M., & Tomasello, M. (2006). Infants determine others' focus of attention by pragmatics and exclusion. *Journal of Cognition and Development, 7,* 411–430.

Moll, H., & Tomasello, M. (2004). 12- and 18-month-olds follow gaze behind barriers. *Developmental Science, 7,* F1–F9.

Moll, H., & Tomasello, M. (2006). Level 1 perspective-taking at 24 months of age. *British Journal of Developmental Psychology, 24,* 603–613.

Moll, H., & Tomasello, M. (2007). How 14- and 18-month-olds know what's new for others. *Developmental Psychology, 43*(2), 309–317.

Moore, C., & Corkum, V. (1994). Social understanding at the end of the first year of life. *Developmental Review, 14,* 349–372.

Moore, C., & Corkum, V. (1998). Infant gaze following based on eye direction. *British Journal of Developmental Psychology, 16,* 495–503.

Moore, C., & D'Entremont, B. (2001). Developmental changes in pointing as a function of attentional focus. *Journal of Cognition and Development, 2,* 109–129.

Myowa, M. (1996). Imitation of facial gestures by an infant chimpanzee. *Primates, 37,* 207–213.

Myowa-Yamakoshi, M., & Matsuzawa, T. (2000). Imitation of intentional manipulatory actions in chimpanzees. *Journal of Comparative Psychology, 114,* 381–391.

Myowa-Yamakoshi, M., Tomonaga, M., Tanaka, M., & Matsuzawa, T. (2004). Imitation in neonatal chimpanzees (*Pan troglodytes*). *Developmental Science, 7,* 437–442.

Nichols, S., & Stich, S. (2000). A cognitive theory of pretense. *Cognition, 74,* 115–147.

Onishi, K. H., & Baillargeon, R. (2005). Do 15-month-old infants understand false beliefs? *Science, 308,* 255–258.

Perner, J., Baker, S., & Hutton, D. (1994). Prelief: The conceptual origins of belief and pretence. In C. Lewis & P. Mitchell (Eds.), *Children's early understanding of mind: Origins and development* (pp. 261–286). Hove, UK: Lawrence Erlbaum.

Piaget, J. (1962). *Play, dreams and imitation in childhood.* New York: Norton. (Original published in 1945)

Povinelli, D. J., & Eddy, T. J. (1996). What young chimpanzees know about seeing. *Monographs of the Society for Research in Child Development, 61* (3, Serial No. 247).

Povinelli, D. J., Reaux, J. E., Bierschwale, D. T., Allain, A. D., & Simon, B. B. (1997). Exploitation of pointing as a referential gesture in young children, but not adolescent chimpanzees. *Cognitive Development, 12,* 327–365.

Rakoczy, H. (2006). Pretend play and the development of collective intentionality. *Cognitive Systems Research, 7,* 113–127.

Rakoczy, H., & Tomasello, M. (in press). Two-year-olds' grasp the intentional structure of pretense acts. *Developmental Science.*

Rakoczy, H., Tomasello, M., & Striano, T. (2004). Young children know that trying is not pretending—A test of the "behaving-as-if" construal of children's early concept of "pretense". *Developmental Psychology, 40,* 38–399.

Rakoczy, H., Tomasello, M., & Striano, T. (2005). On tools and toys: How children learn to act on and pretend with "virgin" objects. *Developmental Science, 8,* 57–73.

Rakoczy, H., Tomasello, M., & Striano, T. (in press). The role of experience and discourse in children's developing understanding of pretend play actions. *British Journal of Developmental Psychology.*

Ross, H. S., & Lollis, S. P. (1987). Communication within infant social games. *Developmental Psychology, 23,* 241–248.

Sabbagh, M. (1999). Communicative intentions and language: Evidence from right-hemisphere damage and autism. *Brain and Language, 70,* 29–69.

Schwier, C., van Maanen, C., Carpenter, M., & Tomasello, M. (2006). Rational imitation in 12-month-old infants. *Infancy, 10,* 303–311.

Searle, J. R. (1969). *Speech acts.* Cambridge: Cambridge University Press.

Searle, J. R. (1995). *The construction of social reality.* New York: Free Press.

Silk, J. B., Brosnan, S. F., Vonk, J., Henrich, J., Povinelli, D. J., Richardson et al. (2005). Chimpanzees are indifferent to the welfare of unrelated group members. *Nature, 437,* 1357–1359.

Sommerville, J. A., & Woodward, A. L. (2005). Pulling out the intentional structure of action: The relation between action processing and action production in infancy. *Cognition, 95,* 1–30.

Sperber, D., & Wilson, D. (1986). *Relevance: Communication and cognition.* Cambridge, MA: Harvard University Press.

Stern, D. N. (1987). The interpersonal world of the infant: A symposium. *Contemporary Psychoanalysis, 23,* 56–59.

Tomasello, M. (1999a). The cultural ecology of young children's interactions with objects and artifacts. In E. Winograd, R. Fivush, & W. Hirst (Eds.), *Ecological approaches to cognition: Essays in honor of Ulrich Neisser* (pp. 153–170). Mahwah, NJ: Lawrence Erlbaum.

Tomasello, M. (1999b). *The cultural origins of human cognition.* Cambridge, MA: Harvard University Press.

Tomasello, M. (in press). Why don't apes point? In N. Enfield & S. Levinson (Eds.), *The roots of human sociality: Culture, cognition, and interaction.* Oxford: Berg.

Tomasello, M., Call, J., & Gluckman, A. (1997). Comprehension of novel communicative signs by apes and human children. *Child Development, 68,* 1067–1080.

Tomasello, M., Call, J. & Hare, B. (1998). Five primate species follow the visual gaze of conspecifics. *Animal Behavior, 55,* 1063–1069.

Tomasello, M., & Carpenter, M. (2005). The emergence of social cognition in three young chimpanzees. *Monographs of the Society for Research in Child Development, 70* (1, Serial No. 279).

Tomasello, M., Carpenter, M., Call, J., Behne, T., & Moll, H. (2005). Understanding and sharing intentions: The ontogeny and phylogeny of cultural cognition. *Behavioral and Brain Sciences, 28,* 675–735.

Tomasello, M., & Farrar, M. J. (1986). Joint attention and early language. *Child Development, 57,* 1454–1463.

Tomasello, M., & Haberl, K. (2003). Understanding attention: 12- and 18-month-olds know what is new for other persons. *Developmental Psychology, 39,* 906–912.

Tomasello, M., Hare, B., & Agnetta, B. (1998). Chimpanzees, *Pan troglodytes,* follow gaze direction geometrically. *Animal Behavior, 58,* 769–777.

Tomasello, M., Hare, B., & Fogleman, T. (2001). The ontogeny of gaze-following in chimpanzees, *Pan troglodytes,* and rhesus monkeys, *Macaca mulatta. Animal Behavior, 61,* 335–343.

Tomasello, M., Kruger, A. C., & Ratner, H. H. (1993). Cultural learning. *Behavioral and Brain Sciences, 16,* 495–552.

Trevarthen, C. (1979). Communication and cooperation in early infancy. A description of primary intersubjectivity. In M. Bullowa (Ed.), *Before speech: The beginning of human communication* (pp. 321–347). London: Cambridge University Press.

Vygotsky, L. S. (1978). *Mind in society: The development of higher psychological processes.* Cambridge, MA: Harvard University Press. (Original work published 1934)

Walton, K. L. (1990). *Mimesis as make-believe.* Cambridge, MA: Harvard University Press.

Warneken, F., Chen, F., & Tomasello, M. (2006). Cooperative activities in young children and chimpanzees. *Child Development, 77,* 640–663.

Warneken, F., & Tomasello, M. (2006). Altruistic helping in human infants and young chimpanzees. *Science, 311,* 1301–1303.

Woodward, A. L. (1998). Infants selectively encode the goal object of an actor's reach. *Cognition, 69,* 1–34.

Wyman, E., Rakoczy, H., & Tomasello, M. (in preparation). Young children's understanding of the context-specificity of pretense.

Zentall, T. (1996). An analysis of imitative learning in animals. In C. M. Heyes & B. G. Galef (Eds.), *Social learning in animals: The roots of culture* (pp. 221–243). San Diego, CA: Academic Press.

5

In the Beginning Is Relation…
And Then What?

PETER HOBSON AND JESSICA HOBSON

OVERVIEW

Our aim in this chapter is to articulate a relational perspective on processes of early development. From an empirical standpoint, we shall adopt the approach of developmental psychopathology and consider how evidence from research in autism serves to illuminate the structure of early interpersonal relatedness. From a theoretical standpoint, we shall take the position that a theory of psychological development needs to begin by characterizing the forms of relatedness that exist between an infant and the social and nonsocial world, and proceed to account for progressively elaborated understandings that the infant and young child acquires about self and other as persons who exist in relation to a shared environment. It is in conjunction with explicit understanding of persons and selves, we shall argue, that children also acquire the conceptual distinction between thoughts (or more basically, attitudes) and things. The reason is that to conceive of oneself as a self among other selves is also to comprehend how given objects and events fall under different descriptions-for-persons. As one aspect of this story, what commences as an essentially cognitive *and* conative *and* affective business of relating to other people and the world, becomes partly reconfigured so that to some degree (but never completely), thinking is emancipated from the immediate exigencies of feeling and will.

One of the fundamental questions that needs to be addressed by anyone who thinks about early development is: What exactly do we mean by "social"? If we want to discriminate between what is social and what is not social in infants' relations with the world, then we need some way of characterizing what each category of relatedness means in terms of infant behavior and experience. It will not do, merely to define social relations as those that have people (or other live creatures) as their focus. This would presuppose much that we need to explain; for example, how it is that what *we* think of as people come to be related to and eventually understood as such by very young children. Moreover, this would overlook how it is possible to relate to a person impersonally, as a kind of thing—something relevant when one considers some aspects of the social relations of children with autism—just as it is possible to relate to things (for example, facelike drawings in the case of young infants) as if they were people.

Indeed it is possible to ask when an infant can be said to have social relations truly or fully at all. From one perspective, at least, it will not suffice that the infant can relate differently to people and things (as famously illustrated by Brazelton, Koslowski, & Main, 1974), because this does not amount to relating to other people as people with their own individuality, their own attitudes, their own status as persons. A similar point has been made about sharing: it is not possible to share until there is sufficient differentiation of the person related to, because by definition a person needs to bring two sets of person-centered experiences in relation to one another for sharing to be taking place. One might even take the view that it is only with the acquisition of a self-concept around the middle of the second year of life, that a child is able to engage in those qualities of relating to others that implicate social relations truly or fully, because, it is claimed (e.g. by Lewis, 1995, and by other authors documented in Draghi-Lorenz, Reddy, & Costall, 2001), only children who have self-concepts can experience "social" or "self-conscious" emotions such as pride, guilt, shame, and embarrassment. So the issue is not simply one that concerns how infants relate to others, but also the degree to which they experience or represent or understand those relations as implicating themselves in relation to other persons *qua* sources of subjective orientation.

THEORETICAL ORIENTATION

"In the beginning is relation" (Buber, 1958). Buber distinguished between I–Thou and I–It relations, and of the former, he wrote: "The 'I' emerges as a single element out of the primal experiences, out of the vital primal words *I-affecting-Thou* and *Thou-affecting-I,* only after they have been split asunder and the participle has been given eminence as an object" (pp. 21–22). Among other philosophers who have reflected upon the structure of early interpersonal experience, the writings of Merleau-Ponty (1964) are especially relevant for the present discussion:

> In perceiving the other, my body and his are coupled, resulting in a sort of action which pairs them [*action à deux*]. This conduct which I am able only to see, I live somehow from a distance. I make it mine; I recover [*reprendre*] it or comprehend it…. (p. 118)

Mimesis is the ensnaring of me by the other, the invasion of me by the other; it is that attitude whereby I assume the gestures, the conducts, the favorite words, the ways of doing things of those whom I confront… [it] is the power of assuming conducts or facial expressions as my own…. (p. 145)

I live in the facial expressions of the other, as I feel him living in mine. (p. 146)

Baldwin (1902) and Cooley (1902) were among psychologists and sociologists who reflected on the contribution of interpersonal experience to children's awareness of self and others. Cooley (1902) wrote,

The immediate social reality is the personal idea…. (p.84)

The personal idea in its more penetrating interpretations involves sympathy, in the sense of primary communication or an entering into and sharing the mind of someone else.…" (p. 102).

Both Cooley and Baldwin considered the emergence of more elaborated forms of self-consciousness and the growth of reflection require that children grasp the nature of other people with minds of their own. This means that *any* kinds of knowledge that entail being aware that one knows such-and-such should be possible only once one has achieved interpersonal understanding. For Baldwin, not only "reflective sympathy" but also reflection itself is "just a relation of separateness created between the ego-self and the alter-self." (p. 233). According to this view, a child comes to adopt a psychological perspective vis-à-vis his or her own self and mental events through adopting appropriate kinds of alternative perspective—where the appropriate kind is one that originates in someone else. G. H. Mead (1934) expounded the relation between such interpersonal role-taking and symbolic thinking thus:

…in order that thought may exist there must be symbols, vocal gestures generally, which arouse in the individual himself the response which he is calling out in the other, and such that from the point of view of that response he is able to direct his later conduct. It involves not only communication in the sense in which birds and animals communicate with each other, but also an arousal in the individual himself of the response which he is calling out in the other individual, a taking of the rôle of the other, a tendency to act as the other person acts. One participates in the same process the other person is carrying out and controls his action with reference to that participation. (p. 73)

In more contemporary writings drawing upon the developmental psychology of infancy, theorists such as Stern (1985), Neisser (1988), and Trevarthen (1979; Trevarthen & Aitken, 2001) have dwelt upon the mechanisms and development of early interpersonal communication. For example, Neisser (1988) echoed Buber's I–

Thou and I–It distinction in contrasting interpersonal and ecological sources of self-knowledge that are based on different forms of information available to the young child. The interpersonal self arises through a special form of direct perception that occurs when the self is engaged in immediate, unreflective social interaction with another person. This aspect of self-development contrasts with the ecological self that develops on the basis of the infant's relations with objects in the world.

One important issue about the development of self–other relations (and social life) on the one hand, and the development of concepts of self and other persons with minds (social knowledge) on the other, is the point at which a child knowingly ascribes to other people qualities associated with the child's own self, on the basis of analogy. A number of current writers (e.g. Carpendale & Lewis, 2004; Hobson, 1991) have cited philosophical arguments such as those of Wittgenstein (1958) to press the critical point that it is not through applying analogy that we *come* to understand and conceptualize the nature of other persons with minds and selves with their own concerns, wishes, and so on. Indeed, the ability to apply analogy from one's own case to that of other people depends upon understanding people-with-minds as selves. This view contrasts with that of writers such as Harris (1989), Meltzoff (2002), Perner (1991), and Tomasello (1999), who have stressed that infants experience others as "like me" but appear to think that understanding self and other as having minds is founded upon the application of analogy from one's own case to that of other people.

Within our framework, the developmental task is not to infuse bodies with minds, but rather to acquire an understanding of how different bodily endowed *people* have their own separate subjective perspectives and "selves" in relation to a common world. This requires that we characterize preconceptual, affectively charged, relational foundations for self-concepts, and provide an account of how the infant moves from *experiencing* to *understanding* person–world psychological relations. In this enterprise, it will be important not to presuppose that certain configurations of feeling, such as those involved in social emotions such as jealousy or coyness, require that an individual has acquired social understanding in the form of self-concepts, when the truth might be that such qualities of relatedness are foundational for the kinds of self-concept we acquire.

In typical development (but to a restricted degree among children with autism), one critical period of transition *toward* understanding self and other occurs at the end of the first year of life, when infants relate to other people as separate centers of psychological orientation toward a common world. As they approach 9 months of age, infants come to take a certain stance or set of attitudes not only toward persons vis-à-vis things, but more specifically toward the *attitudes* of other persons: they share experiences of the world with a caregiver; they show objects, often looking back and forth between the object and the caregiver's eyes; they seek out and relate to the caregiver's affective relation to the world in social referencing; they make and respond to gestural requests; they come to imitate meaningful actions with objects, and so on (e.g., Bretherton, McNew, & Beeghly-Smith, 1981; Carpenter, Nagell, & Tomasello, 1998). Thus 9-month-olds have the requisite forms of attitude toward other people's bodily expressed attitudes well before they can conceptualize the nature of mental states.

It is around the age of 18 months that children do come to acquire a conceptual form of reflective self-awareness, and this is manifest as they begin to show new forms of empathy (e.g., Cummings, Zahn-Waxler, & Radke-Yarrow, 1981; Hoffman, 1975; Zahn-Waxler, Radke-Yarrow, & King, 1979), look up to their parents when proud of achieving something (Stipek, Recchia, & McClintic, 1992), engage in coordinated role-responsive interactions (e.g. Brownell & Carriger, 1990; Hay, 1979; Kaler & Kopp, 1990), and show silly or coy behavior in front of a mirror (Lewis & Brooks-Gunn, 1979). From around this age, toddlers not only make self-descriptive utterances such as "my book" or "Mary eat" (Kagan, 1982; Lewis & Ramsay, 2004), but they may take an active part in talking about people's feeling states such as those of happiness, sadness, or distress (Dunn, Bretherton, & Munn, 1987). Now the child *does* know that other persons are fitting recipients for a kind of analogical reasoning from her own case, and can begin to infer things about the nature of people's minds by conferring attributes on the basis of her own self-experience. Social knowledge transforms and augments social life.

Among the matters that we need to clarify, then, are the processes through which infants experience emotional connectedness with and differentiation from other persons, and how development proceeds in such a way as to promote children's acquisition of *concepts* of self and other. We also need to account for the fact that around the middle of the second year of life, children come to understand what it means to have and to transpose perspectives either from one person to another as in role-responsive linguistic communication, or from one object or setting to another as in the use of symbolic vehicles in play.

In this chapter, we shall be presenting reasons for believing that there is a specific form of social life and intersubjective engagement—one unique to human beings, and probably operative from the early months of life—that not only provides the basis for specifically human forms of sharing and coorientation toward a world held in common, but also structures social experience in such a way that knowledge of self and other, the mind and mind-independent reality, and topic-comment forms of human communication, can be acquired. This involves very young children *identifying with* the attitudes of another person. The critical feature of this particular kind of interpersonal connectedness and communicative exchange is that one person's experience encompasses that of another in such a way that the other's attitude is assumed *in part*, without loss of "otherness" in what is identified with. This statement needs to be qualified, insofar as the other's attitude is assimilated in such a way that it becomes a potential for one's own relatedness to the world (including oneself). Importantly, the process does not necessarily entail that the other is conceptualized as such; on the contrary, we suggest, to arrive at a concept of persons-with-minds a very young child needs to identify with the attitudes of others not only prior to acquiring, but also in order to acquire, such a concept.

In order to ground this abstract formulation in more specific instances of "identifying with," as well as to reflect on broader issues concerning the nature of intersubjectivity, we shall be citing studies of atypically developing children, and in particular research concerning children with autism. Our rationale is that the syndrome of autism involves profound and characteristic impairments in social relations and communication, along with cognitive and language dysfunction. In addition, of course, there is now a body of evidence to suggest that individuals with autism have limited interpersonal understanding, or what has become known as "theory of mind" (e.g. Baron-Cohen, Tager-Flusberg, & Cohen, 1993, 2000). Therefore studies of autism promise to yield insights into the interdependencies among personal relatedness, interpersonal understanding, and conceptually instantiated forms of knowing and thinking about both people and things. More specifically, research in autism may reveal much about the nature and implications of identifying with other people.

CLINICAL DESCRIPTIONS OF CHILDREN WITH AUTISM

Although we shall be concerned primarily with controlled studies of autism, it is worth citing at least a few clinical observations that highlight the children's abnormalities not just in *thinking* about minds, but more centrally, their atypical ways of engaging in *relations with* other individual people. If children with autism are limited in certain forms of social knowledge, and in particular knowledge about other people's minds, then we should consider what might underlie such social-cognitive deficits in terms of the children's perception of and relatedness toward people *as* persons. Kanner (1943) himself pinpointed the pathognomonic disorder in autism as "the children's *inability to relate themselves* in the ordinary way to people and situations from the beginning of life" (p. 242, Kanner's italics). He described how "people, so long as they left the child alone, figured in about the same manner as did the desk, the bookshelf, or the filing cabinet" (p. 246). Kanner recorded a number of instances in which the children related not to what another *person* had just done, but to the hand that was in the way or the foot that stepped upon the child's blocks, or the pin that had pricked or hand that took away a book. Not only this, but often the children failed to appreciate how linguistic utterances were anchored to the perspective of the person who uttered them: for example, when one child stumbled and nearly fell, he said of himself: "You did not fall down." When one 8-year-old child with autism with whom we are acquainted becomes distressed, he says to himself repeatedly: "You don't have to cry."

So Kanner stressed the children's limited engagement with other people *as* people who afford emotional contact and reciprocal communication. Among the additional features he noted were the children's difficulty in using language to convey meaning to others, their often inflexible use of words and abnormal use of the personal pronouns "I" and "you," and the lack of variety in their spontaneous activity. Current-day definitions of the syndrome give additional prominence to the children's lack of creative symbolic play, but Kanner's characterization succeeds in conveying the essential features of the syndrome.

For one further set of clinical descriptions especially relevant for the present chapter, it is worth turning to the writings of Gerhard Bosch (1970), who attempted to delineate "the particular mode of existence of an autistic child" (p. 3). Bosch remarked on the children's difficulty in interpreting the emotional expressions of others, and illustrated how the children often seem to lack a sense of possessiveness as well as self-consciousness and shame. He suggested that "counter-attack or defense is impossible because the child has no experience of attacking or defensive relationship with others" (p. 99). Perhaps most important of all, he emphasized that a "delay occurs in the constituting of the other person in whose place I can put myself...[and]...in the constituting of a common sphere of existence, in which things do not simply refer to me but also to others" (p. 89). In these ways, Bosch framed his account of self- and other-awareness with reference to attitudes implicated in interpersonal involvement. Such attitudes are striking for their presence in typically developing toddlers, but (Bosch suggested) relatively lacking in those with autism. From our perspective, these descriptions are especially important for the emphasis Bosch gives to qualities of interpersonal relatedness that appear to be lacking among children with autism (a viewpoint that is notable for its absence in most "theory of mind" theorizing), and for the prominence he gives to the significance of these children's lack of personal investment in and identification with other individuals.

According to clinical descriptions, therefore, children with autism show a relative lack of a *range* of modes of relatedness toward other people, and this is the case even among those who have achieved some form of self-concept (Hobson, Chidambi, Lee, & Meyer, 2006). Now we turn to controlled studies of what these children do and do not achieve by way of following typical infants' steps toward self/other understanding in the early part of life.

CONTROLLED STUDIES IN AUTISM

We shall focus on studies that illustrate the implications of *identifying with* the attitudes of others in typically developing children, and the effects of a relative absence of this process among children with autism. The initial two studies concern young children, and indicate how those with autism are limited in their person-person-world relations. In the first study, parents described their own observations of their children's interpersonal engagement; in the second, investigators recorded the children's social responsiveness, under controlled conditions. Subsequently we turn to older children and adolescents, and report two studies of nonverbal communication that highlight what intersubjective linkage means, and provide suggestive evidence of how identification yields coordination of bodily anchored expression and experience.

Primary and Secondary Intersubjectivity

We begin by considering interpersonal relations not only in the form of face-to-face engagements (primary intersubjectivity), but also as manifest when a child is responsive to another person's attitudes to the world (secondary intersubjectivity). Wimpory, Hobson, Williams, and Nash (2000) interviewed parents of very young children who were referred with difficulties in relating to or communicating with others. At the time of interview, the undiagnosed children were under 4 years old, and it was only subsequently that 10 children diagnosed with autism were compared with 10 children, matched for age and developmental level, who did not have autism. The parents' reports indicated that not one of the infants with autism had shown frequent and intense eye contact, engaged in turn-taking with adults, or used noises communicatively, whereas half of the control children were reported to show each of these kinds of behavior. There were also fewer infants with autism who greeted or waved to their parents, who raised their arms to be picked up, who directed feelings of anger and distress toward people, who were sociable in play, or who enjoyed and participated in lap games. There were also group differences in the infants' ways of relating to other people's attitudes to the surrounding world. For example, not one of the infants with autism but at least half the infants in the control group were reported to offer or give objects to others in the first two years of life; few children with autism were said to show objects to others or to point, and not one was said to have looked between an object of interest and an adult in joint attention.

The important point here is that young children with autism are not only atypical in their manner of personal relatedness in one-to-one interactions, such as being less connected with other people for their own sake, but they also tend not to engage in sharing or otherwise coordinating their attitudes with those of other people in relation to shared surroundings (e.g., Loveland & Landry, 1986; Mundy & Burnette, 2005; Mundy, Sigman, Ungerer, & Sherman, 1986; Wetherby & Prutting, 1984).

It is a pivotal moment in a typically developing infant's life, when the world changes from a "world-for-me" (unconceptualized as such) to a world that may have meanings-according-to-another-person. The reason is that only when things and events are part of a world that is shared with others, does the possibility of specifically human ways of knowing, whether of people or things, become a possibility (Hamlyn, 1978). Therefore the panoply of person-person-world relations sometimes grouped under the rubric of "joint attention" represents a major advance towards, but not yet the achievement of, social knowledge. For this reason, the relative absence among young children with autism of those forms of joint attention that entail sharing of experience is of serious concern. Here we provide just one illustrative example of a controlled observational study that vividly portrays this limitation.

Empathy and Social Referencing

Sigman, Kasari, Kwon, and Yirmiya (1992) videotaped 30 young autistic children with a mean age of under 4 years, and matched children with and without mental retardation, in the presence of an adult who appeared to hurt herself by hitting her finger with a hammer, simulated fear toward a remote-controlled robot, and pretended to be ill by lying down on a couch for a minute, feigning discomfort (and see Charman et al., 1997, for similar events involving 20-month-olds). The results were that children with autism were unusual in rarely looking at or relating to the adult. When the adult pretended to be hurt, for example, children with autism often appeared unconcerned. When a small remote-controlled robot moved toward the child and stopped about four feet away, the parent and the experimenter, who were both seated nearby, made fearful facial expressions, gestures, and vocalizations for 30 seconds. Almost all the children without autism looked at an adult at some point, but fewer than half the children with autism did so, and they seemed unaffected as they continued playing with the robot.

Here we make a seemingly commonsense, but still controversial, theoretical proposal: that children with autism are not "moved" to adopt another person's attitude and psychological orientation toward a shared world, for the same reason that they are limited in their personal engagement with other persons in one-to-one settings. Adopting the words of Cooley (1902), there is something awry in these children's "primary communication or an entering into and sharing the mind of someone else," such that they are not drawn into another's attitudes when these are directed to what *should* be a shared world.

In order to study this impairment more closely, we turn away from very young children with autism to consider older children and adolescents. Even at this relatively late stage of development, one may discover specific impairments in relatedness toward persons that are especially significant for typical early development. The focus remains upon how individuals with autism differ in their relatedness toward others, but here we seek insight into the *mechanisms* by which even very young human beings are moved to adopt other-centered psychological orientations as one critical step toward social knowledge.

Nonverbal Communication

We conducted a study of patterns of nonverbal communication between adolescents with and without autism as they had a conversation with an adult who was conducting a semistructured "self-understanding interview" (García Pérez, Hobson, & Lee, 2006). The interview had been videotaped some years previously for a study of self-concepts among children and adolescents with autism (Lee & Hobson, 1998), and now we returned to the tapes in order to investigate the patterning of person-with-person bodily/affective coordination during the conversational exchanges. The results were in keeping with previous studies (Capps, Kehres, & Sigman, 1998; Tantam, Holmes, & Cordess, 1993), in that there were surprisingly few and seemingly marginal group differences on behavioral ratings. The principal finding was that when head nods of assent or disagreement were excluded, participants made fewer head-shakes and nods (but not smiles) when the interviewer was talking, and the interviewer made fewer head-shakes and nods when participants were talking. Yet despite the lack of marked group differences in behavioral ratings, reliable "subjective" ratings of affective engagement and smoothness of reciprocal interaction between the conversational partners revealed clear group differences.

It is reasonable to conclude that intersubjective engagement is just that—intersubjective—and that human beings are the best (and arguably, the only) measuring instrument for evaluating whether such engagement is taking place. Not only this, but so, too, a young child's *intersubjective experience* of others may be an irreducible component of social life, and an essential source of social knowledge.

But then, there was also the result on head nodding and shaking. We take the view that by and large, it is appropriate to describe people who speak-with-nodding as "nodding according to themselves." In this respect, the study yielded no significant group difference: compared with control participants, those with autism were only marginally less liable to nod when they were the ones speaking. We also believe it is often the case that when people listen-with-nodding, they are nodding according to themselves-in-identification-with what the other person is conveying through speech and gesture. In other words, when people hear what is said and perceive what is gestured, they play their role in the conversation by making these words and communicative meanings their own, and as one result they are likely to manifest their own corresponding gestures. In this respect, participants *without* autism nodded along with the interviewer speaking, but this kind of nodding was all but absent among the participants with autism. If this interpretation is correct, we are observing subtle but telling signs of a failure of alignment between the subjective orientations of participants in dialogue. Such alignment may be critical for children's sense of involvement with the subjective lives of others.

On the basis of this evidence alone, this interpretation of the interpersonal patterning of bodily gestures is highly speculative. So perhaps we should turn to other manifestations of person-to-person nonverbal communication.

Hello and Goodbye

Our next snapshot is of a quasi-observational study of adolescents with autism. In an attempt to capture something of what interpersonal engagement (or its relative lack) means, Tony Lee and the first author studied what happens in entrances to and exits from such social contact in the course of greetings and farewells (Hobson & Lee, 1998). In what we call our Hello-Goodbye study, we videotaped a group of 24 children and adolescents with autism and a group of matched non-autistic individuals in a standardized situation where they were introduced to, and then departed from, a stranger seated across the room from the door by which they entered and left. Compared with control participants, there were about half as many participants with autism who gave spontaneous expressions of greeting, and a substantial proportion of those with autism failed to respond when the stranger said "Hello." Whereas all the young people without autism made eye contact, and no fewer than 17 smiled, a third of those with autism never made eye contact, and only six smiled. When departing, half the individuals without autism but only three of those with autism made eye contact and said goodbye. Of these, nine of the individuals without autism but not a single autistic individual also smiled. Here it was especially interesting that participants with autism rarely gave a wave of farewell when the investigator called "Goodbye" as the child left through the door, and each of the five who did so made partial and often ill-directed flaps of the hand that were not coordinated with eye contact.

We also asked the raters of our videotapes to make the following judgment about the greeting episode: "Over this period and prior to sitting down, to what degree did you feel that the child engaged with the stranger?" The categories of response were either strongly engaged, somewhat engaged, or hardly, if at all engaged. The independent judges were in good agreement with each other. The results were that 14 of the 24 children without autism were judged to be strongly engaged, and only two hardly, if at all, engaged. In contrast, only two of the 24 children with autism were judged to be strongly engaged, and 13 of them seemed hardly, if at all, engaged.

Now what does this study tell us about the nature of social (or interpersonal) relations, and how might it help us to conceptualize the way in which social life and social knowledge are related? First, intersubjective engagement is not reducible to elements of any individual's behavior. Correspondingly, Kanner's (1943) formulation of autism as an impairment in affective contact between a child and other people is not metaphorical; it is *not* the case that in this context, the words *affective contact* are parasitic on *other* forms of contact, for example, between one's hand and a table. This is important if we are to appreciate that events within the system of child-in-relation-to-other may constitute the appropriate "unit of analysis" of social experience and behavior (Vygotsky, 1962). Indeed, we observed (but did not record) that in the Hello-Goodbye study, however hard the stranger (in fact, the first author) tried to be consistent in the way he greeted and then prompted the departure of each child, it was clear that often his own manner became less fluid and more "forced" when he was relating to children with autism than with control participants. Here it is relevant to recall how 2-month-old infants react when their caregiver adopts a "still-face" (Tronick, Als, Adamson, Wise, & Brazelton, 1978), and how infant-with-caregiver exchanges may be disrupted by introducing a time-lag between the responses of each member of the dyad (Murray & Trevarthen, 1985). It may seem cavalier to compare typically developing infants with adolescents who have autism, but in each case one is witnessing evidence for the presence or relative absence of a basic *level* of interpersonal coordination that is at once behavioral and experiential.

If this is so, then two questions arise. First, is it plausible that children and adolescents with autism fail to develop, or perhaps lose, such qualities of person-to-person engagement because of some deficit in cognitive functioning? Second, if (as we think) this is implausible and if impairments in affective contact are among the primary deficits in autism, is it coincidental that children with this condition have difficulty in acquiring concepts that apply to persons, namely those concepts to do with the workings of the mind such as feelings and beliefs? We believe it is much more likely that children's *concepts* about the mental states of other people are founded upon their experience of *relations with* bodily endowed and psychologically expressive people, and that in the case of autism, limitations in so-called theory of mind are the developmental outcome of affected children's engagement in and experience of personal relatedness with others.

One aim of the Hello-Goodbye study was to capture something of what clinicians have tried to convey in describing how children with autism can sometimes treat other people as pieces of furniture. Greeting and departing are special modes of relating to other people that betray what it means to commence and then curtail a period of engagement with someone else. If one is neither greeted nor bade farewell, then already one misses something of what it means to be treated as a person. Or to turn this around, if a child with autism is not naturally inclined to orientate to and engage with a person who is available for communication, then that child may miss out on part of the *experience* of being in the presence of persons. The point here is that we cannot presume that one greets and bids farewell only *because* one has a concept of persons; a more likely story is that relations that include greetings and farewells (which after all, are present in infants well before there is evidence for concepts of self and other) are foundational for understanding what persons are.

Then there was another feature of the children's relations with the stranger that was disconcerting and telling: the waves of farewell. For nine out of the 14 control participants who waved (and 10 did not do so), the waves were just like the waves you might expect from a typically developing toddler or child. The person orientated (more or less) toward the stranger, the content as well as directedness of the gestured communication was unmistakeable, and the morphology of the wave was unremarkable. So why should these features have been so different among the participants with autism? And why were greetings and waves notable for their absence in the parental reports of young children cited earlier from the study of Wimpory et al. (2000)?

Our reply to this question is to suggest that individuals with autism do not identify with the bodily anchored attitudes and actions of other people, for example, those attitudes and actions that go into the communicative act of waving goodbye. Our hypothesis is that children with autism do not experience what the other expresses from the other's standpoint, and assimilate that person-anchored attitude or action into their own repertoire of possible attitudes or actions. As a result, even when they do wave goodbye, this is not the *same kind* of act as that shown by people who do not have autism. The corollary to our hypothesis about autism, of course, is that among children who do not have autism, the propensity to identify with others is a characteristic and important feature of human psychology.

Again this is a suggestion that needs to be justified by evidence beyond limp waves of farewell. Moreover, the idea of identifying with someone else involves much more than a particular form of imitation. When one person identifies with another, there needs to be some registration of the otherness of the other, what we have referred to as the person-anchored property of the attitudes or actions of the other (and this does not mean the other person as a particular individual, only as a particular instance of a person). We suggest that forms of sharing experiences with someone else have this same configuration, in which something of the experience of the other is encompassed alongside one's own experience in a relational event that has a special phenomenology as well as an essentially interpersonal structure (Campbell, 2002). Therefore we also need evidence that there is a relation between a child's propensity to imitate others with the kind of self/other transposition of action or gesture we observed in the case of waving farewell, and the "sharing" qualities of the child's interpersonal engagement. We explored this relation in the study that follows.

Imitation and Sharing Experiences
In a study of imitation of self–other orientation (Meyer & Hobson, 2004), we tested school-aged children, 16 with autism and 16 without autism, who were matched for chronological age and language ability. The tester and the child sat across from one another on opposite ends of a specially designed testing mat with lines demarcating a central area. The procedures were that the tester demonstrated a brief, simple action to the child immediately after stating "watch this" and then she returned the object(s) to their original positions and instructed the child: "Now you." There were four actions, each presented in one of two orientations on two separate days, yielding eight trials in total. For example, the tester might pick up a small box near herself and rest it on another box near the participant, and then return it to its initial position; or she might pick up the box near the participant and rest it on the box nearest to herself, and then replace it back as before. Or she might pick up a wheel from the center of the mat and roll it close to herself before returning it to its starting-point, or she might pick it up and roll it close to the participant.

As we predicted, the children with autism copied the actions but were significantly less likely to imitate the self–other orientation shown by the tester (for example, by copying the tester's close-to-herself orientation by completing the actions close-to-themselves). While half of the children in the comparison group copied the self–other orientation of the actions on at least half of the eight trials, for example, only three out of the 16 children with autism did so. Here was more direct evidence from tests of imitation that the self–other switches in orientation we considered in the case of waving goodbye do indeed distinguish children with and without autism (Hobson & Meyer, 2005, for additional evidence). On the other hand, the group differences were not absolute and enough variability was present in each group to consider patterns of individual difference.

This gave us the opportunity to explore whether children's propensity to imitate self–other orientation was related to another aspect of social relations we believe to be shaped by identification —interpersonal engagement involving sharing of experience (Hobson & Hobson, 2007). We went back to the videotapes of the children and tester during the demonstration and imitation phases of each of the eight trials with three a priori predictions, as follows: (1) children with autism would contrast with control participants in spending more time looking at the objects acted-upon and less time looking at the tester; (2) participants with autism would show fewer "sharing" looks toward the tester; and, critically, (3) within each group, individual differences in sharing looks (only) would be associated with imitation of self–other orientation. The point of studying different kinds of looking was to determine whether there was something specifically important about sharing looks, over and above the impact of any group differences in joint attention per se. "Sharing looks" were defined as those looks directed to the tester that could be seen as a means to share experience through interpersonal contact. "Checking looks" were defined as those used in order to assess or check out the situation or the tester's attention. "Orientating looks" were those that appeared to occur in direct response to an action, sound, or movement on the part of the tester. Two independent judges showed excellent agreement on these ratings.

Results were that although both groups of children spent most of their time looking at the objects, the children with autism did so for a higher percentage of time, and they looked at the tester for less than half as much time as children in the comparison group. This difference was not specific to a particular quality of joint attention look, as the pattern was similar for sharing, checking, and orienting looks. However, when we considered the qualities of joint attention shown by individual participants, a different pattern was apparent. Eleven of the 16 children with autism compared with only five of the comparison children failed to engage in a single sharing look. This was not the case for other kinds of look, where most of the children in both groups showed at least one checking and at least one orientating look.

Finally, the percentage of time spent looking at the tester overall, as well as the frequency of checking and orienting joint attention looks, were *not* related to propensity to imitate self–other orientation in either group. By contrast, sharing looks were specifically and significantly associated with the children's propensity to adopt a self–other orientation when imitating, both within and across the two groups.

This result suggests that a certain quality of interpersonal engagement, namely, that implicated in sharing looks, is associated with a certain quality of imitation, namely, that in which identifying with the other leads to the *other person's self–other orientation* being transposed to the imitator's own stance (for example, when she-doing-something-near-to-herself becomes me-doing-it-near-to-myself). Although one might interpret these results as showing that one person needs to have some relatively deep contact with another if he or she is to identify with the other's orientation, we believe that identifying with others plays a formative role in sharing experiences. Indeed, we take the view that not only is the structure of infants' social experience configured by identification from early in life (we imagine by 2 months of age, given the qualities of 2-month-olds' sharing emotional experience with someone else), but that this fact distinguishes human beings from other primate species. If this is the case—and it is a radical proposal—might identification also play a role in certain kinds of social emotion that are especially refined in humans? Once again, evidence from autism may help us to consider the role of identification in shaping a person's experience of others.

Self-Consciousness

Here is a study of coyness in which we videotaped matched groups of school-aged children with and without autism (Hobson, Chidambi, Lee, & Meyer, 2006). First, the tester introduced each child to two creatures: "Alien," a small plastic toy figure who unbeknownst to the child, sang a song when his hands were squeezed at the same time; and "Doggie," a small, brown stuffed dog with floppy ears. Each creature (in the tester's hands) engaged in a series of antics. In the Musical Alien condition, the alien jumped up and down on the table, dancing and swinging his long green hair, and finally singing. At each point, the child was invited by the tester to comment on what Alien was doing. These events were designed to be engaging and funny but not to prompt self-consciousness. In the Cuddly Dog condition, Doggie nuzzled first against Alien, then against the tester, and finally turned its attentions to the child, nuzzling him or her on the chin and neck. At each point, the child was invited by the tester to comment on whom Doggie liked. Here we anticipated that when Doggie nuzzled against the participant, this should elicit a coy/self-conscious reaction.

According to reliable ratings by 'blind' judges, the majority of participants in each group showed affective changes in response to Alien's increasingly wild antics. This confirmed that children with autism were not globally unresponsive. For ratings of coyness, on the other hand, there were marked group differences. Nearly half (45%) of participants with autism were judged to show an absence of coyness, whereas this was the case for a minority (11%) of the comparison group. On more specific behavioral measures, interestingly, the children with and without autism were similar in the numbers of children showing self-conscious smiling (10 and 9, respectively) and squirmy movements (11 and 9, respectively). In contrast, 12 of the 19 children without autism but *not a single child with autism* showed a reengagement look following the coyness episode.

These results indicated that although children with autism were self-conscious, there was something specifically lacking in the looks that signaled a return-to-engage-with-this-person. It is this sustained engagement that make coyness so intimate an interpersonal event. Our tentative interpretation relates to a specific aspect of what it means to identify with others, namely that this operates with regard to *particular* persons (by which we do not mean named individuals, rather, an instance of a person in contrast to persons-in-general). Whereas awareness of being the focus of people's attention does not require inter*personal* engagement, and so is relatively spared in children with autism, coyness and some other social emotions such as guilt *do* require the kind of "personal implication" that identification affords. In depth, social life is more than social, it is also interpersonal and intersubjective.

SOCIAL LIFE AND SOCIAL KNOWLEDGE

These studies of nonverbal communication in conversation, greetings and fare-wells, imitation and sharing looks, and finally coyness, are complementary. Each demonstrates one or more facets of intersubjective impairment among individuals with autism. Correspondingly, they point to aspects of social engagement among individuals *without* autism that have potentially far-reaching effects for aspects of cognitive as well as social development. We have stressed the importance of a person's *participation in* other people's bodily expressed attitudes and actions, whereby one is moved to encompass and to some degree adopt the orientation of others alongside or in relation to one's own psychological stance. It is in virtue of this preconceptual and often affectively configured propensity to identify with the attitudes and actions of other individuals that interpersonal psychological engagement is not merging, but rather linkage—there is differentiation as well as connectedness—with profound implications for the growth of social knowledge.

We have said little about the transition from the phase in a typically devel-oping infant's life between the period of person-person-world relatedness at the end of the first year of life, and the time when infancy ends with the explosion of language, the beginnings of symbolic play, and the acquisition of self-concepts around the middle of the second year. Some writers consider that the explana-tion for these changes is to be found in domain-general abilities that reflect brain maturation (e.g. Kagan, 1982; Lewis, 2003), and the abilities in question range from holding two models in mind at the same time (Perner, 1991) to recogniz-ing standards against which one's behavior may be judged (Lewis, 2003). This may be the case, but we consider it to be more likely that such cognitive abilities are the result rather than the cause of social-developmental change. A critical developmental achievement appears to be the transition from experiencing move-ments in attitude toward the world through other persons, to understanding what it is to hold a person-anchored perspective. Once this understanding is in place, then holding such a perspective alongside what is perceived to be the case—for example, being aware that you like what I do not, or holding a view of this box as a toy bed for play—may not be so difficult. From this perspective, the period from 9 to 18 months provides ample opportunity for children to be moved through others to adopt attitudes to their own attitudes. We suspect that whatever else may need to change over this time, it is also critical that the child comes *through this process* to objectify the self as a holder of person-centered attitudes.

This is something that affects the very nature of thinking. Understanding perspectives is critical for grasping how language embodies different takes on the world; it is also what gives rise to the insight that one can apply alternative mean-ings to the materials of play, so that these become symbolic. The idea here is that acquiring symbolically anchored concepts *of anything,* and acquiring the kinds of decontextualization and objectification of the self vis-à-vis the other which are required for the new forms of empathy, role-taking, pride, and so on that appear in the second half of the second year, are intimately intertwined, and develop together. G. H. Mead pointed this out (more or less), many years ago (1934).

If all this is correct, then explicitly conceptualized and specifically human forms of knowledge, including social knowledge of self and other and the relations that exist between persons and the world—including but extending beyond the domain of "theory of mind" concepts such as those of intentions, feelings, beliefs, and so on—are heavily dependent upon forms of social life that implicate the process whereby infants identify with the attitudes and actions of others.

As others in this volume emphasize, much of the social life of infants, both what they express and what they register in others, is bodily manifest: here the social relations that exist are relations between or among *persons*. We adults think that minds and bodies are separable, but infants acquire this way of looking at things through a complex developmental process. In the beginning, they apprehend and respond to what is expressed through other persons' bodies; at the end of the first year, they are moved to adopt others' bodily expressed attitudes toward a world held in common; and by the middle of the second year, they come to conceptualize and think about self and other. Soon after, they are talking about the attitudes or feelings of others, just as they can talk about their own.

We have argued that social life structures thought, and that connectedness and differentiation among thoughts have nontrivial relations with connectedness and differentiation among self and others. In addition, the *contents* of a child's thoughts about self and other are derived from the phenomenology of different modes of relating to others—relations that involve jealousy, wanting contact, feeling distress and joy and rivalry, giving greeting and farewell, having concern, hatred, anger, and so much else besides—many of which have preconceptual roots early in life. It is difficult to overestimate the contributions that social life makes to social knowledge, but a challenge to specify quite what these diverse contributions are.

Acknowledgments

We gratefully acknowledge the children who took part in these studies, and the schools that so generously provided their help and support (Edith Borthwick School, Helen Allison School, Russet House School, Springhallow School, and Swiss Cottage School). We thank Susana Caló, Valentina Levi, and Dave Williams for their careful ratings of videotapes, and Rosa García Pérez and Tony Lee for their substantial contributions to this research. We also appreciate support from the Baily Thomas Charitable Foundation, the Wellcome Foundation, the NHS R&D Levy and the Tavistock and Portman NHS Trust. This text was written while the first author was a Fellow at the Center for Advanced Study in the Behavioral Sciences, Stanford, during an extended visit by the second author.

References

Baldwin, J. M. (1902). *Social and ethical interpretations in mental development.* New York: Macmillan.

Baron-Cohen, S., Tager-Flusberg, H., & Cohen, D. J. (1993). *Understanding other minds: Perspectives from autism.* New York: Oxford University Press.

Baron-Cohen, S., Tager-Flusberg, H., & Cohen, D. J. (2000). *Understanding other minds: Perspectives from developmental cognitive neuroscience* (2nd ed.). New York: Oxford University Press.

Bosch, G. (1970). *Infantile autism* (D. Jordan & I. Jordan, Trans.). New York: Springer-Verlag.

Brazelton, T. B., Koslowski, B., & Main, M. (1974). The origins of reciprocity: The early mother–infant interaction. In M. Lewis & L. A. Rosenblum (Eds.), *The effect of the infant on its caregiver* (pp. 49–76). New York: John Wiley.

Bretherton, I., McNew, S., & Beeghly-Smith, M. (1981). Early person knowledge as expressed in gestural and verbal communication: When do infants acquire a "theory of mind"? In M. E. Lamb & L. R. Sherrod (Eds.), *Infant social cognition: Empirical and theoretical considerations* (pp. 333–373). Hillsdale, NJ: Lawrence Erlbaum.

Brownell, C. A., & Carriger, M. S. (1990). Changes in cooperation and self-other differentiation during the second year. *Child Development, 61,* 1164–1174.

Buber, M. (1958). *I and thou.* 2nd ed. (R. Gregory Smith, Trans.). Edinburgh: T. & T. Clark. (Original work published 1923)

Campbell, J. (2002). *Reference and consciousness.* Oxford: Oxford University Press.

Capps, L., Kehres, J., & Sigman, M. (1998). Conversational abilities among children with autism and children with developmental delays. *Autism, 2,* 325–244.

Carpendale, J. I. M., & Lewis, C. (2004). Constructing an understanding of mind: The development of children's social understanding within social interaction. *Behavioral and Brain Sciences, 27,* 79–151.

Carpenter, M., Nagell, K., & Tomasello, M. (1998). Social cognition, joint attention, and communicative competence from 9 to 15 months of age. *Monographs of the Society for Research in Child Development, 63* (Serial No. 255), 1–143.

Charman, T., Swettenham, J., Baron-Cohen, S., Cox, A., Baird, G., & Drew, A. (1997). Infants with autism: An investigation of empathy, pretend play, joint attention, and imitation. *Developmental Psychology, 33,* 781–789.

Cooley, C. H. (1902). *Human nature and the social order.* New York: Scribner.

Cummings, E. M., Zahn-Waxler, C., & Radke-Yarrow, M. (1981). Young children's responses to expressions of anger and affection by others in the family. *Child Development, 52,* 1274–1282.

Draghi-Lorenz, R., Reddy, V., & Costall, A. (2001). Rethinking the development of "non-basic" emotions: A critical review of existing theories. *Developmental Review, 21,* 263–304.

Dunn, J., Bretherton, I., & Munn, P. (1987). Conversations about feeling states between mothers and their young children. *Developmental Psychology, 23,* 132–139.

García-Pérez, R., Hobson, R. P., & Lee, A. (2006). On intersubjective engagement in autism: A controlled study of nonverbal aspects of conversation. *Journal of Autism and Developmental Disorders.* In Press.

Hamlyn, D. W (1978). *Experience and growth of understanding.* London: Routledge & Kegan Paul.

Harris, P. L. (1989). *Children and emotion.* Oxford: Blackwell.

Hay, D. F. (1979). Cooperative interactions and sharing between very young children and their parents. *Developmental Psychology, 15,* 647–653.

Hobson, J. A., & Hobson, R. P. (2007). Identification: The missing link between joint attention and imitation? *Development and Psychopathology, 19,* 411–431..

Hobson, R. P. (1991). Against the theory of "Theory of Mind." *British Journal of Developmental Psychology, 9*, 33–51.

Hobson, R. P., Chidambi, G., Lee, A., & Meyer, J. A. (2006). Foundations for self-awareness: An exploration through autism. *Monographs of the Society for Research in Child Development, 71* (Serial no. 284), 1–166.

Hobson, R. P., & Meyer, J. A. (2005). Foundations for self and other: A study in autism. *Developmental Science, 8*, 481–491.

Hobson, R. P., & Lee A. (1998). Hello and goodbye: A study of social engagement in autism. *Journal of Autism and Developmental Disorders, 28*, 117–127.

Hoffman, M. L. (1975). Developmental synthesis of affect and cognition and its implications for altruistic motivation. *Developmental Psychology, 11*, 607–622.

Kagan, J. (1982). The emergence of self. *Journal of Child Psychology and Psychiatry, 23*, 363–381.

Kaler, S. R., & Kopp, C. B. (1990). Compliance and comprehension in very young toddlers. *Child Development, 61*, 1997–2003.

Kanner, L. (1943). Autistic disturbances of affective contact. *Nervous Child, 2*, 217–250.

Lee, A., & Hobson, R. P. (1998). On developing self-concepts: A controlled study of children and adolescents with autism. *Journal of Child Psychology and Psychiatry, 39*, 1131–1141.

Lewis, M. (1995). Embarrassment: The emotion of self-exposure and evaluation. In J. P. Tangney & K. W. Fischer (Eds.), *Self-conscious emotions: The psychology of shame, guilt, pride and embarrassment* (pp. 199–218). New York: Guildford.

Lewis, M. (2003). The development of self-consciousness. In J. Roessler & N. Eilan (Eds.), *Agency and self-awareness* (pp. 275–295). Oxford: Clarendon Press.

Lewis M., & Brooks-Gunn, J. (1979). *Social cognition and the acquisition of self.* New York and London: Plenum.

Lewis, M., & Ramsay, D. (2004). Development of self-recognition, personal pronoun use, and pretend play during the 2nd year. *Child Development, 75*, 1821–1831.

Loveland, K. A., & Landry, S. H. (1986). Joint attention and language in autism and developmental language delay. *Journal of Autism and Developmental Disorders, 16*, 335–349.

Mead, G. H. (1934). *Mind, self, and society from the standpoint of a social behaviorist.* Chicago: University of Chicago Press.

Meltzoff, A. N. (2002). Elements of a developmental theory of imitation. In A. N. Meltzoff & W. Prinz (Eds.), *The imitative mind: Development, evolution, and brain bases* (pp. 19–41). Cambridge: Cambridge University Press.

Merleau-Ponty, M. (1964). The child's relations with others (W. Cobb, Trans.) In M. Merleau-Ponty, *The primacy of perception* (pp. 96–155). Evanston, IL: Northwestern University Press.

Meyer, J. A., & Hobson, R. P. (2004). Orientation in relation to self and other: The case of autism. *Interaction Studies, 5*, 221–244.

Mundy, P., & Burnette, C. (2005). Joint attention and neurodevelopmental models of autism. In F. R. Volkmar, R. Paul, A. Klin, & D. Cohen (Eds.), *Handbook of autism and pervasive developmental disorders* (3rd ed., pp. 650–681). Hoboken, NJ: John Wiley.

Mundy, P., Sigman, M., Ungerer, J., & Sherman, T. (1986). Defining the social deficits of autism: The contribution of non-verbal communication measures. *Journal of Child Psychology and Psychiatry, 27*, 657–669.

Murray, L. & Trevarthen, C. (1985). Emotional regulation of interactions between two-month-olds and their mothers. In T. M. Field & N. A. Fox (Eds.), *Social perception in infants* (pp. 177–197). Norwood, NJ: Ablex.

Neisser, U. (1988). Five kinds of self-knowledge. *Philosophical Psychology, 1*, 35–59.

Perner, J. (1991). *Understanding the representational mind.* Cambridge, MA: MIT/Bradford.

Sigman, M. D., Kasari, C., Kwon, J. H., & Yirmiya, N. (1992). Responses to the negative emotions of others by autistic, mentally retarded, and normal children. *Child Development, 63*, 796–807.

Stern, D. (1985). *The interpersonal world of the infant.* New York: Basic Books.

Stipek, D., Recchia, S., & McClintic, S. (1992). Self-evaluation in young children. *Monographs of the Society for Research in Child Development, 57* (1, Serial No. 226).

Tantam, D., Holmes, D., & Cordess, C. (1993). Nonverbal expression in autism of Asperger type. *Journal of Autism and Developmental Disorders, 23*, 111–133.

Tomasello, M. (1999). *The cultural origins of human cognition.* Cambridge, MA: Harvard University Press.

Trevarthen, C. (1979). Communication and cooperation in early infancy: A description of primary intersubjectivity. In M. Bullova (Ed.), *Before speech: The beginning of human communication* (pp. 321–347). London: Cambridge University Press.

Trevarthen, C., & Aitken, K. J. (2001). Infant intersubjectivity: Research, theory and clinical applications. *Journal of Child Psychology & Psychiatry, 42*, 3–48.

Tronick, E., Als, H., Adamson, L., Wise, S., & Brazelton, T. B. (1978). The infant's response to entrapment between contradictory messages in face-to-face interaction. *Journal of the American Academy of Child and Adolescent Psychiatry, 17*, 1–13.

Vygotsky, L. S. (1962). *Thought and language.* (E. Hanfmann & G. Vakar, Trans.). Cambridge, MA: MIT Press. (Original work published 1934)

Wetherby, A. M., & Prutting, C. A. (1984). Profiles of communicative and social-cognitive abilities in autistic children. *Journal of Speech and Hearing Research, 27*, 364–377.

Wimpory, D. C., Hobson, R. P., Williams, J. M., & Nash, S. (2000). Are infants with autism socially engaged? A study of recent retrospective parental reports. *Journal of Autism and Developmental Disorders, 30*, 525–536.

Wittgenstein, L. (1958). *Philosophical investigations* (G. E. M. Anscombe, Trans.).Oxford: Blackwell.

Zahn-Waxler, C., Radke-Yarrow, M., & King, R. A. (1979). Child rearing and children's prosocial initiations towards victims of distress. *Child Development, 50*, 319–330.

6

Experiencing Others
A Second-Person Approach to Other-Awareness

VASUDEVI REDDY

> The confirmation of the other must include an actual experiencing of the other side…. [this]…. is essential to the distinction…between "dialogue," in which I open myself to the otherness of the person I meet and "monologue," in which, even when I converse with her at length, I allow her to exist only as a content of my experience. Wherever one lets the other exist only as a part of oneself, "dialogue becomes a fiction, the mysterious intercourse between two human worlds only a game, and in the rejection of the real life confronting him the essence of all reality begins to disintegrate." (Buber 1923/1958, p. 24, in Friedman, 2002, pp. 354–355)

Martin Buber saw the ability to bridge the experiences of self and other as not only possible, but as necessary for communication, for genuine engagement, and indeed for contact with reality. This is trouble enough for our individualist, Cartesian leanings. In addition, however, by insisting that to allow genuine dialogue (rather than only monologue), this bridging must necessarily involve an actual experiencing of other people rather than a kind of internal capture or re-creation of the other as a part of oneself, his view poses challenges with which recent psychology cannot easily cope.

Can we actually experience "the other side" as he puts it? To answer this in the positive would require the rejection of several centuries of a dualist conviction in a fundamental divide between self and other (and indeed between self and world and between mind and matter) and in the impossibility of any "actual" crossing over.

For such an experiencing of the other we would also need to challenge psychology's deep commitment to mental representations as the route to experience. Mental representations are decidedly "inside" individuals and very much a construction by the self and of the self. Within this (mental representational) paradigm the other can *only* be experienced as a part of oneself. Further, experiencing the other as a potential partner for dialogue would also require that we recognize and be drawn to the "otherness" of the other, to difference rather than just to sameness. The use of recent findings about mirror neurons to explain the perception of sameness between self and other therefore falls short as an explanation; dialogue requires the ability (and motivation) to respond to the other as *different*. Difference in this sense must be profoundly more than simply the absence of sameness: our perception of the *other*ness of the people with whom we engage in dialogue must occur within the experience of the relevance of the other to the self.

If Buber is remotely right, we need an explanation of interpersonal engagement and understanding which is capable both of allowing us to experience other people as more than just a figment of our own consciousness and of dealing with our perception of and attraction to other people as different from the self. We don't really have such an explanation even for adults, let alone for infants. I am going to argue that Buber's emphasis on dialogue and his distinction between *Thou* and *It* highlights a crucial issue in the experience of the other which psychology needs to take seriously. A major problem in discussions of other-awareness has come from conceptualizing the other in the singular: as if, at any moment, there were just one kind of other to be known and related to, as if all other people could be reduced to one homogeneous kind of entity. Differentiating between the different *relations* we can have with others allows us to recognize not only that there are others who are "You's" and others who are "They's," but also the experiential and developmental primacy of the You over the He or She.

In this chapter I will argue that such a second-person approach to self- and other-awareness not only removes the need for controversies between first-person (simulationist) and third-person (theory-theory) accounts (or their recent hybrid offspring), but explains the developmental evidence from infancy in a quite different and more convincing way. From Buber's account, in an I–Thou engagement with an other we *experience* the other in a way that is not available in more reflective, detached I–It relations. Using data from attentional engagements in the first year of infancy I argue that the infant must first experience the other's attention to the self in I–Thou relations before any "appropriate" representational understanding of attention can develop. Indeed, second-person experience may be primary for the awareness of *all* aspects of the world, whether mentality or otherwise. But first, what *is* experience?

EXPERIENCING

...an experience, a very humble experience, is capable of generating and carrying any amount of theory (or intellectual content), but a theory

> apart from an experience cannot be definitely grasped even as a theory.
> It tends to become a mere verbal formula, a set of catchwords used to
> render thinking, or genuine theorising, unnecessary and impossible.
> (Dewey, 1916/1973a, p. 499)

The belief that we have to experience something to "really" know it is easy to find
both in academic psychology and in everyday discourse. We make a distinction,
for instance, between knowing something in theory and knowing it actually, in
practice. In the former there may be awareness of a label to describe something,
or even the grasp of a complex theory about the causes and consequences of a
thing. In the latter there may be the aha experience of *feeling* that something
for oneself after a long time of knowing the theory. This is also significant in
remembering—we can be told about an event in our past or our childhood or we
can remember it ourselves—a feeling which children who have been adopted (and
thus have uncertain access to their pasts) or persons with amnesia of some kind,
are often desperate to experience. We value experience not only in this synchro-
nous sense of direct exposure to (or memory of) sensory events, but also in the
diachronous sense of accumulating such exposure over time (see Bradley, 2004),
with a strong belief in the—albeit vague and mysterious—cumulative effects of
age and experience. The intangibility of the contextual grounding in everyday
interactions that constitutes our cumulative experience of things makes it difficult,
even impossible, to re-create or represent it in the form of rules and abstractions.
This was a lesson painfully learned by the Artificial Intelligence enterprise in the
1970s (Winograd & Flores, 1986). Experience in this sense of grounding in context seems located not in the individual, but outside in real world living and doing,
in practice rather than in plan. In general, what is special about experience seems
to be something about its realness, its nonfictional and nonimaginary character.
Psychology, however, even when it accepts the realness of experience, generally
identifies it with the individual, making it private and inaccessible to others.

Philosophers have waxed both lyrical and baffled about explaining our
mutual awareness of *qualia*—the experience of qualities of things—the taste of
an Alphonso mango, for instance, or the azure of the Aegean over the side of a
ferry, or the smell of the first rains on parched earth. It is this internal, individual
experience of qualia which simulation theorists use to underpin their view of the
divide between self and other. If qualia are the properties of the sensory systems
of individual organisms, they must inevitably belong to a single individual. This
internalization and individualization of experience appears to be a characteristic
of recent Western psychology. In many less industrialized and less individualistic
cultures, the focus on the individual as the locus for psychological experience is
unusual (Frijda & Mesquita, 1994). In some cultures it is more often assumed that
experiences are knowable and shareable by others who are intimately related to
the person. Even in English usage, the sense of experience as a private phenomenon available only to the individual on an internal screen appears to be a recent
phenomenon. Deriving from the Latin *experior* meaning "from trying" or "from
seeking", and referring to that which comes of a motivated and public *action* in

the world, experience should (etymologically speaking at least) mean something which is embodied, motivated, and completely embedded in the world.[1] In this sense, it could refer to an *engagement* with some person or thing. However, the most common usage of this term in Western culture and psychology implies a profound privacy: my experience happens inside me and is only really accessible to me. It is of and for the self. Explorations of distributed and situated cognition which might locate experience outside the individual are marginal and not widely accepted.

Within this assumption of privacy, the question inevitably arises of the role played by individual intellect and capacity in experiencing things. What makes the individual capable of experiencing something that happens in the outside world? Is experience an automatic consequence of events, or is it dependent on some more intellectual construction? Cognitive psychology has traditionally reserved the term for those events or phenomena which are not merely sensed, but *made* sense of in some more reflective and meaningful way. It is often argued that the individual needs to act reflectively upon external events for those events to be available on the internal screen.[2] Even in discussions of affect—which could be seen by some as a basic prerogative of many organisms—the distinction is often made between *having* an emotion and *experiencing* it. Many animals (and young human infants) are seen to *have* emotions, but the subjective experience of these same emotions, the feelings, are seen as limited only to a few, perhaps only to humans (post-infancy). Organisms are believed to have pain but not feel it;[3] they may have hunger but not experience it; they may have distress but not feel sadness or loss. Within those theories where affective feelings or affective experiences are seen as mediated by higher cortical processes (Damasio, 2003; Le Doux, 1996; Lewis, 1995) emotion is seen as a physiological mechanism which can bypass experience. Subjective experience—of individual emotion as well as of the external world of events—is seen as reserved for those organisms which are capable of some reflective capacity. Young infants and most nonhuman animals must therefore be essentially zombie-like in this view of emotion and experience (Panksepp & Smith-Pasqualini, 2005).

The evolutionary absurdity of this view is challenged by what Panksepp calls the "Affective Neuroscience" view, which sees feelings (affective experiences) as emerging from subcortical processes, without the necessity for higher cortical systems (Panksepp, 1998). Affective consciousness, according to this view, was originally an ancient subcortical function of the brain, serving an adaptive role in keeping organisms in a state of action readiness (Panksepp & Smith-Pasqualini, 2005). Similarly, in relation to human infancy, the affective neuroscience view implies that feeling states are a primary aspect of consciousness and the subjective affective experiences of infants emerge from and motivate their interactions with the world. I am going to assume that affective consciousness is present in human infants at least from birth—that human neonates are affectively motivated and perceive the world with an affective tone. The either–or question of whether an event is experienced or not is better transmuted into a question of the details:

asking *what* exactly an individual organism (with species-specific potential) can subjectively experience at different ages, in different states and contexts.

These debates have obvious implications for any consideration of development where an experience of the other is seen as vital for dialogue and interpersonal awareness. We are left with a crucial question, which needs also to be asked of adults: *What* do infants experience of other people? If direct experience is important for really knowing something, what *can* we directly experience of other people? Within the traditional individualist and dualist metaphysics we are only allowed to (if that) directly experience the physical properties of other people. We cannot experience their *experiences*. It is precisely this contrast and this problem that is captured in the problem of other minds as expressed in Cartesian theory[4] and in more recent developmental accounts through the contrast between perception and proprioception. Perception is seen as the experience of information about the world and proprioception as the experience of information internal to the self. Information about people is therefore seen as existing, neatly divided, either in the form of third-person perception (about others) or in the form of first-person proprioception (about the self).

But let's look more closely at this question of perception and proprioception in relation to experiencing other people. Following the challenges posed by ecological and activity theories to information processing approaches to perception (Bernstein, 1967; Gibson, 1979), it is now widely accepted that all perception involves proprioception (see also Shotter, 2006 on consciousness as a product of the mingling of the inner and the outer). Proprioception is normally thought of as internal information about movement and posture. However, internal information must also consist of affective feelings, however mild they are. Perception, always embedded within the organism's activity in the world, must happen within an affective and motivated field of proprioceptive experiences of interest, responsive feelings, attitudes, and impulses to act. Perception cannot be disinterested and therefore what you perceive of the outside must always be affectively linked to the inside, as argued for instance by Heidegger (Dreyfus, 1995), and empirically demonstrated by Gestalt psychology. Similarly, proprioception too always involves the perception of relation to the world or "ex-proprioception" (Lee, 1993). Information from inside the body or the self is always information about relation to the world. Two radical changes must therefore be involved in how we conceptualize perception and proprioception: one, the difference between the internal and the external in terms of information is no longer possible to maintain, and two, for both perception and proprioception the information experienced involves affective feelings.

These shifts in conceptualization of perception and proprioception impact dramatically on the question of what we perceive of other people. The distal perception of other people's physical properties must always include the perceiving individual's own affective feelings. Similarly, the proprioception of the perceiving individual's own movements and posture must always include (in it) the perception of the other person's affective expressions toward the self. Not only, then, is the perceptual experience of the other always colored by the *self's-feelings-toward-the-other*, but the proprioceptive experience of the self is colored by the *other's-feelings-toward-the-self*. These perceptual, proprioceptive experiences of self and other are therefore inevitably interconnected and indivisible and much more so within engagement than outside. More importantly for developmental theory, they are also mutually constitutive. *Self-feelings-to-other* must be affected by *other-feelings-to-self*, and vice versa. Separating the two is not a psychologically feasible enterprise either experientially or developmentally. Experiencing other people, then, must occur within the experience of the self's response to the other (and conversely, the experience of the self must occur within the experience of the other's response to the self). Both in terms of *what* is experienced and in terms of *where* this experience is located, there is a greater affective permeability than maintained by traditional theories. Why is this important for developmental theories?

TRADITIONAL CONTROVERSIES IN UNDERSTANDING PEOPLE: FIRST PERSON VS. THIRD PERSON

The best known of modern approaches to the problem of other minds is the theory-theory approach—one which could be described as a third-person approach. Essentially adopting a rationalist and deductive approach to the existence and nature of other minds, the theory-theory is unconcerned with experience in the sense of the "feeling" or "actual" knowing that we have talked about. Experience is seen as the accumulation of *information* about minds, not the taste or feel of mental qualities. According to this view we do not directly experience *any*one (whether self or other) in terms of psychological features, but must stipulate these from information about physical movements and patterns of events. This leaves us with exactly the kind of theoretical knowing that offends those who prize direct experience. We are left, in this view, with experience neither of self nor of other. It is a third-person approach because others are seen from some sort of intellectual or reflective distance as a he or a she rather than as a you.

What we might call first-person theories—simulation or "like me" theories of mind—reject the absurdities of such purely deductive knowledge of other minds and root knowledge of other people in the direct experience of the self. This actual or qualic experience is believed to be necessary to a deep and appropriate knowledge of others (Gordon, 1993). This is, of course, a version of the Cartesian privileged access to self. Theorists who adopt a first-person approach vary in the specific developmental route to knowledge of others that they advocate, ranging from explicit analogical inference to simple reference to internal states or models (Harris, 1992). Most first person approaches posit a developmental discovery of the similarity of self to other before experience of the self can be extended to apply to others. Some place this discovery as occurring well into infancy at around 9 or 12 months through the deductive construction of an intentional schema (Barresi & Moore, 1996a) or "like me" representations (Tomasello, 1999) while others place it pretty much at birth (Meltzoff & Moore, 1997). In essence, however, and common to all these views, is the point that it is the experience of something in the self that is *then* extended to others in imagination.

There are many problems with this position, such as the impossible fragility of knowledge which is based on an N of one, which have often been offered from a third-person perspective (e.g., Gopnik, 1993). From Buber's perspective one problem with this focus on the self is that others' psychological qualities could never actually *be* experienced. When we engage with another person all we could experience of them is that in them which is identical to that in ourselves. While it is undoubtedly the case that our understanding of others is often drawn from our own experiences, sometimes explicitly so, the assumption that we can *only* experience the self is problematic. If it were the case that recognition of others as psychological beings, or the awareness of some psychological quality in others, were based only on the recognition of their similarity to the self, then other persons are not really being recognized as others at all. You might say that we would merely be recognizing (or experiencing) the *self in the other.*

In the recent psychological literature on how we develop an understanding of others there is still an opposition between these two approaches, both assuming a spectatorial relation between self and other (Thompson, 2001). The alternative of a second-person solution, despite its older philosophical pedigree (Hobson, 1989; Shotter, 1989) is only recently beginning to be explored (Bogdan, 2005; Gallagher, 2001; Gomez, 1996; Reddy, 1996, 2003; Thompson, 2001). This omission can be clearly seen in two theoretical reviews attempting to portray a picture of the problem involved in understanding people as people and outlining current solutions to it. John Barresi and Chris Moore (1996a) expressed it thus: how does the infant (or any other organism) connect two qualitatively very different kinds of information about intentional activity—first-person information about the self (the world in relation to self) and third-person information about others (movements and spatiotemporal relations to the world)? To put it another way, how does first-person proprioception become understood as similar to third-person perception? How do infants get to know that both involve the same sort of subjective experience? They plumped for a conceptual solution: an intentional schema, developing at the end of the first year of life, built from considerable data of experiencing self and other together, which serves to hold both types of information together under one categorical umbrella. Once this umbrella has been built it is then available for interpreting all new data about mentality—whether obtained in the first person or the third person (Barresi & Moore, 1996a). The problem in their view is the bridging of this gulf between first-person and third-person information. A second-person solution cannot be entertained within the assumptions of the problem.

Another thorough and comprehensive discussion on intentionality more recently published by Sommerville and Woodward (2005) mentions at least four different contenders for explaining *how* the infant might come to be aware of the goal structures of other people's actions. These are (a) explanations based on innate modules (e.g., Baron-Cohen, 1995), which by definition are not explanations at all; (b) explanations based on action production leading through reflection and simulation to an understanding of others' actions (e.g., Meltzoff & Moore, 1997, Tomasello, 1999); (c) explanations based on action production leading to expertise and a selective focusing of attention on relevant features of others' actions (e.g., Gibson, 1969; Gibson & Pick, 2000); (d) explanations based on observation of others' actions leading to greater experience of goal structures and cues and thence to their use in understanding actions (e.g., Baldwin & Baird, 2001), and possibly a variant (d[1]) involving experience of associations and probabilities in movements leading to the development and application of a teleological stance (e.g., Gergely, 2003). In common terms we could think of (b) as a simulation theory account, one which favors the direct experience of the self as the answer to how we understand others. That is, it is the matching of the direct experience of the self to what little we know of the other that allows us to understand the other. This is a first-person route to the other—getting to the other through the self. We could think of (d) and especially (d[1]) as something like theory-theory accounts, positing the development of a broad based deduction about mentality from observation of others' actions. Here too, there is no mention of a second-person route.

Why does this alternative (i.e., the second-person route) not surface in the literature? There may be several reasons, but I think two are key: One, the familiar Platonic separation of the domain of knowing as distinct from the domain of feeling and doing (see for instance, Marková, 1983). The disconnection of knowledge from action and emotion (its disembodiment) in relation to the issue of social knowing has meant that people have been presented with nothing more than a representational bridge between them in order to begin dialogue. Affective engagement as a bridge that both involves and enables knowing has not entered the picture. But more interesting for the moment is a second reason, which is related to the neglect of affect. In the classic formulation of the problem of other minds or in treatises on knowing other minds, the other has always been seen (very oddly) as some sort of unitary entity. All other minds have generally been equated as constituting the third person, someone other than the self (they are not believed to differ in either the structure or the modalities of the informational sources; Barresi & Moore, 1996b). Within this defacing of the other the infant has no choice but to wait for an abstract representational awareness of the other as a person. *Does* the other have a (psychological) face?

A SECOND-PERSON APPROACH TO AWARENESS OF OTHERS: WHAT IS IT ABOUT?

Central to a second-person approach is relation and therefore necessarily a pluralization of the other. If we are talking about others in relation (that is, if others are necessarily perceived in self–other relation), then there must be not *one* other, but many. There are people whom we are in engagement with and whom we address as you, and there are people whom we might observe from a psychological distance and whom we might refer to as he or she. In Buber's terms, we are in an I–It relation with the people whom we refer to in the third person as he or she, whereas when we address someone as you we are in an I–Thou relation with them. What is the difference between the two? In a powerful paper with the first use of the term in this context, Shotter (1989) expresses the distinction in the following manner:

> First- and second-persons (plural or singular) are, even if in fact non-personal or inanimate always personified (with all that that implies for the "personal" nature of their relation), and are thus, so to speak, "present" to one another, in a "situation". By contrast, third-persons need not be personified (they can be "its"); nor are they present as such to other beings or entities; nor are they necessarily "in a situation". Indeed, the category is so non-specific that it may be used to refer to absolutely anything, so long as it is outside of, or external to, the immediate situation jointly created in the communicative activities between first- and second-persons. (p. 2)

Many philosophers argue that being addressed by another person as a you is vital for existing as a self, as an I. Hegel talks about the importance of being "recognized" by another consciousness for existing as a consciousness oneself and Bakhtin (1981) talks of the person as "the subject of an address." Something about the attention of another when it is directed to us is vital for our very existence. William James thought of attentional neglect by others—simply never being noticed—as the worst possible torture we could ever experience (James, 1890); to be not noticed by others may involve not being seen at all, or being seen as a thing of some kind rather than as a person to be addressed. Referring to Nietzsche's idea that "the You is older than the I," Shotter among others argues that the I is constituted by the you (Shotter, 1989). It is when I as an individual am noticed by someone who talks to me as a person, who addresses me as a you, who recognizes me as an individual consciousness, that I begin to exist as a self. What is vital for developmental psychology, and for the specific question of other-awareness is a further point: in order for this constitutive effect to happen, the individual must not only be perceived by another person as a you but must perceive—or in some way experience—this perception! If you could not discriminate between being addressed as a you and being treated as a he or she, there *could* be no constitutive influence of the you on the I. The presumption within some developmental theories that infants cannot perceive another's perception of the self or another's attitude toward the self would therefore create a serious problem for the infant (who would be unable to recognize that he or she was being addressed as a you).

Avoiding the chicken and egg traps that are inevitable when we adopt a linear causal theory of the you leading to the I or vice versa, John Macmurray's notion of the "field of the personal" might be helpful (Macmurray, 1961). The recognition of the other as a person and the recognition of the other's recognition of the self as a person may be a simultaneous feature of the adopting of what Macmurray calls a "personal attitude." In direct engagement with another we are in a personal relation with them, a second-person relation, which involves a different kind of knowing. We are open to the other in a way which is not possible within a more detached or disengaged third-person observation of another person.

The distinction between second-person and third-person relations in terms of the degree of emotional openness to the other and the information held for the individual is evident in everyday interactions. In the former the intensity and relevance of our emotional response to the acts of the other is different and usually greater. Your feeling/perception of your mother turning and frowning at you is different from your feeling/perception of your mother turning and frowning at your brother. Your feeling/perception of a baby's sudden quivering lip as you say hello to her is quite different from when you observe the baby reacting in the "same" way to someone else's hello. Your feeling/perception when your lover smiles when he or she catches your eye, is quite different from seeing him or her smile at someone else. It matters powerfully whether the other mind that you observe is turned toward you or toward someone else. The expressions—the frown, the smile, the tears—may be literally the same, but the "information" they hold for you is phenomenally different. Of course, acts that we merely *observe* can also arouse emotional response in us—when we watch a movie for instance or witness an interchange on the street. But because these observed acts are less complexly intertwined with our own prior actions and are likely to be less significant for our next action, our emotional response to them is often likely to be less intense and less meaningful for us. Acts which we perceive as directed toward us, on the other hand, can matter intensely and often *must* matter to us if we are to survive. The difference of emotional response in us as perceivers cannot *but* change the perceived information about the other—being a you to another therefore influences not only the nature of the self, but the nature of the other.

Given the profound mutually constitutive nature of the you and the I, it seems problematic to describe the nature of our experience of the you in the individualistic terms of information. However, even considered as information, acknowledging the difference between second-person and third-person relations changes the problem of other minds posed in terms of the profound gap between first-person proprioception and third-person perception. The perception of the other who is addressing their attention and actions to you inextricably involves your proprioception of your responses to them, dissolving the apparent mystery of the connection between self and other. A second-person psychology is (and needs to be) an affective science which is based not just on the adaptive role of subjective experience of affect within oneself, but on the adaptive and interpersonally constitutive role of the intersubjective experience of affect.

I will take one example to illustrate the primacy of second-person relations and their significance for awareness of other minds: the awareness of attention. Infants' engagements with other people's attending through the first year show a sequence of development in which early I–Thou engagements allow the emergence of a more reflective and I–It grasp of attending. And the difficulties which children with autism have in responding or initiating appropriately in emotional terms to others' attention suggest that it is not an awareness of the mechanics of attending which is problematic in autism but its emotional significance— a problem with I–Thou rather than I–It relations.

Experiencing Others' Attention
Can we *experience* others' attention? In the enormous literature on the issue of infant awareness of others' attention, the question of experiencing attention is not usually asked. Instead, the focus of research has tended to be on the triangular coordination of attention on external objects, with the reasoning that this provides the first evidence of the infant's representation of the other's attentional states as psychological rather than physical phenomena. The premise underlying this reasoning is of course the fundamental assumption that psychological states in others are only inferable—neither perceivable nor experienceable. Such triangulation in joint attention is not clearly evident until the end of the first year, appearing to support the premise that attention as a psychological phenomenon is perceptually inaccessible—for depictions of earlier attentional triangulations see Fivaz-Depeursinge and Corboz-Warnery (1999). This premise is used sometimes to explain the late appearance of joint attention relative to the awareness of intentional actions.

Recent studies have shown that infants as young as 5 months can recognize the intentional directedness of even disembodied arms reaching for objects on a screen (Woodward, 1998, 1999). Debates about habituation studies notwithstanding, such early discrimination between another person reaching *for* a specific thing as opposed to *just* reaching is intriguing. It is even more intriguing because it appears that if (with the help of velcro-covered mittens!) they are given prior experience of reaching for the objects themselves, even 3-month-olds make such discriminations (Sommerville, Woodward, & Needham, 2005). Woodward argues that this early recognition of intentional directedness (compared to attentional directedness) is possible because the connection between the reaching arm and the object is perceivable, while the connection between a looking eye and its object is not. The latter, it is commonly assumed requires a representational connection for its directedness to be grasped. However, if we accept the self as an object of attention (and it would indeed be bizarre not to do so, given that our most obvious and intense experiences of others' attention comes from having it directed to ourselves) then there is no longer any need to posit an intervening entity to connect attention with its objects. Because it is *experienced* in emotional reactions, attentional directedness is perceivable too!

Two streams of evidence support the argument that the experiencing of attention is primary. The evidence from the sequence of development in typically developing infants suggests that experiencing others' attention directed to the self is chronologically prior to (responses to and actions upon) others' attention directed to other things in the world. Second, the evidence from atypical development and from some experimental studies of typically developing infants suggests that the affective experiencing of attention is necessary for further exploration of attention and the development of complex attentional engagements. Problems in dyadic attentional engagements may lie at the root of problems in triangulation and representation of attention known to exist in some disorders: different affective experiences may lead to very different understandings of attention.

THE CHRONOLOGICAL PRIMACY OF THE EXPERIENCE OF ATTENTION

Mutual attentional engagements from the first few months of life in human infancy are well documented (Adamson & Bakeman, 1991; Bateson, 1979; Stern, 1985; Trevarthen, 1977; Wolff, 1987). However, they are rarely (with the exception of Trevarthen and Adamson & Bakeman) taken into serious consideration in discussions of the infant's awareness of attention. The standard story about the awareness of attention usually begins with joint attention at somewhere between 9 and 12 months of age (Bates, Camaioni, & Volterra, 1976; Tomasello, 1999). Bates and colleagues in their landmark study saw the triangulation of infant, other, and external object as signaling the discovery of attention—a conclusion warranted by the simultaneous development of protoimperative pointing, protodeclarative pointing, and tool use—although see Camaioni, Perucchini, Bellagamba, and Colonnesi (2004), for findings that are not consistent with the simultaneous development of declarative and imperative pointing. The reasons for the neglect of mutual attention as implying any awareness of attention center around a metaphysical definition of attention as an internal and representational entity (see Reddy, 2003, 2005 for a discussion). Some theorists even take the terms of this definition to imply that in order to be of interest as a psychological quality, attention (or any other mental state such as intention or belief) *must* be unobservable (Penn & Povinelli, in press).

However, as we can see from Table 6.1, there is a rich variety of attentional engagements evident through the first two years both predating and following the cluster of triangulation phenomena at the end of the first year (see also Reddy, 2003, 2005 for an extended discussion). The theoretical reduction of attention-awareness to joint attention does violence to these data. There are three features of these early attentional engagements that are significant for the claim that the infant experiences others' attention when it is directed to the self. First, the emotional responses evoked by others' attention are complex and varied even when directed to the 2-month-old infant. Positive, negative, indifferent, and ambivalent reactions to others' attention are evident at 2 months as well as later. This similarity of affective response to attention suggests a similarity of the affective meaning of attention for the infant. Second, part of the claim of a joint attention revolution is the idea that attempts to *direct* attention emerge for the first time at the end of the first year as manifest in protoimperative and protodeclarative (and now protoinformative, Liszkowski et al., 2006) pointing. However, on the contrary, one can see from Table 6.1 that infant initiations and directing actions upon others' attention are common from the first few months onward. Third, and linked to

Table 6.1 Attentional engagements between human infants and others in the first two years

Age	Kinds of attentional engagements
2–4 months	Responding to onset of mutual attention with smiling (Wolff, 1987; even when involving artificially posed adults: Caron et al., 1997; D'Entremont et al., 1997; Hains & Muir 1996; Muir & Hains, 1999) with ambivalent or coy reactions (Reddy, 2000), with negative emotional reactions (Brazelton, 1986), and with indifference (personal observation).
	Discriminating 5-degree deflections of gaze in mutual gaze (Symons, Hains, & Muir, 1996)
	Mutual gaze leads to better gaze following to other objects (Farroni et al., 2003), and to more communicative exchanges (Muir & Hains, 1996).
	Directing others' attention when it is absent by different "calling" vocalizations (Kopp, 1992; personal observation)
4–7 months	Responding to tickling, playing games with the body
	Waiting for the initiation of games? (evidence unclear)
7–10 months	Responding to attention to self and to the activities of the self with positive, negative, ambivalent, and indifferent emotional reactions
	Discriminating others' gaze direction to frontal targets (Butterworth & Jarrett, 1991)
	Directing or seeking to maintain others' attention to self by repeating actions for effect, engaging in clowning and showing off (Reddy, 2005)
10–12 months	Responding to attention to distal objects, gaze following (Butterworth & Jarrett, 1991; Moore & Corkum, 1998)
	Directing attention to distal objects through protodeclarative, protoimperative, and protoinformative pointing (Bates et al., 1976; Camaioni et al., 2004; Liszkowski et al., 2006; Tomasello, 1999)
14–20 months	Responding to others' attention to performance by the self with ambivalence and embarrassment (Lewis et al., 1989; Reddy, 2001)
	Discriminating gaze to distal objects in nonvisible space (Butterworth & Jarrett, 1991)
	Directing others' attention to non-present objects (on the basis of previous contact) by selective showing, giving on request, pointing (Reddy & Simone, 1995; Tomasello & Haberl, 2003)
20–36 months	Responding to and directing others' attention to normative aspects of performance by the self (Lewis, 1995)

these continuities is the fact that there is a gradual "expansion" over the course of the first two years in the infant's grasp of the objects with which others' attention can be engaged.

This is in fact the principal change over the first two years: the expansion of the objects to which others' attention can be directed in order to elicit these

Table 6.2   The infant's awareness of the expanding objects of others' attention

(From) Age	The object of others' attention which the infant is aware of	Attentional engagements with these objects
2–4 months	Self	Responding: *Pos, neg., indiff., coy* Directing: *Calling other*
4–7 months	Self-body	Responding: *Enjoys tickle, games, clapping* Directing*?* (evidence unclear)
7–10 months	Self acts Directing*: Clowning, showing-off, teasing*	Responding: *Enjoying, ambivalent*
10–14 months	Distal objects	Responding: *Gaze following* Directing: *Pointing, showing, etc.*
15–20 months	Objects in time	Responding? (evidence unclear) Directing: *Telling re past events, selective showing*

reactions. As can be seen from Table 6.2, the infant's responses to and acts upon others' attention, initially limited to attention to the self, expand over time to include, after the first three or four months, attention directed to the body (although there is little clear data of attentional engagements in such games), then in the second half of the first year to attention directed to actions by the self such as in showing-off and clowning. Finally, by the end of the first year attentional engagements with others involve distal objects—the traditional landmarks of joint attention in clear gaze following and pointing. But even after the emergence of such distal triangulation, the engagement with the objects of others' attention continues to expand, including, around the middle of the second year, attentional objects which may not even be present at the time; that is, objects which others had attended to in the past and objects which others have not yet attended to (Reddy & Simone, 1995), although recent findings (Tomasello & Haberl, 2003) suggest that this may occur even earlier (around 12 months).

THE CONSTITUTIVE ROLE OF THE EXPERIENCE OF ATTENTION

Experiencing of others' attention directed to the self may not only be developmentally primary, but developmentally *necessary*. The affective experiencing of attention to the self *must* be central to the meaning that attention subsequently has for the individual and for the actions that the individual performs with others' attention. This prediction (Reddy, 2003) applies not only to typical development—where the early experience of attention must motivate and shape further actions upon or with attention—but also to disorders in development. If for some reason—whether due to difficulty in the infant or in the caregivers—the infant has not been able to *experience* mutual attention in the way that we typically understand it to happen, then further awareness of attention must develop in a different—atypical and inappropriate—direction. There is, of course, a circularity here: the affective experience of attention influences the infant's engagement with others' attention, which influences the experience of attention.

The early experience of attention depends not only on the infant's biological predisposition to a particular perceptual/proprioceptive/emotional response to attention to the self, but on what then happens in the engagement. Infants engage in dyadic attentional interactions with adults from minutes after birth. What happens if the adult does not engage with the infant? What happens if the infant is distressed or unable to engage? What happens if the infant finds the engagement disturbing and negative? What attention means to the infant must depend heavily on such histories. We can guess that an *absence* of emotional response to attention to self will divorce the infant's developing understanding of attention from any experiential reality of attention until it can be analogically inferred. We can guess that a largely *negative* (distressing) or neutral (disinterested) experience of emotional response to attention to self must inhibit further engagements with attention, leading to a spiraling negativity of affect, and influence the nature of later conceptual understanding of attention. And we can guess that a largely *positive* experience of attention to self must enhance and encourage further initiations of attentional engagement as well as lead to a spiralling positivity in experiencing and conceptualizing attention. Absence of emotional involvement with others' attention—to its various objects—could be seen as directly influencing the absence of emotional responses to attention as we see in typically developing infants. The understanding that is developed outside of emotional engagement may be a more logical, deductive, projective understanding.

We do not know enough about problems in early attentional engagements to test these predictions. Some hints come from studies of maternal depression (Hatzinikolaou, 2003; Stanley, Murray, & Stein, 2004), and others come from studies of much older children with autism. We do know that children with autism have difficulty disengaging from attention and show resistance to bids for mutual attention (usually gaze; see Adamson, McArthur, Markov, Dunbar, & Bakeman, 2001; Leekam & Ramsden, 2006). It certainly seems to be the case that mutual attentional engagements in children—not infants—with autism are problematic. Most interestingly for this prediction, they show some impairments in emotional reactions to mutual attention. Chidambi (2003) for instance, showed that the coy reactions evident at the onset of mutual attentional engagements and shown by the 2- and 3-month-old typically developing infant are not shown by older children with autism. Even when the mutual attentional situation is intensely intimate older children with autism did not show such reactions while a matched group of children with other disabilities did. Why is this? It could be that children with autism are unable to experience others' attention emotionally, *as* attention. Or it could be that, as Caldwell (2006) argues, in autism the child experiences others' attention, only too intensely—but is unable to deal with it appropriately. In either case, mutual attentional engagements are not typical in autism and although we would need developmental data to explore this further (e.g., from systematic home videos) this atypicality may lead to the further secondary impairments of attention that we associate with autism (such as inability to "understand" or to produce protodeclarative pointing, to follow gaze, etc., see also Reddy, Williams, & Vaughan, 2002). Children with autism appear to have difficulties with the affective experience of attention as well as with the contextual grounding of attentional engagements; that is, with the *experience* of others' attention in both the synchronic and diachronic sense. Any problems or differences from the norm in how one experiences others' attention to the self must lead to further atypicalities in more complex attentional engagements and in the conceptualization of attention. The evidence on attentional engagements in autism appears to support this picture.

Evidence from typical development also supports the prediction that the affective experience of attention directed to self is a prerequisite for the further development of an appropriate (or typical) understanding of attention. There are intriguing findings from recent experimental studies that gaze following of sorts can occur even in 3-month-olds, but only if mutual attention is first established (Farroni, Mansfield, Lai, & Johnson, 2003). Similarly, others' gaze has been shown to lead to smiles and communicative behavior in the early months but only if prior mutual gaze has occurred (Hains & Muir, 1996). Something in the phenomenon of mutual attention—in this case mutual gaze alone —appears to be responsible for motivating the infant's actions upon and explorations of the other's attentional shifts.

An intriguing study that looks at influences on infant gaze of adults' hands also emphasizes the importance of mutual attention, but approaches this issue from a very different direction. Amano and colleagues (2004) found that when very young infants are presented with the averted profile of an adult, they continued looking at it for a few seconds before turning to look at the adult's hand (which may have been holding an object). If the adult's gaze remained on them, however, the infants did not bother much with looking at the adult's hand even if the adult's hand had an object in it. The absence of attention—which may translate directly into the absence of the subjective experience involved in receiving it—may either release the infant more quickly to explore further afield or even drive the infant directly to seek the objects linked with its absence. The infant's attentional shifts in both these studies make the most sense if we assume that the infant is aware of the other's attention as a psychologically directed act. It may be because, in mutual attention, this directedness is experienced by the infant to herself as the object, that the shift to other targets can occur. If the infant did not feel the other's attention to herself, she would have little more than academic curiosity as a motive to explore the other's attention to the world. It is this affective awareness of others' attention to the self that allows infants to develop a broader (and eventually conceptual) awareness of others' attention.

Adults, however unwittingly, play their own motivational part in broadening the infant's grasp of the objects (beyond the self) that other persons can and do attend to. Parents, we know, do things at the fringes of infants' abilities—working in a Vygotskyan zone of proximal development (Vygotsky, 1934/1962;

Rogoff, 2003). And infants, like most juvenile mammals, seek and enjoy novelty and exploration. When they are around 3 or 4 months old infants are known to shift their own attentional interests from mutual attentional engagements to the environment around them (Trevarthen, 1977; Vedeler, 1994). The waning of the infant's exclusive focus on them moves the adults to start doing more and more exaggerated actions—moving the infant's feet, singing songs, starting to invite the infant into rhythmic games and so on—to regain the infant's attention. The infant's horizon of adult actions therefore expands to include focus on parts of the infant's own body. This expansion must have consequences: on the one hand marking the infant's body parts as separate entities (objects of attention), and on the other making the process of engagement instantly more complex and essentially triadic. It would be surprising if the infant, faced with these new complexities and potential targets of attention, did not then herself bring them into interactions with adults. The motive for expanding objects of attention then becomes clear—the infant's horizons expand mutually—infants seek more novelty and adults provide more complexity. When the two combine, infants' awareness of attention expands further.

CONCLUSIONS

Approaches to the question of how humans come to be aware of the psychological qualities of people often begin with the postulation of a gap between proprioceptive experience of the self and perceptual experience of the other leading to the continued offering (and opposition) of first-person and third-person bridges across the gap to awareness of other minds. A second-person alternative is based upon drawing a distinction between different kinds of perception of other minds depending upon the relation between self and other. Other minds in direct engagement with the self call upon affective responses and actions in a different way from other minds toward whom the self is in a more detached, spectatorial relation.

I have argued that the awareness of other minds must begin in the actual experiencing of the other within the self in second-person relations. Attentional engagements beginning from very early infancy show a similarity in emotional responses to other people's attention through the first year, with attempts to direct others' attention starting much earlier than is evident in joint attention to distal objects. Through the first year there is a developing awareness of the objects to which others' attention *can* be directed. The meaning of attention for infants (that is, their awareness of attention) must be based upon their affective experience of it, and must change with and depend upon the nature of their developing involvement with others' attentional engagements. Atypical awareness of others' attention, as in autism, appears to be based upon atypical affective experience of attention in mutual attentional engagements. Beginning with the affective experience of attention to self in mutual attentional engagements there must be a profound circularity between such experience and further attentional engagements and further affective experience.

If this explanation, of how we come to be aware of other minds in general or of others' attention in particular, is valid, it must apply beyond infancy. Even in adulthood it must be the case that it is engagement of this sort with the objects of each others' attention that continues to expand our awareness of what kinds of things can be attended to and what kind of thing attention is and could be. At the root of such expanding awareness, however, must be the affective experience of others' attention, when it is directed in the first instance, to the self. Social life can only lead to social knowledge if it involves social feeling.

Notes

1. See Trevarthen (in press). Dewey makes this point lucidly:

    Experience does not go on simply inside a person. It does go on there, for it influences the formation of attitudes of desire and purpose. But this is not the whole of the story. Every genuine experience has an active side which changes in some degree the objective conditions under which experiences are had.... We live from birth to death in a world of persons and things which in large measure is what it is because of what has been done and transmitted from previous human activities. When this fact is ignored, experience is treated as if it were something which goes on exclusively inside an individual's body and mind. It ought not to be necessary to say that experience does not occur in a vacuum. (Dewey, 1938/1973b, p. 516)

2. Psychology's commitment to construal and constructivism makes experience of the world very difficult for simple organisms. The Cartesian distinction between *res extensa* and *res cogitans*—between the psychological and the material—is strongly visible in this commitment. The individual can become conscious of (that is, can experience) the material world of events only through an intervening process— some kind of imaginary or constructive act. While Descartes saw all external events as not directly experienceable by the individual, modern psychology draws more subtle distinctions between perceiving (as a sensory phenomenon) and experiencing (as a meaningful and interpretive phenomenon).

3. The continuing academic need for experiments with chickens (e.g., Dawkins, 2006) and even with mammals such as cats, testing whether pain or discomfort is actively and effortfully avoided, are testament to the general conviction that the subjective experience of feelings is separable from emotion. In human ontogeny too, it was not so long ago that newborns were believed not to *feel* pain (crying notwithstanding) and therefore not in need of anesthesia for surgery.

4. Coupled with the fairly general conviction that we have to experience something to really know it, this tendency to view experience as private makes it of course impossible to actually experience anything or anyone outside the self. We are back to a Cartesian Square One in terms of the problem of knowing other people!

References

Adamson, L. & Bakeman, R. (1991). The development of shared attention during infancy. In R. Vasta (Ed.), *Annals of Child Development* (Vol. 8, pp. 1–41). London: Jessica Kingsley.

Adamson, L. B., McArthur, D., Markov, Y., Dunbar, B., & Bakeman, R. (2001). Autism and joint attention: Young children's responses to maternal bids. *Journal of Applied Developmental Psychology, 22,* 439–453.

Amano, S., Kezuka, E., & Yamamoto, A. (2004) Infant shifting attention from an adult's face to an adult's hand: A precursor of joint attention. *Infant Behavior and Development, 27,* 64–80.

Bakhtin, M. (1981). *The dialogic imagination: Four essays by Mikhail Bakhtin* (M. Holmquist, Ed.; C. Emerson & M. Holquist, Trans.). Austin: University of Texas Press.

Baldwin, D., & Baird, J. (2001). Discerning intentions in dynamic human action. *Trends in Cognitive Sciences, 5,* 171–178.

Baron-Cohen, S. (1995). *Mindblindness: An essay on autism and theory of mind.* Cambridge, MA: MIT Press.

Barresi, J., & Moore, C. (1996a). Intentional relations and social understanding. *Behavioural and Brain Sciences, 19,* 107–154.

Barresi, J., & Moore, C. (1996b) Response to commentaries. *Behavioural and Brain Sciences, 19,* 142–149.

Bates, E., Camaioni, L., & Volterra, V. (1976). Sensorimotor performatives. In E. Bates (Ed.), *Language and context: The acquisition of pragmatics* (pp. 49–71). NewYork: Academic Press.

Bateson, M. C. (1979) The epigenesis of conversational interaction. In M. Bullowa (Ed.), *Before speech.* New York: Cambridge University Press.

Bernstein, N. (1967). *The coordination and regulation of movements.* London: Pergamon.

Bogdan, R. (2005) Why self-ascriptions are difficult and develop late. In B. Malle, F. Bertram, & S. D. Hodges (Eds.), *Other minds: How humans bridge the divide between self and others* (pp. 190–206). New York: Guilford.

Bradley, B. (2005). *Psychology and experience.* New York: Cambridge University Press.

Brazelton, T. B. (1986). The development of newborn behavior. In F. Faulkner & J. M. Tanner (Eds.), *Human growth: A comprehensive treatise* (Vol. 2, pp. 519–540). New York: Plenum.

Buber, M. (1937). *I and thou.* London: T&T Clark. (Original work published 1923)

Butterworth, G., & Jarrett, N. (1991). What minds have in common is space: Spatial mechanisms serving joint visual attention in infancy. *British Journal of Developmental Psychology, 9,* 55–72

Caron, A., Caron, R., Roberts, J., & Brooks, R. (1997). Infant sensitivity to deviations in dynamic facial-vocal displays: The role of eye regard. *Developmental Psychology, 33,* 802–813.

Caldwell, P. (2006). Speaking the other's language: Imitation as a gateway to relationship. *Infant and Child Development, 15,* 275–282.

Camaioni, L., Perucchini, P., Bellagamba, F., & Colonnesi, C. (2004). The role of declarative pointing in developing a theory of mind. *Infancy, 5,* 291–308.

Chidambi, G. (2003). *Autism and self-conscious emotions.* Doctoral dissertation, University College London.

D'Entremont, B., Hains, S. M. J., & Muir, D. (1997). A demonstration of gaze following in 3- to 6-month-olds. *Infant Behavior and Development, 20,* 569–572.

Damasio, A. (2003) *Looking for Spinoza.* Orlando, FL: Harcourt.

Dawkins, M. S. (2006). Through animal eyes: What behaviour tells us. *Applied Animal Behaviour Science, 100,* 4–10.

Dewey, J. (1973a). Democracy and education. In J. J. McDermott (Ed.), *The philosophy of John Dewey: The lived experience*. New York: Capricorn Books. (Original work published 1916)

Dewey, J. (1973b). Experience and education. In J. J. McDermott (Ed.), *The philosophy of John Dewey: The lived experience*. New York: Capricorn Books. (Original work published 1938)

Dreyfus, H. L. (1995). *Being in the world: A commentary on Heidegger's Being and Time, Division 1*. Cambridge, MA: MIT Press.

Farroni, T., Mansfield, E. M., Lai, C., & Johnson, M. H. (2003). Infants perceiving and acting on the eyes: Tests of an evolutionary hypothesis. *Journal of Experimental Child Psychology, 85*, 199–212.

Fivaz-Depeursinge, E., & Corboz-Warnery, A. (1999). *The primary triangle*. New York: Basic Books.

Friedman, M. (2002). *The life of dialogue* (4th ed.). London: Routledge

Frijda, N. H., & Mesquita, B. (1994). The social roles and functions of emotions. In S. Kitayama & H. R. Markus (Eds.), *Emotion and culture: Empirical studies of mutual influence* (pp. 51–87). Washington D.C.: American Psychological Association.

Gallagher, S. (2001). The practice of mind: Theory, simulation or primary interaction? *Journal of Consciousness Studies, 8*, 83–108

Gergely, G. (2003). The development of understanding of self and agency. In U. Goswami (Ed.), *Blackwell handbook of child cognitive development* (pp. 26–46). Malden, MA: Blackwell.

Gibson, E. (1969). *Principles of perceptual learning and development*. New York: Appleton-Century-Crofts.

Gibson, E., & Pick, A. (2000). *An ecological approach to perceptual learning and development*. New York: Oxford University Press.

Gibson, J. J. (1979). *Ecological approach to visual perception*. Boston: Houghton Mifflin.

Gomez, J. C. (1996). Second person intentional relations and the evolution of social understanding. *Behavioural and Brain Sciences, 19*, 129–130

Gopnik, A. (1993). How we know our minds: The illusion of first person knowledge of intentionality. *Behavioural and Brain Sciences, 16*, 1–14.

Gordon, R. M. (1993). Self-ascriptions of belief and desire. *Behavioural and Brain Sciences, 16*, 45–46.

Hains, S., & Muir, D. (1996). Infant sensitivity to eye direction. *Child Development, 67*, 1940–1951.

Harris, P. (1992). From simulation to folk psychology. *Mind and Language, 7*, 120–144.

Hatzinikolaou, K. (2002). *The development of empathy and sympathy in the first year.* Unpublished doctoral dissertation, University of Reading, U.K.

Hobson, R. P. (1989). On sharing experiences. *Development and Psychopathology, 1*, 197–203.

Kopp, C. B. (2002). Commentary: The co-developments of attention and emotion regulation. *Infancy, 3*, 199–208.

LeDoux, J. E. (1996). *The emotional brain: The mysterious underpinnings of emotional life*. New York: Simon & Schuster

Lee, D. N. (1993). Body-environment coupling. In U. Neisser (Ed.), *The perceived self: Ecological and interpersonal sources of knowledge* (pp. 43–67). New York: Cambridge University Press.

Leekam, S. R., Hunnisett, E., & Moore, C. (1998). Targets and cues: Gaze-following in children with autism. *Journal of Child Psychology and Psychiatry, 39*, 951–962.

Leekam, S. R., & Ramsden, C. (2006). Dyadic orienting and joint attention in pre-school children with autism. *Journal of Autism and Developmental Disorders, 36*, 185–197.

Lewis, M. (1995) Embarrassment: The emotion of self-exposure and evaluation. In J. P. Tangney & K. W. Fischer (Eds.), *Self-conscious emotions: The psychology of shame, guilt, pride and embarrassment* (pp. 199–218). New York: Guildford.

Lewis, M., Sullivan, M. W., Stanger, C., & Weiss, M. (1989). Self development and self-conscious emotions *Child Development, 60,* 146–156.

Liszkowski, U., Carpenter, M., Striano, T., & Tomasello, M. (2006). 12-and 18-month-olds point to provide information for others. *Journal of Cognition and Development, 7,* 173–187

Macmurray, J. (1961). *Persons in relation.* London: Faber and Faber.

Marková, I. (1982) *Paradigms, thought and language.* New York: Wiley.

Meltzoff, A., & Moore, M. K. (1997). Explaining facial imitation: A theoretical model. *Early Development and Parenting, 6,* 179–192.

Moore, C., & Corkum, V. (1998). Infant gaze following based on eye direction. *British Journal of Developmental Psychology, 16,* 495–503.

Muir, D., & Hains (1999). Young infants' perception of adult intentionality. In P. Rochat (Ed.), *Early social cognition: Understanding others in the first months of life* (pp. 155–188). Mahwah, NJ: Lawrence Erlbaum.

Panksepp, J. (1998). *Affective neuroscience: The foundations of human and animal emotions.* New York: Oxford University Press.

Panksepp, J., & Smith-Pasqualini, M. (2005). The search for the fundamental brain/mind sources of affective experience. In J. Nadel & D. Muir (Eds.), *Emotional development: Recent research advances* (pp. 5–30). New York: Oxford University Press.

Penn, D. C., & Povinelli, D. J. (in press). On the lack of evidence that non-human animals possess anything remotely resembling a "theory of mind." *Philosophical Transactions of the Royal Society of London.*

Reddy, V. (2003). On being the object of attention: Implications for self-other-consciousness. *Trends in Cognitive Sciences, 7,* 397–402.

Reddy, V. (2005). Before the "Third Element": Understanding attention to self. In N. Eilan, Howerl, C., McCormack, T., & Roessler, J. (Eds.) *Joint attention: Communication and other minds: Issues in philosophy and psychology.* New York: Oxford University Press

Reddy, V., & Simone, L. (1995). *Acting on attention: Towards an understanding of knowing in infancy.* Paper presented at the Annual Conference of the Developmental Section of the British Psychological Society, Strathclyde, Scotland.

Reddy, V., Williams, E., & Vaughan, A. (2002). Sharing humour and laughter in autism and Down syndrome. *British Journal of Psychology, 93,* 219–242.

Rogoff, B. (2003). *The cultural nature of human development.* New York: Oxford University Press.

Shotter, J. (1989) Social accountability and the social construction of the you. In J. Shotter & K. J. Gergen (Eds.), *Texts of identity.* London: Sage.

Shotter, J. (2006). Vygotsky and consciousness as *con-scientia*, as witnessable knowing along with others. *Theory and Psychology, 16,* 13–36.

Sommerville, J., & Woodward, A. (2005). Pulling out the intentional structure of action: the relation between action processing and action production in infancy. *Cognition, 95,* 1–30.

Sommerville, J., Woodward, A., & Needham, A. (2005). Action experience alters 3-month-old infants' perception of others' actions. *Cognition, 96*, B1–B11.

Stanley, C., Murray, L., & Stein, A. (2004). The effect of postnatal depression on mother–infant interaction, infant response to the still-face perturbation, and performance on an instrumental learning task. *Development and Psychopathology, 16*, 1–18.

Stern, D. (1985). *The interpersonal world of the infant.* New York: Basic Books

Symons, L. A., Hains, S. M. J., & Muir, D. W. (1998). Look at me: 5-month-olds' sensitivity to very small deviations in eye-gaze during social interactions. *Infant Behavior and Development, 21*, 531–538.

Thompson, E. (2001). Empathy and consciousness. *Journal of Consciousness Studies, 8* (5–7), 1–32.

Tomasello, M. (1999). Social cognition before the revolution. In P. Rochat (Ed.), *Early social cognition: Understanding others in the first months of life* (pp. 155–188). Mahwah, NJ: Lawrence Erlbaum.

Tomasello, M., & Haberl, K. (2003). Understanding attention: 12- and 18-month-olds know what is new for other persons. *Developmental Psychology, 39*, 906–912.

Trevarthen, C. (1977). Descriptive analyses of infant communicative behaviour. In H. R. Schaffer (Ed.), *Studies in mother–infant interaction: The Loch Lomond Symposium* (pp. 227–270). London: Academic Press.

Trevarthen, C. (in press). Moving experiences: Perceiving as action with a sense of purpose. In G.-J. Pepping & M. A. Greally (Eds.), *Closing the gap: The scientific writings of David N. Lee* (pp. 1–20). Mahwah, NJ: Lawrence Erlbaum.

Vedeler, D. (1994). Infant intentionality as object-directedness: A method for observation. *Scandinvian Journal of Psychology, 35*, 343–366.

Vygotsky, L. (1962). *Thought and language.* Cambridge, MA: MIT Press. (Original work published in 1934)

Winograd, T., & Flores, F. (1986). *Understanding computers and cognition: A new foundation for design.* Norwood, NJ: Ablex.

Wolff, P. H. (1987). *The development of behavioral states and the expression of emotions in early infancy: New proposals for investigation.* Chicago: University of Chicago Press.

Woodward, A. (1998). Infants selectively encode the goal object of an actor's reach. *Cognition, 69*, 1–34.

Woodward, A. (1999). Infants' ability to distinguish between purposeful and non-purposeful behaviours. *Infant Behaviour and Development, 22*, 145–160.

7

Social Knowledge as Social Skill
An Action Based View of Social Understanding

MAXIMILIAN B. BIBOK, JEREMY I. M. CARPENDALE, AND CHARLIE LEWIS

The literature on social cognitive development has witnessed continuing interest in the development of infants' and children's understanding of the psychological world (e.g., Carpendale & Lewis, 2006). This interest derives from two observations: (1) the importance of social understanding in enabling children to navigate successfully through the complex and novel social worlds in which they find themselves, and (2) that such social understanding is so evidently lacking in children with autism. There have been ongoing theoretical debates about how best to conceptualize the development of children's social understanding. Notwithstanding such debate, any theory that addresses children's social understanding must necessarily rest upon a prior conceptual framework of presuppositions regarding the nature of knowledge and the mind. Typically, these presuppositions are: (1) minds are private and hidden; (2) we only have direct access to the contents of our own mind; (3) we must infer the mental states of others via their observable behavior; and, (4) knowledge takes the form of representations in the mind that match the world. In this chapter we scrutinize these often unexamined presuppositions. In particular, we outline and critique the representational view of mind assumed in most work on children's social understanding, more commonly known as children's "theories of mind." As an alternative we present an action-based, constructivist account that avoids fundamental errors endemic to the representational view of mind. We argue that children's social understanding can be explicated in terms of social skills that give children the potential to engage in social interaction.

It is one thing to claim the representational view of mind is problematic; it is another to offer a viable alternative. Indeed it has been suggested, in the absence of an adequate alternative, that such a view of the mind may be regarded as an existence proof; if there is no viable alternative, then such a view of the mind must be the case—there is no other option (Bickhard & Terveen, 1995). In this chapter we argue that there is a viable alternative to the representational or inferential view of mind assumed by "theory of mind" researchers. From the perspective of a constructivist, action-based approach, we contend that an understanding of mind develops within the context of the continuous interactions that individuals have with their social environments. That is, mind finds its origin in activity. We also explicate the view of language that follows from this approach and discuss how it is linked to social development.

THE REPRESENTATIONAL VIEW OF MIND

If we are concerned with how children develop social knowledge, we must begin by examining assumptions regarding the nature of knowledge and its development on which theoretical frameworks are based. In the theory of mind field, knowledge is generally approached from within a representational framework. According to this view, knowledge either takes the form of innate representations (nativism), or is attained by abstracting mental representations from the sensory stimuli that we experience (empiricism). Thus, central to the representational view of knowledge is the theoretical tenet that the mind contains representations that stand in a relation of "aboutness" with a state of affairs in the world. That is, representations, re-present, they present again, a state of affairs in the world; representations stand in for things-in-themselves (Bickhard & Terveen, 1995; Campbell & Bickhard, 1986), or act as a substitute for them.

The relation between the representational view of knowledge and "mental states," as they are portrayed in the theory of mind literature, is easy to see. Debate in the 1990s (Carruthers & Smith, 1996) hinged on the idea that for children to demonstrate false belief understanding they must necessarily understand that other people and they themselves have mental representations that are causally antecedent to the actions they perform in the world. The representational view holds that children must understand that these representations are "about" the world, and thus may be either accurate or inaccurate (i.e., true or false). Perner's (1991) theory, in particular, rests on the assumption that if children demonstrate false belief understanding they have a theory of mind in which knowledge is representational in nature (aboutness) and accounts for how those representations cause or explain the actions of others.

On the face of it, such a view of the mind has an intuitive appeal, which is evident in the following example. When others challenge us to guess what number between 1 and 10 they are thinking of it does intuitively seem as if they have a representation (e.g., a picture) of the number in their mind's eye. Moreover, they have direct access to this representation and we do not; after all, this is why they are challenging us in the first place. For us to figure out the number, it also intuitively appears as if we go through a process of inference using all available information. However, we agree with a school of thought that holds that, for all of its allure, such a view of the mind and knowledge is, at its core, untenable. To explain why this is the case, we must first examine more fully how it is that representations come to accurately reflect the world about us.

If knowledge is mediated by representations, how do we compare two representations in order to claim that one represents knowledge of the world and the other does not? The answer is simple enough. To constitute knowledge, a given representation must accurately match the world. But there is a problem with this answer. According to the representational view of knowledge, we only know the world through our representations; that is their point; they are "about" the world. Yet to make a judgment regarding the truth or falsity of the match would require that we have direct access to both our representations and the world of things-in-themselves in order to compare the two. If they are congruent with each other, then the match is held to be true, and so the representation is indeed knowledge about the world. Yet, this is precisely the function that representations were meant to serve; if we could access the world directly, why would we need representations in the first place? Consequently, we are left in a logical position in which we are unable to determine if our representations are either true or false, as we have no standard against which to compare them. For this reason, knowledge-as-mental-representations cannot actually be claimed to constitute any form of knowledge about the world at all (Bickhard & Terveen, 1995; Chapman, 1999; Piaget, 1970).

To clarify this argument, we need to identify the difference between a causal and an epistemic relation between representations and the world. Suppose photons of light strike the retina, and as a result one experiences an image, say of a piece of fruit. This is a causal relation; the photons could be said to have caused the representation of a piece of fruit. However, the same causal relation could take place between these photons and a camera. The camera could be said in a sense to contain information that is accessible to persons, but the camera does not know anything. And even if the information was transferred to a computer the computer would not know anything (Bickhard & Terveen, 1995; Kenny, 1991; Müller, Sokol & Overton, 1998). Although causal mechanisms (e.g., neurological processes) are necessary before someone can potentially know about the world, it is not possible for such causal processes to account for knowledge about the things that representations may be causally matched with. Thus, an interpreter or homunculus would have to be added to the model to interpret or make sense of the information (Bickhard & Terveen, 1995; Kenny, 1991). But to do this, such an interpreter must also be in possession of a representational mind and so would require his or her own interpreter, and so forth and so on. Needless to say, no one wants a model that is flawed in this way (at least when the incoherence is explicitly pointed out).

Further, this causal relation does not mean that my representation must be accurate. I may be in error. Perhaps it was actually a child's toy that caused the representation, an error that is only recognized later after the fact. For such a causal relation to be claimed to be accurate, the thing-in-itself and my representation must be in a logical relation of matching. For instance, Q and q are logically related. To know this we must first have access to both terms, Q and q, and then know that they logically go together. However, if we just have Z, we cannot determine the logical relation that is to be established. Our representation of Z may have been triggered by z or some error, such as 7. To determine how a representation logically matches the world, we need access to both to determine the nature of the logical relation (i.e., correct or incorrect). But, as previously stated, if all I have epistemic access to are my representations then I am unable to go about establishing such a relation. Consequently, the only way such a logical relation could be established is if representations actually carried their own truth value. Moving back to the earlier example, if some photons triggered a representation of Z in my mind, the only way it could be said to be true that Z represents z (which I have no access to) is if I just take such a relation for granted. Thus, Z is assumed to have been caused by z, so Z is taken as being a true representation of the world without ever checking if such is the case. But, if such were the case, my representations would no longer be "about" the world, but instead only true-in-themselves (i.e., self-contained). As argued by Putnam (1981, emphasis in original), "thought words and mental pictures do not *intrinsically* represent what they are about" (p. 5). At this point, representations could no longer be said to represent anything about the world. Representations, therefore, cannot be claimed to be either true or false in relation to the world, as it is impossibly to check upon their accuracy.

But what does this have to do with children's theory of mind or social understanding? The importance of this argument can be seen at play in the very terminology used within the field—understanding of *false* belief. Specifically, in the theory of mind literature beliefs are conceptualized as taking a representational form, yet, as argued, no mental representation taking the form of a corresponding match with the world can ever be determined to be either true or false. It is not so much a matter of determining which beliefs are true and which are false. Rather, given the representational view of knowledge, no belief as a mental representation could ever be determined to be true or false. Children, therefore, simply cannot attain social understanding in the manner proposed by the theory of mind literature.

What then are the implications of the representational view of knowledge when thinking about the development of children's social knowledge? Under the representational view of knowledge, our understanding of the world is mediated through our representations. We only have direct private access to our representations; we do not have direct access to the world. Our experience of the world, therefore, is individually private. It is commonly supposed that in order to demonstrate false belief understanding, children must infer the hidden mental representations of others in order to know how to predict or explain their actions. It is only through inference that one private and publicly inaccessible mind can determine the contents of another private and publicly inaccessible mind. As such, this tacit assumption regarding the nature of the mind frames the very research question driving the theory of mind field: How do children acquire knowledge of other minds—or put differently, how do children come mentally to represent for themselves the representations occurring in the mind of another person? At this point the argument against the representational view of knowledge and the nature of the mind has come full circle. Knowledge as mental representations presupposes a private, publicly inaccessible view of the mind, which in turn creates the very problem children are allegedly required to solve. To solve this problem children are required to develop a theory of mind. At its core, the mystery of how children discover or infer the mental representations in the minds of others is a conceptual artifact that necessarily follows from the representational view of knowledge.

One difficulty recognized by some theorists concerns the development of the representations themselves. To know about the world requires the possession of a matching representation. If this is the case though, individuals could not recognize anything new because they would not have a matching representation. As we do in fact recognize new features of our environment, some theorists have assumed in response that representations must be innate (Fodor, 1985). However, shifting the problem to evolution does not solve it. The reason for this is because the development of representations is a logical problem in which the truth value of the match between a representation and the thing in the world it represents must be determined; it is not a causal problem. If the development of representations could be solved by evolution then it could be solved just as well in the process of development (Bickhard & Terveen, 1995). In the area of social development, some researchers have claimed that children's understanding of the mind as representational is prespecified in innate modules (e.g., Baron-Cohen, 1995; Leslie, 1994). Rather than solving the problems that we outline above, this approach simply assumes that the logical issue of comparing internal representations with the outside world is innately pregiven in the computational organization of the modules. As a result, it suffers from the same problems of representationalism, since it posits the same representation–world relations assumed by the theory-theory perspective.

The same holds for simulation accounts of social understanding (e.g., Harris, 1991; Johnson, 1988). Simulation accounts criticize the notion of theory of mind because the hypothesized representational processes of such theories are too complex to account for the social understanding of children, particularly preschoolers. Instead, they suggest that rather than forming theories, individuals simply imagine (i.e., simulate) another person's perspective on the world. Through simulation, individuals generalize from their own mental states to the world. However, from this perspective there is no account of how anyone, particularly children, can even begin to compare how their own private sensations relate to anything or anyone out there. Elsewhere, we have pointed out problems with the claim that it is possible for children to introspect on mental states like beliefs and intentions to determine the mental states of other persons (Carpendale & Lewis, 2004, 2006).

AN ACTION-BASED APPROACH TO MIND

The development of representations has implications for how children understand the social world. That we learn about people by interacting with them is a statement that few people would contest. As bodily beings we engage in actions that change our social environment; we talk, touch, play, and do things with other people. But how do we know what changes or outcomes we have produced in the social environment through our actions? Through representations? If our representations mediate our knowledge of the world, yet the effects produced by our actions in our social and physical environments are unmediated by such representations (the environment knows nothing of our representations), then a conceptual division can be said to exist between representation and action. Although one may argue that representations are antecedent to our actions, the effects produced by our actions must also be represented to be known. As argued though, representations cannot be said to be either true or false because we cannot check upon their accuracy. Consequently, we cannot unite the effects of our actions with our representations of those effects; the effects of our actions have no relation with the accuracy of our representations of those effects. How then are we to learn about the social world? The inability to check the accuracy of our representations effectively precludes the possibility of learning about our world (Bickhard & Terveen, 1995). Nonetheless, we still do have the ability to interact skillfully in that world.

What if one rejects the representational conception of knowledge and the theories of social development based on it? An alternative view of knowledge is constructivism, according to which we know the world directly in terms of the actions by which we transform our environment. From an action-based approach, knowledge is the unmediated, embodied ability to interact directly *in* and *with* our environment; "Knowing is effective action, that is, operating effectively in the domain of existence of living beings" (Maturana & Varela, 1987, p. 29). From birth, infants gradually develop schemes, sensorimotor patterns of activity, regarding what they can do with aspects of the world (Piaget, 1936/1963). Infants know the world in terms of the potential outcomes they can produce through their interaction with the environment (Bickhard & Terveen, 1995; Watson, 1972). Such knowledge is not representational information "about" the world that mediates our relation with our environment. The expectations that infants develop through their interaction are, therefore, not representations, nor are they objects in the mind, but instead are *embedded* and *implicit* in the very structure of the activities that they perform in the world (Brooks, 1991).

Thus, in contrast to the empiricist view of mind, under an action-based model of mind, cognition is *embodied* (Overton, 1994). The individual is not an epistemologically *passive* witness of representations originating from sensory inputs from a world "out there," and which mediates his or her behavior and relation with that world. Rather, cognition is understood in terms of an embodied, epistemologically *active,* agent embedded directly in interaction *with* and *within* the world; "People act and understand through their bodies acting in the world, not through a disembodied mind or brain" (Fischer & Bidell, 2006, p. 316). Such an agent is epistemologically active because his or her actions are not indirectly mediated by knowledge that takes the form of representations. Instead, the agent knows the world in terms of the actions that he or she can exercise upon it; knowledge is inherent in developing interactive skills. Thus, it is to be able functionally to relate to the world to achieve a given goal.

One example of the difference between representational and action-based approaches to cognition indicates why embodiment is sometimes viewed with perplexity. It is how we as adults tend to assume that objects intrinsically possess certain attributes by which we designate them as targets for the exercise of particular skills. Consider a child's toy ball: We typically think of such an object as possessing attributes or properties that match our representations of objects that can be thrown, kicked, bounced, or rolled. Consequently, if our representation of an object possesses an attribute that allows us to throw it, then our representation affords us the opportunity actually to pick it up and engage in our throwing skills. In an action-based approach to cognition this notion is reversed. We delineate objects in our environment precisely because those very attributes were first constructed through the practical interactions we have had with them. That is, our skills actually codetermine the very properties of those objects. Knowledge is constructed through interaction in order to achieve a given goal, which itself is the product of such interaction. For an infant a toy ball has none of the aforementioned attributes. Rather, by interacting with the ball, infants learn the skill of "rolling a ball." This skill is usually learned and practiced in interaction with others. Repeated experience allows infants to know that a ball is something that can be rolled; that is, we ascribe to objects the attributes they have because of functional outcomes of our skilled interaction with those objects. The final outcome of our skillful interaction with the world is then perceived as pregiven and apparently calling for such forms of interaction in the first place.

How then does an embodied action-based view of the mind lead to a greater understanding of children's developing social knowledge? Although infants begin life with no clear distinction between the physical world and the people who surround them, the experience they have of interacting with objects is very different from that of interacting with people. Piaget focused on how infants develop knowledge of the physical world, and he only made occasional remarks about the development of personal, social, or affective schemes (Piaget, 1945/1962, p. 207). In this chapter we extend an action-based approach to children's construction of social knowledge.

Social Skills

With respect to how children develop an understanding of the social world, we propose that such development may be profitably conceptualized in terms of social skills. Broadly defined, a skill is a "constantly adapting, regulated activity structure" that is context-specific (Fischer & Bidell, 2006, p. 322). Social skills are those abilities that individuals manifest as they come to coordinate their activities with those of others. We emphasize that they are rooted in activity and consist of the practical abilities that children come to develop in particular types of situations and social contexts. Early social skills are exemplified in infants' actions as they engage in particular forms of interaction such as following pointing gestures, directing others' attention by pointing, giving objects, and gaze following. These forms of interactions, and others falling under the umbrella term *joint attention behaviors*, necessarily involve knowledge of other people. It is this practical knowledge, manifested directly in action, which defines social skills and permits successful interaction with others in particular situations. With continued development, children gradually combine these basic skills at coordinating attention in increasingly complex and various ways. It is from the resulting set of skills developed through this process that recent theorists have abstracted and referred to as children's "theory of mind."

The choice of the everyday language term *skill* affords a number of theoretical and conceptual advantages (Fischer, 1980). Skills undergo development; people train, improve, and refine their performance on individual activities. Moreover, such development is understood to be a gradual process, with varying degrees of proficiency observed between people throughout the process. Skills are abilities (rather than capacities which are innate) that are constructed by individuals in which they coordinate various resources (e.g., biological, neurological, sociocultural) in context-specific patterns of actions to achieve a specific goal (Fischer, 1980; Fischer & Bidell, 2006). In contrast to explicit theoretical knowledge (e.g., a "theory of mind"), skills are practical, atheoretical, goal-directed, and develop in context through practice. Social skills, therefore, necessarily develop through practice within particular social environments they are meant to engage. They cannot exist prior to social interaction, for they only make sense within social contexts. Finally, they are applicable across contexts occurring within domain-specific areas (Fischer, 1980; Fischer & Bidell, 2006). Hence, the skills an infant learns through interaction with his or her parents are applicable to other persons as well. For these reasons, social knowledge can be conceptualized as the gradual development of social skills, which children manifest with varying degrees of proficiency in their actions with others, and which are contextually relevant for particular social activities.

A gradual, piecemeal view of development follows from an action-based approach to social understanding and the notion of skills. There are various forms of evidence supporting this gradual view of social development (Carpendale & Lewis, 2004, 2006), including a microgenetic study of the development of false belief understanding that shows fluctuating task performance and no sudden insight (Amsterlaw & Wellman, 2006). This view contrasts with the more common, and we argue misleading, view of development whereby children develop a "theory of mind" and show a qualitative shift in social understanding. Such a shift is argued for in the interpretation Wellman, Cross, and Watson (2001) provide for their meta-analysis of almost 600 conditions using false belief tasks. These tasks gained a foothold in the literature precisely because they appeared to represent an indicator that children acquire a representational view of both mind and knowledge. As we have argued, one of the strengths of the concept of skill is that it does not commit us to the presence–absence dichotomy inherent within the representational view of knowledge. If the research question in the theory of mind field is in fact an artifact of the representational view of knowledge, then such a qualitative shift in understanding is equally an artifact resulting from the representational view in an attempt to answer that question. We contend that this is one of the key reasons why progress in understanding the development of children's social understanding has been theoretically hampered: Both the research question and the proposed answer of a qualitative shift find their origin in an untenable empiricist view of knowledge. As such, the empiricist view becomes self-fulfilling, with the result that no empirical finding lies beyond the scope of its interpretative framework. The qualitative shift, which is so central to the "theory of mind" literature, may simply show that children get better at this task in the course of their fourth year, a stage when most areas of psychological functioning improve (Scholl & Leslie, 2001). When viewed from a social skills perspective, shifts in development are regarded in terms of the improvement and coordination of skills rather than as the acquisition of a sudden insight into the workings of the mind.

The term *skill* can also clarify the issue of internalization in development. The notion of internalization is common but the associated assumptions are rarely explicated, resulting in the view that knowledge can be passively transmitted. From our perspective, social skills, like all skills, only develop through individual practice within the context of their application, specifically in this case social interaction. They cannot involve a simple process of cultural assimilation. Other persons may facilitate the process of skill acquisition by modifying the environmental context, or decomposing the skill into elementary units. However, facilitators cannot transmit this to another person, nor can that person internalize such a skill. Rather, children come to master skills (Wertsch, 1993). We do not internalize interactions; rather, we develop the ability to engage in and maintain those interactions, although the cultural contexts in which a skill develops may texture its expression (Fischer & Bidell, 2006). Such a conceptual position helps overcome the theoretical incommensurability existing between individualistic and socially oriented views of children's development of social understanding.

As an analogy of how children develop social skills within social interaction, yet without the former being constituted by the latter, consider what is presupposed in developing the ability to play tennis. One can only cultivate this skill while playing; practicing in the batting cage may improve one's swing, but tennis, by its very nature, is interactive. For this reason, it can only be learned in interaction with another player. Moreover, the skill developed only makes sense in the context of the environmental conditions necessary for a game to occur; without an opponent to play against, such a skill may be of little value. Conversely, the skills that individuals exercise simultaneously codefine the environments they experience. Unless two people each possess a rudiment of skill for playing tennis, a game cannot occur, because they simultaneously codefine the environment. It is the skills of two people that permit them to continue the joint interactive environment known as a tennis match. We do not talk about internalizing the ability to play tennis through the process of playing with experts. Rather, we may talk about improving particular skills and becoming a better player.

As just illustrated, there is a bidirectional relation between skills and the environments in which they are exercised by individuals. It is this very matter of bidirectionality that resolves the dilemma erected by the representational view of the mind and knowledge. By enabling individuals to interact with the environment surrounding them, skills consequently enable individuals to have knowledge of that very environment in terms of the potential outcomes they can achieve by exercising them in that environment (Bickhard & Terveen, 1995). More simply stated: "When all one has is a hammer, everything starts looking like a nail." That is, one's skills enact, disclose, or bring forth, one's environment-as-skill-domain (Maturana & Varela, 1987; Varela, Thompson, & Rosch, 1991). We distinguish objects from the greater environmental background because it is our skills that define them as meaningful and important to us. In contrast to the representational view of knowledge, one does not have representations that correspond with an environment out there that is independent of our interaction with it. Rather, one knows an environment in terms of how to act to get it to produce specific and anticipated results, not what an environment is like in and of itself, existing objectively and independently of oneself. Concurrently, the demands of the environment impose a selection pressure that constrains what actions will ultimately lead to successful interaction (Bickhard & Terveen, 1995). The environment, by placing demands on individuals, does not specify which actions will come to constitute a successful interaction, but only "triggers" their development (Maturana & Varela, 1987, p. 75). However, whatever actions lead to successful interactions are so in relation to the individual, not the environment out there. In this manner, knowledge achieved by skill formation bridges the Cartesian gulf between the objective and subjective. One knows the world in terms of potential interactions that can be exercised on it, and that knowledge-as-interactive-potential is directly related to that external world, as the external world codetermines what skills could ultimately be developed. In this way, the supposedly objective and representational forms of knowledge "about" the world are factored into the very structure of a skill, although they can never be said to be actually represented. Rather they can only be accounted for because what is ultimately known about the world is the potential outcomes one can produce in the environment through skillful interaction. In such a view, the objective demands of the environment do not need to be cognitively computed by any rules, algorithms, or theories, as is assumed from a representational perspective, and which is evidenced in the "theory of mind" literature. Instead, such computations have been "off-loaded onto the environment" (Wilson, 2002) because the demands of the environment are already intrinsically accommodated within the codetermination of a skill's structure.

Learning to walk is an example of how a knowledge-as-interactive-potential manifests itself in terms of skill, because in this case it is clear that representational thought or insight cannot play a causal role. This skill is the result of practice. To achieve the goal of walking, children must coordinate the various resources they have at their disposal, such as balance, muscle coordination, patterns of actions, within the constraints of the environment. At first they stand up, take a step, and then fall down. With continued practice, children learn to walk for longer periods of time. Through the gradual coordination of all of these resources they construct the skill. However, walking has no meaning independent of the physical environment because it is the result of the interaction between children *and* the environment. The environment places constraints and demands upon their activity. To walk successfully they must balance themselves against both the forces of gravity and any unevenness in the terrain. If children grew up on a space station with zero gravity, such constraints would be absent. Yet, without those environmental constraints, a goal such as walking would not be meaningful. Perhaps children on a space station would learn to move about by pushing off from the walls. Moreover, such walls might never be understood as something one could potentially walk upon. Conversely, though, walking is codefined by having legs. For a snake, walking could never make any possible sense. The skill of walking then is the embodied, interactive, outcome of children coordinating their resources with the demands of the environment.

It is possible to abstract two components of skills. On the one hand, they are the coordination of the individual's resources, and on the other hand, they are contingent upon the demands of the environment. These two components are interdependent. For instance, the working of legs within a gravitational field allows for the coordination we know as walking. Without either legs or gravity, this skill could not exist. Indeed researchers within a dynamic systems perspective have shown that infants demonstrate walking movements soon after birth, but these seem to disappear when their increased weight prevents such actions and reappear when the infant is, for example, partly submerged in water (Thelen & Smith 1994).

It is because of the fact that the coordination of our resources is *directly contingent* upon the world, via our embodied condition, that such coordination manifests direct and unmediated knowledge of the world. A representational mind, contemplating the representations that mediate its relation with the world, would lack such a direct connection with the world and could, therefore, only make inferences about the world. As previously discussed, this is the traditional framing of the "theory of mind" research program. The ability of individuals to achieve their goals through the coordination of their resources with the contingencies of the environment is the defining characteristic of a skill. Such coordination may be called learning, and later when directly reflected upon may be called explicit knowledge. That is, our explicit knowledge finds its origin in our embodied, skillful, interaction with the world.

SKILLS DEVELOP IN A SOCIAL ENVIRONMENT

Having provided a framework of what a skills approach to development might look like, and the many ways in which it contrasts with the representational view of knowledge, it is vital to consider how such skills develop. Unlike the physical world, the social environment affords new interactive potentials so that social interaction and social knowledge necessarily emerge together.

From the moment of birth, infants are embedded in a social world (Richards, 1974). They are necessarily cared for by their parents and other caregivers. Although this statement is true from the perspective of an observer (Hobson, 2002/2004; Piaget, 1977/1995), it does not as yet capture the social environment from the perspective of infants who are still learning how to enact, or bring forth such an environment by way of their slowly changing social skills. Thus, what needs to be explained is how infants actually begin to engage with others as social beings, rather than physical objects. It is to this end that the remainder of this chapter is focused.

At first newborns lack sufficient skills to interact with, or differentiate out, the social sphere from the greater environmental context. Initially this process of differentiating is driven by the parents who fit in their interaction bids around their babies' spontaneous gestures (Stern, 1977), or act as a "biological echo" (Hopkins, 1983). For infants, parents easily constitute the most demanding interactive element of the sociophysical environment. In Baldwin's (1906) discussion of the difference between the child's experience of persons and things he writes that things have a "stay-putness" whereas "persons are actually intrusive; they go off like guns on the stage of his panorama of experience; they rise and smite him when he least expects it; and his reactions to them are about equally divided between surprised gratifications and equally surprised disappointments" (p. 60). People, unlike objects, are dynamic and come to comprise a separate environment with which infants must learn to interact if they wish to attain certain outcomes. For the infant, parents *are* the social environment; they are not simply *in* the social environment. By placing interactive demands upon infants, parents are epistemologically no different from any other environment in which infants develop relational, interactive skills. The development of social skills, therefore, brings forth the social environment.

This notion of parents and other caregivers forming the infant's social environment represents a departure from the misunderstanding that social development is simply an unfolding of an individual's skills, which research in the 1970s worked so hard to dispel (e.g., Newson & Newson, 1975; Schaffer, 1977). Under an action-based approach, people, as social environments, offer infants an opportunity for the development of skills as does the physical world. Of course infants also provide an environment for parents to operate in (Sameroff & Chandler,

1975). Skills, having a dual component, accord both to environmental demands, and the resources of the individual. To interact with their caregivers, infants must construct skills that accord to the behaviors (i.e., environmental demands) of those people. Yet, parents themselves exercise relational skills that they manifest in their own behavior. Consequently, infants come to develop social skills in response to those of their parents. Moreover, both parents and infants share the same collection of human resources, owing to their shared mutual condition of human embodiment. Given this identity of resources, infants inevitably come to construct social skills which are reciprocal to those of their parents. That is, as the social skills of the parents behaviorally manifest themselves to infants as a social environment, the social skills infants develop to interact with that environment will necessarily complement the same set of skills that originally created that very environment. Through embodied interaction with their parents, in the context of daily social practices, such as bathing, feeding, and play, infants come to develop skills that match and coordinate with those of their parents.

This development of reciprocal skill sets between parents and infants enables the latter to construct the self–other distinction. The psychological construct of self is itself another skill that infants construct through interaction. However, the development of the self–other distinction does not occur as a single transitional event. Through daily interaction with their parents, infants gradually reach a position whereby prior coordinations themselves begin to be coordinated (Fischer & Bidell, 2006). This metacoordination, the management of skills, constitutes the first sense of self for the infant. Similarly, owing to an identical construction in their parents (i.e., environmental demand), infants are able to enact, or bring forth, their parents as other through the application of their new skill of self (Carpendale & Lewis, 2006, ch. 4; Carpendale, Lewis, Müller, & Racine, 2005).

Studies of the self have often suggested that infants gain a sense of self at about 15 to 20 months when they appear to realize that a mirror shows a reflection of themselves—they touch their own face when they see a smear of rouge which has surreptitiously been put there (Lewis & Brooks-Gunn, 1979). Although such milestones are of interest there is no a priori reason why the ability needed to perform such a task emerges suddenly and needs to be described in terms of the acquisition of a single and fundamental capacity to distinguish self from other. They might be the culmination of a complexity of different skills, which commonly coalesce at approximately the same age in children. We contend that the ability to interact with another and become aware of the self in such interactions must be the product of the child's history of such interactions. This is a view that has been dominant in large areas outside the theory of mind tradition, notably attachment theory (Bowlby, 1969), but also in perspectives established in opposition to the theory of mind tradition (Reddy, 2003). This view of skills being coordinated and combined is very much in keeping with Piaget's view of "reciprocal assimilation" (Piaget, 1936/1963, e.g., pp. 106, 120–121, 230–231). Through the continuation of this process, infants thereby continue to build more complex social skills upon earlier and more rudimentary practical skills of interaction (e.g., joint attention, gaze following, etc.), and thereby come to develop more complete knowledge of the social world.

The piecemeal and gradual view of development that follows from our approach contrasts with the way that Carpenter, Nagell, and Tomasello (1998) interpret their longitudinal study of infant social development. They assessed 24 infants monthly from 9 to 15 months of age and reported that various measures of joint attention such as gaze following, point following, and the use of imperative and declarative gestures all emerge at about the same time, suggesting that the development of an underlying insight is responsible for their co-occurrence. However, in a cross-sectional study of 60 infants between 8 and 14 months of age no correlations were found between the following joint attention behaviors: gaze following, social referencing, and imitation (Slaughter & McConnell, 2003). One point to note about Carpenter et al.'s study is that they assessed an age of emergence for each of the joint attention behaviors. We would be cautious about this interpretation because it does not allow for the possibility that such skills gradually improve.

LANGUAGE AS SKILL

Beyond infancy, children's interaction within the social world increasingly occurs through the use of language. As previously stated, advanced forms of skill develop and build upon more rudimentary basic level skills (Fischer & Bidell, 2006). The capacity for joint attention provides infants with further knowledge of the social environment in terms of expectations of interactive potentials. This serves as the foundation upon which language development comes to be based. However, these rudimentary social skills are still practical in their application; they are not yet reflective. Infants are able to manifest their social knowledge in interaction, but they cannot reflect on this social knowledge that they manifest, and which is inherent within the structure of their social interactions by which they engage the social world.

The question is, then, with respect to false belief understanding and other forms of social understanding, how is it that infants come to make the transition from this practical, lived knowledge, or skill of engaging with others, to a reflective social understanding that allows them to talk about the psychological world and pass false belief tests? The key to accounting for this transition is language. However, to explicate fully how this occurs, it is first necessary to examine the nature of language, and how its traditional conceptualization has been influenced by the representational view of knowledge.

The common approach to understanding language has been described as a code model (Turnbull, 2003), which makes the same assumptions as the representational view discussed at the start of the chapter. According to the code model, language works by encoding meaning into words that are then transmitted to others, who in turn decode those words to recover the intended meaning. Words, therefore, are viewed as linguistic representations that stand in for explicit mental representations (Campbell & Bickhard, 1986). At its core, the code model of language is the inevitable result of applying the representational view of knowledge to language; it is how one private, publicly inaccessible mind transmits ideas to another private, publicly inaccessible mind. For this reason, the code model of language suffers from the same problems previously discussed with the representational view of knowledge. Specifically, if language takes the form of a correspondence, a match, between words and a private, hidden mental representation, then there is no way to determine the accuracy or truth value of such a match (for further critique of the code model; see Turnbull, 2003).

Consider for a moment an example provided by Quine (1960). Suppose a linguist visiting another country does not speak the language. On an outing with one of the locals they both observe a rabbit scurrying by. In response the local says "Gavagai." What is the linguist to make of this cryptic utterance? More specifically, what mental representation is the linguist to match up with this word? Does such an utterance mean "rabbit," "pest," "good omen," "lunch," or maybe "bad luck"? There is nothing intrinsic to the word that informs someone if the word even stands in for a mental representation. For all the linguist knows, his local guide may have sneezed in midsentence or, worse, misused the word. That is, the truth value regarding the correct or incorrect usage of the word cannot be determined because the linguist does not have epistemic access to the private mental world of the local language speaker. As a consequence, given the epistemology underlying the code model of language, it becomes evident that no language speaker could ever learn language in this fashion, nor can language even function in such a manner.

In keeping with an action-based approach to cognition, language is not viewed as a representational means to communicate mental concepts. Instead, it is described as an activity itself, with the meaning of words determined by their interactive usage and indexical location within a sequence of social interaction (Budwig, 2000; Budwig, Wertsch, & Uzgiris, 2000; Turnbull, 2003). Specifically, meaning is based upon circumstances of shared understanding, achieved by the coordination of complementary skills. To the extent that two individuals share social practices in which they both have developed a skill set in response to the environmental demands imposed by the other, do they mutually understand each other, even if only on a lived, practical level (Maturana & Varela, 1987).

Think about the everyday event, for instance, in which two people attempt to get through the same doorway. There is that awkward moment when the two people are engaging in a practical, embodied, nonreflective, interaction in which they attempt to negotiate who should go through the doorway first. Both go forward, both stop and fall back, one person waits and without a response from the other person proceeds to enter the doorway, only to have the other person attempt the same action, both in turn then fall back, and so on. This example demonstrates how both individuals are coordinating complementary skills, in that although neither has said a word, both modify their actions to fit with the other's, and each in turn understands what the other's actions mean. Such occurrences do not last long, however, with both persons quickly reaching a coordination of actions, resulting in both eventually getting through the doorway. Neither person needs to make mental inferences on a reflective level as to what the other person's actions mean, although the coordination of action could be described in this way. Rather, on the basis of a history of embodied interaction with others, both people in this situation understand the actions of the other person on a nonverbal, practical level. Without the shared embodied practice of physically bumping into people in doorways, both persons would not share, or *embody*, the same meanings as to what their physical actions mean.

From this example, it can be seen that at its fundamental level, shared meaning is the result of the interactive usage of actions. This is to be understood in the way that one uses a tool to interact with the environment. A hammer has meaning for us to the degree that it can be used to transform the environment, such as hammering in nails. Similarly, words have the meanings they do because of the things one can do with them to transform the social environment enacted by one's social skills, such as doing things together with other people to achieve a shared goal. On this view, language is an abstraction from more rudimentary social skills that permit interaction between people.

Words attain their meaning because they co-occur and are based upon these prior social skills (Racine & Carpendale, in press-a). The word *look*, for instance, may be rooted in joint attention and declarative pointing. By their co-occurrence within a dyadic relation, the word becomes a new social skill that infants can use to transform the social world, specifically, to direct the attention of others. But without the prior social skill developed through the shared practice of declarative pointing, which both parents and infants embody, such a new skill could not occur. But words can be used in many different forms of interaction to convey different meaning, and "look" is no exception. To illustrate this consider a study by Maridaki-Kassotaki, Lewis, and Freeman (2003) capitalizing upon the fact that in Greek there are two competing words for the verb to *look*. One, *kitazo*, is used with young children to engage in seeing, as in "Look!" The other, *psahno*, usually refers to the act of looking when searching. When questioned about which verb they would use when talking about someone acting on a false belief, parents said they would use *psahno*. However, Maridaki-Kassotaki et al. found that even 5-year-olds struggled with the false belief task when this verb was used, but 3-year-olds sailed through when *kitazo* was used, even though both verbs take the same complement "for" (*na vro*). These contrasting findings suggest that the child's understanding of such psychological terms is rooted within their interactions involving the use of such terms: the question with *kitazo* alerts the listener to the act of Maxi's "looking" and the need to identify Maxi's perspective on events is thus accessible.

As another analogy of words as interactive usage, suppose, for instance, that one was camping and needed to drive in tent pegs but had no hammer on hand. To resolve this problem one simply picks up a flat rock and proceeds to pound the tent pegs into the ground. In this instance the meaning of the rock is that of a hammer, owing to the functional usage to which one puts it in order to transform the environment. If the meaning of the rock was not the result of the potential functional interactive outcomes one could produce, then all the possible meanings and consequential uses of the rock would have to be mentally bound to one's mental representation of "rock." That is, from the representational perspective we would require representations for rock-as-rock, rock-as-paperweight, rock-as-doorstop, rock-as-ornament, or rock-as-projectile.

Such a position immediately produces what has been termed the "frame problem" of mental representations, or a "frame of reference problem" (Bickhard, 2001). Given the infinite uses one could potentially make of a rock, if the representational view of knowledge is to be maintained, then one would require an infinite number of representations to account for all of the potential uses one could make of a rock. The problem with this lies in the fact that we can use rocks in novel situations that we have never before encountered, yet if this is the case then where did the requisite mental representations needed to guide our actions come from? This problem arises from the representational view of the mind but it does not occur for a constructivist, action based view of knowledge.

Notice that all the uses one can make of a rock result from the actions, or skills, that one can exercise upon it in a specific environment, such as driving in tent pegs. That is, usage is context dependent and indexical to the interactive sequence of actions occurring in that context (the environment). One would not understand the usage of rock-as-hammer unless the environment supported the exercise of such a skill. By extension of this analogy, language is the usage of words that produce socially interactive outcomes, dependent upon the location in the sequence of social interaction in which they are used. It must be stated, however, that the particular usage language is put to is guided by the potential socially interactive outcomes it can produce, and it is those outcomes that ultimately give words their meaning; *not* the other way around, with some predefined meaning linked to words thereby enabling them to produce those social outcomes; "Language is an ongoing process that only exists in languaging, not as isolated items of behavior [i.e., words]" (Maturana & Varela, 1987, p. 210). It is this ability to use language indexically within a sequence of interaction, rooted in social practices and skills, which grants language its flexibility. This is why, given an appropriate context, insults can be a form of endearment, and in another context, politeness can be insulting.

With the acquisition of language, children's social skill development continues through their social and linguistic interaction with others. Through a process of continuous coordination of new and prior skills (i.e., coordinations themselves) children continue to increase their ability successfully to interact with the social world. Language use, as simply a more complex form of activity, allows children the opportunity for increasingly complex forms of interaction. Although initially its use is built upon prior interactive social skills, with continued development language itself begins to constitute another resource available to children for their use in social coordinations. This allows children simultaneously to develop conceptual knowledge as they learn how to use words that pertain to the embodiment of those concepts as practical skills. The development of conceptual knowledge via language allows children self-reflectively to contemplate at a new level what was previously a practical and nonverbal form of knowledge. From this point on, the process of acquiring advanced social skills is inseparable from the process of learning how to use language (Carpendale, Lewis, Susswein, & Lunn, in press).

FORMS OF INTERACTION: HUMAN INFANTS AND CHIMPANZEES

If social development and language acquisition are as intimately connected as claimed, then does such a position entail cultural relativism? That is, given the multiplicity of natural languages and culturally specific social practices around the world, would not each culture develop its own unique and idiosyncratic form of social knowledge? The action-based approach presented so far would indeed acknowledge that at higher levels of abstraction such cross-cultural differences may become more apparent. Yet, given the human form of embodiment and environmental regularities across the world, such as caring for infants, physiological needs for shelter and food, or coordination of group activity to achieve goals, human beings across the world will universally share a common and uniquely human form of interaction with both the world and each other. At the same time there are biological differences between species and these permit us access to uniquely human forms of knowledge, not available to other species. Of course, the same holds for those species with respect to us, but early nonverbal forms of communication form the basis of later language and the acquisition of mental state terms which refer to the mind.

If, as proposed, the commonality of the human condition allows human beings inevitably to develop a unique and specifically human form of social understanding, how then does such a view fit with recent work on the social understanding of primates, and chimpanzees in particular? As stated, social skills develop through a bidirectional coordination of an organism's resources with its environment. Therefore, on these two counts humans differ from chimpanzees. One difference is that human infants are born helpless, relative to chimpanzee newborns, and must therefore receive more and different care by parents (Portmann, 1944/1990). This results in an environmental problem space that is specific to humans, but not chimpanzees. Owing to the extended length of helplessness that human infants experience, the inevitable result is that human infants are faced with the necessity of learning to make requests (Carpendale et al., 2005). For chimpanzees though, the need to make requests does not arise in quite the same way owing to the chimpanzee infant's relative autonomy. Although young chimpanzees do develop some forms of requests (Tomasello & Camaioni, 1997), those in the wild fail to make triadic pointing gestures. However, when cared for in captivity, with the resulting decrease in autonomy and different environmental demands that this entails, chimpanzees in fact have been observed to use pointing gestures to make requests (Leavens, Hopkins, & Thomas, 2004). Such individuals must develop new social skills to interact effectively in their new environment, such as pointing to make requests (Racine & Carpendale, in press-a).

Yet another form of interaction that seems to be uniquely human, and which is not observed in young chimpanzees, is sharing attention with others. Young chimpanzees do not seem to be interested in sharing with others what they are paying attention to; that is, showing objects or toys (Tomasello & Carpenter, 2005). However, this is a ubiquitous occurrence in human parent–infant dyads (Carpenter et al., 1998). Even young chimpanzees who have been mostly raised by humans still do not understand cooperative interaction, which is a common human form of interaction, but they are better at understanding competitive interaction (Tomasello & Carpenter, 2005). What then are the personal resources or environmental differences between humans and chimpanzees that account for this observed difference? Specifically, what preconditions are needed to develop the shared practices of joint attention?

Many biological adaptations may be required, but chief among them would undoubtedly be a predisposition to find the interactive outcomes of joint engagement intrinsically rewarding. However, this does not necessarily imply the existence of a social gene, for clearly there are many social species. What this means instead is that in the event that joint engagement occurs, human infants find the emotional outcome produced by this joint interaction enjoyable. This does not imply that enjoyment of joint interaction is genetically encoded; only that human infants are genetically predisposed to find certain emotional outcomes enjoyable. Similarly, infants display a preference for sweet tastes, but this does not imply that they have a genetic preference for candy. It must also be noted that children with autism, although being confronted with the same environmental demands as normally developing infants, do not appear to be as interested in engaging with others (Hobson, 2002/2004). The autism-like symptoms displayed by many of the children raised in Romanian orphanages shows that environmental factors can account equally for deficits in social skills (Hobson, 2002/2004). As stated before, social skills result from the coordination of the individual's resources with the demands of the environment.

TALK ABOUT THE PSYCHOLOGICAL WORLD

Having provided a theoretical framework for an action-based approach to mind, conceptualized with respect to the ordinary language term *skill*, this chapter arrives back where it started. If mental state concepts, such as talk about beliefs, desires, and intentions, are not representational mental states, then what role do they play in children's social understanding? As discussed, children first acquire social skills in the context of early dyadic relationships with their parents. Concurrently, however, children are similarly developing skills to interact with the physical world. As such, two epistemological streams of development may be conceptualized as occurring: one social, the other physical. Chapman (1991) discussed the triadic interaction resulting in the convergence of these two streams in terms of an "epistemic triangle," in which it is held that any understanding of an object of knowledge is mediated through interactions between members of a culture. Throughout this chapter we have been discussing the development of triadic interaction. In triadic interactions the child and adult who previously interacted dyadically, now coordinate their actions together with respect to a facet of the physical world. By definition, within triadic interactions, people coordinate attention with another person within social interaction toward an aspect of the world.

Within triadic interaction, the use of psychological language referring to intentions, beliefs, and desires allows children to conceptualize the epistemic relation that results from the exercise of various skills performed with another person in relation to both the physical and social environments, and to share that understanding with other people. Words referring to the psychological world do not gain their meaning by referring to hidden inner mental entities (i.e., representations). Instead young children use these words as tools to accomplish outcomes in triadic interactions of shared understanding. Thus, children come to do things like state their intentions, or deny that they did something on purpose, or ask for permission, but these are not reports of inner states. Rather, the usage of these mental state terms allows children to coordinate their skills, both for the social and physical environments, to achieve a given goal with another person. When children say that they want some juice, this is not to say that they are reporting upon an inner mental state of desire and an inner representation of a glass of juice. Instead what children are doing is skillfully using the word *want* to coordinate their activity with that of their parents to achieve a potential interactive outcome of having something to drink. The use of psychological language is the way in which we go about coordinating our actions with those of others. The gradual means by which children begin using psychological language in various ways in the process of coordinating their interaction with others is nicely charted in Budwig's (2002) longitudinal study of young children and their parents' use of the term *want*.

Once children are able to talk about the psychological world, the next step in their development is to be able to talk about the psychological world in the absence of another person being present to respond to them. That is, they can talk as if they were addressing another person, and later they can imagine another person's response. In short, they can now talk to themselves, as if they were addressing someone else. This egocentric speech (Piaget, 1923/1959; Vygotsky, 1934/1986) reveals reflective understanding because children can now begin to anticipate another's response, and in this sense take the role of another person. This becomes most explicit with language, but given that we assume that this is derived from earlier forms of shared interaction, some forms of reflection may be possible before the use of words.

From the action-based approach outlined here, this ability involves neither the internalization of dialogue, nor the internalization of another person into the mind of the child. Rather, egocentric speech is the consequence of the continuation of skill development. Specifically, it occurs when skills begin to become coordinated, creating instances of recursion, and by extension self-reflection (Campbell & Bickhard, 1986). That is, a given set of skills can become the environmental context upon which other new constructed skills operate. In this sense, children can be said to have internalized dialogue with others, and in a way this is metaphorically correct. If it were not for the development of a prior repertoire of triadic interaction with others, those skills in turn would not be available to act as a new environmental context for the exercise of the newly emerging self-reflection. More accurately, however, the interlocutor who participates with a child in triadic interactions is never even metaphorically internalized within the cognition of the child. Rather, knowledge of the interlocutor has always been present in a practical, nonverbal form, and therefore, inherent in the very actions that manifest the child's triadic skills. Only later, when they are able to use language in place of, and to reflect on, this practical knowledge of the interlocutor, do children begin to engage in egocentric speech.

Once children begin to engage in egocentric speech, things quickly become more complex, as they can now make use of language to talk about past and future events. The reason for this is that to speak of temporal events one needs to be able to talk about the self or someone else (i.e., the "internalized" interlocutor) at some moment in time. This in turn allows for the understanding of simple situations of joint attention in which the question of whether or not others are attending to a situation is fairly obvious, to be extended to more complex situations involving whether or not someone attended to something in the past (e.g., did Maxi see the chocolate being moved). It is finally at this point in development, once all the prerequisite skills have been developed, that children can correctly answer questions of false belief. Children now begin to understand words such as *look*, *think*, and *know* in terms of actual and potential interactions involving self, others, and the world. This, in turn, allows for further development of a more complex understanding of the social, emotional, and moral world.

CONCLUSION

In this chapter we have outlined the representational view of the mind, according to which knowledge consists of the possession of mental representations that correspond to, or match, aspects of the world. We have argued that if knowledge were to take the form of mental representations then we would never be able to compare such representations against the world to check upon their accuracy. At best, such representations could only be compared against other representations, at which point they could no longer be said to be "about" the world. Thus, the representational view of knowledge is incapable of accounting for the development of knowledge. Similarly, the problems with the representational view of knowledge are necessarily shared with, and underlie, the commonly held representational theory of mind. These problems, therefore, carry over into the theory and research on children's social cognitive development.

As an alternative we have proposed an action based approach to the development of social understanding, according to which knowledge consists of understanding the potential opportunities for interaction with the world; that is, we know the world in terms of what we can do with it. Expanding upon this action-based view of knowledge, we have attempted to demonstrate the potential productivity of framing a "theory of mind" or social understanding in terms of social skills that develop within the child's interaction with others. For instance, we suggest that evidence of early social understanding, such as pointing gestures, should be understood in terms of social skills that emerge within particular activities with others, rather than as actions driven by mental representations. Similarly, early theory of mind competencies assessed through task variations can be conceptualized as assessments of subcomponent skills that are likely to underlie success on more traditional tasks. Moreover, as social skills build upon each other and become coordinated, a developmental sequence in social understanding can be elucidated. The forms of interaction that we are describing in terms of social skills are situations in which children and adults share understanding, and this is the basis for language. Words can be added to such shared practices and language then makes more complex forms of social understanding possible. Theoretical advantages such as these, and others, cannot be secured in any framework that continues to conceptualize social understanding in terms of representational knowledge.

References

Amsterlaw, J., & Wellman, H. M. (2006). Theories of mind in transition: A microgenetic study of the development of false belief understanding. *Journal of Cognition and Development, 7,* 139–172.

Baldwin, J. M. (1906). *Thoughts and things: Vol. 1. Functional logic.* New York: Macmillan.

Baron-Cohen, S. (1995). *Mindblindness: An essay on autism and theory of mind.* Cambridge, MA: MIT Press.

Bickhard, M. H. (1999). Interaction and representation. *Theory and Psychology, 9,* 435–458.

Bickhard, M. H. (2001). Why children don't have to solve the frame problems: Cognitive representations are not encodings. *Developmental Review, 21,* 224–262.

Bickhard, M. H., & Terveen, L. (1995). *Foundation issues in artificial intelligence and cognitive science: Impasse and solution.* Amsterdam: Elsevier.

Bowlby, J. (1969) *Attachment and loss: Vol 1. Attachment.* Harmondsworth: Pelican.

Brooks, R. A. (1991). Intelligence without representation. *Artificial Intelligence, 47,* 139–159.

Budwig, N. (2000). Language and the construction of the self. In N. Budwig, I. C. Uzgiris, & J. V. Wertsch (Eds.), *Communication: An arena of development* (pp. 195–214). Stamford, CT: Ablex.

Budwig, N. (2002). A developmental-functionalist approach to mental state talk. In E. Amsel & J. P. Byrnes (Eds.), *Language, literacy, and cognitive development: The development and consequences of symbolic communication* (pp. 59–86). Mahwah, NJ: Lawrence Erlbaum.

Budwig N., Wertsch, J. V., & Uzgiris, I. C. (2000). Communication, meaning, and development: Interdisciplinary perspectives. In N. Budwig, I. C. Uzgiris, & J. V. Wertsch (Eds.), *Communication: An arena of development* (pp. 1–14). Stamford, CT: Ablex.

Campbell, R. L., & Bickhard, M. H. (1986). *Knowing levels and developmental stages.* Basel, Switzerland: Karger.

Canfield, J. V. (1999). Folk psychology versus philosophical anthropology. *Idealistic Studies, 29,* 153–172.

Carpenter, M., Nagell, K., & Tomasello, M. (1998). Social cognition, joint attention, and communicative competence from 9 to 15 months of age. *Monographs of the Society for Research in Child Development, 63* (Serial No. 255).

Carpendale, J. I. M., & Lewis, C. (2004). Constructing an understanding of mind: The development of children's social understanding within social interaction. *Behavioral and Brain Sciences, 27,* 79–96.

Carpendale, J. I. M. & Lewis, C. (2006). *How children develop social understanding.* Oxford: Blackwell.

Carpendale, J. I. M., Lewis, C., Müller, U., & Racine, T. P. (2005). Constructing perspectives in the social making of minds. *Interaction Studies, 6,* 341–358.

Carpendale, J. I. M., Lewis, C., Susswein, N., & Lunn, J. (in press). Talking and thinking: The role of speech in social understanding. In A. Winsler, C. Fernyhough, & I. Montero (Eds.), *Private speech, executive function, and the development of verbal self-regulation.* Cambridge: Cambridge University Press.

Carruthers, P., & Smith, P. K. (Eds.). (1996). *Theories of theories of mind.* Cambridge: Cambridge University Press.

Chapman, M. (1991). The epistemic triangle: Operative and communicative components of cognitive development. In M. Chandler & M. Chapman (Eds.), *Criteria for competence: Controversies in the conceptualization and assessment of children's abilities* (pp. 209–228). Hillsdale, NJ: Lawrence Erlbaum.

Chapman, M. (1999). Constructivism and the problem of reality. *Journal of Applied Developmental Psychology, 20,* 31–43.

Fischer, K. W. (1980). A theory of cognitive development: The control and construction of hierarchies of skills. *Psychological Review, 87,* 477–531.

Fischer, K. W., & Bidell, T. R. (2006). Dynamic development of action, thought, and emotion. In W. Damon & R. M. Lerner (Eds.), *Handbook of child psychology: Vol. 1.Theoretical models of human development*(6th ed., , pp. 313–399). New York: Wiley.

Fodor, J. A. (1985). Fodor's guide to mental representation: The intelligent auntie's vademccum. *Mind, 94,* 76–100.

Goldberg, B. (1991). Mechanism and meaning. In J. Hyman (Ed.), *Investigating psychology: Sciences of the mind after Wittgenstein* (pp. 48–66). London: Routledge.

Harris, P. L. (1991). The work of the imagination. In A. Whiten (Ed.), *Natural theories of mind* (pp. 283–304). Oxford: Blackwell.

Heil, J. (1981). Does cognitive psychology rest on a mistake? *Mind, 90,* 321–342.

Hobson, P. (2004). *The cradle of thought: Explorations of the origins of thinking.* New York: Oxford University Press. (Original work published 2002)

Hopkins, B. (1983). The development of early non-verbal communication: An evaluation of its meaning. *Journal of Child Psychology & Psychiatry, 24,* 131–144.

Johnson, C. N. (1988). Theory of mind and the structure of conscious experience. In J. W. Astington, P. L. Harris, & D. R. Olson (Eds.), *Developing theories of mind* (pp. 47–63). New York: Cambridge University Press.

Kenny, A. (1991). The homunculus fallacy. In J. Hyman (Ed.), *Investigating psychology: Sciences of the mind after Wittgenstein* (pp. 155–165). London: Routledge.

Leavens, D. A., Hopkins, W. D., & Thomas, R. K. (2004). Referential communication by chimpanzees (*Pan troglodytes*). *Journal of Comparative Psychology, 118*, 48–57.

Leslie, A. M. (1994). Pretending and believing: Issues in the theory of ToMM. *Cognition, 50*, 211–238.

Lewis, M., & Brooks-Gunn, J. (1979). *Social cognition and the acquisition of the self.* New York: Plenum.

Maridaki-Kassotaki, K., Lewis, C., & Freeman, N. H. (2003) Lexical choice can lead to problems: What false-belief tests tell us about Greek alternative verbs of agency. *Journal of Child Language, 29*, 145–164.

Maturana, H. R., & Varela, F. J. (1987). *The tree of knowledge: The biological roots of human understanding.* Boston: Shambhala.

Mead, G. H. (1912). The mechanism of social consciousness. *The Journal of Philosophy, Psychology and Scientific Method, 9*, 401–406.

Mead, G. H. (1922). A behavioristic account of the significant symbol. *The Journal of Philosophy, 19*, 157–163.

Mead, G. H. (1934). *Mind, self and society.* Chicago: University of Chicago Press.

Mead, G. H. (1977). *George Herbert Mead on social psychology* (Anselm Strauss, Ed.). Chicago: University of Chicago Press.

McDonough, R. (1989). Towards a non-mechanistic theory of meaning. *Mind, 98*, 1–21.

McDonough, R. (1999). Bringing cognitive science back to life. *Idealistic Studies, 29*, 173–214.

Meltzoff, A. N., Gopnik, A., & Repacholi, B. M. (1999). Toddlers' understanding of intentions, desires, and emotions: Explorations of the dark ages. In P. D. Zelazo, J. W. Astington, & D. R. Olson (Eds.), *Developing theories of intention* (pp. 17–41). Mahwah, NJ: Lawrence Erlbaum.

Müller, U., Sokol, B., & Overton, W. F. (1998a). Constructivism and development: Reply to Smith's commentary. *Developmental Review, 18*, 228–236.

Newson, J., & Newson, E. (1975) Intersubjectivity and the transmission of culture. *Bulletin of the British Psychological Society, 28*, 437–446.

Overton, W. F. (1994). Contexts of meaning: The computational and the embodied mind. In W. F. Overton & D. S. Palermo (Eds.), *The nature and ontogenesis of meaning* (pp. 1–18). Hillsdale, NJ: Lawrence Erlbaum.

Perner, J. (1991). *Understanding the representational mind.* Cambridge, MA: MIT Press.

Piaget, J. (1959). *The language and thought of the child.* New York: Meridian Books. (Original work published 1923)

Piaget, J. (1962). *Play, dreams and imitation in childhood.* New York: Norton. (Original work published 1945)

Piaget, J. (1963). *The origins of intelligence in children.* New York: Norton. (Original work published 1936)

Piaget, J. (1970). *Genetic epistemology.* New York: Norton.

Piaget, J. (1995). *Sociological studies.* London: Routledge. (Original work published 1977)

Pinker, S. (1994). *The language instinct.* New York: Harper Perennial.

Portmann, A. (1990). *A zoologist looks at humankind.* New York: Columbia University Press. (original work published 1944)

Putnam, H. (1981). *Reason, truth and history.* New York: Cambridge University Press.

Putnam, H. (1988). *Representation and reality.* Cambridge, MA: MIT Press.

Quine, W. V. O. (1960). *Word and object.* Cambridge, MA: MIT Press.

Racine, T. P., & Carpendale, J. I. M. (in press-a). The embodiment of mental states. In W. F. Overton, U. Müller, & J. Newman (Eds.), *Body in mind, mind in body: Developmental perspectives on embodiment and consciousness.* Mahwah, NJ: Lawrence Erlbaum.

Racine, T. P., & Carpendale, J. I. M. (in press-b). The role of shared practice in joint attention. *British Journal of Developmental Psychology.*

Reddy, V. (2003). On being the object of attention: Implications for self-other consciousness. *Trends in Cognitive Science, 7,* 397–402.

Richards, M. P. M. (Ed.). (1974). *The integration of a child into a social world.* Cambridge: Cambridge University Press.

Russell, J. (1996). *Agency: Its role in mental development.* Hove, UK: Lawrence Erlbaum.

Sameroff, A., & Chandler, M. J. (1975). Reproductive risk and the continuum of caretaking casualty. In F. D. Horowitz, M. Hetherington, S. Scarr-Salapatek, & G. Siegel (Eds.), *Review of child development research* (Vol. 4, pp. 187–244). Chicago: University of Chicago Press.

Schaffer, H. R. (Ed.). (1977). *Studies of mother–infant interaction.* London: Academic Press.

Scholl, B. J., & Leslie, A. M. (2001). Minds, modules, and meta-analysis. *Child Development, 72,* 696–701.

Slaughter, V., & McConnell, D. (2003). Emergence of joint attention: Relationships between gaze following, social referencing, imitation, and naming in infancy. *Journal of Genetic Psychology, 164,* 54–71.

Stern, D. (1977). *The first relationship.* Cambridge, MA: Harvard University Press.

Thelen, E., & L. Smith (1994). *A dynamic systems approach to the development of cognition and action.* Cambridge, MA: MIT Press

Tomasello, M. (2003). *Constructing a language: A usage-based theory of language acquisition.* Cambridge, MA: Harvard University Press.

Tomasello, M., & Camaioni, L. (1997). A comparison of the gestural communication of apes and human infants. *Human Development, 40,* 7–24.

Tomasello, M., & Carpenter, M. (2005). *The emergence of social cognition in three young chimpanzees. Monographs of the Society for Research in Child Development, 70*(Serial No. 279).

Turnbull, W. (2003). *Language in action: Psychological models of conversation.* Hove, UK: Psychology Press.

Varela, F. J., Thompson, E., & Rosch, E. (1991). *The embodied mind: Cognitive science and human experience.* Cambridge, MA: MIT Press.

Vygotsky, L. (1986). Thought and language. Cambridge, MA: The MIT Press. (Original work published 1934)

Watson, J. S. (1972). Smiling, cooing and "the game." *Merrill Palmer Quarterly, 18,* 323–340.

Wellman, H. M., Cross, D., & Watson, J. (2001) Meta-analysis of theory of mind development: The truth about false belief. *Child Development, 72,* 655–684.

Wertsch, J. V. (1993). Commentary. *Human Development, 36,* 168–171.

Wilson, M. (2002). Six views of embodied cognition. *Psychonomic Bulletin & Review, 9*(4), 625–636.

Wittgenstein, L. (1968). *Philosophical investigations.* Oxford: Blackwell.

8

Relationships and Children's Discovery of the Mind

JUDY DUNN

My topic is the links between two domains of psychology that are usually studied quite separately: children's close relationships, and their *discovery of the mind*—Janet Astington's (1993) term for the remarkable growth in children's curiosity about and understanding of people's feelings and thoughts during the preschool years. No one who has been around children between 18 months and 3 years can fail to be impressed by the extraordinary blooming of their sophistication and their increasingly effective powers of teasing, deceiving, joking, and comforting, their skills of conciliation, of companionship in shared fantasy play, all of which reflect some understanding of what others are thinking or feeling. Increasingly during the third year their discussion of mental states explicitly reflects their understanding of mind. Each of these features illustrates how closely communicative skills and understanding of mental states are linked, and how central they are to the development of children's relationships.

However, children's understanding of mind has been chiefly studied in terms of their success in "false belief" tasks, rather than in terms of their behavior in the context of their relationships. There has been a tremendous growth of research using the false belief paradigm (1,021 papers published between 2000 and 2004 according to PsychInfo), and the meta-analysis conducted by Wellman and colleagues of 178 of the best of these studies showed that most children succeed in these tasks by 4 to 5 years of age (Wellman, Cross, & Watson, 2001).

However, naturalistic studies of children in the context of their families, or with close friends, show that their powers of comforting, teasing, deception, sharing an imaginative world, their talk about why people behave the way they do are all evident well before they successfully or reliably pass false belief tasks. The classic study by Newton and colleagues (Newton, Reddy, & Bull, 2000), in which mothers were trained to record their children's deceptive behavior, and the children were also tested with conventional false belief tasks, established three key points. First, the 3-year-old children who were studied engaged in all the different types of deception that were shown by the 4-year-olds. Second, deception was shown by children who failed the false belief tasks. Third, and most importantly for my argument here, the children's attempts to deceive were largely made in situations of emotionally charged opposition to parents.

Why should there be this discrepancy between children's early understanding that is revealed in their close relationships, and the later development of mind reading as shown in their performance on false belief tasks? A number of suggestions have been made concerning this apparent precocity of toddlers and 2- to 3-year-olds within their families in terms of understanding the other people in their world. First, it could be the familiarity of family members that is important—children have had ample opportunity to observe and anticipate how their parents and siblings behave and react. Second, it could be the significance of the particular relationship to the children—clearly more immediately important than the behavior of a puppet in a task designed by a psychologist. Third, it could be that in interactions with a parent or an older sibling, the partner "scaffolds" the interaction to support the child's understanding. And fourth, it should be noted that the observations of children in their families have provided evidence of their understanding of *emotions, motives, and intentions*, rather than their understanding of *beliefs*, and it is this understanding of beliefs that is the focus of the theory of mind/false belief tasks. All these suggestions are plausible; the key point is that it matters to children that they should understand why their family members behave the way they do—the issue is the children's motivation to understand and the emotional context of family interactions. The three themes of my argument here are that (1) the motivation to understand others is part of relationships; (2) emotion is central in relationships and a cornerstone of the early stages of understanding mind; (3) communication is central to relationships and to the growth of an understanding of mind.

Note that in considering these themes, I will be focusing on children after the first year of life. This is not to suggest that the first year is unimportant in the growth of reading minds and emotions: we know that infants are extremely sociable and interested in other people, and that joint attention with others is a cornerstone of the early stages of understanding others (Baron-Cohen, 2000; Carpendale & Lewis, 2006). The significance of the changes in infant behavior that reflect the growth of understanding others as intentional agents has been supported by a variety of research methods, which highlight the skills that emerge around 9 months (Carpenter, Nagell, & Tomasello, 1998; Rochat & Morgan, 1998;

Rochat, Morgan, & Carpenter, 1997; Tomasello, 1999). It is the early development in mind reading that takes place *after* this initial and crucial stage of understanding others that is my focus here

NORMATIVE PATTERNS

Children's motivation to understand others shows up in a host of different aspects of their behavior, of which just one example is their curiosity about others, evident in their questions about others (Dunn, 1988), in their narratives, and in their comments. A classic study of children's early causal statements and questions (Hood & Bloom, 1979) showed that it was psychological rather than physical causality that interested 2- and 3-year-olds. The children discussed motivation and intention, and there was a gradual shift from expressing causal relations in connection with their own intentions towards referring both to their own and to other people's actions and intentions (Bloom & Capatides, 1987). In our own studies the children talked about other people from 18 months on, the pattern changing during the second and third year from questions and comments focused chiefly on people's whereabouts, feelings, and actions, to an increasing interest in their feelings, perceptions, and in social rules, and during the third year, in their mental states (Dunn, 1988). The analyses of the CHILDES data set has been particularly valuable in providing longitudinal evidence from naturalistic conversations within the family on the developmental changes in children's interest in others (Bartsch & Wellman, 1995). Before we turn to these data, the issue of emotion has to be considered. We should note that from the first year through the preschool years, family life and interactions with friends are full of emotional drama. With siblings, for instance, our observational studies have shown that an average of 21% of interactions are characterized by intense negative emotions, while with mothers, 10% are intensely negative (Dunn, 1993). And this significance of emotion is clear in the CHILDES data set. Bartsch and Wellman (1995) show that children talk appropriately about certain emotional states in advance of similarly appropriate talk about cognitive states (thoughts and beliefs). This is illustrated, for instance, in the children's use of *contrastives*, when they explicitly contrast their own state with that of another person. Contrastive use of emotions—*happy, sad, afraid*—was evident by 2½ years of age, as the following example from Ross, aged 2½, illustrates:

Father: Marky's mad at your Daddy (Marky is Ross's older brother)
Ross: But I'm happy at my Dad.

Contrastive use of mental states—*think, know, remember, believe,* and *dream* only appeared later. Bartsch and Estes (1996) make an important developmental point from these and other data, when they point out that very young children explain people's actions initially in terms of feelings and desires, and through their own experiences, especially those that involve emotional issues, they come to incorporate the notion of belief in the understanding of people's actions. What is so important about this proposal is that it suggests an understanding of *cognitive* states arises from an earlier understanding of *emotional* (noncognitive) states. The work of Bartsch and her colleagues makes clear that communication, understanding of mind and relationships are closely linked in normative development. This is especially clear when we consider individual differences.

INDIVIDUAL DIFFERENCES

In every aspect of children's social understanding, and in the use they make of this understanding in their relationships, individual differences are marked. Some children are already in their second year stars at manipulating the feelings of their siblings and parents through teasing and jokes, others are less adept. Some continually ask questions about their social world, and wrestle with the puzzling replies they get, and others simply don't show such curiosity. There is no necessary connection between the factors that influence normative development and the development of these differences, though it is quite possible that influences on the one are also important for the other. While the initial studies of theory of mind were focused very much on normative development, more recently there has been a welcome increase in research that focuses on individual differences. In what follows, my concern is with this research on individual differences, and I draw in particular on five longitudinal studies we have carried out in the United States and in England (Dunn, 1988; Dunn, Brown, Slomkowski, Tesla, & Young-blade, 1991; Dunn & Cutting, 1999). Each of these studies involved naturalistic observations of children at home and with their friends, together with assessments of their social understanding using standard theory of mind tasks, emotion understanding tasks, assessments of language development, and assessments of their close relationships with interviews of children and parents.

As a starting point, consider the findings from what was one of the first studies of individual differences in theory of mind (Dunn et al., 1991). When the children in this study were 40 months old, their performance on a theory of mind assessment was examined. Individual differences in their success were marked, and exploration of factors earlier in the children's lives that were related to these differences highlighted three very different aspects of their relationships with their mothers and siblings. Forty percent of the variance in the children's success on the mindreading tasks was attributable to these three aspects of their relationships. First, children who had engaged in more frequent cooperative play with their older siblings (in particular shared pretend play) were more likely to be successful on the false belief tasks. Second, children who had participated in discourse about feelings and other minds with other family members were particularly successful, and third, children whose mothers and older siblings had engaged in frequent disputes were also more successful. These findings suggest that very different social processes within the family may be related to individual differences in the growth of mindreading abilities. More recent research has highlighted further aspects of children's social experiences: attachment quality

(Meins, Fernyhough, Russell, & Clarke-Carter, 1998); parental education (Cutting & Dunn, 1999); and attitudes (Ruffman, Perner, & Parkin, 1999; Ruffman, Slade, Devitt, & Crowe, 2006). In what follows I want to focus in particular on the aspects of communication that appear to be important in the development of the understanding of the mind.

COMMUNICATION AND UNDERSTANDING OF MIND

A wealth of research has now shown that engaging in discourse about inner states is linked to later success in understanding of mind and emotion, whether this is assessed in terms of success on theory of mind tasks, or in terms of observations of interactive behavior (Astington & Jenkins, 1995; Dunn et al., 1991; Howe, 1991; Hughes & Dunn, 1998; Meins et al., 1998). What aspects of these discourse experiences foster the growth of understanding of mind and emotion? We have begun to unpack what is happening in conversations about inner states that may foster the growth of understanding of mind, by asking the following questions: Do particular contexts foster discourse about inner states? Do these depend on the quality of the relationships between child and partner? Does the pragmatics of the discourse matter? Are the characteristics of the interlocutor important?

The Importance of Particular Contexts

A number of studies have shown that in the context of shared pretend play, children are particularly likely to engage in talk about inner states (Astington & Jenkins, 1995; Dunn & Cutting, 1999; Howe, 1991; Hughes & Dunn, 1997). A comparison of the frequency of talk about inner states in which children engaged with their mothers, their siblings, and their friends showed that it was with their friends that children participated particularly often in discussions about inner states, and this was most likely to be in the context of shared pretend narratives. As we will see, shared pretend is a core feature of early friendships (Gottman, 1983), and developing a make-believe narrative with a friend frequently involves description of why the protagonist behaves in certain ways, and what his feelings are.

Another candidate for a context that was especially rich in discussion of inner states was conversations about the past. It has been argued that engagement in narratives may well be a process through which the development of understanding of mind and emotion is influenced (Bruner & Feldman, 1993). Bruner and Feldman's proposal is that patterns of narrative scaffold the metacognition about intentions that lies at the core of theories of mind. Studies in which mother-and-child were asked to talk about different episodes such as occasions in the past when particular emotions were expressed have shown that such discourse has a high frequency of talk about the *causes of emotion*, and *mind–emotion* connections (Cleveland & Reese, 2005; Hudson, 2004). And in a study of naturally occurring narratives about the past, Brown (1995) showed that such early narratives were not emotionally neutral. Rather, it was the emotional dramas in children's lives that prompted the children to embark on telling coherent stories about the past, especially their negative emotional experiences. Compare the following two narratives from a 3-year-old; in the first, he sequences events both temporally and causally:

1. Child to sibling as he runs into the house from the garden: "I came running back 'cause I saw two snakes and I was scared so I runned back!"
2. In comparison, a happy experience was simply conveyed: Child to sibling: "I peed by myself, Ryan!"

Parallel findings are reported by Hudson and her colleagues (Hudson, Gebelt, Haviland, & Bentivegna, 1992), showing that children were more likely to use a plotted story structure and to include a discussion of cause and consequence when the story involved anger or fear than when telling happy stories. Brown (1995) also made an important point concerning the pragmatic setting in which the children marshaled their story-telling skills: talk about negative past events was most frequent when children were attempting to influence another person's behavior. This was in contrast to talk about happy or neutral events which occurred most often when children were not attempting to get the person to do something.

Negative emotions expressed by children were also the context in which mothers were especially likely to talk about feelings; in our Pennsylvania study mothers' references to feelings were twice as likely when the children were expressing distress or anger than they were when the children were happy or neutral in terms of emotional expression (Dunn, 2004).

However, before we draw conclusions about the causal significance of these patterns of association, we should face the possibility that these particular social contexts, which are especially rich in discourse about inner states, reflect the quality of the relationships between the child and interlocutor—and that what underlies the association with later understanding of mind is not the context per se, but the quality of the relationship. We know that the construction of shared fantasy with another child—the context which we know is likely to be rich in discourse about inner states—depends on the quality of the relationship between the two children. For example, close and affectionate friendships between young children are associated with shared pretend play, as are close sibling relationships (Dunn & Cutting, 1999; Dunn & Dale, 1984; Gottman, 1983). Gottman sees such shared pretend as a core feature of early friendships. Sibling relationship quality, too, is associated with shared pretend play (Dunn & Dale, 1984; Youngblade & Dunn, 1995). And studies of mother–child relationships and discourse that fosters understanding of mind have identified mind-mindedness as a key quality in mothers' talk (Meins et al., 1998). It is evident that discourse linked to later understanding of mind flourishes in certain relationships. So the causal question remains: Is it the content of the discourse that is important for later understanding of mind or the quality of the relationship in which these conversations take place?

Pragmatics of the Discourse
In a parallel way, we can ask whether the conversations that are linked to later understanding of mind are characterized by particular pragmatic qualities. That

is, are the pragmatic intentions of the speakers linked to the later understanding of mind? The answer from one study is yes. In our Pennsylvanian study we examined the correlations between mothers' causal talk and the children's emotion understanding, taking into account the pragmatic context of the conversations. The results showed that while there was a positive correlation between mothers' causal talk and children's later emotion understanding when the conversation took place in a context of shared positive interaction, when the mothers' causal talk was in a controlling context, the correlation with later emotion understanding was *negative*. So we have seen that while most studies of inner state discourse and its links to children's later understanding have focused on the *content* of the discourse, in fact there are other aspects of these conversations that may be crucial—the social context, the quality of the relationship between child and other, the pragmatics of the discourse—what each person is attempting to "get done" in the conversation. Finally we have to consider *who* the child's interlocutor is—the characteristics, personality, cognitive skills of the other person for instance. This turns out to be of real importance, and brings us back to the issue of relationships.

Are the Characteristics of the Interlocutors Important?

In our London study of young friends, we began by recruiting 120 3-year-olds, from local nursery classes and their friends. The criteria for selecting friends were those developed by Howes (1996) in her classic studies of young friends: they included observation, interviews, reports by nursery staff and by mothers. On two occasions a week apart the pairs of friends were videotaped as they played alone (without an observer present) in a room at school, with a set of dressing up clothes and toys. They were also assessed on a variety of theory of mind tasks, language development, emotion understanding, and moral development (Dunn, Cutting, & Fisher, 2002). These children were then followed up after they had made the transition to school: after they had been at school for a year, we interviewed them about their school experiences, including questions about their friends, and their moral understanding.

The key question we addressed was this: what earlier factors accounted for the individual differences in the social understanding the children showed about their friends at school, and in the quality of the friendship? Three important findings stood out from our longitudinal analyses. First, the children's own emotion understanding and their language skills as preschoolers were correlated with their later friendship quality. Second, and independently, the emotion understanding and language skills of the *preschool friend* also were correlated with the children's insight and friendship quality at school. That is, the identity and characteristics of the friends mattered, in terms of the child's later relationships. And third, of particular interest, the interactive experiences of child and friend in the preschool period were also independently correlated with the child's school age friendship (Dunn et al., 2002). The frequency of shared pretend play between child and friend, and their communicative success were correlated with the child's friendship quality 2 years later. What was particularly striking was the evidence from children who made the transition to school without their preschool friend; that is, the children who had to make new friends at primary school, because their preschool friend had been sent to a different school. The pattern of findings was clear: both the identity of their preschool friend, and the shared experience of pretend play and smooth communication with this preschool friend independently predicted the children's insight into their new friend, and their liking for this new friend. Again, the significance of the relationship framework is highlighted.

These findings provide support for Howes's (1996) speculations on the significance of early friendships. She argued that early friendships may form internal representation of relationships during the preschool period on which children draw in their subsequent relationships. What is important here is the evidence that children's conversational experiences are important not solely in terms of the development of a cognitive skill or individual characteristic, but in terms of the children's dyadic relationship experiences.

An example drawn from a very different developmental study makes a similar point. This is a program of research on the development of children rescued from Romanian institutions and adopted into UK families (Rutter & the English and Romanian Adoptees (ERA) study team, 1998; Rutter, Kreppner, & O'Connor, 2001). The design of the study makes it possible to compare the outcome of children who were rescued from the institutions at different points with a control group of UK adopted children: those rescued before 6 months, by 12 months, 24 months, and later. The children have now been followed up at 4, 6, 11, and 13 years. Two points from the rich array of findings that highlight the links between the children's early deprivation and their later development concern their friendships as 11-year-olds. First, the children who were adopted before 6 months did not differ from the control group children in terms of difficulty in making friends, whereas those who were adopted after 6 months were significantly more likely to report difficulties in their friendships. Second, the children were interviewed extensively about their friends, and the frequency of references to mental states and feelings during these interviews were coded. Again, the differences were striking: the children adopted after 6 months, and especially those adopted after 24 months, were much less likely to refer to their friends' feelings and inner states; they also were most likely to have difficulties in making friends (Kreppner, 2003). Of course such findings cannot in themselves illuminate the mechanisms underlying the associations; however, they show in especially dramatic form the significance of the deprivation of early relationships for later developments in social understanding and relations with peers.

RELATIONSHIPS AND EARLY SOCIAL UNDERSTANDING

What then are the key developmental questions we need to address? First, is early social understanding related to later relationship quality? To summarize the evidence that the answer is *yes,* consider the findings on friendship (Dunn, 2004).

The longitudinal research has shown that early mind reading skills are associated with more connected conversation between children and their friends, an interactive style which involves smoother communication in which each speaker is tuned in to the other's intentions and interests; these early skills are associated with more shared and more elaborate imaginative engagement between friends—a key feature of early friendship; they are linked to more insight into the friends' needs and feelings at later points, more skill at resolving conflict, and more moral sensitivity (Dunn, Cutting, & Demetriou, 2000; Hughes & Dunn, 2000). Three longitudinal studies of young friends (one in the United States, two in Britain) showed that children with particularly close, intimate friendships were more likely to give interpersonally oriented justifications concerning moral issues (Dunn, 1995; Dunn et al., 2000; Hughes & Dunn, 2000). That is, these studies highlighted the links between the friends' shared imaginative play in the preschool period and their moral orientation years later.

Second, do the associations go the "other" way too—is early relationship quality related to later social understanding? Again, the answer is *yes,* as has been shown in studies of mother–child attachment and communication (Meins et al., 1998; Meins, 1997), sibling relationship quality (Dunn, 1993), and friendship quality and moral development (Dunn et al., 2002). A further point about a relationships approach to the development of understanding mind is that it highlights how important it is for children to be able to put together thoughts, actions, and feelings over time in explaining people's actions over time. This time dimension is a defining feature of relationships (Hinde, 1979), and it is a core aspect of the growing understanding of mind, as the studies by Lagattuta and Wellmann (2001, 2002) have shown, with their evidence that conversations about negative emotions have a high concentration of talk about the past, about causes of emotions, and about mind–emotion connections.

The implications of this research linking relationship quality and later social understanding are several. First, it seems highly likely that the causal patterns are bidirectional, from relationships to sociocognitive development and vice versa. Second, the unpacking of the role of children's language skills in these associations has shown that it is not solely the content of conversations that is important. It is not only talk about the mind and feelings that matters: it is who you talk with and why you do so that are important. That is, as noted elsewhere (Dunn & Brophy, 2005), talk may be the most powerful mediator influencing the growth of understanding of mind, but the quality of the relationship within which such talk takes place influences the talk. And the evidence on young children shows us that the very early signs of understanding other minds are present when children are trying to "get things done" in their close relationships: teasing, managing conflict, cooperating in shared pretence, where it is crucial to understand what the other person is thinking or planning, anticipating what a sibling is doing to gain parental attention. Children discover the mind because of their relationships, just as they learn to talk because of their relationships. Second, in these relationships, emotion is core, and is a key part of children's curiosity about why people behave the way they do.

The important next steps are to pursue the questions raised by the evidence to date on the links between relationships and understanding of mind: to clarify how the patterns of association differ for the same child in his or her different relationships—for instance the different significance of language in sibling and friend relationships (Cutting & Dunn, 2006). We need to understand what governs how children *use* their understanding in particular relationships, to appreciate the network of relationships within which children develop and use their understanding of mind, and finally to pursue the fruitful intervention studies currently being conducted (e.g., Lohmann, Tomasello, & Meyer, 2005), if we are to make progress in understanding the causal processes underlying the associations between children's early relationships and their understanding of others.

References

Astington, J. W. (1993). *The child's discovery of the mind.* Cambridge, MA: Harvard University Press.

Astington, J. W., & Jenkins, J. M. (1995). Theory of mind development and social understanding. *Cognition and Emotion, 9*, 151–165.

Baron-Cohen, S. (2000). Theory of mind and autism: A fifteen year review. In S. Baron-Cohen, H. Tager-Flusberg, & D. J. Cohen (Eds.), *Understanding other minds: Perspectives from cognitive neuroscience* (pp. 3–20). Oxford: Oxford University Press.

Bartsch, K., & Estes, D. (1996). Individual differences in children's developing theories of mind and implications for metacognition. *Learning and Individual Differences, 8*, 281–304.

Bartsch, K., & Wellman, H. M. (1995). *Children talk about the mind.* Oxford: Oxford University Press.

Bloom, L., & Capatides, J. B. (1987). Sources of meaning in the acquisition of complex syntax: The sample case of causality. *Journal of Experimental Psychology, 43*, 112–128.

Brown, J. R. (1995). *What happened? Emotional experience and children's talk about the past.* Unpublished manuscript.

Bruner, J., & Feldman, C. (1993). Theories of mind and the problems of autism. In S. Baron-Cohen, H. Tager-Flusberg, & D. Cohen (Eds.), *Understanding other minds: Perspectives from autism* (pp. 267–291). Oxford: Oxford University Press.

Carpendale, J. I. M., & Lewis, C. (2006). *How children develop social understanding.* Oxford: Blackwell.

Carpenter, M., Nagell, K., & Tomasello, M. (1998). Social cognition, joint attention, and communicative competence from 9 to 15 months. *Monographs of the Society for Research in Child Development, 63.*

Cleveland, E. S., & Reese, E. (2005). Maternal structure and autonomy support in conversations about the past: contributions to children's autobiographical memory. *Developmental Psychology, 41*, 376–388.

Cutting, A. L., & Dunn, J. (1999). Theory of mind, emotion understanding, language and family background: Individual differences and inter-relations. *Child Development, 70*, 853–865.

Cutting, A. L., & Dunn, J. (2006). Conversations with siblings and friends: Links with between relationship quality and social understanding. *British Journal of Developmental Psychology, 24*, 73–87.

Dunn, J. (1988). *The beginnings of social understanding.* Cambridge, MA: Harvard University Press.

Dunn, J. (1993). *Young children's close relationships: Beyond attachment* (Vol. 4). Newbury Park, CA: Sage.

Dunn, J. (1995). Children as psychologists: The later correlates of individual differences in understanding of emotions and other minds. *Cognition and Emotion, 9,* 187–201.

Dunn, J. (2004). *Children's friendships: The beginnings of intimacy.* Oxford: Blackwell.

Dunn, J., & Brophy, M. (2005). Communication, relationships and individual differences in children's understanding of mind. In J. W. Astington & J. Baird (Eds.), *Why language matters for theory of mind* (pp. 50–69). Oxford: Oxford University Press.

Dunn, J., Brown, J., Slomkowski, C., Tesla, C., & Youngblade, L. (1991). Young children's understanding of other people's feelings and beliefs: Individual differences and their antecedents. *Child Development, 62,* 1352–1366.

Dunn, J., & Cutting, A. (1999). Understanding others, and individual differences in friendship interactions in young children. *Social Development, 8,* 201–219.

Dunn, J., Cutting, A., & Demetriou, H. (2000). Moral sensibility, understanding other, and children's friendship interactions in the preschool period. *British Journal of Developmental Psychology, 18,* 159–177.

Dunn, J., Cutting, A., & Fisher, N. (2002). Old friends, new friends: Predictors of children's perspectives on their friends at school. *Child Development, 73,* 621–635.

Dunn, J., & Dale, N. (1984). I a Daddy: 2-year-olds' collaboration in joint pretend with sibling and with mother. In I. Bretherton (Ed.), *Symbolic play: The development of social understanding* (pp. 131–158). San Diego, CA: Academic Press.

Gottman, J. M. (1983). How children become friends. *Monographs of the Society for Research in Child Development, 48* (Serial no. 201).

Hinde, R. A. (1979). *Towards understanding relationships.* London: Academic Press.

Hood, L., & Bloom, L. (1979). What, when, and how about why: A longitudinal study of early expressions of causality. *Monographs of the Society for Research in Child Development, 44* (Serial no.).

Howe, N. (1991). Sibling directed internal state language, perspective-taking, and the sibling relationship. *Child Development, 62,* 1503–1512.

Howes, C. (1996). The earliest friendships. In W. M. Bukowski, A. F. Newcomb, & W. W. Hartup (Eds.), *The company they keep: Friendship in childhood and adolescence* (pp. 66–86). New York: Cambridge University Press.

Hudson, J. A. (2004). The development of future thinking: Constructing future events in mother–child conversation. In J. M. Lucariello, J. A. Hudson, R. Fivush, & P. J. Bauer (Eds.), *The development of the mediated mind: Sociocultural context and cognitive development* (Vol. xii, 274, pp. 127–150). Mahwah, NJ: Lawrence Erlbaum.

Hudson, J. A., Gebelt, J., Haviland, J., & Bentivegna, C. (1992). Emotion and narrative structure in young children's personal accounts. *Journal of Narrative and Life History, 2,* 129–150.

Hughes, C., & Dunn, J. (1997). "Pretend you didn't know": Preschoolers' talk about mental states in pretend play. *Cognitive Development, 12,* 477–499.

Hughes, C., & Dunn, J. (1998). Understanding mind and emotion: Longitudinal associations with mental-state talk between young friends. *Developmental Psychology, 34,* 1026–1037.

Hughes, C., & Dunn, J. (2000). Hedonism or empathy? Hard-to-manage children's moral awareness, and links with cognitive and maternal characteristics. *British Journal of Developmental Psychology, 18*, 227–245.

Kreppner, J. M. (2003). *Friendship quality, friendship representations, and understanding of mental and emotional states in children following severe emotional deprivation.* Unpublished Ph.D. dissertation, University of London.

Lagattuta, K. H., & Wellman, H. M. (2001). Thinking about the past: Early knowledge about links between prior experience, thinking, and emotion. *Child Development, 72*, 82–102.

Lagattuta, K. H., & Wellman, H. M. (2002). Differences in early parent–child conversations about negative versus positive emotions: Implications for the development of psychological understanding. *Developmental Psychology, 38*, 564–580.

Lohmann, H., Tomasello, M., & Meyer, S. (2005). Linguistic communication and social understanding. In J. W. Astington & J. Baird (Eds.), *Why language matters for theory of mind* (pp. 245–265). Oxford: Oxford University Press.

Meins, E. (1997). *Security of attachment and the social development of cognition.* Hove, UK: Psychology Press.

Meins, E., Fernyhough, C., Russell, J. T., & Clarke-Carter, D. (1998). Security of attachment as a predictor of symbolic and mentalising abilities: A longitudinal study. *Social Development, 7*, 1–24.

Moore, C. (1999). Intentional relations and triadic interactions. In P. Zelazo, J. Astington, & D. Olson (Eds.), *Developing theories of intention: Social understanding and self-control* (pp. 43–61). Mahwah, NJ: Lawrence Erlbaum.

Newton, P., Reddy, V., & Bull, R. (2000). Children's everyday deception and performance on false-belief tasks. *British Journal of Developmental Psychology, 18*, 297–317.

Rochat, P., & Morgan, R. (1998). Two functional orientations of self-explanation in infancy. *British Journal of Developmental Psychology, 16*, 139–154.

Rochat, P., Morgan, R., & Carpenter, M. (1997). The perception of social causality in infancy. *Cognitive Development, 12*, 537–561.

Ruffman, T., Perner, J., & Parkin, L. (1999). How parenting style affects false belief understanding. *Social Development, 8*, 395.

Ruffman, T., Slade, L., Devitt, K., & Crowe, E. (2006). What mothers say and what they do: The relation between parenting, theory of mind, language and conflict/cooperation. *British Journal of Developmental Psychology, 24*, 105–124.

Rutter, M., & the English and Romanian Adoptees (ERA) study team. (1998). Developmental catch-up, and deficit, following adoption after severe global early privation. *Journal of Child Psychology and Psychiatry, 39*, 465–476.

Rutter, M. L., Kreppner, J. M., & O'Connor, T. G. (2001). Specificity and heterogeneity in children's responses to profound institutional privation. *British Journal of Psychiatry, 179*, 97–103.

Tomasello, M. (1999). Having intentions, understanding intentions, and understanding communicative intentions. In P. Zelazo, J. Astington, & D. Olson (Eds.), *Developing theories of intention: Social understanding and self-control* (pp. 63–75). Mahwah, NJ: Lawrence Erlbaum.

Wellman, H. M., Cross, D., & Watson, J. (2001). Meta-analysis of theory of mind development: The truth about false belief. *Child Development, 72*, 655–-684.

Youngblade, L. M., & Dunn, J. (1995). Individual differences in young children's pretend play with mother and sibling: Links to relationships and understanding of other people's feelings and beliefs. *Child Development, 66*, 1472–1492.

9

The Constructive Role of Asymmetry in Social Interaction

GERARD DUVEEN AND CHARIS PSALTIS

INTRODUCTION: SOCIAL INTERACTION
AND COGNITIVE DEVELOPMENT

In his account of the development of moral judgment Piaget (1932) introduced a fundamental distinction between different types of social relationship, or more specifically he attributed different types of psychosocial processes to different forms of social relationship. Where there is *constraint* because one participant holds more power than the other the relationship is asymmetrical, and, importantly, the knowledge which can be acquired by the dominated participant takes on a fixed and inflexible form. Piaget refers to this process as one of social transmission, and he refers to the way in which the elders of a tribe initiate younger members into the patterns of beliefs and practices of the group. Similarly where adults exercise a dominating influence over the growing child, it is through social transmission that children can acquire knowledge. By contrast, in *cooperative* relations, power is more evenly distributed between participants so that a more symmetrical relationship emerges. Under these conditions authentic forms of intellectual exchange become possible because the partners have the freedom to project their own individual thoughts, consider the positions of others, and defend their own independent points of view. In such circumstances, where children's thinking is not limited by a dominant influence, the conditions exist for the emergence of constructive solutions to problems, or what Piaget refers to as the reconstruction of knowledge rather than social transmission. Here the knowledge which emerges is open, flexible, and regulated by the logic of argument rather than being determined by an external authority. In short, cooperative relations provide the arena for the emergence of operations, which for Piaget requires the absence of any constraining influence, and is most often illustrated by the relations which form between peers.

Piaget's argument is in part motivated by his critical response to Durkheim's sociology. While he recognizes much that is of value in Durkheim's work, he also considers its limitations, insofar as it focuses only on the constraining influence of one generation over the succeeding one. This is one particular way in which Durkheim's theory is oriented toward understanding what it is that holds societies together, and as Mosocvici and others have suggested, such a view neglects to consider the equally important process of how societies change (cf Duveen, 2000a). Piaget's response to Durkheim is framed as an ontogenetic argument, but he too is concerned with the prospects for change, in this case of cognitive structure. In basing his argument on a distinction between different types of social relationship, Piaget takes the adult–child and the child–child relation as the ideal types of what he identifies as constraint and cooperation. Of course he is also aware that while ideal types may have analytical utility, they do not always describe empirical realities very clearly. Here, for instance, it would be absurd to ignore the multiple ways in which child–child relations might take asymmetric forms as one child dominates the other, or the way in which it may be possible for adults to interact in more symmetrical ways with children. It is the distribution of power in the relationship which is central for Piaget, and he insists that it is only under conditions of symmetry that children experience the autonomy necessary for the construction of operational structures. Indeed, so closely did the relationship between cooperation and cognitive development appear to Piaget that in a later work he remarks that "they constitute two indissociable aspects of a single reality that is at once social and individual" (Piaget, 1977/1995, p. 145). And in his comments on Vygotsky, Piaget also notes that "there is an identity between intra individual operations and the inter individual operations which constitute *co-operation*, in the proper quasi-etymological sense of the word" (Piaget, 1962, pp. 13–14). And he goes on to observe that the reason for this identity is that "actions, whether individual or interpersonal, are in essence co-ordinated and organized by the operational structures which are spontaneously constructed in the course of mental development" (Piaget, 1962, p. 14).

Vygotsky too considers social relationships as fundamental to the development of psychological processes. But in Vygotsky's (1978) account we do not find any distinction between types of social relationship comparable to that found in Piaget. When he formulates his *general genetic law of cultural development* he frames it simply as the internalization as an intrapsychological category of a function initially established between people as an interpsychological category. And when he gives this general principle a specific expression as the *zone of proximal development* he refers explicitly to asymmetric situations, in which one partner (adult or more capable peer) uses his or her expertise to guide the activity of the other partner (see Duveen, 1997, for a discussion of this point). This formulation emphasizes that the asymmetry in the relationship is one of expertise (or perhaps one should say more precisely that it is an asymmetry in the availability of forms of semiotic mediation), but as always it is difficult to disentangle knowledge and power. Thus while both Piaget and Vygotsky emphasize the importance of social relationships for psychological development they do so in rather different ways. Vygotsky's emphasis on asymmetrical relations seems to elide any reference to the kind of constructive activity which Piaget suggests is the core of development. Yet, at the same time, Piaget's abstract theoretical scheme is not without its problems and difficulties either. Piaget himself never undertook any systematic research into the relations between social relations and psychological development, so it is perhaps not surprising that we do not find any clear account of how children (or any other social actors) come to establish cooperative relations rather than relations of constraint. In Piaget's account these two different social relations appear rather as two distinct states of affairs, each with its own properties. But the world in which social actors encounter one another is above all a world constituted around differences, which may be differences in prestige, in authority, in knowledge, or along a multiplicity of other dimensions. Each dimension of difference is itself a potential source of asymmetry in social relations, so that it becomes important to ask how it is possible for cooperative relations to emerge from the communicative exchanges of interaction.

THE HYPOTHESIS OF SOCIOCOGNITIVE CONFLICT

A central contribution to our understanding of the ways in which social interaction may be related to cognitive development came from the experimental program of research in Geneva initiated by Willem Doise and his colleagues, Gabriel Mugny and Anne-Nelly Perret-Clermont (cf. Doise & Mugny, 1984; Doise, Mugny, & Perret-Clermont, 1975; Perret-Clermont, 1980). By re-presenting some of Piaget's classic experimental investigations as problems for pairs (and sometimes triads) of children, this research was able to focus on the consequences of interaction for children's cognitive development. In their designs, children's performance on a pretest enabled the researchers to control the composition of pairs of children who would be invited to work on the same problem together in an interaction phase, and the outcomes for individual children could be established through subsequent posttests and by comparing the performance of children who had participated in such an interaction with a control group who had not. Using this design, these "social-Genevan" researchers were able to establish that children did indeed benefit from working with another child, especially when their partner was more advanced in his or her understanding of the task. In their work these authors also reported some other interesting observations. First, in a number of cases they reported that children produced novel arguments in the posttest; that is, they produced arguments which they had not heard from their partner during the interaction phase. This was one important element sustaining their claim that in these circumstances children's development was the product of a structural reorganization of their cognitive functions, rather than simply imitation of their partner. Second, on a more complex task of spatial perspectives they also observed that children working together could produce solutions which were in advance of what either child had achieved in their pretest. As well as providing further evidence that in these situations children were not simply imitating their partners, such observations can also be seen as questioning the Vygotskian assumption about the necessity for a difference in expertise as a facilitator of development. While there have been some studies which have claimed not to have been able to replicate these effects (Russell, 1982; Russell, Mills, & Reiff-Musgrave, 1990), the weight of evidence clearly supports the productive role of social interaction. Not only did Doise and Mugny (1984) find similar effects across a range of tasks, but a number of other studies have also reported congruent findings (Ames & Murray, 1982; Bearison, Magzamen, & Filardo, 1986; Mugny, De Paolis, & Carugati, 1984; Perret-Clermont, 1980).

To explain their experimental results, Doise and his colleagues introduced the hypothesis of sociocognitive conflict (Doise & Mugny, 1984; Doise, Mugny, & Pérez, 1998; Mugny, De Paolis, & Carugati, 1984; Perret-Clermont, 1980), by which they meant that in these interactions different perspectives on the task were embedded in the social relations between the children tackling it, and that by facilitating the expression of different perspectives these interactions were also contributing to the resolution of the conflict between these perspectives. Thus, where Piaget himself had suggested that cognitive development emerged through the child's confrontation with conflicting perspectives, this hypothesis framed this process as a function of social relations.

While this hypothesis of sociocognitive conflict appears to be theoretically coherent, some problems are clearly evident. First, in the Genevan research it was never possible to identify specific features or characteristics of the interaction which could be linked to outcomes for individual children, so that sociocognitive conflict remained a general inference about what had happened rather than an observable feature of the interaction. And second, not every child who participated in an interaction with a peer made progress on a posttest. To explain this differential effect of interaction, Doise and his colleagues drew on theories of social influence to suggest that while some children were able to work toward a constructive resolution of the conflict (envisaged as similar to the process of innovation in minority influence), others achieved only a relational resolution, a kind of compliance to the power and authority of the more developed child, which did not lead to the emergence of any more developed understanding. But again, this distinction, while theoretically interesting, is really a post hoc interpretation rather than a direct observation of the interaction (and one could add in parenthesis here that while the Vygotskyian proposition that development consists in the internalization of interpsychic relations as intrapsychic relations, his work offers no explanation of why some interactions may not lead to internalization).

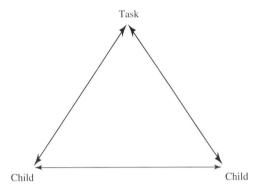

Figure 9.1   The triadic structure of relationships.

Notwithstanding these problems, the work of these "social Genevans" nevertheless also introduces a clearer theoretical frame through its focus on the triadic relationships among child-child-task as the fundamental unit for analysis. In other words, theoretical explanations for the relations between social interaction and cognitive development need to consider the relations between the children as well as between the children and the task (Chapman, 1991, also introduces a similar idea).

This emphasis on triadic relationships is important for a number of reasons. First, it serves to establish a distinction with classical Piagetian accounts which have tended to emphasize the dyadic relationship between subject and object, child and task. Actually, whether this is best characterized as a distinction or a clarification is perhaps a moot point. While there has always been a clear orientation toward the significance of social interaction in Piaget's work (e.g., Piaget, 1977/1995; and the contributions to Carpendale & Müller, 2004), it is not clear whether this extends to encompassing a triadic model of development. In his methodological comments on the clinical interview Piaget shows himself to be a very sensitive analyst of the intricacies of the relationship between interviewer and child (Duveen, 2000b), even to the point of recognizing the potential structuring influence of the interviewer. Yet when he turns to theoretical explanations of development, social influences are given less weight than the autoregulative process of equilibration, with the former being considered one of the necessary but not sufficient conditions for intellectual development, while only the latter acquires the status of being both necessary and sufficient. Even in his most sociological writings, Piaget (1932, 1977/1995) hesitates over whether social interaction can ever be seen as having a constitutive role in the genesis of structures. At best he usually restricts himself to analyzing the homologies he finds between structures of operations on the one hand and structures of interaction on the other, with both being driven by the rationality implicit in the logic of the coordination of actions. In his broader considerations of the factors in mental development, Piaget always insisted on the necessary role of social interactions, while maintaining that they were not a sufficient condition for development (e.g., Piaget & Inhelder, 1969). Thus, while social relations might be considered a constituting element in the development of operations, for Piaget they did not constitute the whole. By contrast, the hypothesis of sociocognitive conflict suggests precisely a constitutive role for social interaction in the ontogenesis of intelligence.

Second, the emphasis on a triadic structure of relationships also opens a theoretical space for considering intellectual development as a social-psychological process, in particular to the genetic social psychology of Serge Moscovici which has also emphasized the triadic structure of self-other-object as the central unit of analysis (Moscovici, 1972, 1976, 1980; and also Marková, 2003). Indeed, Moscovici's work on social influence should be seen as an important element in the formation of the hypothesis of sociocognitive conflict. For Moscovici, it is precisely the forms of communication within interaction which structure different modalities of social influence, and in particular he draws a distinction between compliance (often described as majority influence) in which patterns of communication lead to the public acceptance of a position, and conversion (or innovation, and often described as a minority influence) in which patterns of communication induce cognitive reorganization. Indeed, in his research he has demonstrated that minorities can be influential to the extent that they are able to structure communications within interactions in such a way as to induce precisely a form of reflection which generates a process of reorganization. There is clearly a parallel between Moscovici's description of these different forms of social influence and Piaget's distinction between constraint and cooperation as types of social relation (cf. Butera & Mugny, 2001; Doise, Mugny, & Pérez, 1988; Duveen, 2001; Psaltis, 2005a). The hypothesis of sociocognitive conflict suggests that development through interaction is envisaged as a kind of conversion process or innovation generating cognitive reorganization, and hence the significance of Doise and Mugny's (1984) observations of novelty in posttests following interactions since they provide an index of such reorganization.

In Moscovici's theory, the capacity for minorities to generate change by influencing majorities is viewed as a function of the behavioral styles which they adopt. This has led researchers (Doise, Mugny, & Pérez, 1998; Leman & Duveen, 1999) to suggest that interactions between children be considered as communicative exchanges framed as social influence processes. Emler and Glachan (1985), for instance, linked the argumentative style of conservers with what Moscovici described as the behavioral style of consistency, since their operational grasp of the task was more likely to provide constant support for their argument throughout the discussion. More generally, Moscovici's discussion of behavioral styles can be seen as related to Piaget's (1932, 1977/1995) distinction between social relations of cooperation, which foster the emergence and resolution of conflicts of centration and thus provide the context in which the child is able to reconstruct knowledge, and social relations of constraint in which knowledge is not reconstructed but simply accepted because of the prestige of the source. Piaget defines the relation of cooperation as "reciprocity between autonomous individuals" (1977/1995, p. 232). Piaget also emphasizes the importance of reflection for cognitive development which he sees as linked with relations of cooperation, and notes "reflection is not spontaneous to individuals" (p. 234) but rather arises through social interaction, since the conscious realization of the methods and procedures of one's actions are less fruitful when an individual's action is not reflected in that of others; that is, when cooperation does not complete pure individuality.

Third, the triadic view also enables a clearer perspective to emerge on the character of the communication between the children themselves as they work together on a task. In this respect, research on sociocognitive conflict may also be connected with research on peer interaction from the Vygotskyian perspective, where the emphasis has been more on the process rather than the outcome, which has also led to a greater reliance on more ethnographic forms of research. In looking at interactions between more and less capable peers, Tudge (1992), for instance, suggested that verbalization of reasoning by both partners was a condition under which cognitive growth is more likely to occur during peer collaboration, and specifically that the more competent partner had to verbalize his or her reasoning and the less advanced child had to accept it.

A focus on the communicative demands of the task situation also gave rise to a second generation of studies derived from the initial research on the theme of sociocognitive conflict. These studies (Perret-Clermont, Perret, & Bell, 1991; Perret-Clermont & Schubauer-Leoni, 1981; Schubauer-Leoni & Grossen, 1993; Schubauer-Leoni & Perret-Clermont, 1997; see also Perret-Clermont, 1994) have also been more focused on questions of process, and in particular on the pragmatics of the communication between adult and child in the testing situation, emphasizing the form of communicative contract established between them.

SOCIAL INTERACTION, SOCIAL IDENTITY, AND SOCIAL REPRESENTATIONS

As children work together on a task, the dynamics of the interactions between them may be shaped by a number of different influences. There may be differences between them in their initial levels of understanding of the problem, but any conversation also embraces other sources of difference and conflict, each of which has the potential to influence the form and shape of the conversation which emerges between the children. Thus it becomes important to consider what it is that children bring into these conversations, the background knowledge which, while it may often be implicit, nevertheless exercises an influence. Children may be attentive to the academic or social reputation of their partner, for example, or the character of their relationship with their interlocutor within a broader social network. While it would be interesting to consider the influence of asymmetries derived from such sources (cf. Psaltis, 2005b), gender, or rather, social representations of gender, is a persistent influence, introducing a complex dynamic into conversation. Children not only enter a conversation with their own sense of their gender identity, but also bring to it expectations about their partner and the appropriate forms of interaction which derive from their shared representations of gender (Lloyd & Duveen, 1992). What a child, whether a boy or a girl, expects of a partner in terms of authority or power in this kind of interaction differs according to the gender of the partner. Such expectations may, of course, be challenged or modified through the course of the interaction—talk itself can also always be productive in this sense—but gender remains a pervasive influence in children's conversations. A first exploration of this idea came in the work of Leman and Duveen (1999) which modified the design used by Doise and his colleagues by controlling the gender composition of the pairs of children participating in the interaction. In this study children were engaged with one of Piaget's (1932) moral judgment dilemmas (which contrasts judgments about the consequences of an action with judgments about intentions), and the pretest established whether the child was oriented toward a heteronomous or autonomous solution. Four different dyads could then be formed by controlling both gender and initial level of development (see Table 9.1; all of the children in this study were aged 9–10 years).

Analysis of the interactions within each of these pair types showed that the *Fm* pairing was distinctive in several ways—these conversations took longer to reach an agreed solution than any other pair type, and the girl had to deploy a wider and more sophisticated set of arguments to persuade her partner. Of course this is also the pair type where the initial level of understanding is most strongly contrasted with expectations derived from representations of gender—generally the boys do not expect their female partners to take a leading or assertive role in the conversation, and their initial resistance to the girls' argument leads to both longer conversations and the broader set of arguments deployed by the girl.

It is instructive to review the form of these different conversational patterns. In the first example (an *Mf* pair), it is the boy, James, who opens the conversation, but he does so through an assertive statement which sets out his perspective while leaving little space for the girl, Nadia, to challenge, or even participate in the agreed solution to the task. Her contribution to the solution is the simple repeated monosyllable "Yeah".

Table 9.1 Pairings achieved by manipulating gender and developmental level in Leman and Duveen (1999)

Autonomous	Heteronomous
M	m
M	f
F	f
F	m

Note: M=Boy, F=Girl. Upper case letters refer to the autonomous child, lower case letters refer to the heteronomous child.

Example 9.1: Nadia & James

1. J: He's not as bad 'cos he only opened the door to get tea but he's naughtier 'cos he's not meant to be having sweets.

2. N: Yeah.

3. J: So he's naughtier?

4. N: Yeah

5. J: Go get him back in then. Go say we're finished.

6. Experimenter enters.

7. N: That one.

8. J: That one.

In the second example (an *Fm* pair), it is again the autonomous child who opens the conversation, but this time Jade takes a noticeably different approach. Instead of asserting what the answer is, she opens a space for dialogue by asking Leon why he thought John was the naughtier of the two boys in the vignettes. By doing so she opens the problem space for discussion, and as the conversation proceeds she allows Leon the opportunity to articulate his own perspective, while also bringing forward arguments of her own which highlight aspects of the situations described in the vignettes which Leon has not taken into consideration.

Example 9.2: Jade & Leon

1. J: That's David and that's John. Why did you think John was naughtier?

2. L: Because he's broke more cups and he's also knocked over a table.

3. J: Yeah but his mum said that when his mum called him for dinner she didn't tell him that there was a table behind the door and…to be careful did she? But David….

4. L: David…

5. J: But David, he's naughtier 'cos he got up on a chair and he was stealing sweets.

6. L: Yeah, but his mum was out.

7. J: Yeah, but his mum still called him for dinner and she didn't tell him that there was a table behind the door, did she? What one d'you think?

8. L: Well, he's only broken one cup so how's that being naughty, he's only broken one cup? And he's broken about six…

9. J: But his mum, she called him down for dinner.

10. L: Yeah.

11. J: And his mum never told him there was a table behind the door and he pushed it a little bit. 'Cos he just pushed it open and she never told him that there was a table behind the door when she called him down to dinner did she? So I've got a point, ain't I? But he, he knows where the cups are. He knew that them cups were in there but he just went up.

12. L: Yeah, but I've got a point because he's broken more cups.

13. J: Don't make no difference, his mum never told him.

14. L: Right then, so it was him.

15.   Experimenter enters.

16. L: David.

17. J: David.

Where Nadia is a passive presence in her conversation with James, Leon is an active participant in his conversation with Jade. James, it seems, is oriented toward solving the problem, and Nadia is accorded only an instrumental recognition in his strategy. Since they have been asked to reach an agreed solution, he needs to secure her agreement, and shows little interest in her understanding. Jade, by contrast, from the opening of her conversation recognizes Leon as an active agent in the dialogue, seeking to secure agreement through persuasion. Although these conversations are very different, they can both be seen as proceeding from the same underlying representation of gender, one in which the dominant and author-itative position in tackling a problem and structuring a conversation is marked as masculine. James exploits the power this gives him, while Jade finds a discursive solution to escaping such gendered framing of the conversation.

These two examples illustrate clearly the features of what Doise and his col-leagues described through their hypothesis of sociocognitive conflict. Where Example 9.2 indicates a constructive resolution of the task, Example 9.1 cor-responds to what they described as a relational resolution. Naturally one wants to know whether this difference in the form of the conversation has any conse-quences for the children involved. What do Nadia and Leon carry away from this interaction? Are there any traces of these different conversational experiences visible in their later moral thinking? Unfortunately the design of the study by Leman and Duveen did not include any posttests, so that it is not possible to answer these questions about these children. However, Psaltis and Duveen (2006, 2007) in a study using the familiar conversation of the amount of liquid task used the same manipulation of gender and developmental level embedded in a design with both pretests, posttests, and control groups (see Table 9.2).

In this study[1] 70 pairs of children (aged 6.5 to 7.5 years), distributed more or less evenly across the four pair-types, participated in the interaction phase, with a further 44 children serving as the control groups (28 boys, *Cm*, and 16 girls,

Table 9.2 Design of the Psaltis and Duveen (2006, 2007) study

Pretest	Interaction	Delayed posttest
	Four Pair types (Mm, Mf, Ff, Fm)	
Controls		**Controls**
(Cm, Cf)		(Cm, Cf)

Note: M = Boy, F = Girl; C = Control group. Capital letters refer to the conserving child, lower case letters to the non-conserving child.

Cf). In the interaction phase of the study most of the conservers successfully per-suaded their non-conserving partners to agree that the amounts of the water were the same (59 out of 70 pairs reached an agreement of equality, and the pairs reaching an agreement of inequality were randomly distributed across the pair-types), and as Table 9.3 shows, performance on the posttest showed clearly the benefits of the interaction for the non-conservers: 34 out of 70 non-conservers (49%) made progress on the posttest compared to only 7 out of 44 (16%) in the control groups. However, comparisons between each pair-type and the corresponding control group showed a clear effect only for the *Fm* group, with a marginal effect for the *Mm* group and no effects for either the *Ff* or *Mf* groups.

As in the social-Genevan studies, the analysis of the posttests also investigated the use of novel arguments (that is arguments which the non-conservers had not heard during the interaction phase) as a stricter criterion of progress and a clearer index of cognitive reorganization. Again while the overall comparison is significant, there is considerable variation among the pair types. Non-conservers interacting with a female conserver (i.e., groups *Ff* and *Fm*) made more use of novel arguments than non-conservers interacting with a male conserver (i.e., groups *Mf* and *Mm*).

CONVERSATION TYPE AND DEVELOPMENTAL PROGRESS

While these analyses indicate some relationship between the gender composition of the pairs and outcomes for the non-conservers, the relationship is clearly a

Table 9.3 Progress made from pretest to posttest by gender composition of the group

		Pair type					
	Group	Mm	Mf	Ff	Fm	Cm	Cf
1	No progress	10	11	8	7	24	13
2	Progress without novelty	6	7	4	6	n/a	n/a
3	Progress with novelty	2	0	3	6	n/a	n/a
4	Global (total) progress	8	7	7	12	4	3

Note: M = Boy, F = Girl. Upper case letters refer to the conserving child, lower case letters refer to the non-conserving child.

complex one. In all pair-types there are non-conservers who make progress on the posttest as well as some who do not, so that no unequivocal relationship between gender composition and outcome can be established. Similarly, closer analyses of the details of the argumentative strategies employed also showed complex relationships between gender composition and outcomes. However, stronger and clearer relationships emerged when the data were analyzed at a molar level by taking the whole conversation as the unit of analysis. By avoiding the fragmented picture given by focusing on specific conversational features, this approach enabled both the sequential nature of the conversations as well as the modalities of resolving the conflict to be taken into account. A review of all the transcripts of the interactions revealed the existence of four distinct types of conversation. As well as considering the joint response given by each pair, the strategy for identifying conversational types also focused on the contributions of the non-conserving child, since the development of the interaction depended largely on their response to the conserving child's assertion of equality.

While the majority of interactions resulted in a conserving response as the joint answer, in a small minority of cases the pairs also came to agree on a non-conserving answer. In such instances the non-conserver persuaded the conserving partner, and such conversations were classified as *Non-conserving* type.

The first type of conversation which resulted in an agreement on a conservation response could be described as having the form of direct conformity, since no resistance was present during the discussion, and such conversations were classified as *No Resistance*.

Conversations where the non-conserver offered an argument in support of his or her position at least once during the interaction seemed qualitatively different from such direct compliance, so that conversations of this type were described as *Resistance*.

In some discussions there were also indications from the non-conserver that agreement with the conserving position was the product of genuine progress. Such indications of understanding could be expressions of the a-ha moment such as "Oh, now I understand!" "I see, you are right!"; or moments where original non-conservers appropriated and used conservation arguments themselves, either elaborated arguments or unelaborated general assertions. A characteristic of these discussions was also that after the turn where the indication of understanding was given the original non-conserver offered no further resistance to the conserving argument. These types of conversations were described as *Explicit Recognition*.[2]

As Table 9.4 indicates, the relationship between conversation type and outcome for the non-conserver is both clearer and stronger than was the case for the gender combination of the pairs. Specifically, two of the conversation types have a clearly identifiable relationship with progress on the posttest. None of the participants in *Non-conserving* conversations made progress, while nearly all of the children who participated in *Explicit Recognition* did show progress on the posttest. Further, almost half of the children from *Explicit Recognition* conversations also made use of novel arguments in their posttest (which accounted for nearly all of the novelty observed in the posttest), suggesting that this conversation type is

Table 9.4 Progress on the posttest by conversation type

		Conversation types			
		Non-conserving	No Resistance	Resistance	Explicit recognition
1	No progress	11	7	16	2
2	Progress without novelty	0	6	9	8
3	Progress with novelty	0	1	2	8
4	Global (total) progress	0	7	11	16

particularly linked to cognitive reorganization. The other two conversation types, *No Resistance* and *Resistance*, have more mixed results, with only about half of these children showing progress on the posttest, and for those who do progress there is very little evidence of novelty in the posttest.

While the relationship between conversation type and outcome is stronger than that between pair type and outcome, analysis also showed that conversation type was not independent of pair type. Indeed, instances of all four conversation types were observed in each of the gender combinations. The most distinctive pair types were *Mf* and *Fm*, with many more instances of *No Resistance* in *Mf*, and more *Resistance* and *Explicit Recognition* in the *Fm*. When the data were broken down by all three variables, conversation type, pair type, and outcome, the cell sizes were too small for statistical comparisons. However, some patterns were clearly visible. Where the original non-conserver made progress with novelty on the posttest following an *Explicit Recognition* conversation, this was overwhelmingly in pairs in which there was a female conserver rather than a male conserver. And while progress is not exclusively restricted to *Explicit Recognition*, the children who made progress without novelty following a *No Resistance* conversation were nearly all females who had participated in an *Mf* pair.

The complexities of the relations between the gender composition of the pairs, the form of communication established between them, and outcomes illustrates the openness and unpredictability of interaction. While the composition of a particular pair type may influence the formation of a particular conversation type, it does not determine it. Further, while the establishment of a particular conversation type may influence the outcome, it also does not determine it. True, all of our non-conservers will eventually achieve conservation, but the process of reaching it could be very important in terms of the timing or the modality of knowledge obtained. The evidence here suggests differences in the stability of knowledge depending on the ways that it is legitimized through different conversation types. To understand how these conversations are structured in different ways so as to generate different opportunities for development it is necessary to examine in more detail the different ways in which children participate in each conversation type. In doing so an important focus for attention is on the ways in which children acquire access to the problem space and the different forms of social recognition which this implies.[3]

Non-conserving

Characteristically in these conversations it is the non-conserver who initiates the discussion, and in doing so sets the frame for the conversation as a whole. Most of these discussions were quite short, and in many instances the conserving child did not support his or her original position even once. However, most of the conservers regained their conserving level in the posttest, suggesting that such discussions largely involved the establishment of a relation of social constraint between the two partners introduced by factors related to other sources of asymmetry such as gender or academic reputation (in fact, the majority of the non-conservers who won the argument were considered academically stronger students in comparison to their partners by their teachers, and girl conservers were twice as likely as boys to submit to the non-conserver's view.)

A revealing symptom of the constraint prevailing in these conversations is that in some of them the non-conserver moved to force an ending to the conversation by underlining the need for agreement. In the following example of *Non-conserving* discussions that follow, this urgency for premature closure can be seen in turn 8.

Example 9.3: Mf dyad Non-conserving

1. C: This is bigger…my glass is bigger.

2. N: Yes but mine is smaller than yours.

3. C: The water is equal!

4. N: No…. This is more.

5. C: The water here is equal with yours because if we pour it in there it will be the same.

6. N: It isn't…. This is small.

7. C: Yes but the glass is bigger…

8. N: That means that the water is more…Do you agree?… Do we agree?…(long pause)

9. Experimenter: What did you agree?

10. N: That his glass is bigger and he has more…

11. Experimenter: Do you both agree?

12. C: Yes.

No Resistance

Constraint is also characteristic of the *No Resistance* conversations, though this time it is exercised by the conserver. As can be seen in Example 9.4 they do not leave much space for the non-conserver to be given any kind of recognition, except a kind of *instrumental recognition* as the conserving child seeks to find agreement in order to meet the requirements of the task set by the experimenter. In this type of conversation it is nearly always the conservers who initiate the discussion and then in a condensed and consistent manner support their view. Notably in turn 3 in Example 9.4 the conserver frames the conversation in a highly structured way in which the non-conserver's contribution is anticipated, as though they were simply being asked to fill in the conversational slots generated by the conserver. This type of conversation occurred most frequently between male conservers and female non-conservers (cf. Psaltis & Duveen, 2006) suggesting that gender asymmetry contributes to the establishment of this form of constraint.

Example 9.4: Mf dyad No Resistance

1. C: Wasn't this (water in glass C) equal a while ago, when he poured it?

2. N: Yes.

3. C: This is a tall glass and that's why they are equal should we call him?

4. N: Yes.

5. C: (opens the door and calls the experimenter back)

6. Experimenter: (comes back to the room) What did you agree?

7. N: Equal.

8. C: Equal.

Interestingly, as Table 9.4 shows, half of the non-conservers who participated in *No Resistance* conversations nevertheless showed progress on the posttest. Overwhelmingly, however, these were non-conserving girls interacting with a conserving boy, suggesting that these conversations were dominated by expectations derived from social representations of gender. Yet, as the progress evidenced by these girls suggests, compliance is not always the same as passivity, though in these cases it was largely progress without novelty.

Resistance
Resistance is a less constrained conversation type than the previous two since by definition the non-conservers support their original non-conserving position. Again it is generally the conserver who sets the frame by initiating the discussion, but as the non-conserver now begins to defend their position the conversations not only become longer, but also introduce a different form of participation for the children. What kind of conflict emerges in these conversations and how is it resolved? Generally in these conversations it is indeed a sociocognitive conflict (Doise & Mugny, 1984) that emerges in which different points of view are clearly expressed. In these conversations, the conserver also provides some clearer invitation for the non-conserver to reflect on the problem, indicating there is also

a clearer recognition of the non-conserver as a thinking agent. Both of these features can be seen in Example 9.5, where the conserver can also be observed introducing more elaborated conserving arguments in turn 11 in response to the non-conserver's repeated assertion of inequality, until the original non-conserver agrees on conservation.

Example 9.5: Fm dyad Resistance

1. C: They are equal. They are equal! I say they are equal, equal.

2. N: No they are not!

3. C: They are equal!

4. N: But yours is here. (points to the level of water)

5. C: Equal.

6. N: And mine [is

7. C: [equal

8. N: Here! (points to the level of the water in the transformation glass C)

9. C: But they are equal! Equal! We had both glasses and they were equal.

10. N: Mine is up to here and yours is up to here. (points to the level of water in glass C and glass A)

11. C: But they are the same! It's just that the glass is bigger and it can take more, that's why.

12. N: OK should we tell him?

13. C: Yes.

14. N: Come!

15. Experimenter: What did you agree?

16. N: Equal.

17. C: Equal.

Explicit recognition
This type of conversation has some of the same features which were evident in *Resistance* conversations, though as they develop the child who was originally a non-conserver comes to a clearer recognition of conservation. Again it is generally the conserver who establishes the frame, though interestingly in a small minority of cases the non-conserving child actually began the conversation by adopting a conserving position, presumably due to spontaneous progress between the pretest and interaction phases. In some conversations *Explicit Recognition* came after the non-conserving child had not only been exposed to a conserving

argument, but had also resisted it at least once by supporting their original position, a type illustrated in Example 9.6.

Example 9.6: Mm dyad Explicit Recognition

1. C: What should we do? Should we say the same? That we have the same?

2. N: No, I have more, you have less.

3. C: But, this is taller and that is wider…it's the same….

4. N: It's the same thing….

5. C: No…this is short, it's small….

6. N: That is small, but is wider…. If we put it in here it will be the same! That means it's the same!

7. C: Should we say that it's the same?

8. N: OK.

9. Experimenter: Did you agree?

10. C: Yes, it's the same water.

11. N: Yes.

In this example, questioning by the conserver invites the non-conserver to take responsibility for the task and provides an opportunity for reflection. The initial resistance of the non-conserver fades as the conserver restates their argument. By turn 6 the non-conserver has taken advantage of the opportunity for reflection by providing a clear argument for conservation, leading to agreement with their partner.

There were also conversations where explicit recognition came after the non-conserver was exposed to a conservation argument by their partner without any explicit resistance by the non-conserver. In these instances the conserver generally adopts a more didactic strategy, as in Example 9.7, where the turn by turn construction of the joint solution is mostly controlled by the conserver. The conservation argument is skilfully built. The non-conserver contributes to the building of the argument by answering the questions of the conserver who asks questions that draw the non-conserver into reflection. Here there is clearly recognition of N as a thinking subject by C, who is looking for recognition of their own arguments. In turn 8 N explicitly recognizes conservation (it might be argued that this is beginning to happen from turn 4).

Example 9.7: Fm dyad Explicit recognition

1. C: This glass (glass C) had the same water with that one (glass B) right?

2. N: Yes.

3. C: This glass (glass B) had equal water with that one (glass A) right? As we have said here, it's the same when we poured it in here (glass C) should we have more?

4. N: No…so the glass is bigger.

5. C: Yes, only the glass is bigger.

6. N: Yes.

7. C: Therefore is it more in here or are they equal?

8. N: Equal, it looks more because the glass is bigger.

9. C: Yes!

10. N: OK

11. C: Come! (calls the experimenter)

12. Experimenter: What did you agree?

13. N: Equal.

14. C: Equal.

15. N: It's just that her glass (glass C) is bigger.

As these illustrations indicate, the conversation types vary in the forms of participation established between the children. As always in conversation, the partner who initiates the discussion exercises some measure of control by setting the frame for the exchange. But there are clearly different ways of establishing control. In the *Non-conserving* and *No Resistance* conversations this control is exercised in a way that limits the access of the other child to the problem space, so that in doing so the child who takes the dominant position extends only an instrumental recognition of the partner. In both of these conversation types the dominant child frames the conversation by aligning the initial asymmetries of knowledge between the children with other asymmetrical dimensions of the situation stemming from representations of gender or of academic ability so that the conversations as a whole remain bounded by the expectations derived from these representations. While this strategy is sufficient to induce compliance from their partner, these conversations are not associated with any persistent change in the understanding of the dominated partner.

Where there is *Resistance,* the conserving child has to find a strategy for persuading his or her partner, which usually involves some form of sustained argument for conservation. Here the problem space of the task becomes more accessible to the non-conserving child, who is able to take on a measure of responsibility for its solution and thus establish a clearer recognition for themselves as an autonomous agent or thinking subject. Lastly, in *Explicit Recognition* there is a clearer sense of the problem space being accessible to both children, and the conserver is more clearly oriented to a form of persuasion in which the non-conserver is stimulated to reflect on their understanding of the task. In both of these conversation types, the initial asymmetries of knowledge take on a more positive or constructive role in the conversation, which consequently can sometimes move outside the limits associated with representations of gender or academic ability. As it does so, a different kind of social relation becomes established between the children in which both are recognized as thinking subjects contributing to the solution of the task. This is clearest in the *Explicit Recognition* conversations, where the non-conserver's reflection on their understanding is highlighted, resulting not only in greater evidence of developmental progress, but also in clearer evidence of cognitive reorganization in the extent of novelty in their posttest discussions.

CONCLUSION: FROM MICROGENESIS TO ONTOGENESIS

In returning to the vexed question of the relations between social interaction and cognitive development we have argued for the benefits of extending the analysis of the details of how conversations take shape and form for understanding the ways in which they may also structure the development of children. In this sense, development can be seen to proceed from the microgenesis of the emergence of shared representations of the task to the ontogenesis of cognition. At the center of this process through which social interaction influences and structures development are the different forms of participation through which children engage in the conversations. Where the child becomes an active participant in addressing and solving the task, then he or she also enters into (joint) ownership of the problem space of the task. A balanced triadic structure of child-child-task is established in which not only can different viewpoints be expressed, they can also be coordinated in a way in which each child is recognized as an active contributor to achieving the solution. In short, in these circumstances, children engage with their peer and the task as active agents, responsible for their own perspective and responsive to the perspective of the other. Participation in this sense is the cooperative moment at the heart of children's interactions, and if it is not always necessary for participation to occur for children to demonstrate progress on the posttest (cf the *Mf* girls who progress), then it does seem to be the case that only participation in this sense can lead to the interiorization which enables the child to produce novelty in the posttest.

Participation, though, is not the inevitable consequence of children interacting, but rather something which emerges from the particular type of conversation which is established between them as they address the task. It is in shaping the type of conversation that asymmetries between the children can be seen to have a significant role. Where the asymmetry is given a negative expression, the conversation remains bound by the different expectations associated with the asymmetry itself. Where the asymmetry becomes a more positive force it is because the contrasts, conflicts, and tensions it establishes lead to the conversation escaping from the limits set by prior expectations, thus opening the prospect of both children participating in the solution to the task. Consequently we also need to revise Piaget's distinction between constraint and cooperation. Rather than being construed as independent states of affairs, they need to be seen as social relations established through the processes of interaction. Indeed, the achievement of a cooperative relation may be just a moment within the flux of interaction, but it is a moment in which asymmetric relations between children can take on a constructive role leading to the emergence of more symmetric relations.

As with the "social Genevans," our approach to the study of social interaction and cognitive development is grounded in a social constructionist perspective, with its assumption that psychological activity is always the product of communication between different voices (cf. Marková, 2003). This perspective differs from Piaget's own constructionism precisely in relation to this assumption. In his brief comments on the first studies by Doise and his colleagues, Piaget (1976) himself raised this question by asking whether this research concerned the source of operations or their structure. Concretely, the question becomes one of asking whether social interaction is not only the context for disequilibration, but also provides the resources for the emergence of new forms of structure (that is for reequilibration). This, however, is not a straightforward or simple empirical question, in the sense that what can be observed might be uniquely interpretable from one theoretical perspective or the other. It is only through the theoretical work of interpretation that the constitutive or causal factors in development appear intelligible in relation to observable phenomena. In Piaget's own work, his analyzes of equilibration are likewise interpretations of observable phenomena. Our emphasis on the ways in which different types of conversation generate different outcomes for the participants is a step toward a broader effort to establish a social constructionist perspective on intellectual development.

As we have suggested earlier, our analyses of the relations between social interaction and cognitive development are derived from a triadic epistemology framed as the interdependence between the child, the other, and the object. Others (for example, Chapman, 1991; Schubauer-Leoni & Perret-Clermont, 1997; Zittoun, Cornish, Gillespie, & Psaltis, 2007) have also emphasized the need for such a triadic epistemology, and also remarked on the way this moves beyond the classical dyadic epistemological frame of Piagetian theory. Working through the consequences of adapting such an epistemology without simply abandoning Piaget's genetic epistemology is a challenge which still needs to be met.

Notes

1. Details of the statistical analyses of these data can be found in Psaltis and Duveen (2006).
2. Interrater agreement for the four conversation types was excellent (Cohen's Kappa=0.82, $p < 0.001$).
3. Details of this qualitative analysis are in Psaltis and Duveen (2007). In the transcripts, C indicates the conserving child, N the non-conserving child. This study was undertaken in Cyprus, and the transcripts are translated from the original Greek-Cypriot dialect.

References

Ames, G. J., & Murray, F. B. (1982). When two wrongs make a right: Promoting cognitive change by social conflict. *Developmental Psychology, 18,* 894–897.

Bearison, D., Magzamen, S., & Filardo, E. K. (1986). Socio-cognitive conflict and cognitive growth in young children. *Merrill-Palmer Quarterly, 32,* 51–72.

Butera, F., & Mugny, G. (Eds.). (2001). *Social influence in social reality: Promoting individual and social change.* Ashland, OH: Hogrefe and Huber.

Carpendale, J., & Müller, U. (Eds). (2004.). *Social interaction and the development of knowledge.* Mahwah, NJ: Lawrence Erlbaum.

Chapman, M. (1991). The epistemic triangle. Operative and communicative components of cognitive development. In M. Chandler & M. Chapman (Eds.), *Criteria for competence: Controversies in the conceptualisation and assessment of children's abilities* (pp. 209–228). Hillsdale, NJ: Lawrence Erlbaum.

Doise, W., & Mugny, G. (1984). *The social development of the intellect.* Oxford: Pergamon.

Doise, W., Mugny, G., & Pérez, J. A. (1998). The social construction of knowledge, social marking and sociocognitive conflict. In U. Flick (Ed.), *The psychology of the social* (pp. 77–90). Cambridge: Cambridge University Press.

Doise, W., Mugny, G., & Perret-Clermont, A. N. (1975). Social interaction and the development of cognitive operations. *European Journal of Social Psychology, 5,* 367–383.

Duveen, G. (1997). Psychological development as a social process. In L. Smith, P. Tomlinson, & J. Dockerell (Eds.), *Piaget, Vygotsky and beyond* (pp. 67–90). London: Routledge.

Duveen, G. (2000a). The power of ideas. Introduction to S. Moscovici, G. Duveen (Ed.), *Social representations: Explorations in social psychology* (pp. 1–17). Cambridge: Polity Press.

Duveen, G. (2000b). Piaget ethnographer. *Social Science Information, 39,* 79–97.

Duveen, G. (2001). Representations, identity, resistance. In K. Deaux & G. Philogene (Eds.), *Representations of the social* (pp. 257–270). Oxford: Blackwell.

Emler, N., & Glachan, M. (1985). Apprentissage et developpement cognitif. In G. Mugny (Ed.), *Psychologie sociale du developpement cognitif* (pp 71–92). Bern: Peter Lang.

Leman, P. J., & Duveen, G. (1999). Representations of authority and children's moral reasoning. *European Journal of Social Psychology, 29,* 557–575.

Lloyd, B., & Duveen, G. (1992). *Gender identities and education.* London: Harvester Wheatsheaf.

Marková, I. (2003). *Dialogicality and social representations: The dynamics of mind.* Cambridge: Cambridge University Press.

Moscovici, S. (1972). Society and theory in social psychology. In J. Israel & H. Tajfel (Eds.), *The context of social psychology* (pp. 17–68). London: Academic Press.

Moscovici, S. (1976). *Social influence and social change.* London: Academic Press.

Moscovici, S. (1980). Towards a theory of conversion behaviour. In L. Berkowitz (Ed.), *Advances in experimental psychology* (Vol. 13, pp. 209–239). London: Academic Press.

Mugny, G., De Paolis, P., & Carugati, F. (1984). Social regulations in cognitive development. In W. Doise & A. Palmonari (Eds.), *Social interaction in individual development* (pp. 127–146). Cambridge: Cambridge University Press & Maison des Sciences de l'Homme.

Perret-Clermont, A.-N. (1980). *Social interaction and cognitive development in children.* London: Academic Press.

Perret-Clermont, A.-N. (1994). Articuler l'individuel et le collectif. *New Review of Social Psychology, 3,* 94–102.

Perret-Clermont, A.-N., Perret, J. A., & Bell, N. (1991). The social construction of meaning and cognitive activity in elementary school children. In. L. B. Resnick, J. M. Levine, & S. D. Teasley (Eds.), *Perspectives on socially shared cognition* (pp. 41–62). Washington, D.C.: American Psychological Association.

Perret-Clermont, A.-N., & Schubauer-Leoni, M.-L. (1981). Conflict and cooperation as opportunities for learning. In P. Robinson (Ed.), *Communication in development* (pp. 203–233). London: Academic Press.

Piaget, J. (1932). *The moral judgement of the child.* London: Routledge & Kegan Paul.

Piaget, J. (1962). *Comments on Vygotsky's critical remarks concerning* The Language and Thought of the Child *and* Judgement and Reasoning in the Child. (Anne Parsons, Trans.). Cambridge, MA: MIT Press.

Piaget, J. (1976). Postface. *Archives de psychologie, 44,* 223–228.

Piaget J. (1995). *Sociological studies.* London: Routledge. (Original work published 1977)

Piaget, J., & Inhelder, B. (1969). *The psychology of the child.* London: Routledge & Kegan Paul.

Psaltis, C. (2005a). Communication and the construction of knowledge or transmission of belief: The role of conversation type, behavioural style and social recognition. *Studies in Communication Science, 5,* 209–228.

Psaltis, C. (2005b). *Social relations and cognitive development: The influence of conversation types and representations of gender.* Unpublished doctoral dissertation, University of Cambridge.

Psaltis, C., & Duveen, G. (2006). Social relations and cognitive development: The influence of conversation type and representations of gender. *European Journal of Social Psychology, 36,* 407–430.

Psaltis, C., & Duveen, G. (2007). Conservation and conversation types: Forms of recognition and cognitive development. *British Journal of Developmental Psychology, 25,* 79–102.

Russell, J. (1982). Cognitive conflict, transmission, and justification: Conservation attainment through dyadic interaction. *Journal of Genetic Psychology, 140,* 283–297.

Russell, J., Mills, I., & Reiff-Musgrove, P. (1990). The role of symmetrical and asymmetrical social conflict in cognitive change. *Journal of Experimental Child Psychology, 49,* 58–78.

Schubauer-Leoni, M.-L., & Grossen, M. (1993). Negotiating the meaning of questions in didactic and experimental contracts. *European Journal of Psychology of Education, 8,* 451–471.

Schubauer-Leoni, M.-L., & Perret-Clermont, A.-N. (1997). Social interaction and mathematics learning. In P. Bryant & T. Nunes (Eds.), *Learning and teaching mathematics. An international perspective* (pp. 265–283). Hove: Psychology Press.

Tudge, J. (1992). Processes and consequences of peer collaboration: A Vygotskian analysis. *Child Development, 63,* 1364–1379.

Vygotsky, L. S. (1978). *Mind in society: The development of higher psychological processes.* Cambridge, MA: Harvard University Press.

Zittoun, T., Cornish, F., Gillespie, A., & Psaltis, C. (2007). The metaphor of the triangle in theories of human development. *Human Development, 50,* 208–229.

10

Selves and Identities in the Making
The Study of Microgenetic Processes in Interactive Practices

MICHAEL BAMBERG

CONSTANCY, CHANGE, AND DEVELOPMENT

Current developmental theorizing faces a number of dilemmas, if not aporias. The three most relevant ones that provide offspring for different approaches within developmental psychology are (1) the "identity dilemma," posing the question: how it is possible to consider oneself as the same in the face of constant change; (2) the "uniqueness dilemma": whether it is possible to consider oneself as unique in the face of being the same as everyone else (and vice versa); and (3) the "construction" or "who-is-in-charge-dilemma": asking whether it is the person who constructs the world the way it is, or whether the person is constructed by the way the world is. Answers that view these dilemmas in terms of the dialectics between (1) constancy and change; (2) uniqueness/specificity and generality/universality; and (3) two directions of fit, the person-to-world and world-to-person direction of fit, point out correctly that one is not thinkable without the other. Of course, these three dilemmas are highly interwoven. It could be argued that the construal of sameness and difference across time forms a presupposition for constructing others and self as same and different, which in turn can be said to be a basic building block for constructing and changing the world in a productive way. However, when it comes to doing developmental inquiry, that is, exploring how actual changes and constancies play each other out and are made sense of in the actual lives of human beings, in particular from the perspective of those who

live these lives, we are confronted with the additional dilemma that we can't take
the perspective of both of the opposing principles simultaneously, but rather seem
to be forced to choose.

In the following, since I will centrally be concerned with identity and the
analysis of emergent identity, I will focus mainly on the identity dilemma and
begin by an analysis of how it surfaces in developmental inquiry. I will first work
across current theorizing in developmental inquiry in order to lay the groundwork
for a microgenetic approach to identity analysis, one that is grounded in the traditions of Wernerian *Aktualgenese* but also enriched by current work in discourse
analysis and microethnography. Let me start out with some rather simple reflections on time and what we consider the same across the weathers of time and what
we consider change.

In principle, it seems that our developmental theorizing about constancies
and change in time are very much in line with the way we make sense of them
in our everyday talk as recurrent phenomena. Time seems to be stoppable in the
form of "moments." When we look from an angle that spans across these moments
and takes these moments as boundaries, imagining one at the left and the other at
the right, we can see what has changed and what has remained the same. Thus, it
seems, constancy and change only and always occur across a certain time span.
The moments that seem to hold and constrain this time span can bind together
for longer or shorter durations. They can construe periods of global or more local
time (such as the history of the human species, i.e., phylogenesis), the evolution of
communities (such as small groups like families or friendship networks), or larger
cultures and societies as in "histories of civilization" (sociogenesis), or changes in
the history of an individual organism from embryo to adulthood/maturity (ontogenesis). Moments as "substantial" points in time help to tie events into a particular sequential structure and at the same time serve to differentiate the structure
under consideration from previous and subsequent event structures. In principle,
the span of interest can also consist of a series of very brief snapshots of moment-
to-moment, such as what happens between stimuli and reactions, the way Sander
(1930) and Werner (1926/1959, 1948) attempted to capture the processes of the
genesis of a percept or a thought (microgenesis).

Underlying these apparently *natural* constructs of the relation between continuity and change seem to be, nevertheless, a number of metaphors that allow
us to think and talk about time as stoppable, that is, as viewing the flow of time
as consisting of a series of (underlying) moments. Bickhard (this volume) characterizes this view as an outcome of the longstanding tradition of a "substance
metaphysics" by use of which we attribute "substance" to how time "moves on" in
the form of "substantial" continuous moments, as if one moment follows another
moment, ultimately adding up to what is perceived as the flow of moments into
"time." According to this view, "stasis…is the explanatory default, and any purported change requires explanation" (Bickhard, this volume). It is interesting to
note that according to this view the substance or meaningfulness of moments
comes to existence only as the result of its history—the previous moments that

happened before. Bickhard's alternative, to take continuous change as the under-lying principle for the possibility to abstract stasis from it, is very much in line with Bergson's approach to "reality as a process" (Bergson, 1913/2001). Accord-ing to this process-orientation, "the real" exists only as a constant and undivided flux; only by adopting a perspective that is equivalent with the substance view can we arrest time and take a perspective that moves us "above" and "out of" the flux of time so that time becomes available and disposable.

A way to better understand the difference between these two very different approaches to constancy, change, and development is by a closer consideration of how events and states, as two oppositional time frames, are differentiated. Events are constructs that emerge by perspectivizing temporal contours by the attribution of temporal boundaries (cf. Verkuyl, 1972; Weinrich, 1964). More spe-cifically, events of differing duration such as a dropping needle, traffic accidents, weddings, or someone's adolescence come to existence by way of establishing a boundary to the left (the beginning of the event) and a boundary to the right (its ending). What is happening in the middle is held together by these two bound-aries, giving it focus and current relevance. Simultaneously, it demarcates this event from previous and subsequent events. Similarly, states are also constructs; however, they emerge by taking a perspective that opens up, or better yet does *not* tie a happening to a particular temporal contour. Following such construction procedures, states such as being asleep, being alive, and the earth rotating around the sun can be created. Note that I am presenting both binding and unfolding pro-cedures as constructions rather than representations of the way the world is. This is not to say that these events or states do not exist or are only fictional products of some—individual or cultural, unwanted or agreed upon—binding and unfolding processes; not at all. Rather, the binding and unfolding activities are constitutive as perspectives from which events and states, constancies and change, and ulti-mately time and space *are constructively made use of.* They require identifying a figure and ground from the perspective of an agent who actively takes part in communal and individual meaning-making processes.

The way substance and process views of constancy and change (as well as event and state) can be brought into a relationship is by way of using the visualiza-tion of figure and ground in the common representations of a vase or jar versus the mirror image of the silhouette of a human face (see Figure 10.1). Whereas the left pictorial representation is more likely to be "recognized" (interpreted) as an image of two faces, the pictorial representation to the right is immediately recognizable as a vase. However, with a certain amount of effort, it is possible to reverse these interpretations and see the mirror image of two faces in the right picture and the contours of a vase in the left. And while one can say, at some more abstract level, that both pictures lend themselves to both interpretations, it is not possible to see both images at the same time. The reason is that what provides the ground for the figure is reversed in the two interpretive acts; figuring and grounding, the way they result in one or the other interpretation in this particular example, are mutually exclusive.

Figure 10.1 Figuring and grounding as mutually exclusive acts. (Courtesy of Kaiser Porcelain, LTD and the ITS Division of Clark University)

In our efforts to make sense of constancy and change, I am arguing, we are in a similar situation. While the substance-perspective attempts to focus and foreground aspects of change, using moments of substance as the basis, the process-perspective yields change to do the grounding work in order to highlight the emergence of moments. Whereas the act of grounding and figuring orients toward one such interpretation, the other is necessarily inaccessible. Only with a total reorientation of what was formerly the ground and now is turned into the figure can we move from one interpretive orientation to the other. To argue to access or engage orienting toward both at the same time is impossible and resembles the act of "Mambo #5."[1] Beginning to attend to the identity dilemma along those lines, and in similar ways to the "uniqueness" and "construction dilemma," clarifies that there is no resolution to these dilemmas, especially no simple resolution. Rather, both sides of the dilemmas can be viewed as two different kinds of approaches that sharpen the focus of a lens and concentrate on different aspects of the overall constellation. And although a sharper focus is beneficial for what is considered relevant, it loses sight of what becomes viewed to be peripheral.

Taking these insights back to our engagement with developmental inquiry, we are now in a better position to clarify that development does not exist in the form of changes out there, the way they seem to occur in "real time." Rather, and here I am taking up on Kaplan's (1983a, 1983b) clarification, it is not possible to read off development from people's actions and behaviors. Instead, development is a (value—and often valuable) perspective used to make sense of changes (in the light of constancies) and constancies (in the light of changes). It always presupposes a value-orientation from where changes and constancies are made sense of in an overall move toward a meaningful and as such positive telos. In light of the above discussion then, it should be obvious that seemingly neutral changes and constancies cannot be read off from individuals' isolated actions and behaviors, either. What we, as humans, consider stable and what we consider mutable requires a position from where we bring figure and a ground into a relationship. If constant temporal flux is the ground, then we bring out constancies as figures that can stand off against this ground. However, if we take constancies as the ground, we are figuring, so to speak, and highlighting what we consider to be relevant changes. Consequently, the perspective from where figure and ground are brought into a relationship can rarely be claimed to be neutral—but will turn out to be, in all likelihood, "developmentally colored" toward a telic orientation.

MICROGENESIS, MICROANALYSIS, AND POSITIONING

As mentioned in the opening section of this chapter, microgenesis has been part of a longstanding tradition of doing developmental inquiry (cf. Sander, 1930; Werner, 1948; and for overviews Lavelli, Panrtoja, Hsu, Messinger, & Fogel, 2005; Siegler, 2006), although the U.S.–European tradition, with its focus on children growing up and becoming adults, has neither particularly welcomed nor embraced this way of developmental theorizing. Its roots in Friedrich Sander's and Heinz Werner's original notion of *Aktualgenese* (which is probably best translated as "actual becoming" or "occasioning"—later termed by Werner in his English writings *microgenesis*), this notion was designed to open up the exploration of changes in percept or thought formation in very brief sequences of moments. For instance, the process of visual recognition was broken down experimentally in order to gain insight into the processes that then were taken to underlie how perceptual images were slowly being grasped and transformed into full consciousness (Werner, 1948, p. 348f.).

While still anchored firmly in the substance perspective of relating permanence and change, *Aktualgenese*/microgenesis nevertheless has opened up methods of inquiry that supposedly could arrest microgenetic processes of development by minimizing the temporal distance between moments—with the tendency of moving closer, if not "inside" the origins of the moment itself. In other words, while more macrodevelopmental processes were more clearly driven by the final outcome of developmental changes, the study of microdevelopmental processes not only credited the local contexts within which changes take place, but also simultaneously repositioned the moment itself with a potential genesis of its own. Naturally, this would imply a considerable weakening of the substance perspective and constitute a move in the direction of a process-orientation. At the same time, the procedures to investigate how moments become interpreted as meaningful by humans in concrete contexts would open up the terrain to qualitative methods such as closer (participant) observations, interviewing or projective testing, and microanalytic analyses of social interactions.

To put this differently, crediting the moment of an experience as the cornerstone for learning or other developmental transformations meant that it would be possible to integrate such moments into developmental theorizing and developmental inquiry. Transformational experiences that seemed to be tied up in moments abound in accounts of how we have learned to ride a bike, tie our shoes, or in other situations in which the kind of a-ha experience represented the breakthrough into a new and transformative practice or repertoire of performances.[2] However, although abundant in everyday accounts of how we experience development, such transformative breakthrough moments have been notoriously absent in developmental theorizing and empirical inquiry. This may have been partly due to the fact that in traditional developmental theorizing moments by themselves cannot be scrutinized for changes (and therefore become tucked away into the realm of personal anecdotes) and partly because the technology to capture such moments and prepare them for microscopic analysis has only recently progressed to a point where this seems to be possible.

While most microgenetic research has been accomplished in the field of cognitive development (summarized in Siegler, 2006), some more recent work has attempted to apply microgenetic methodology in the field of brain processes (Brown, 2002) and social development (c.f., Fogel, 1995; Fogel, de Koeyer, Bellagamba, & Bell, 2002; Lavelli et al., 2005.) With the exception of Brown's (2002) theory, which is explicitly grounded in the process-orientation of Bergson, almost all microgenetic research is anchored in the substance approach to change and constancy. Nevertheless, there have been a number of interesting innovations that provide a good platform for further developmental theorizing and applications in developmental inquiry.

Let me start out with Siegler's (2006) three main properties that he holds as central for the application of microgenetic methods, which are:

1.   Observations span the period of rapidly changing competence.

2.   Within each period, the density of observations is high, relative to the rate of change.

3.   Observations are analyzed intensively, with the goal of inferring the representations and processes that gave rise to them. (Siegler, 2006, p. 469)

While the first two properties are relevant, it is the third that has become the center of innovative research strategies, marrying the method of doing microgenesis with the Wernerian focus on microcontext and Vygotskyan focus on sociocultural macrocontexts. As an attempt to better understand the processes that give rise to novel representations and competencies at more "developed" levels of differentiation and integration, Saxe's (1988, 1998, 2002) analysis of the microcultures of math practices (inside and outside of classroom interactions) presents illuminating examples of how developmental inquiry has become invigorated by microgenetic approaches. In a nutshell, Saxe argues:

> In collective practices, joint tasks are accomplished…through the interrelated activities of individuals. In such joint accomplishments, individual and collective activities are reciprocally related. Individual activities are constitutive of collective practices. At the same time, the joint activity of the collective gives shape and purpose to individuals' goal-directed activities. (pp. 276–277)

Consequently, the study of the emergence of mathematical knowledge starts with minute descriptions of concrete interactional practices, within which the knowledge originally is "housed." From here, by engaging in these practices (here as "doing" mathematics), particulars of these practices become routinized and transformed over time into competencies and representational capacities that may reach deeply into the representations of beliefs and values.[3] The focus on the situated and local management of context—managed by individuals in interaction—was a central characteristic of what emerged as a new wave in the analytic inquiry of microgenetic development.

Microgenetic processes have been at the heart of some functionalist approaches to children's language development where processes have been examined in mother–child interaction (Budwig, 1995, 2000, 2003) and early book-reading activities (Bamberg, 1987, 1997a, in press) in order to show how developmental changes occur in concrete action contexts under highly specific conditions. Using video- and audiorecorded data of coconstructed activities between children and more capable others, we were able to show how local accomplishments at the level of joint actions could function as resources for differentiations that appeared later on the plane of individual functioning. Building on Werner and Kaplan's (1963/1984) *orthogenetic principle*, according to which development is defined in terms of increasing differentiation and hierarchic integration in human functioning, we developed and presented techniques that document microgenetic changes as changing qualities in children's form–function coordination (Bamberg, Budwig, & Kaplan, 1991). In recent years I have systematically extended this approach to a more fine-grained analysis of how identities and a sense of self first become differentiated at the level of interactions in order to become consequently integrated into repertoires that can productively be employed in new interactions in new situations. Notably, in these types of analyses, I have continually tried to refine our descriptions of face-to-face interactions in moment-to-moment situations in order to better understand how participants work out issues of sameness and difference in real time and contribute as active agents to differentiations and higher levels of sophistication of their own individual competencies and social-relational work with one another (Bamberg, 2004a, 2004b; Bamberg & Georgakopoulou, in press).

In the process of developing and refining microanalysis as the proper means to deal with the process of microgenesis, it became clear that we were not dealing with the development of relational or dialogic *knowledge* at the intrapsychological level.[4] Rather, we were dealing with the construction of actual relations and dialogues in real-world time and situations. Our endeavors of developing microscopic descriptions of human activities in interactions became spurred by recent advances in the work of Garfinkel (1967), Goffman (1981), Kendon (1990), and Scheflen (1974), resulting in what is probably best characterized as a turn to microethnography (see Streeck & Mehus, 2005, for an excellent overview of the emergence of this field). Central to microethnography are (1) the level of microscopic attention to situated local contexts as being under construction and constantly changing through the activities performed by the interactants (as "in the making"); (2) the central role of language as constitutive of these contexts, though in concert with other multimodal actions (such as postural configurations, gaze, prosodic delivery, and suprasegmentation); and (3) the analysis of the sequential performance and online negotiation of moment-to-moment interactions. Thus, a microethnographically informed analysis of the sequential arrangement of interaction is the most constructive way, within a process-oriented framework, to guide inquiry into the genesis of how people *make*[5] sense of themselves and others, ultimately linking up the micro with the macro.

In recent articles, we have tried to promote and apply this type of micro-ethnographic analysis to psychology under the heading of *positioning analysis* (Bamberg, 1997b, 2003; Bamberg & Georgakopoulou, in press). The term *positioning* has been contrastively refined and redefined with reference to earlier forms of positioning analysis (Davies & Harré, 1990; Harré & van Langenhove, 1999; Hollway, 1989). The purpose of this redefinition has been to focus more effectively on the construction or who-is-in-charge-dilemma; that is, the apparent contradiction between the agentive organism as positioning him- or herself, and the societal, sociocultural constraints seemingly "always and already" at work positioning "the subject." Positioning analysis along these newly defined lines studies how people as agentive actors position themselves—and in doing so become positioned.

To clarify, it is important to note that, for microanalytic purposes, it is the subject's actions that form the starting point of the analysis. From there, the next step is the sequential arrangement between interactants that ties actions into configurations within which these individual acts become recognizable as actions and meaningful interactive encounters.[6] Obviously, this type of functional analysis is reminiscent of the analysis of brief moments as moment-to-moment processes in which meaningful events emerge —though note that this analysis explicitly makes the agentive role of the person central for the genesis of meaningful interactions. This is not to deny the existence of social constraints that "allow" for certain actions (and interactions), disallowing others. However, rather than taking these kinds of constraints as preexisting macrostructures to form the starting point for our analytic inquiry, we view them as *products* or *outcomes* of individual actions in interactions. While a macroanalytic approach would start with a concept of the subject as primarily socially constructed by outside, societal forces resulting in actions and activities that somehow reflect these constraints, we propose a different route. Taking off from micro- and sociogenesis as the local and situated formation sites of identity and otherness, the particular focus here is on practices in which subjects evoke (or position themselves vis-à-vis) dominant discourses or master narratives (Bamberg, 2004b), thereby effectively linking up to the macro of our social world. Positioning a sense of self in interactive practices opens the door to analyzing empirically how interactants make locally relevant whether and how they want to be understood in alignment with such dominant discourses or in opposition to and subverting them.

This model of positioning proposed in previous works (Bamberg, 1997b, 2004a; Bamberg & Georgakopoulou, in press) affords us the possibility of viewing identity constructions as twofold: We are able to analyze the *way* the referential world is constructed, with characters (such as self and others) in time (then) and space (there). Simultaneously, we are able to show how the referential world is constructed as a function of the interactive engagement, where the way the referential world is constructed points to how the teller "*wants to be understood*"; or more appropriately, to how tellers index a sense of self. It is precisely this groundedness of self and identity in sequential, moment-to-moment interactive engagements that is at best undertheorized and at worst dismissed in traditional developmental inquiry.

In the following, I will illustrate identity work through positioning in brief moments of interactions by turning the tables on a typical interview elicitation scenario (in which the researcher elicits monologic answers to explore aspects of the researched participant) to see what happens when the researched participants (in this case, a group of 10-year-old boys in a working-class East Coast American elementary school talking to one another in the presence of the moderator) engage in identity work that attends to peer group roles, dynamics, and shared interactional history on the one hand, and to the interview situation (including the moderator) on the other hand. I am consciously choosing to work with a brief segment that occurred in an interview situation to make tangible the point about the necessity of including moment-to-moment interactions in the main agenda of identity analysis as a form of developmental inquiry that is apt to be linked to the construction of more macroaspects of the social world we live in.

The sequence of discourse activities that I will analyze next routinely gets dismissed by developmental researchers since it does not seem to represent any developmental points worthy of study. However, I hope to be able to show that the microanalysis of a particular interaction segment is more than just the exemplification or illustration of a theoretical entry and methodological inclination. The functionalist orientation vis-à-vis talk in interaction as tools to constitute worlds, and in these worlds a sense of self, captures aspects of how this sense of self is manufactured in this particular site of engagement. As such, this reveals the processes within which selves are under construction. Entering the microgenesis of identity from this perspective, I propose to look into *one* concrete site of engagement in which senses of self are tried out and negotiated. What follows is an empirical analysis of the procedures (repertoires) used by speakers in order to establish a particular sense of self in and through their talk. The analysis will pay particular attention to the formation of a sense of self in the face of seemingly different discursive pulls[7]: one toward a sense of (unrelational) masculinity according to which it is uncool to invest in relationships with girls and the other pulling toward a seemingly more relational stance, according to which it is okay, if not cool, to "be involved" or "have a girl friend."

"No One Ever Liked That Girl": Identity Formation as Process—Selves in the Making

The excerpt I will analyze at the microlevel stems from a group discussion session in which four 10-year-old boys and an adult (male) moderator are sitting around a table and talk about—broadly speaking—what it means to be a 10-year-old. This was the topic under which the participants had been recruited, and this phrase had been used as the opener for the discussion session. The excerpt comes from a time well into the discussion and reflects to a large extent the way the interaction was structured by the interactants. The interactions were video- and audiotaped and transcribed by using a simplified transcription that presents each turn as a unit—the length of pauses marked by dots (.) or giving the full length (1 sec), and overlaps marked by square brackets by [, and latching-on by //. Contextual remarks such as gestures and gaze directions are in triangular brackets <>. I will abstain from giving more information such as the socioeconomic background of the participants, their standing in school, their relational histories, and what we learned about the boys' families and the boys' private lives in the course of our study, since this type of information may call for interpretive categories that may or may not be relevant for a better understanding of the participants' interactions in this particular situation. In essence, we are attempting to bring as little pre-formed knowledge as possible to the work with this excerpt in order to see what categories they actually make relevant (in the sense of interactively attending to) in their talk.

Analyzing the excerpt microethnographically means that we attempt to follow the five interactants in their mutual constructions of each other and themselves in their moment-by-moment interaction. This way, we assume, we will be able to "lay open" the *how* of the genesis of identities and selves in *this* piece of interaction; that is, we will scrutinize how the interactants position themselves using macrocategories and recreating them in their business of making sense of each other. Through these activities they form a sense of who they are. "Analyzing" here will consist of determining the acts in their sequence that led to some understanding of the overall structure of the interaction at the microlevel; the analysis thus is meant to be quite different from simply paraphrasing what the interactants are saying. It also attempts to avoid bringing outside categories prematurely to the interpretive business at hand.

Topical flow

The topic that was in the process of being negotiated at the onset of the excerpt, mainly between Martin and the moderator, was on Kimberly, a female character in the TV series *The Power Rangers*. This is a topic that the moderator (in turn 2: "*what about that?*") seemingly attempts to make relevant for the other participants by eliciting others' responses. Victor, in turn 3, responds by initiating his own question, picking up and repeating the moderator's exact lexical phrase to introduce his question ("*what about*"), and keeps one aspect of the topic the same ("*Kimberly*"). However, in what follows, it becomes clear that he changes the topic to another character, Kimberly Spears, and continues by reformulating his "*what about Kimberly Spears*" question, seemingly making it more precise, by asking whether anyone *ever liked that girl*. The phrasing suggests a *dispreferred* answer. Martin's request (turn 4) for clarification of the initial question is followed by the repetition of the name (turn 5), suggesting that Martin's question was heard by

Table 10.1 Transcript of the whole interaction (Lines 1–40)

Participants: Mod—Moderator; Martin; Victor; Wally; Stanton

1	Martin	…I'd say like (.) Kimberly↑(.) the Power Ranger↓
2	Mod	what about that↓
3	Victor	d'know Kimberly Spears↓ (1sec) did anyone ever like that girl↑
4	Martin	who
5	Victor	Kimberly Spears↓
6	Mod	who [is that
7	Victor	[I think Stanton did
8	Mod	who is Kimberly Spears
9	Wally	I do [not know↓
10	Mod	[is she (.) is she a (.)
11	Victor	it was a girl who used to uh go to our school (.) she she moved um
12	Wally	who liked Britney that was in Mrs. [Petrie's class
13	Victor	[no Britney Longlanderthat was Louis (.) that was Louis Martinez//
14	Stanton	//fine I kind of liked her(1 sec)
15	Wally	ha:a[\<high pitch> \<gaze toward Stanton; pointing with left hand at Stanton; briefly shifting gaze to Victor, then back to Stanton>
16	Victor	[I knew it I knew [it I knew it (.) that girl used to always have like a fruit punch thing around her mouth=
17	Stanton	[a little bit
		=I know (.) no chapped lips
18	Victor	yeah, chapped lips (.) like she had like this big thing that used to go eeuw// \<encircles his mouth with both hands - with high pitch noise]
19	Stanton	//no it was like over here \<motions just a little under and around his left edge of his mouth>
20	Mod	and you you think it was from [fruit punch?
21	Wally	[there was this one girl (.) there was this one girl
22	Victor	\<gazing at and nodding in response to Moderator's question> she must have gone] \<lifting up a pretend cup and pretending to drink with a slurping noise>
23	Stanton	[there's two other people I like that aren't in the school anymore↑
24	Martin	who
25	Stanton	no one
26	Martin	you can't tell them
27	Victor	Brittany [Long
28	Wally	[Britney =Long
29	Victor	=I know that↓ you used to always hang around Britney Long (.) Britney Long (.) Britney Longlander↑//
30	Stanton	//Britney Britney
31	Martin	I think James Mason likes Christine Janson
32	Wally	Christine liked James uh [James Heisen before
33	Stanton	[Stephanie(.) not Stephanie [that's in school now (.) Stephanie//
34	Wally	[at the beginning of the year yeah she told us *(continued)*

Table 10.1 Continued

35	Victor	//Gonsalves↑//
36	Stanton	//no↓ she's not in school anymore (.) and (1 sec) Shannon <smiling and coming up from resting-on-table position>
37	Victor	eoh and you liked Shannon she was so ugly I [ha:te her <moves both hands up to his head – covers his eyes – pulls his hat down>
38	Stanton	[yeah she's annoying but
39	Mod	(1 sec) alright [see….
40	Victor	[she's a tattletale

Victor only as an acoustic issue. The moderator (turn 6) follows up on Martin's previous request, by now more overtly asking for further specification about this girl (*"who is that?"*). Victor, whose turn (7) overlaps with the moderator's request, follows up on his own earlier question (whether anyone liked this girl) by giving the answer (*"I think Stanton did"*). To summarize thus far: Victor initiates a new topic, a girl that supposedly is not likable; he asks whether anyone ever liked that girl, implying that nobody would, and then gives the answer to his own question, suggesting that one of the participating boys, namely Stanton, actually likes (or liked) her.

In terms of analyzing how Victor crafted the implication that one of the participants liked an "unlikable girl," we may want to ask which other way he could have phrased his question. One suggestion is that he could have addressed Stanton more directly by, let's say, "You liked Kimberly Spears, who is an unlikable person." However, for reasons unclear at this point, he chose a highly indirect way to formulate what clearly can be construed as a challenge, since liking something or somebody "unlikable" requires some form of explication on the part of the person who has been implicated. However, there is no immediate response from Stanton. Instead, the subsequent turns (8–13, lasting for exactly 15 seconds) center first on some more information about Kimberly Spears, and from there move the conversation to other girl–boy relations. A more fine-grained analysis of these turns would reveal, although I do not have the space to lay this out in detail, that the emerging activity frame in these few turns is one of gossiping about who in their peers is "going" with whom. If this is correct, then Victor's implication of Stanton retrospectively has turned into a de facto statement that Stanton "was going out with" Kimberly Spears. This is something that up to turn 13 had not been rejected but neither was it supported by anyone. It seemed to have become currently irrelevant. The flow of the conversation had moved on to another, seemingly more interesting, topic.

It is at this moment (turn 14) that Stanton formulates what becomes the answer to Victor's original question (turn 3), but he simultaneously counters Victor's challenge with turn 7: Stanton's *"fine"* in turn-initial position clearly marks his answer in contrast to what was laid out as expected. In other words, Stanton clearly contextualizes the dispreferred orientation that Victor had suggested and decidedly counters it. At the same time, he hedges his answer carefully: he only "*kind of*" liked the girl under discussion. This modification is further specified by "*a little bit*"—a turn by Stanton that fully overlaps with Victor's response to Stanton's previous turn. The reaction to what in the sequential arrangement of the moment-by-moment actions of the participants is becoming an "admission" is in line with the dispreferred orientation of the initial question: Victor's (turn 16) repetition (three times) of his "knowing" (past tense: "*I knew it*") functions to align his audience to the sequence of his previous actions: my (Victor's) challenge of you, Stanton, was and is legitimate. Wally's reaction to Stanton's "admission" is equally telling: He points at Stanton and outright laughs, though he first reassures his reaction by a quick gaze check towards Victor, the initiator of this sequence of moments, signaling that the target of his laughter is Stanton. At this point it is unclear as to why Stanton's admission is "laughable," unless we are about to bring in a categorical interpretation that men who "are going" with partners who aren't likable are the laughing stock of other men. However, this could surmount a premature closing of what is in the midst of emerging in the conversation of the participants. Additionally it is from an adult vantage point; that is, not necessarily from the orientation that these 10-year-olds are in the business of working up.

A quick look into a different modality will strengthen and confirm the analysis of what is emerging here in the participants' moment-by-moment interactions. At the time of the delivery of his question (turn 3), Victor's body and gaze are fully oriented toward the moderator, suggesting that his question is clearly in response

Table 10.2 Transcript of lines 7–14 (including gaze and duration)

			Gaze direction/ object handling	Time duration between turn 7 and turn 14
7	Victor	[I think Stanton did	brief gaze to Stanton	_____
8	Mod	who is Kimberly Spears		↓↓
9	Wally	I do [not know↓	full gaze to Stanton	↓↓
10	Mod	[is she(.) is she (.)		↓↓
11	Victor	it was a girl who used to uh go to our school (.) she moved um	shifting gaze to Mod	15 sec
12	Wally	who liked Brittany that was in Mrs. Petrie's class	Stanton handling object	↓↓
13	Victor	[no Britney Longlander↑ that was Louis (.) that was Louis Martinez//	<displaying disinterest>	↓↓
14	Stanton	//fine I kind of liked her	___	↓↓

to the moderator's question. Although it is not an answer, it nevertheless picks up on the moderator's suggestion to open the floor for turns from others; that's what he is following up on. At the point in time where he explicitly refers to and implicates Stanton (turn 7: *I think Stanton did*), he shifts gaze for a split-second to Stanton (turning his head but immediately turning it back) while maintaining his overall body orientation vis-à-vis the moderator. Then, when the moderator explicitly asks for more information, Victor turns more fully to Stanton, as if an answer is expected to come from Stanton. Then Stanton, who was resting his head on the table, upon hearing his name raises his head. However, he keeps his gaze fixed on an object that he simultaneously handles. He returns shortly afterwards to his former position, lowering his head and resting his chin on his hands on the table. He maintains this position another 10 seconds and does not move up his chin during the performance of his turn (14: *fine I kind of liked her*). However, when challenged by Wally (turn 15) and Victor (turn 16), Stanton moves his head up. He delivers his modification "*a little bit*," expressed with a bright smile, then moves his head back into a resting position again. In sum, this brief description of the sequential arrangement of body posture and gaze orientation adds to a better understanding of what actions are sequentially at play in the construction of some integrated sense of what is going on.

In the following, I will limit my analysis to two small parts of the subsequent actions between the participants. Victor's characterization of Kimberly in turn 18 as having "*like a fruit punch thing around her mouth*" orients toward the category of "slob" or "baby" (or both). It is countered by Stanton by a turn-initial agreement (*I know*), but then he negates (*no*), and subsequently corrects Victor's claim, making clear that her lips looked the way they looked due to being chapped. Stanton's implication can be heard along the lines that chapped lips can happen to anyone; they are not Kimberly's fault, while drinking fruit punch resulting in fruit-punch lips is. In other words, Stanton's remarks can be understood in terms of his action-orientation as fending for Kimberly. Subsequently, Victor responds (turn 18) with a turn-initial consent (*yeah, chapped lips*) but then continues with a slurping noise, which may be understood as insisting on his earlier fruit punch version. He further characterizes Kimberly's lips in terms of a rather largely affected area. In parallel to his previous move, Stanton (turn 19) opposes Victor's version (*no*) and describes the affected area to be much smaller (*it was like only here*). Again, while Victor's descriptions of Kimberly can be taken to downgrade her appearance and her character, something that is in line with his original and opening characterization of Kimberly as "unlikable," Stanton's descriptions are fending off and can be understood as upgrading Kimberly as a potentially likable character.

The second segment I briefly want to analyze is consequent to Stanton's further admission in turn 23, namely that he liked two other *people*, none of them at their school anymore. While it is noteworthy that these two girls are referred to as "people" and that neither of them is said to be at their school anymore, I want to focus on how this statement assists Stanton in involving the other participants in

Table 10.3 Transcript of lines 16–21

16	Victor	[I knew it I knew [it I knew it (.) that girl used to always have like a fruit punch thing around her mouth=
17	Stanton	[a little bit
		=I know (.) no chapped lips
18	Victor	yeah, chapped lips (.) like she had like this big thing that used to go eeuw// <encircles his mouth with both hands - with high pitched noise]
19	Stanton	//no it was like over here <motions just a little under and around his left edge of his mouth>
20	Mod	and you you think it was from [fruit punch?
21	Wally	[there was this one girl (.) there was this one girl

a guessing game as to who these girls might be. Note that he was not pressed for more information on girls, in particular girls he liked; so the subsequent rounds of individual turn-taking actions are clearly (re-) initiated by him. Then, when he discloses the name of the second girl, Shannon (turn 36), since nobody seems to remember the first girl, Victor starts out with an evaluative sound (*euw*) and a question that is rhetorically formatted to display a nonpreferred response (*you liked Shannon*), followed by two ultimate negative assessments (*she was so ugly*

Table 10.4 Transcript of lines 23–40

23	Stanton	[there's two other people I like that aren't in the school anymore↑
24	Martin	who
25	Stanton	no one
26	Martin	you can't tell them
27	Victor	Brittany [Long
28	Wally	[Britney =Long
29	Victor	=I know that you used to always hang around Britney Long (.) Britney Long (.) Britney Longlander↑//
30	Stanton	//Britney Britney
31	Martin	I think James Mason likes Christine Janson
32	Wally	Christine liked James uh [James Heisen before
33	Stanton	[Stephanie(.) not Stephanie [that's in school now (.) Stephanie//
34	Wally	[at the beginning of the year yeah she told us
35	Victor	//Gonsalves↑//
36	Stanton	//no↓ she's not in school anymore (.) and (1 sec) Shannon <smiling and coming up from resting-on-table position>
37	Victor	eoh and you liked Shannon she was so ugly I [ha:te her <moves both hands up to his head—covers his eyes – pulls his hat down>
38	Stanton	[yeah she's annoying but
39	Mod	(1 sec) alright [see….
40	Victor	[she's a tattletale

and *I ha:te her*). In parallel to Stanton's earlier activities of fending for Kimberly, he starts his turn (38) by an initial agreement (*yeah*) but then considerably down-grades Victor's evaluation by describing her "only" as "*annoying*"; followed by "*but*," suggesting a list of further attributes disagreeing with Victor and working toward an upgrading of Kimberly.

Summary

Attempting to answer the question of what the participants are talking *about*, or what the overall topic of the conversation is that holds it together thematically, Victor and Stanton both refer to three female characters (actually, there are more, but I only analyzed these three). The characters are drawn up in some evoked past events that are not further specified: Kimberly Spears, Shannon, and Stanton. It is the relationship between Stanton and these two girls, respectively, that is under discussion—whether he actually "liked" these girls. Now, we could have started out with the question: What does it mean for a 10-year-old boy to like a girl, and we could have speculated about that. Instead, we decided to make this question more specific by asking: What does it mean to get caught liking a girl by one's male peers? The investigation focused on this question by analyzing the discursive means that are employed when becoming implicated in exactly this.

One important aspect of the discursive means employed were particular characterizations in the sense of designing or fashioning characters in the realm of the talked about. As we could see, Stanton carefully positions Kimberly and Shannon in the referred-to world of the there-and-then in order to position him-self in the here-and-now of the group discussion. And equally, Victor positions Kimberly, Shannon, and Stanton in the there-and-then in order to position him-self in the here-and-now to display a sense of how he understands gender and gender relationships. In that sense, the interaction between the two boys, Victor and Stanton, into which the other participants are pulled, is not really about those girls, but about themselves, individually as well as in this group. Both of them engage in some very careful positioning of the characters in the there-and-then of the referred-to world and themselves in the here-and-now of this interaction, signaling that they are maneuvering in between two pulls.

At first glance, these two pulls can be characterized in terms of coming across as finding girls attractive versus not being interested in girls. As such, both boys can be heard as juggling two "dominant discourses": One according to which they can be seen as being invested in girls where "going with" constitutes a potential gain in social capital, and the other in which they come across as not attracted to girls, where hanging out with girls and "doing girl-stuff" is uncool. This is what one might expect in preadolescent and adolescent (American) boys, where girls "have cooties" and are characterized as "yuck." However, behind this superficial characterization that traditionally tends to inscribe these contradictions in par-ticular developmental phases of growing up heterosexual (Maccoby, 1998), two more powerful conceptual orientations seem to be lurking: These pulls can be characterized as two master narratives (or dominant discourses) that position narrators in quite different ways. The two conflicting master narratives in this case are a dependent, soft and caring, more feminine sense of self on the one hand, and an independent, strong, noncommittal, and more masculine sense of self on the other. Whereas the first is used by Stanton to position himself regarding girls, Victor employs the second to position himself as different and in contrast to girls. Victor and Stanton, in their discursive maneuvers between these two positions, can be shown as constructing two distinguishable orientations as ways of making sense of themselves (and each other).

CONCLUSIONS

The above analysis, performed on the sequential arrangements of interactions among the five participants, has revealed aspects of the genesis of how people make sense of themselves and others—here with emphasis on the interactive practices of 10-year-old young males. As has been demonstrated, the analysis was not attempting to access sense-making as intrapsychological activities in the mind, but *in the activities* among participants—positionings of self and others in the social domain of talk-in-interaction. And it should be noted that the analysis was not solely relying on language as linguistic activities and strategies. It is the body that is analyzed in concert with other bodies, with language taking a somewhat central role but always deeply embedded within other multimodal actions (such as postural configurations, gaze, prosodic delivery, and suprasegmentation). Local contexts and situated meanings are constituted and continuously produced and reproduced in concert with these actions. What became notable in the analysis of the sequence under consideration was how sense-making as a moment-to-moment process is grounded in the developmental dynamics of integration and differentiation: While the individual acts in their sequential arrangements were seen as becoming progressively differentiated, they also were viewed as simultaneously becoming integrated into larger meaningful units, thereby contributing to some overarching understanding of what is being accomplished in terms of the genesis of identities and selves in local, situated activities (*Aktualgenese*).

Of course it could be argued that the participants must have had access to the kinds of pulls in the form of master narratives prior to the specific encounter analyzed. In one way or another, they must have heard or been exposed to them before, so they can call them into being by drawing up positions vis-à-vis these master narratives. However, previous exposure does not result necessarily in complicity or in counterpositions. At best, the argument of previous exposure may lead participants to try out positions, without prematurely fixing them as positions—and this is precisely what we are able to show by way of microanalytically delineating the maneuvers that lead to the identification of positions. Further analysis into the ways these maneuvers are negotiated could lay open how, in spite of the competitiveness of the individual moves of the interactants, they still result in something that can be characterized in terms of (male) solidarity and probably even harmony.[8] Speaking sociogenetically, the participants use the interaction to test out masculinity discourses, manipulate them for different purposes in order to check for potential gains and losses, while overall still striving for some form of relational stance among each other.

Starting from the assumption that moment-by-moment changes are the ground against which events begin to stand out and then can be integrated into larger, overarching configurations that are socially and individually meaningful, we can begin to appreciate how a process-orientation can be productively used for empirical work in developmental inquiry. Along similar lines, work within this type of approach to development and change (and constancy) equally contributes to a better understanding not only of the identity dilemma, but also to how identity becomes constituted as same and different from others (the sameness dilemma) and how the individual agentively construes him- or herself and is constantly being construed by social, outside forces (the construction dilemma). The assumption that process is a natural ingredient of meaning construction that reaches deep into the formation of selves and identities, opens up new challenges for developmental psychologists and forms a particularly exciting frontier for empirical contributions that attempt to link the micro and the macro of our social world.

Notes

1. Mambo #5, a 1999 hit by Lou Bega, has become an MTV expression for "wanting to have too many things at the same time." See for the wording of the song: http://www.lyricsondemand.com/onehitwonders/mambo5lyrics.html
2. This is not to deny that there are other possible accounts of learning in the form of a history of trials and errors, possibly mixed with a good amount of rewards and punishments; or, alternatively, accounts that build on our genetic endowment and sociocultural constraints in the form of socialization practices.
3. Interestingly, micro- and sociogenesis both complement one another in these practices: What can be viewed on the one hand as the emergence of individual accomplishments of means-end relations (e.g., in the form of counting practices), on the other hand appears as communal practice that has the potential of resulting in the joint experience of intimacy and belonging as emergent relations among the participants, thereby reaffirming the process of "practicing."
4. Positing relationality or dialogicality as intraorganismic "substances" is asking for a very traditional type of developmental inquiry, namely one that centers on their unfolding at moments in ontogenesis–rather than along micro- and sociogenetic lines (i.e., investigating how relationality and dialogicality are actually established in the time and space of moment-by-moment interactions).
5. Making sense is meant very literally: While sense-making traditionally is a figure of speech for the mental activity of "understanding," here we are appealing to the activity of sense construal—in action and interaction between people—and only in subsequent steps in the head or in the mind of individuals.
6. Note how this resembles the developmental principle of *integration* and simultaneous *differentiation* into some overarching, holistic organization.
7. "Discursive pulls" are discursively organized types of making sense; although they can be analyzed as having an existence outside of concrete interactions and exercis-

ing a certain rhetorical power over individuals and their actions, our analysis below only attends to these "pulls" insofar as participants of the interaction actually evoke the categories and display these "pulls" in their interactions.

8. Note how both Victor and Stanton start each of their turns marking an overall agreement before detailing their disagreement. And note further how their exchanges display an overall sense of tentativeness and playfulness.

References

Bamberg, M. (1987). *The acquisition of narratives: Learning to use language.* Berlin: Mouton de Gruyter.

Bamberg, M. (1997a). A constructivist approach to narrative development. In M. Bamberg (Ed.), *Narrative development—Six approaches* (pp. 89–132). Mahwah, NJ: Erlbaum.

Bamberg, M. (1997b). Positioning between structure and performance. *Journal of Narrative and Life History, 7,* 335–342.

Bamberg, M. (2000). Critical personalism, language, and language development. *Theory & Psychology, 10,* 749–767.

Bamberg, M. (2003) Positioning with Davie Hogan—Stories, tellings, and identities. In C. Daiute & C. Lightfoot (Eds.), *Narrative analysis: Studying the development of individuals in society* (pp. 135–157). London: Sage.

Bamberg, M. (2004a). "We are young, responsible, and male": Form and function of "slut-bashing" in the identity constructions in 15-year-old males. *Human Development, 47,* 331–353.

Bamberg, M. (2004b). Considering counter narratives. In M. Bamberg & M. Andrews (Eds.), *Considering counter narratives: Narrating, resisting, making sense* (pp. 351–371). Amsterdam: John Benjamins.

Bamberg, M. (in press). Sequencing events in time or sequencing events in story-telling? From cognition to discourse—With frogs paving the way. In J. Guo, S. Ervin-Tripp, & N. Budwig (Eds.), *Festschrift for Dan Slobin.* Mahwah, NJ: Erlbaum.

Bamberg, M., Budwig, N., & Kaplan, B. (1991). A developmental approach to language acquisition: Two case studies. *First Language, 11*(1), 121–141.

Bamberg, M., & Georgakopoulou, A. (in press). Small stories as a new perspective in narrative and identity analysis. *Text & Talk.*

Bergson, H. (2001). *Duration and simultaneity* (F. L. Pogson Trans.). Manchester: Clinamen. (Original work published 1913)

Brown, J. W. (2002). *Self-embodying mind: Process, brain dynamics and the conscious present.* Barrytown, NY: Midpoint Trade Books.

Budwig, N. (1995). *A developmental-functionalist approach to child language.* Mahwah, NJ: Lawrence Erlbaum.

Budwig, N. (2000). Language and the construction of self: Linking forms and functions across development. In N. Budwig, I. Uzgiris, & J. Wertsch (Eds.), *Communication: An arena of development* (pp. 195–214). Stamford, CT: Ablex.

Budwig, N. (2003). Context and the dynamic construal of meaning in early childhood. In C. Raeff, J. Benson, & J. Kruper (Eds.). *Social and cognitive development in the context of individual, social, and cultural processes.* London: Routledge.

Davies, B., & Harré, R. (1990). Positioning: The social construction of selves. *Journal for the Theory of Social Behaviour, 20,* 43–63.

Fogel, A. (1995). Development and relationships: A dynamic model of communication. *Advances in the Study of Behavior, 24,* 259–290.

Fogel, A., de Koeyer, I., Bellagamba, F., & Bell, H. (2002). The dialogical self in the first two years of life: Embarking on a journey of discovery. *Theory and Psychology, 12*, 191–205.

Garfinkel, H. (1967). *Studies in ethnomethodology.* Englewood Cliffs, NJ: Prentice Hall.

Goffman, I. (1981). *Forms of talk.* Oxford: Blackwell.

Harré, R., & van Langenhove, L. (1999). Introducing positioning theory. In R. Harré & L. van Langenhove (Eds.), *Positioning theory: Moral contexts of intentional action* (pp. 14–31). Oxford: Blackwell.

Hollway, W. (1989). Gender difference and the production of subjectivity. In J. Henriques, W. Hollway, C. Urwin, C. Venn, & V. Walkerdine (Eds.), *Changing the subject: Psychology, social regulation and subjectivity* (pp. 227–263). London: Methuen.

Kaplan, B. (1983a). A trio for trials. In R. Lerner (Ed.), *Developmental psychology: Historical and philosophical perspectives* (pp. 185–228). Hillsdale, NJ: Erlbaum.

Kaplan, B. (1983b). Genetic-dramatism: Old wine in new bottles. In S. Wapner & B. Kaplan (Eds.), *Toward a holistic developmental psychology* (pp. 53–74). Hillsdale, NJ: Erlbaum.

Kendon, A. (1990). *Conducting interactions: Patterns of behavior in focused encounters.* New York: Cambridge University Press.

Lavelli, M., Pantoja, A. P. F., Hsu, H., Messinger, D., & Fogel, A. (2005). Using microgenetic designs to study change processes. In D. M. Teti (Ed.), *Handbook of research methods in developmental science* (pp. 40–65). Malden, MA: Blackwell.

Maccoby, E. E. (1998). *The two sexes: Growing up apart, coming together.* Cambridge, MA: Belknap Press.

Sander, F. (1930). Structure, totality of experience, and gestalt. In C. Murchison (Ed.), *Psychologies of 1930* (S. Langer, Trans., pp. 188–204). Worcester, MA: Clark University Press.

Saxe, G. B. (1988). The mathematics of child street vendors. *Child Development, 59*, 1415–1425.

Saxe, G. B. (1998). Candy selling and math learning. *Educational Researcher, 17*, 14–21.

Saxe, G. B. (2002). Children's developing mathematics in collective practices: A framework for analysis. *The Journal of the Learning Sciences, 11*, 275–300.

Scheflen, A. (1974). *How behavior means.* Garden City, NY: Doubleday/Anchor.

Siegler, R. S. (2006). Microgenetic analyses of learning. In W. Damon & R. M. Lerner (Series Eds.) & D. Kuhn & R. S. Siegler (Vol. Eds.), *Handbook of child psychology: Vol. 2. Cognition, perception, and language* (6th ed., pp. 464–510). Hoboken, NJ: Wiley.

Streeck, J., & Mehus, S. (2005). Microethnography: The study of practices. In K. L. Fitch & R. E. Sanders (Eds.), *Handbook of language and social interaction* (pp. 381–404). Mahwah, NJ: Lawrence Erlbaum.

Verkuyl, H. J. (1972). *On the compositional nature of aspects.* Dordrecht, The Netherlands: Reidel.

Weinrich, H. (1964). *Tempus: Besprochene und erzählte Welt.* Stuttgart, Germany: Kohlhammer.

Werner, H. (1959). *Einführung in die Entwicklungspsychologie* (4th ed.). Munich: Johann Ambrosius Barth. (Original work published 1926)

Werner, H. (1948). *Comparative psychology of mental development.* New York: International Universities Press.

Werner, H., & Kaplan, B. (1984). *Symbol formation: And organismic-developmental approach to language and the expression of thought.* Hillsdale, NJ: Lawrence Erlbaum. (Original work published 1963)

11

The Anthropology of Moral Development

CHRISTOPHER R. HALLPIKE

INTRODUCTION

As an anthropologist I believe that Piagetian studies of moral development can greatly increase our understanding of moral thought in simple, nonliterate societies, but many anthropologists would vigorously oppose such a claim. Relativists would say that there is no such thing as moral development, because all moral rules are arbitrary social conventions that vary from one society to another. Others would agree that there has been moral development in the course of history, but claim that this has been the result of increasing social complexity, and that social facts can never be explained by individual psychology.

ANTHROPOLOGY AND PSYCHOLOGY

Ethnocentrism is our normal attitude of mind. We naturally assume that the ideas and values of our own society are obviously right, and one of the most valuable achievements of anthropology has been to make us aware of this illusion by the study of other cultures. It has made us realize that different ways of thinking about the world are possible, and shown us how beliefs and values develop in a social context and why they may vary from one society to another and, for that matter, within societies. There were good social reasons why Spartan values, for example, were different from Athenian values, and in modern society why the qualities of leadership, courage, and discipline that are quite understandably valued by soldiers do not have such an obvious relevance in the lives of academics.

Unfortunately, a moderate relativism of this sort, which recognizes that different values and moral codes may be appropriate in different social circumstances easily degenerates into the facile belief that there are no common principles underlying the moral ideas of different cultures, but only an endless variety of customs and attitudes. To quote a famous anthropologist, Sir Edmund Leach, "The content of moral prohibitions varies wildly not only as between one society and another but even within the same society as between one social class and another, or between one historical period and another. Breathing apart, it is difficult to think of any kind of human activity which has not, at one time or another, been considered wrong" (Leach 1968, p. 49). Leach states explicitly that there is really no distinction between social conventions and moral rules, but merely customs that are different: for example, "It is wrong to wear outdoor shoes in a mosque; in some Catholic churches it is wrong for a woman to bare her head," and there are no principles of a more fundamental kind that underlie them. But there is in fact an obvious common principle here, that there should be special rules of dress in sacred places, and this rule ties in with other rules about respect and deference.

This type of facile relativism is not only very boring—what intellectual challenge is there in merely noting cultural differences and not trying to discover their underlying principles—but ignores the obvious fact that human life is essentially a social life, and that, everywhere in the world, social life has certain fundamental constraints that are inescapable and universal.[1] All societies, therefore, have notions of respect, and of insult and joke, of truth and lie, of property and theft, of gift and reciprocity, and will be concerned with such basic issues as what sorts of actions are approved and disapproved (moral rules); and what aspects of character are admired and despised (virtues and vices).

An older and more scholarly tradition in anthropology has long noted, from a wealth of ethnographic and historical evidence, that while there are many cross-cultural universals of this type, the way in which people think about certain basic moral issues changes in relation to the degree of social complexity. The moral thinking that is typical of hunters and gatherers is in some respects different from that found in tribal societies, which in turn differs from the ethical principles of the literate civilizations of antiquity and the world religions. Some of the best established ways in which moral thinking has developed are as follows:

1. The range of moral concern has steadily extended from one's immediate kin and neighbors to include human beings as a whole. "The best established trend is the extension of the range of persons to whom moral judgements apply; it is not so much the sense of duty to a neighbour that had varied as the answer to the question who is my neighbour" (Ginsberg 1944, p. 19).

2. The concept of duty begins simply with the proper performance of one's specific social roles. "In the early stages of ethics rights and duties do not attach to a human being as such. They attach to him as a member of a

group" (Hobhouse 1929, p. 233). Only much later does it become the general principle of moral obligation, in which it becomes possible to think of other people as individual moral beings regardless of their social status.

3. The most elementary concept of justice is that of equal exchange, of reciprocity, of good for good and bad for bad. Only in more complex societies does it develop more fully into an explicit concept of the Golden Rule, to mentally taking the place of others, and into concepts of social fairness, as between different classes, or between rulers and subjects.

4. There is a general development from conventional to principled morality. One aspect of this is a growing distinction between the duties of custom and law, on the one hand, and those of a purely moral nature on the other, between social conventions and natural law. This is related to the ability to think about society as a whole and to criticize it on general moral grounds such as justice. Another aspect of the development of principled morality is the kind of justification for doing what is right. "There gradually emerges the notion that goodness is something which the mind can apprehend as self-sustained and independent of external sanctions. Among simpler peoples, as described by anthropologists, the sanctions behind customary rules are relatively external and prudential" (Ginsberg 1944, p. 23).

5. This process is related to another major dimension of moral development that has been observed by anthropologists and historians, which is the growing awareness of the inner life of the individual, and of the mind in its cognitive aspects, as necessary to understanding why other people behave as they do, and how it would feel to be in their place. So we find a development from predominant concern with the act and its consequences towards the recognition of subjective factors of motive and intention. This development is closely related to another aspect of moral development, from a morality of *shame*, the consciousness that one has offended against an external, social rule, to that of guilt, an inner conviction of wrongdoing with its essential element of self-condemnation.

6. A further aspect of this growing awareness of the inner life is a clearer articulation of the idea of virtue in relation to the self. Members of simple societies can easily give lists of what are regarded as desirable qualities—generosity, bravery, good temper, and so on—and these are remarkably similar cross-culturally. But there is no analysis of the essential elements of character that allow people to perform well as moral agents, such as the cardinal virtues of Plato and Aristotle; the virtues in simple societies are simply lists of attributes that remain unsynthesized, a *bag of virtues*, as Kohlberg has described them.

Some anthropologists would claim that these different modes of thought just reflect an increase in social complexity: greater size and division of labor, political centralization, the development of formal legal systems, urbanization and commerce, and the decline in importance of traditional kinship obligations, and so on. According to Mary Douglas, for example, "In the course of social evolution, institutions proliferate and specialize...one inevitable by-product of social differentiation is social awareness, self-consciousness about the processes of social life" (1966, p. 91), which is also said to be responsible for a growing differentiation between subjective and objective, natural law and social law, and personal and physical notions of causation. In this view, different modes of thought have to be explained by social factors, and any recourse to psychology must be vigorously rejected, for reasons that have been very clearly stated by Max Gluckman (1949–1950):

> Perceptions, emotions, evaluations of right and wrong, ideas of the causes of events—in short, whole systems of thought and feeling—...exist transcendentally, independently of the individuals in whom they appear. They are what the French sociologists call *collective representations*, which pass from generation to generation, learnt in behaviour, contained in proverb and precept, in technology and convention and ritual, and, with the development of writing, in books. A man's psyche is social, not organic (p. 75)...an individual's emotional reactions and his complex ideas for dealing with his fellows and with nature are derived from his culture (pp. 73–74).

In this model, the basic cognitive processes of the human mind are thought to be innate and the same everywhere, and the only differences between people's ideas are produced by the particular culture in which they grow up. Every culture has a certain content of ideas and categories embodied in its language, technology, customs, rituals, and so on, and these are replicated in the mind of the individual rather like preformed pieces of a jigsaw puzzle being slotted into place. The mind here plays an essentially passive role, that of an empty bucket being gradually filled with cultural content.

But I am sure the reader will have noticed some marked similarities between the historical development of moral thinking, and the development of moral thinking in the individual, both in Western society and cross-culturally, as described by Piaget, Kohlberg, and other developmental psychologists. I will very briefly summarize some of their general conclusions here. These are that children initially understand society in the form of concrete relations between individuals, in an atomistic, unsystematized fashion, yet with a rigid notion of rules and conventions. Rules are obeyed for fear of the consequences; right is what is fair, an equal exchange, a deal; no distinction is made between social and natural law; there is little awareness of the mental states of others, or of the mind in its cognitive aspects; responsibility is objective, so that punishments should be for actions rather than for motives and intentions, and the self is externally defined by size, gender, and so on.

The development of a sense of social order involves greater awareness of social roles, and the idea that what is right involves living up to the expectations of others, and having good motives. The social order is seen as authoritative, although the social and natural law are still not clearly distinguished. Gradually society comes to be understood in a more systematic manner, and hierarchical structures and role differentiations are understood more clearly. What is right consists in maintaining the society as a whole, and more distinction is made between intentions and actions when awarding punishment.

Finally, conventions are understood as arbitrary rules that might have been different, adopted for the general good of society, while moral principles are distinguished from custom and law. The individual is distinguished from society, and it becomes possible to think of moral obligations to all human beings, regardless of the society to which they belong. One's own society can become the subject of criticism, and hypothetical social orders can be discussed. The idea of the self becomes predominantly defined by psychological and spiritual attributes, and is much more differentiated and integrated; the cognitive functions of the mind are realized, and the self can be the judge of the self.

It is important to remember that these results were initially obtained from the study of children and adolescents in Western society, although later validated cross-culturally (Hallpike 2004). But if the anthropologists are right and children acquire their culture by simply copying the ideas of adults, then why should there be any resemblance between the moral ideas that anthropologists have recorded for simple preliterate societies, and those that developmental psychologists have found among children brought up in the very different circumstances of modern liberal industrial society? And why, since societies are so different, should there be the kinds of cross-cultural developmental universality that psychologists have reported as well? The answer is that Gluckman, Douglas, and the whole of their anthropological tradition are wrong, and the learning process is not one of passive assimilation at all, but an active process in which the child experiments with his environment and incorporates his experience into his own cognitive structures. This means that children's representations of the world in causality, space, time number, and moral thinking, for example, are not simple if inadequate copies of the adult culture in which they are being socialized, but differ systematically from it.

Children have to assimilate information about their society and institutions to their existing cognitive structures, so that we find systematic differences between the ways in which children understand society and that of adults. If the mind had only content, which was processed in an identical manner by all human beings, these differences between the way in which children understand the world and that of adults would be incomprehensible. Adults do not teach children, for example, that there is more liquid in the tall thin glass than in the short fat one—why, then, should preoperational children typically think that there is? Nor do adults correct children in such matters, since they are usually oblivious to the special characteristics of children's thought.

But if collective representations are not simply copied by children, but are actively assimilated into their cognitive structures, then Gluckman's clear distinction between collective representations and individual thought processes is an illusion. Collective representations, like the game of marbles or parliamentary democracy, may have been produced by social collaboration, but they all have to be learned and handed on from one generation to the next by *individuals*, and because individuals can only transmit ideas as each individual understands them, their cognitive capacities must have a fundamental influence on the collective representations that they learn, develop, and pass on to subsequent generations.

Moreover, it is hard to see how an increase in social complexity, by itself, could explain very much about the major developments in moral thinking. Why, as social complexity increased, and the traditional tribal system of obligations based on kin groups and respect for age was eroded by states, conquest warfare, urbanization, and commercialization, did moral thought not simply become more bewildered and incoherent? Why should increasing social differentiation inevitably produce more self-consciousness about the processes of social life, or greater awareness of the difference between the objective and the subjective, or between natural law and social law, as Mary Douglas claims? Why did cultural differences with their neighbors lead the Greeks to distinguish between social convention and natural law, when tribal peoples, who are also well aware of cultural differences, simply respond by saying, "they have their customs and we have ours"?

There is a general correlation between the historical and the psychological development of moral thinking, but it cannot be explained simply as a product or reflection of growing social complexity by itself, but by a dialectical relationship between social and psychological factors. To appreciate how this works we need to distinguish between social institutions, as such, and the kinds of intellectual activity that are involved in getting through life in societies at different levels of complexity, with the levels of cognitive skill that such activities produce. While social systems and institutions are in a sense created by people, much of this occurs without deliberate planning or conscious purpose. This is not only true of modern political and economic systems, but in the institutions of simpler tribal societies. So it is normal for complex institutions to develop in ways that their members do not fully grasp, and therefore in some respects our society is as alien to our understanding as the natural world. The adoption of agriculture and the development of complex institutions based on descent and age, political centralization and the development of the state, urbanization, trade, and conquest warfare have an institutional logic of their own, and complex hierarchical organization and specialization of function can develop without conscious planning. People then have to grapple with these social changes, but what they make of them and how they interpret them will depend on the level of their cognitive development.

Now certain social activities are closely related to the development of higher cognitive functioning: notably planning, coordination, differences of opinion and debate, and settlement of legal disputes, and these intellectual activities are also closely related to social complexity in its broader aspects. Here the development of centralized government, the state, has particular relevance, because this greatly intensifies the degree of planning and coordination needed for raising taxes, organizing public works, planning conquest warfare, legal and theological debate, commercial calculations, and, with the advent of literacy, schooling. Literacy combined with mere rote learning, as in the scribal schools of ancient Egypt and Mesopotamia, has no significant cognitive consequences, but schooling and formal education that involve taking the pupils out of the context of their normal daily lives and their active participation and discussion with their teachers is of particular importance. It is closely involved with the ability to explain verbally one's reasons for making particular choices in test situations, and it also seems to develop the search for rules for the solution of problems, and the awareness of one's own mental operations (Scribner & Cole 1981). Besides schooling of this type, cross-cultural research has shown that other social factors are also closely related to cognitive development in moral thought. Interaction with non-kin in an urban environment, involvement in commercial relations, leadership, participation in state level institutions, and experience of cultural diversity are all stimulating factors (Edwards 1975; Harkness, Edwards, & Super, 1981). But here again, we must emphasize that a problem does not present itself: it has to be recognized as one, and this requires those with the cognitive ability to do so.

Social institutions can be understood at very different cognitive levels, and as higher cognitive capacities develop, notably in a society's leaders and decision makers, traditional social issues such as paternal authority, the claims of customs to be obeyed, and people's responsibility for their actions, will be thought about in new ways. Should a father be obeyed simply because he is the father and begot his children, or should he be obeyed because of his moral qualities and experience? Should we obey rules because the ancestors established them, or because they are our customs, or because all societies must have rules to function properly? If a person does not mean to injure someone, should we take this into consideration? How should we treat strangers who are unrelated to us? If I do something wrong and don't get caught, does it matter?

As societies become more complex they also create a range of new issues for people to reflect upon, for example: Where written law codes exist, there is a potential conflict between the letter of the law and the moral claims of equity. The moral implications of conquest are a relevant problem for empires that have to establish stable relations with their subject peoples—how far are the claims of justice valid, for example?—and there may be a need to reconcile different cultural codes of law and ethics within a single political and jural system, as in the Roman *jus gentium*. How far can a commercial morality be distinguished from the rest of our moral obligations? Do vendors, asks Cicero, have the moral duty of declaring the defects of what they are selling to prospective purchasers? But these issues only become problems when people actually recognize them as problems, and this in turn will depend on the degree of their cognitive development.[2] The social problems of, say, Greece, India, and China in the first millennium BC would not, therefore, have automatically produced Kohlberg's Stage 5 moral thinking unless there had been an educated class, and philosophers to do the thinking that was involved.

Now the importance of the model of moral development provided by the psychologists is that it shows us the types of moral thinking that people will find easiest in this process of reflection on their society. It is a basic principle of cultural evolution that people will do, not what is most adaptive, *but what is easiest in the circumstances,* and this applies as much to thinking as to doing, and as much to moral thinking as to thinking about the natural world. It is therefore perfectly possible, in a cognitively undemanding milieu, for elementary cognitive structures to be viable and to persist indefinitely. For example, it was possible for the Tauade, a people whom I studied in Papua New Guinea, to have no words for numbers higher than two because in their simple circumstances they had managed to get along without them, and in my earlier book *The Foundations of Primitive Thought* (Hallpike, 1979) I showed in detail that it was possible for preoperational thinking about number, time, space, causality, and classification to be perfectly adequate in simple societies.

Because some ways of thinking about society are harder than others, they will naturally tend to occur later in any developmental process. For example, the ability to conceptualize one's society as a total system, or to comprehend the nature of ideological conflict only develops in adolescence, if at all, as does the ability to understand one's own mental processes. This has very profound consequences for the history of moral development, because it explains one of its most striking features to which I have not so far referred: the absence of higher levels of moral thinking in traditional small-scale societies. There is absolutely no sociological reason why hunter-gatherers, for example, should not say explicitly that one should treat others as one would like to be treated oneself, but they do not: what they actually say is that one should not cause trouble. There is nothing about the higher stages of moral reasoning, such as Kohlberg's Stage 5, that would make them *unworkable* among hunter-gatherers or simple agriculturalists, and we know that moral reasoning in some small agricultural groups, such as Hutterite colonies, or Israeli *kibbutzim,* may be at Stage 4 or 5 (Snarey 1985, Table 2).

We actually find a predominance of Kohlberg's Stage 2 moral thinking among hunter-gatherers and some shifting cultivators not because it is directly determined by the social structure, or because in some Darwinian fashion it is selected for because it is more adaptive, but simply because, first, it is adequate to the social conditions, and second, it is an easier mode of thought than Stage 3. Although it might be thought that it would be impossible to sustain a functioning social order unless the predominant level of moral and social reasoning among the adult members of a society were at Kohlberg's Stages 3 or 4, the Conventional Level, we shall see that this need not be the case at all.

While the developmental psychologist is primarily concerned with the ontogeny of moral development as this occurs within an existing society, the anthropologist, on the other hand, also has to relate moral development to the general process of social evolution, and I would now like to look at this interaction between moral thinking and the development of the social order in more detail. It would be impossible, within the limits of this paper, to consider the whole range of this process, and I shall therefore concentrate on the anthropological evidence about social orders in which Kohlberg's Preconventional Stage 2, and Conventional Stage 3 moral thinking predominate. My particular interest here is to see how it is possible for the simpler forms of moral thinking to be adequate for a viable social life, and why particular forms of social life do or do not stimulate reflection on moral issues.

ATOMISTIC SOCIETIES

The simplest form of human society is that of hunter-gatherer bands, on which we have a good deal of evidence from modern ethnography. The main features of these types of society are, first of all, their small size, with each band having an average population of about 25 to 50 because of the very limited carrying capacity of hunter-gatherer ecology. Families are the largest form of kin groups, and we do not find the clans or lineages typical of agricultural and pastoral societies, and there are no formal age-grouping systems either. Individuals can move easily from one band to another, especially when social friction occurs. There is no form of hereditary chieftainship or similar political authority. Although headmen may exist, they are not hereditary, and their limited influence is essentially informal and persuasive, operating through the force of personality and example rather than from a generally accepted duty of obedience on the part of band members. While the older generations are generally respected by their juniors, neither they nor headmen have any judicial functions by which they might settle disputes, and there are no persons who have the authority to act as go-betweens, or arbitrate in disputes. Disputes are settled by public pressure and ridicule, mutual avoidance, compensation, or vengeance. So there is no opportunity to develop any body of law or to think about criteria for dispute settlement, and there are very limited occasions for planning, other than hunting, or for the coordination of group activities.

The personal qualities most approved are those such as sharing, and generosity, and avoiding disputes and fighting, all of which are obviously of great practical relevance in daily life, but there is no appeal to abstract principles such as moral obligation or the Golden Rule. Someone may say, "If struck on one side of the face, you turn the other side toward the attacker" (Gardner 1966, p. 394), but on closer examination this does not express forgiveness of one's enemies in the Christian or Stoic manner, but is simply practical advice to avoid fighting within the group. The most important means of maintaining social solidarity among hunter-gatherers is the constant exchange of gifts, and this not only includes the sharing of meat from the hunt, but the exchange of everyday objects and possessions.

Bands, therefore, are collections of individuals, and while there is a great emphasis on reciprocity and a constant exchange of gifts between individuals and the sharing of game, there is also a great deal of envy[3] and lack of mutual trust outside the circle of one's immediate relatives. Ethnographers have frequently commented on the individualistic quality of these societies, the emphasis on personal autonomy and independence, and low levels of interpersonal concern and mutual assistance (Barry, Child, & Bacon, 1959; Holmberg 1969; Howell, 1989; Marshall, 1976; Woodburn, 1968).

It has also been observed (Gardner, 1966; Morris, 1976, 1991) that while the members of such societies obviously have a great deal of practical knowledge of their environment, "not only are their taxonomic systems limited in scope but they have a relative unconcern with systematisation" (Morris 1976, p. 544). Gardner refers to this as *memorate knowledge*, that is, knowledge based on personal, concrete experience, and it has been noted as a characteristic of a wide range of hunter-gatherer societies, as well as some shifting cultivators.

For example, a hunter was asked in a court case in Canada how many rivers there were in his territory, but could not say. This was not because he did not know, but because it had never occurred to him to count them. The hunter knew every river in his territory individually and therefore had no need to know how many there were. Indeed, he would know each stretch of each river as an individual thing and therefore had no need to know in numerical terms how long the rivers were either. Verbal counting systems are often very poorly developed among hunter-gatherers, with no word for numbers beyond two or three. Rather than using named lunar months, time reckoning tends to be by the sequence of activities throughout the year. Basic color terms are often restricted to black/white, while the chromatic colors are designated by a wide variety of terms based on actual objects.

I emphasize this relative lack of developed taxonomic thinking because it extends to social relations as well as to the natural world, and Gardner, for example, says of the Paliyans, "Just as [they] have problems with natural taxonomy, they manifest difficulty providing models or rules to describe social practices such as residence "(Gardner 1966, p. 398).

It should also be noted that religion has very little significance as a mode of social control. Although some forms of behavior may be believed to incur the anger of supernatural beings, and therefore to incur unpleasant consequences for the offender and possibly the whole community, these are predominantly ritual offenses such as laughing at animals or throwing leeches on the fire, rather than social offenses such as assault, theft, and quarreling.

Many of the societies of shifting cultivators of Papua New Guinea have characteristics that are markedly similar to hunter-gatherer bands because, until the introduction of the sweet potato in the last two to three hundred years, they lived in small groups that were heavily dependent on foraging. I conducted fieldwork from 1970 to 1972 among the Tauade in the high mountains of Papua (Hallpike 1977), and much of what I observed among them fills out what we have seen of the moral structure of hunter-gatherer societies.[4] They were shifting cultivators of sweet potato and pig rearers, which allowed them to produce a large surplus of food for ceremonial exchange, but it was clear that land and pig ownership had greatly increased the scope of status competition, quarrels, and the level of violence and this adds an entirely new element to atomistic societies of the hunter-gatherer type.

The level of violence in Tauade society was not, therefore, a necessary aspect of its atomistic organization, and there are other shifting cultivators and hunter-gatherer societies with much less violence but essentially the same structure of moral system. On the other hand, the lack of normative development at the level of Stage 2 moral thinking made it particularly easy for an ethos of revenge to flourish in Tauade society, as we shall see.

The total population was about 6,000, split into local groups of around 200 which were divided into small clans. These were very vague, and although they nominally owned tracts of land the clans were dispersed among a number of different hamlets, whose membership changed often and had many of the atomistic features of hunter-gatherer bands. The nuclear family was the primary unit of cooperation, but people often went off to live for long periods with close relatives and in-laws in other local groups because these ties are very important. Members of the same hamlet, like bands, tried to avoid arguments and fights, and in each hamlet of any size there was the familiar New Guinea figure of the Big Man.

Big Men traditionally were often war leaders, organizers of competitive feasts and dances, and orators, and there were a number of these in every local group. Each was supported by a clique of followers comprised of relatives and friends, but the Big Men were not called on to mediate in disputes. The managerial functions of the Big Men prevented their role developing into an inherited office, and it simply faded away when they became old. At the other end of the social scale were the rubbish men, usually unmarried, of unimpressive characters and poor, who could be killed with relative impunity, especially by Big Men,.

The attributes of the Big Man and the rubbish man express fairly concisely the dominant values of Tauade society: success is based on power, wealth, generosity, violence, and sexual prowess, and those who cannot compete in the struggle for these are treated with contempt. They are not, obviously, entirely indifferent to social order, without which competition for the good things in life would itself be impossible for them. For the Tauade a "good" man is one who facilitates cooperation, especially for feasts and dances, by his powers of coordination, and is prepared both to offer and accept compensation in the settlement of disputes. Such a man is a strong man, and for the Tauade, therefore, strength is the basis of "goodness" as they conceive it, so that might and right are essentially indistinguishable. Conversely, meanness, weakness, and antisocial behavior, such as disrupting ceremonial exchanges go together also. Since power and strength are the only qualities that were respected, being old, as such, was despised, not respected; it was normal for elderly men to bind their heads in bark cloth to hide the shame of their baldness, and there was therefore no class of elders who could act as mediators in disputes. The absence of proper forums for the discussion and settlement of disputes meant that there was no opportunity for group leaders to take the initiative in articulating legal and moral norms that could have led to a higher awareness of the requirements of the wider social order.[5]

Without hereditary clan leaders or elders to act as mediators, all disputes had to be settled by face-to-face confrontation between the parties and their supporters, but, as we shall see, their morality was basically relativistic, in the sense that something was wrong if it injured one's friends, but all right if it injured one's enemies, and so there were no normative principles to which they could appeal. If the culprit was in a good mood a peaceful settlement might be reached, but if not, then violence was likely. This applied to the Australian administration, as well, when it tried to mediate:

> It is very seldom that a dispute between two [groups] can be settled to the satisfaction of both parties. The losing party, almost invariably, feels that it has been unjustly done by and, to them, the decision is unsatisfactory…it rankles in the minds of the losers until it develops into such magnitude that it can only be settled by "pay-back" or by an outbreak of open warfare. (Hallpike 1977, p. 211)

Disputes were extremely common, particularly over pigs, gardens, and women, and while there was great affection within the nuclear family and to some extent with close cousins, beyond this narrow circle personal relations were suspicious and hostile. The Tauade are extremely proud and liable to take offense, so that insult, or something perceived as an insult, easily led to violence, and there was a very high level of violence not only between but within local groups. An insult or injury to a close relative or friend in particular could provoke violent rage, and the homicide rate, for example, in the traditional precolonial society was of the order of 1/200 per annum.

For example, one night an elderly retired Big Man found that his son's wife was sleeping with a lover in her hut while her husband was away, so in a rage he set fire to the hut with them both inside. They escaped, but the next morning he came to me, as his friend, and asked me to write a letter to the Assistant District Commissioner, to have them both prosecuted for adultery. He was a very intelligent and charming old gentleman, but was most surprised when I said that this was not a good idea, as the ADC would probably prosecute him for attempted murder instead: "But I did it because I was angry. I was very upset."

The response to homicide could either be the payment of compensation by the killer to his victim's relatives, or alternatively they might kill a relative of the killer, or even some unrelated person from his local group. When homicides occurred within the local group the killer would usually go and live elsewhere for a while until anger had cooled.

Not surprisingly, there was no word for peace in the Tauade language, and their closest approximation to this idea was a situation in which strangers met each other and established friendly relations by an exchange of their sisters in marriage. Dyadic relationships of this sort between friends were very important, and also involved exchanges of pork and acts such as the ceremonial planting of Cordyline as an act of sympathy for a friend in mourning. I think it is fair to say that they saw their society basically as a network of relationships between individuals, not as a structure of institutions, a social order, whose maintenance had a normative claim on everybody, while groups were nothing more than collections of individuals. This was an extremely simple form of social organization, but none of my informants was able to discuss Tauade society with me or give me any general outline of its institutions. In one sense they *knew* perfectly well how their society was organized, but this understanding was based on a great mass of concrete personal knowledge about individuals in terms of which their social relationships were ordered. It would therefore have been very difficult for a Tauade to have articulated this type of knowledge into general statements about their local groups, clans, and hamlets.

Pay-back, *kakit*, together with pride, was a basic principle of Tauade society; it included returning one good deed for another, as well as a bad one, ceremonial gift-exchange in which the killing of pigs was central, the exchange of women in marriage, compensation for injury (both physical and for hurt feelings), and vengeance, which might involve physical assault and homicide, burning down people's houses, or destroying their pandanus trees, their most valuable form of property.

But while they clearly had the idea that reciprocity, both for good and evil, was basically right and fair because that was a transaction between individuals, their moral judgments were basically relativistic, relative, that is, to their personal connection to the parties involved. Theft, adultery, arson, assault, and homicide were not seen as wrong in themselves, as offenses against the social order, but as injuries to a particular individual. So one's attitude to someone who had stolen a man's pig, or seduced his wife, or burned his house down, or killed him very much depended on whether or not he was a close relative or friend or from one's own hamlet.

I found it extremely difficult to elicit general value judgments or moral rules from the Tauade, beyond vague categories of good/bad or, more frequently, strong/weak. For example, someone said to me about one patrol officer, who had been dismissed from the government and imprisoned for the unlawful punishment of natives: "Yes, he was bad: he burned our houses, and killed our pigs, and beat us; but he was good because he was like us and understood our customs." They too, if they had had the power, would have liked to do just the same, and there was no sense here of any appeal to wider standards of cruelty or injustice. The same unwillingness to make general moral statements, unrelated to specific people and situations, has been generally reported by anthropologists in Papua New Guinea. "Pressed for an evaluation, their usual reply is a neutral 'I don't know,' and it is exceedingly difficult to ascertain if the act is regarded as right or wrong" (Read 1955, p. 282).

There was no category of accidental homicide, and vengeance was taken or compensation demanded in the usual way regardless of whether or not the killing had been intended. The anthropologist Kenneth Read provides a good example, from the very similar society of the Gahuku-Gama, of this irrelevance of intention when assessing responsibility. Read had a close friend whose wife was expecting a baby down by the river. The birth was obstructed, and they asked Read for his advice. He said that she should be taken to the local hospital as quickly as possible, and they immediately agreed. After she had been carried to the hospital, accompanied by her husband, he came back to Read's hut and said,

> "If this woman dies you cannot stay with us." For a moment I looked at him without speaking, not even sure that I had heard him correctly. Then he hurried on, answering the question I had not asked. "If she dies they will say it was your fault. You saw their faces when we brought her back from the river. They were saying she should not go to the hospital. They said she should stay here, and if she dies no one will talk to you. Leave us, go away. Brother, you cannot stay here any longer." (Read, 1966, p. 86)

The villagers did not like the hospital because it had many strangers and enemies as patients whose evil magic might have endangered the woman, but she was in fact safely delivered of a daughter. "Later that evening, the villagers came to my house as usual, but their attitude was distinctly different, informed by a new familiarity, a new ease and acceptance. A short time before they had been ready to blame me if she had died, now they credited me with her successful deliverance" (Reid, 1966, p. 86).

Just as acts, not intentions were what counted, so too it was not wrongdoing as such that mattered but being found out. It caused a man shame, *katet*, to call him a liar, but the shame consisted in saying it openly to him in front of other people, not because he felt an inner sense of wrongdoing, guilt, in breaking a moral obligation to tell the truth.

It might be argued, however, that atomistic societies like the Tauade seem to resemble in one way more complex civilizations, since in both cases the individual is not under the overriding claims of status and membership of corporate groups. But in the first place, in atomistic societies the relations between individual and group are not equilibrated by such principles as "everyone should do his or her part for the common good," or "might is not right" because as we have seen, there is no idea of a social order. There is simply self-assertion, counterbalanced by group pressure or personal violence. Second, there is no idea of principled opposition to convention and popular feeling—there are no idealistic rebels against the majority point of view, and in a culture dominated by fear of ridicule that is hardly surprising. Third, despite the autonomy of personal choice, there was certainly no idea of the pure individual who deserves our concern simply as a fellow human being. Obligations to others were primarily defined by their social status: parents, siblings, in-laws, fellow clan or hamlet member, someone to whom one owed pork, and so on. Those who had no claim to consideration on the basis of their social status, such as strangers, could be, and often were killed as the result of personal whim.

Finally, there was certainly no capacity for articulate introspection, or the analysis of the states of mind of others in the explanation of their behavior. The striking exception to this was a remarkable man, Casimiro Kog. He had had no schooling, and only spoke Tauade, but he had worked for many years with the Fathers of the Catholic Mission helping them to express the concepts of Christian doctrine most appropriately in the Tauade language, and in translating the Bible. He was not only highly intelligent, but this exposure to debate and discussion, and to alien concepts, meant that his level of cognitive functioning was very much higher than that of his fellow Tauade. His texts were remarkable and unique for several references to what the protagonists in his stories were thinking as an explanation of their actions.

For example, a Big Man of group A invited the people of group B to take refuge with him after their defeat in warfare, and after several years held a feast to mark the eventual return of the B to their own land. A number of other groups had been invited to this feast, including group C, neighbors of the B. Some of the C men were relatives of the B, and had looked after their gardens and pigs while the B were away. They told the B how their gardens and pigs were getting on, and they all cried together. The Big Man was very angry to see this, and wanted his own group A to kill both the B and the C. Why should he have had this reaction? Casimiro's explanation was as follows: "What he thought was that it was not the responsibility of his group to look after the B, and if the C were so sorry for them now, they should have taken care of them in the first place. He was angry because he had looked after the B, and now they were being friends with the C though the C had abandoned them in the past." I had other informants whom I knew well, and with whom I spent many hours discussing similar cases, but if I asked them why so-and-so had done something, the standard answer would be that his insides were hot, or cool, as the case might be.

Again, he wanted to explain to me that only the Big Men had the *authority* (a concept for which there was no word in Tauade) to give the orders for the *polo* (bull-roarer enclosure) to be erected, and so he said, "In your country only the government can print money; so with us only the Big Man could give the order for the *polo*."

Tauade culture also conforms to Gardner's and Morris's model of *memorate culture* in other ways. Color terms are idiosyncratic and concrete, related to the hues of specific objects, and the only basic terms are *black/dark* and *white/light*, plus *red*. They have no verbal numerals beyond *single* and *pair*, and counting is performed on fingers and toes. There is no calendar or any form of time reckoning, and while they have a word for the moon, they do not use the lunar cycle to calculate time. They have words for the places where the sun rises and sets, but these are not used as directional indicators and they have no general spatial orientations at all. While they have words for various plants, trees, animals, and birds, these are not integrated into a general classificatory system, and there is little in the way of a general symbolic ordering of the natural and social worlds.

There are obviously some significant resemblances between the moral thinking of atomistic societies and Kohlberg's Preconventional Level, in which moral judgments are based not on respect for authority but on fear of the consequences of disobedience, and consequently on doing what one wants as long as one is not caught. Stage 2, is characterized as individualism, instrumental purpose, and exchange:

> *What is right:* Following rules only when it is to someone's immediate interests and needs and letting others do the same. Right is also what's fair, what's an equal exchange, a deal, an agreement.

> *Reasons for doing right:* To serve one's own needs or interests in a world where you have to recognize that other people have interests, too.

> *Social perspective of Stage:* Concrete individualistic stage. Aware that everybody has his own interest to pursue and these conflict, so that right is relative (in the concrete individualistic sense). (Kohlberg 1984, p. 174)

There is also a rigid and inflexible attitude to convention and taboo, guilt consists in being found out, and responsibility is objective with little interest in motive or intention.

Stage 2 moral systems can therefore operate quite satisfactorily in small groups where everyone knows everybody else, because the mechanisms of direct reciprocity, group pressure, and avoidance, in particular, are adequate forms of social control.[6] Even a highly agonistic type of Stage 2 moral system, such as that of Tauade society is still perfectly viable on a permanent basis. But as societies increase in size and complexity, small groups of family and friends,[7] and the devices of reciprocity and group pressure, are not enough, and we now need to see what further developments take place.

TRIBAL SOCIETIES OF CORPORATE ORDER

The shift to agriculture inherently allows larger and more permanent groups to form, and I shall refer to these societies as based on "corporate order." While this process may take many centuries, the need to cope with exponential increases in the number of social relationships and new forms of property in land and stock produce profound changes in the social order.

People who live in large, permanent groups must find ways of dealing with neighbors too numerous to be known individually. One of the major steps facilitating progress to larger group size appears to have been the development of systems to categorize, identify, and stereotype group members (Cohen 1989, pp. 23–24).

These groups are considerably wider in membership than the familistic and cooperative groups of atomistic societies, and are based on the simple principles of descent, age, birth-order, gender, and residence, while smiths, potters, and other craftsmen are also often distinguished from farmers and take on hereditary status. Descent groups, in particular, often develop into hierarchical structures of clans, subclans, lineages, and so on, but while *we* would conceptualize these as hierarchies of logical classes and class inclusions, it is quite possible to think of them as simply like a tree, with the different levels of the hierarchy correspond-ing to the trunk, branches, twigs, and so on.[8] We must not imagine that people sat down and deliberately planned these new institutional structures, as we might set up a new committee system, and I shall return to this question of social under-standing later.

The Konso of Ethiopia, among whom I conducted fieldwork from 1965 to 1967 (Hallpike, 1972) are a good example of this type of social order and present a very different picture from the Tauade. They are a highly structured society of advanced agriculturalists living in south-west Ethiopia, traditionally pagans, not Christians, living in around 30 large villages of up to 3,000 inhabitants each. Traditionally, membership of these villages was very stable, and families lived in the same village for generations, because the rest of their lineage lived there and because their land was also next to the village. There were nine clans dis-tributed among all the villages, and each clan was divided into small lineages, whose members all lived in the same village. The head of each lineage inherited his office which involved, in particular, blessing his kin and mediating in their disputes. The villages were organized in three regions, at the head of which was a primarily religious figure who performed annual rituals for all the villages of his region, mediated in battles between the villages and in cases of accidental homicide, supervised the complex age-grading system, and received tribute from the villages of his region. Each region also had a pair of sacred drums—the drum was a symbol of peace—that circulated round the villages. Dyadic relations and gift exchange were much less important than among the Tauade: the emphasis was not on the giving of things but on performing one's duties to one's neighbors in the ward and village, to one's fellow lineage members, one's working party, one's fellow age-set members, and so on.

Age was a very important basis of respect, and the villages were governed by councils of elders; there was a council for each village, and one for each of the wards into which every village was divided. Elders were elected informally by the heads of households in their ward on the basis of their personal qualities. The Konso were very clear what they should be—knowledge of affairs, self-con-trol, good temper, authority, and so on. The councils discussed political issues, ordered the punishment of criminals, and mediated in disputes between men of different lineages.

I must also add that they had a 12-month calendar which they kept in syn-chrony with the solar year by periodically repeating a month, a verbal numeral system that could express hundreds and thousands, a fairly systematic taxonomy of plants and animals, and a set of specific terms for types of social groups, cat-egories, and relationships, of a kind that was entirely lacking among the Tauade.

Waqa, the Sky God and god of rain, though remote, was concerned that men should live at peace and not quarrel, lie, steal, or murder. It was believed that he would withhold the rain from villages where there was too much quarrelling, and Waqa was also invoked when two men swore oaths in a dispute over land, and it was believed that he would strike the liar dead. But while in such cases Waqa was believed to punish wrongdoers directly, generally he was thought to have delegated his authority to the elders, for whom as I have said there was great respect, and they were supposed to work in harmony with the warriors to maintain peace and order. While Waqa was a moral god, it should also be noted that there was no idea that sin would be punished and virtue rewarded in the next life. Rewards and punishments came in this life.

No clear distinction is made between the social and natural world, so that their complex social order is linked by a set of rich symbolic associations with the natural and cosmic order. Waqa, the Sky God, was closely linked with men, and with the elders in particular, while the other cosmic principle, the Earth, was associated with women, fertility, and food; each of the nine clans had important associations with a variety of natural phenomena; and they believed that the social harmony promoted by the age-grading system helped the crops to grow. We have here "a small scale society which sees the working of the 'universe' as closely involved in the particularities of its own social system and the personal relationships this contains" (Gluckman 1967, p. 237). Piaget also found that

> the child, up to the age of about 7–8, always regards the notion of law as simultaneously moral and physical. Indeed, we have tried to show that until the age of 7–8 there does not exist for the child a single purely mechanical law of nature…. In short, the universe is permeated with moral rules. (Piaget 1932, pp. 188–189)

This type of symbolic order is very effective in giving people a sense of the intellectual coherence of their society, but is highly resistant to critical analysis and discussion.

In small groups, which continue for generation after generation in the same place, with a simple technology, it is easy to develop institutions based on principles which do not have to be made explicit. While the members of such societies know, in an implicit sense, how their society works, this knowledge often cannot be expressed in an articulate and coherent way.

I remember once having a conversation with a young man of about 25, who had attended the mission school for two or three years, on the subject of the Konso age-grading system, in which elders, warriors, and boys are organized in a hierarchy of groups based on generational seniority. I tried to express to him the idea that the different grades each had their own work to do in relation to the whole society and was surprised to discover that he did not find this at all easy to grasp. With the advantage of Piagetian hindsight it now seems likely that what he found difficult was to think of the age organization as a whole, as a total system, to which the component groups and categories made their distinctive contribution. Of course, he was perfectly well aware of the distinctive role expectations of elders, warriors, and boys, but he could not combine this knowledge into a conscious and articulate model of the total age-grouping system. His knowledge remained implicit and inarticulate. Compare this case with the reflections of a medieval European cleric on a traditional order very similar in type to that of the Konso:

> The society of God, which one thinks of as one, is divided into three orders: some pray, others fight, and others work. These three orders live together and cannot be separated. The services of one permit the services of the other two. Each in turn lends its support to all. (Dubuisson, 1975, p. 37).

None of the Konso, in fact, was able to give me a concise and coherent account of how their age-grading system worked, and it is therefore possible for the members of these tribal societies to *operate* complex institutions which form a total order of considerable complexity by knowing a set of specific rules that apply to them, yet without the ability to grasp consciously that total order, or to be able to see and articulate how the component parts fit together for the whole.

On the other hand, the emergence of well-defined social institutions, political and religious authority, and associated processes of mediation in this type of social order to which I have referred, have made possible the development of clear normative structures. There was a general idea that some moral consideration was due to people from one's region and from other parts of Konso; they were often encountered at the various markets, for example, and the nine clans existed in all the neighboring tribes as well, so this extended the notion of common humanity to these people as well. To kill a stranger whom one met on the road was definitely considered a sinful act that Waqa would punish.

With increased political authority go more effective judicial procedures, involving the mandatory intervention of third parties, usually village councils and heads of descent groups, who typically function not only as mediators in private disputes but also as the agents of the political group as a whole to punish those offenses against the group which impair its solidarity and harmony. These can now be treated as a distinct type of offense, different from an injury to an individual, a crime rather than a tort. Leadership roles give to a minority the opportunity to reflect more deeply on social issues than ordinary people, and such tribunals are obviously the principal means for the development of articulate norms of conduct binding on all group members, and which can be appealed to in disputes. Among the Konso there were, for example, accepted legal rules for the sale and rent of land and houses, and for compensation in case of damages of various kinds, and for the conditions under which men without land worked for rich landowners.

They also distinguished between deliberate and accidental homicide: the man who killed someone accidentally would go for sanctuary to the home of an official in his village, the Father of the Drum, who would then take him to the home of the regional priest who would mediate with the victim's kin for compensation. But deliberate and accidental homicide can be distinguished on the basis of observable facts without the sort of psychological probing of individual motives with which we are familiar. In societies such as the Konso, motives were generally imputed to people on the basis of their actions, and on social stereotypes of age, gender, and so on. As Gluckman says of Lozi justice,

> The judges…concern themselves, even when they state the law's rules, with internal moral states…but these internal moral states and motivations are inferred from the actions of parties. Motives follow logically from the actions of the parties…. Guilt and innocence of motive are determined from the facts…. Here the judges work…with a set of psyches specified for the various categories of persons who come before them—fathers, children, husbands, wives, and so forth. (Gluckman, 1965, p. 230)

In particular, having good will toward others is a normative expectation, and this is assessed on the basis of people's actions, as in the following example. One day a man came to me saying that his baby was ill with diarrhea, and asking for medicine. Some men were sitting with me, and I said to them, "This is very difficult for me. You all know how easily babies die from diarrhea. If I give this man medicine for his baby and it dies, you will blame me and say that I killed it." "No," they said, "If you give him medicine and the baby dies, that is God's will. But if you refuse him the medicine, that will show that you do not care if the baby dies or not." So I gave him the medicine and I am glad to say that his baby got better. Unlike the Gahuku-Gama and the Tauade, my intentions were relevant, but they were inferred from what I did.

In these societies the individual is not the type of relatively free agent typical of atomistic societies but, on the contrary, interacts with other people on the basis of his membership of various groups, especially his descent group. It becomes very much easier for individuals to think of one another in terms of their social roles and their associated duties, and hence to judge the behavior of others in terms of their fullfilment of role obligations. The development of formal institutions to adjudicate disputes also allows social norms to be more clearly articulated, so that moral judgments can be given a more objective, nonrelativistic basis in terms of the social order, rather than the personal relations of friendship and enmity between the individual disputants that we find in atomistic society.

What people should and should not do in such a traditional scheme of social order is prescribed in terms of status, and discussion of moral dilemmas centers on ambiguities of status—the elder who behaves badly, the young man who displays wisdom beyond his years—not on general problems of duty or justice. In these traditional societies, dominated by corporate obligations, there is little or no scope for exercising authority in ways that are clearly antisocial or dishonest, and so a whole range of dilemmas with which we are familiar in our kind of society can scarcely occur at all.

For example, in the modern Konso capital of Karate a young Christian Konso was employed as a government storekeeper. One day, he was asked to sign a receipt for some barrels of food-oil that had not in fact been delivered to the store, but had been stolen before they had arrived. He told the missionary that he had wrestled the whole night with God, and quoted to him a biblical text about things which could be a benefit for a time, but which then proved to be a curse. He finally refused to sign the receipt and lost his job. In this new type of urban, politically centralized society it is possible for the authorities to act in dishonest ways that create severe moral dilemmas for the virtuous individual. But is it hard to imagine a comparable type of dilemma in traditional Konso society because no one would have had the power to dismiss someone from a job, and there were no paid jobs anyway, and resources were not distributed by a central agency. It is therefore not surprising that the analysis of duty and virtue in ways that are called for in this example is not of much relevance in the traditional type of society, and for this reason we do not find such distinctively ethical concepts as duty, moral obligation, virtue, or justice, in societies of this sort.

In relation to justice, Havelock (1978) says of Homeric society,

> if justice be identified as the central principle of modern morality, con- ceptually defined, oral societies could get on very well without it. What they did rely on for cohesion—as does any society—was a set of propri- eties, of general rules of behaviour which in sum total constitute "what is right"...these "rules" are not abstracted from what is done—that is, they occur incidentally—and they need not add up to a system which can be consistently formulated. (p. 53)

So, as Havelock says, "Those who are 'unjust' are those who behave 'wan- tonly', 'recklessly', 'in disregard of the rules'" (Havelock, 1978, p. 183), and this applies very well to societies like the Konso.

Rather than thinking in terms of abstract rules of justice or duty the Konso think in terms of the general way of life, in which everyone does what is conven- tionally expected of them. Such common expressions as *porra koteeta*, "the way to behave," *akama achaato*, "how you should live," or *aaka tampeeta*, "ancestral custom" are essentially appeals to people's knowledge of this conventional order in which the way to behave does not need detailed individual calculations with reference to abstract criteria. So, too, among the Navaho,

> Since the responsibilities [to different categories of kin] are accepted without question, many ethical problems, which in our society are set- tled by individual moral judgment, hardly arise. With us, questions of parental authority, support of the incompetent, distribution of wealth (including generosity and hospitality) have constantly to be solved anew. The Navaho can depend upon his social code to settle most of them; individual judgment plays a small role. (Reichard, 1963, p. 124) [9]

Peace, *nakayta*, was a word that the Konso constantly used, not only in greet- ings but as a fundamental value. While they were a notably brave and warlike people, and men who had killed enemies in battle were commemorated by spe- cial statues on their graves, their basic ideal was nevertheless one of community harmony between the different generations, and hence the age-grading system within the village, within the wards, and within the lineage, and it was the responsibility of the elders and the lineage heads to maintain this.

Truth, *dukaata*, was another basic value closely linked to the idea of peace and the social order. The liar, like the thief, was particularly despised as the destroyer of social order and trust, and sincere discussion was the ideal means by which disputants spoke their minds and settled their differences. It was on the basis of these values that they judged the Amhara, who had conquered them in the 1890s, to have done wrong in taking money and property by force and by enslaving some of the Konso, and generally disrupting the proper order of society, "spoiling the land," as they expressed it.

In these societies the moral order is therefore the same as the corporate order itself which cannot be assessed by more abstract criteria independently of that order: "The traditional way of life is hence taken for granted and there is no critical assessment of the validity or usefulness of customary practices and beliefs" (von Fürer-Haimendorf, 1967, p. 208).

The characteristic features of moral thought in corporate societies correspond with Kohlberg's Conventional Level, Stage 3 in a number of respects:

> *(a) What is right.* Living up to what is expected by people who are close to you or what people generally expect of people in your role as son, brother, friend, etc. "Being good" is important and means having good motives, showing concern about others. It also means keeping mutual relationships, such as trust, loyalty, respect, and gratitude.

> *(b) Reasons for doing right.* The need to be a good person in your own eyes and those of others. Your caring for others. Belief in the implicit golden rule. Desire to maintain rules and authority which support stereotypical good behaviour.

> *(c) Social perspective stage.* Perspective of the individual in relationships with other individuals. Aware of shared feelings, agreements, and expectations which take primacy over individual interests. Relates points of view through the concrete golden rule, putting yourself in the other person's shoes. Does not yet consider the generalized system perspective [that we find with state-level institutions]. (Kohlberg, 1984, p. 174)

While substantial numbers of persons in these societies will presumably be at Kohlberg's Stage 3, we should note Kohlberg's distinction between an implicit, "concrete" awareness of the Golden Rule, and the ability to formulate it in explicit form. The Konso seem to have had an implicit understanding of the Golden Rule before they encountered it from Christianity, and it is very instructive to see how they construe it. The following is a commentary by an educated Konso Christian, Ato Korra Gara, on Mt. 7.12, "Do to others what you want them to do to you":

Do not wish the harm that you don't want for yourself to happen to others. What you wish a man to do to you, do the same for him. That means, for example, if you have a problem, and want someone to help you with that problem, you help him in the same way. As you have a problem, and ask for help about it, don't forget that everyone who has a problem needs help like you.

The Konso to whom I read this exposition agreed enthusiastically with it, but it is not concerned with the individual who is searching for a general rule of how to behave to others, and who thus mentally changes places with them. It is firmly based on the realities of social life and the need for good will and mutual assistance in a small, face-to-face community. I have found no positive confirmation in cross-cultural research on the ethnographies of tribal peoples that the Golden Rule is explicitly formulated, and one clear disconfirmation (Ladd 1957, p. 272).

But there may be some important differences between the modes of thinking among leaders and nonleaders (e.g., Edwards, 1975). In their study of the Kipsigis of Kenya, Harkness and colleagues (1981) found significant differences in this respect. For example, with regard to paternal authority,

All of the men [leaders and nonleaders] agreed that children should always obey and respect their father, but in the eyes of the leaders, a man should command natural respect through his own superior moral qualities. His authority should be maintained through being reasonable and nonarbitrary, and he should teach his children to obey willingly for the common good of the family…. According to the non-leaders, however, the head of the household was simply a strong man, a ruler. (p. 599)

Similarly, one feature of traditional stories told by the Kuranko of West Africa is this distinction between personal attributes and social status, but some individuals were much more aware of this than others. One very intelligent man said to Jackson (1982, p. 110), the anthropologist:

Even if a person is a child, but behaves like an elder, then he is an elder…. Even if a person is old and senior, if he behaves like a child then he is a child. Therefore, this matter of seniority comes not only from the fact that one is born first, or from the fact that one is big and strong; it also concerns the manner in which a person behaves and does things…I am speaking now, but some of these words of wisdom which I am explaining to you are not known by everyone.

This was true, and as Jackson (1982) says, "Other informants tend to play down such attributes as cleverness, preferring a fairly doctrinaire definition of status superiority/inferiority, which emphasizes birth order position alone" (p. 111).

Again, it was found in the Kipsigi study that ideas corresponding to "con-science" were expressed by some of the leaders, but not among the ordinary men (Harkness et al., 1981):

> The idea of conscience, as described by leaders and non-leaders, varies from an inner voice, or self-judgment, to an outwardly oriented concern about wrongdoing and fear of punishment or disapproval. Conscience as an inner voice or self-judgment was best expressed by one of the lead-ers: "You remain unhappy because you have something in your heart that will draw you to a shadow of being afraid of something that you have done to someone else. Because you will charge yourself accord-ing to your heart that you were not right at that time" (Leader B, stage 3[4])…. Most men, however, displayed approval or punishment-oriented concepts of conscience. (p. 600)

Jackson (1982) reports a similar experience among the Kuranko:

> When Kuranko people asked me what prevented me from wronging oth-ers, I would endeavour to explain that my conscience and scruples did so. I would say that a kind of voice inside me spoke out against my "bad thoughts" (*miriye yugume*). Such a view was regarded as down-right ridiculous, and I would be assured that it was the fear of the other person's *hake* which made me do right, not the inner voice. [A person's *hake* is a kind of magical force that will take retribution on you if you do wrong to an innocent person, even if he is unaware of it.] (pp. 29–30)

There are, then, some important continuities between the moral thinking of corporate and atomistic society. Status is still the primary determinant of per-sonal value, and acts still retain a much greater significance than motives or inten-tions. There is not much more awareness of the inner life of the individual and of motives and intentions than in atomistic societies, and still no thinking about thinking. The "ethical" remains embedded in the religious and the legal, and is not abstracted as a distinct body of principles. The virtues remain a "bag" of socially desirable attributes, and there is no idea of the possibility of a principled rejection of the customs and institutions of one's society. While the notion of order does give an important emphasis to the idea of truth, and that right and wrong are somehow part of the nature of things, and appeals can be made to divine commandments, the predominant emphasis in moral thought still tends to be, as Ginsberg says, relatively prudential and external, on shame rather than on guilt and the awareness of what is good in itself, while morality is still essentially public rather than private.

CONCLUSIONS

In this chapter I have tried to show how Stage 2 and 3 moral thinking can be the norm in simpler societies because at this level of social organization elementary methods of social control are sufficient to maintain a viable society. In atomistic societies of very small groups, we saw that reciprocity and gift exchange, group pressure, and avoidance and mobility are adequate, even without mediation, and this type of society only requires Stage 2 moral thinking. In societies of corporate order, much larger populations are organized into groups based on the ascriptive principles of descent, age, and gender, and on residence. These can provide the basis for authority and mediation, and allow the formulation of clear social norms and moral codes. The social order is linked to the natural order by symbolism: coherence can be given to complex social structures by the symbolic order, which people do not understand in a rational and articulate way, and the religious use of the natural order—the sky, rain, sun, etc.—can give authoritative status to the moral code. People can operate within this social order simply with a knowledge of their specific role requirements, and a grasp of the system as a whole is unnecessary, so that Stage 3 thinking is adequate for ordinary people although it may be questioned by those in positions of leadership.

Social evolution does not wait, of course, on cognitive development, and was produced by such processes as the adoption of agriculture, urbanization, conquest warfare, the state, writing, and industrialization. But I have tried to show that the development of cognitive skills has nevertheless been an integral part of the process by which people reflected on their own society and developed new collective representations. The fundamental contribution of developmental psychology here is to show us what types of thinking are easier than others, and once we know this we can see that a certain stage of moral thinking will be adequate in societies at one level of complexity, but inadequate at higher levels. It will also tell us why the more advanced levels of moral thinking are not found in the simpler societies although they would be perfectly workable in them, and why there should be so many cross-cultural resemblances in moral thinking between very different societies which are at roughly the same level of complexity.

Notes

1. I have shown in detail in my book (Hallpike, 2004, pp. 15–36) that claims that *all* knowledge, including moral judgments, is culturally relative are absurd. As the philosopher Bernard Williams summed it up, "The assertion that all truths are relative requires a non-relativistic justification" (cited in P. Munz, 1993, p. 132) and I shall not refer to it again.
2. While one can see why the development of formal law courts would have made it easier to articulate clearer moral norms, there is no connection, as such, between the development of formal courts and the investigation of intention. In ancient Greek law courts,

   > Except in [obvious cases such as accident and self-defense] the Greeks long felt unable to delve into men's mental states for the purpose of distinguishing different degrees of guilt. Methods of legal proof, particularly among peoples in early stages of legal development, have to rely upon outward phenomena of the plainest sort in order to draw inferences as to the existence and nature of responsibility for human conduct. (Jones, 1956, p. 261)

Or again, medieval European states were much more complex than tribal societies, but their courts had as much difficulty in handling the subjective aspect of criminal responsibility. In the words of Pollock and Maitland (1923),

> In medieval England, the law…still finds grave difficulties in its way if it endeavours to detect and appreciate the psychical element in guilt and innocence. 'The thought of man shall not be tried, for the devil himself knoweth not the thought of man':- thus at the end of the Middle Ages spoke Brian C. J. in words that might well be the motto for the early history of criminal law. It cannot go behind the visible fact. Harm is harm and should be paid for. (pp. 474–475)]

3. Lee (1979) makes a special note of the relation between egalitarianism and envy among the !Kung. One of his informants said,

> When a young man kills much meat he comes to think of himself as a chief or a big man, and he thinks of the rest of us as his servants or inferiors. We can't accept this. We refuse one who boasts, for some day his pride will make him kill somebody. So we always speak of his meat as worthless. (Lee, 1979, p. 49)

4. Woodburn (1968) describes a very similar Hadza disposition to cut the superior person down to size.

> There are certain universal features of the moral systems [of Papua New Guinea] *qua* systems. Shame, as noted, is probably universally present. In that sense they might be categorized as "shame cultures" as opposed to "guilt cultures".…. Another universal feature is that the moral code, along with whatever sanctions support it, is always group specific. That is, the moral rules do not apply beyond some known and finite body—the clan, the parish, and alliance of parishes, or at most a language group.…. Still another universal feature is that moral rules are not abstracted from their social context or their locus in the system. The people do not think of a category "morality" as opposed to other aspects of behavior. (Langness, 1973, pp. 197–198)

5. There was also no idea of the punishment of wrongdoing by gods or spirits, or other forms of supernatural retribution, and while they did hold ceremonial pig killings and dances to which members of other local groups were invited, these were not intended to promote peace and social harmony but were competitive displays of virility and power: hospitality on such occasions was a way of humiliating one's guests by one's wealth and generosity, with boastful speeches, and ritualized violence by guests against their hosts.

6. Gorsuch and Barnes (1973) also reached similar conclusions from their research among the Caribs of Honduras:

> The respondents, for example, seem to express a real concern with helping others, a concern seldom found in stage 2 in the United States. They were concerned not because of a moral norm within the culture, but *because they could reasonably expect to have the favour returned to them.* [Again]…the possible violation of norms were not perceived as a live option *because group pressures would be immediately applied.…* In a sense, therefore, personal and village interests converge sufficiently so that one need not move above a stage 2 to be an accepted individual of that culture and to have a functional society [my emphases]. (pp. 296–297)

7. "Primary reference groups such as family and friends provide role-taking opportunities suitable for the types of interpersonal thinking involved in stages 1 and

2. However, primary reference groups are not sufficient to promote higher moral thinking because children must be able to take a generalized social perspective in order to attain moral stages 3 and above" (Edwards, 1975, p. 520).

8. While segmentary descent groups are very common, these may not be conceptualized as hierarchies of logical classes in relationships of class inclusion, but simply as parts of a whole as branches are of a tree (partitive membership). A good example is that of the Maenge of New Britain:

> All the clans existing in the Maenge country are said to have evolved from one another through a process of repeated scission, the first clan having emerged from a tree stump. Not only is a vegetal origin thereby ascribed to mankind, but the current conceptualization of the differentiation process itself is also based on a vegetal metaphor. Indeed, all the descent groups are seen in their relations to one another as arranged like limbs, branches, and twigs along the bole of a tree. This representation, which is still adhered to by everybody, is of outstanding importance because it gives the Maenge a means of ordering the advents of their different clans and subclans in a fixed series which is agreed upon. Thus, although most people cannot retrace their descent even to the founder of their minimal group, either their local subclan or its local branch, they do know what senior group theirs has arisen from, and conversely who are their juniors. (Panoff, 1969, p. 163)

Thus while superficially the Maenge clan system might appear to be a classificatory system employing class inclusion, on closer examination it proves to be a classic case of a graphic image of partitive membership (Hallpike, 1979, p. 219).

9. The Navahos do not need to orient themselves in terms of principles of abstract morality. They get their orientation from face-to-face contacts with the same small group of people with whom they deal from birth to death. In a large, complex society like modern America where people come and go and where business and other dealings must be carried on by people who never see each other, it is functionally necessary to have abstract standards which transcend an immediate concrete situation in which two or more persons are interacting. (Kluckhohn & Leighton, 1974, p. 314)

References

Barry, H., Child, I., & Bacon, M. K. (1959). The relation of child training to subsistence economy. *American Anthropologist, 61*, 51–63.

Cohen, M. N. (1989). *Health and the rise of civilization.* New Haven, CT: Yale University Press.

Douglas, M. (1966). *Purity and danger.* London: Routledge & Kegan Paul.

Dubuisson, D. (1975). L'Irlande et la théorie des "trois ordres." *Revue de l'Histoire des Religions, 188*, 35–63.

Edwards, C. P. (1975). Societal complexity and moral development: A Kenyan study. *Ethos, 3*, 505–528.

Edwards, C. P. (1981). The comparative study of the development of moral judgment and reasoning. In D. A. Wagner & H. W. Stephenson (Eds.), *Handbook of cross-cultural human development* (pp. 248–279). San Francisco: W. H. Freeman.

Fürer-Haimendorf, C. von (1967). *Morals and merit: A study of values and social controls in South Asian societies.* London: Weidenfeld & Nicolson.

Gardner, P. M. (1966). Symmetric respect and memorate knowledge. *Southwestern Journal of Anthropology, 22,* 389–415.

Ginsberg, M. (1944). *Moral progress: Frazer lecture.* Glasgow: Glasgow University Press.

Gluckman, M. (1949–1950). Social beliefs and individual thinking in primitive society. *Memoirs and Proceedings of the Manchester Literary and Philosophical Society, 91,* 73–98.

Gluckman, M. (1965). *The ideas of Barotse jurisprudence.* New Haven, CT: Yale University Press.

Gluckman, M. (1967). *The judicial process among the Barotse of Northern Rhodesia (Zambia)* (2nd ed.). Manchester: Manchester University Press.

Gorsuch, R. L., & Barnes, M. L. 1973. Stages of ethical reasoning and moral norms of Carib youths. *Journal of Cross-Cultural Psychology, 4,* 283–301

Hallpike, C. R. (1972). *The Konso of Ethiopia: A study of the values of a Cushitic people.* Oxford: Clarendon Press.

Hallpike, C. R. (1977). *Bloodshed and vengeance in the Papuan mountains: The generation of conflict in Tauade society.* Oxford: Clarendon Press.

Hallpike, C. R. (1979). *The foundations of primitive thought.* Oxford: Clarendon Press.

Hallpike, C. R. (1986). *The principles of social evolution.* Oxford: Clarendon Press.

Hallpike, C. R. (2004). *The evolution of moral understanding.* Prometheus Research Group: http://www.prometheus.org.uk

Harkness, S., Edwards, C. P., & Super, C. M. (1981). Social roles and moral reasoning: A case study in a rural African community. *Developmental Psychology, 17,* 595–603.

Havelock, E. A. (1978). *The Greek concept of justice: From its shadow in Homer to its substance in Plato.* Cambridge, MA: Harvard University Press.

Hobhouse, L.T. 1929. *Morals in evolution* (6th ed). London: Chapman & Hall.

Holmberg, A. (1969). *Nomads of the long bow: The Siriono of Eastern Bolivia.* New York: Natural History Press.

Howell, S. (1989). *Society and cosmos: The Chewong of peninsular Malaysia* (2nd ed.). Oxford: Clarendon Press.

Jackson, M. (1982). *Allegories of the wilderness: Ethics and ambiguity in Kuranko narratives.* Bloomington: Indiana University Press.

Jones, J. W. (1956). *The law and legal theory of the Greeks.* Oxford: Clarendon Press.

Kluckhohn, C. (1960). The moral order in the expanding society. In C. H. Kraeling & R. M. Adams (Eds.), *City invincible: A symposium in urbanization and cultural development in the ancient Near East* (pp. 391–404). Chicago: Chicago University Press.

Kluckhohn, C., & Leighton, D. (1974). *The Navaho* (2nd ed.). Cambridge, MA: Harvard University Press.

Kohlberg, L. (1984). *The psychology of moral development: The nature and validity of moral stages.* San Francisco: Harper & Row.

Ladd, J. 1957. *The structure of a moral code. A philosophical analysis of ethical discourse applied to the ethics of the Navaho Indians.* Cambridge, MA: Harvard University Press.

Langness, L. L. (1973). Ethics. In I. Hogbin (Ed.), *Anthropology in Papua New Guinea* (pp. 187–206). Melbourne: Melbourne University Press.

Leach, E. R. (1968). *A runaway world? 1967 Reith lectures.* Oxford University Press.

Lee, R. B. (1979). *The !Kung San: Men, women and work in a foraging society.* Cambridge: Cambridge University Press.

Marshall, L. (1976). Sharing, talking, and giving: Relief of social tension among the !Kung. In R. B. Lee & I. De Vore (Eds.), *Kalahari hunter-gatherers* (pp. 349–371). Cambridge, MA: Harvard University Press.

Morris, B. (1976). Whither the savage mind? Notes on the natural taxonomies of a hunting and gathering people. *Man* (n.s.), *11*, 542–557.

Morris, B. (1991). *Western conceptions of the individual.* New York: Berg.

Munz, P. (1993). *Philosophical Darwinism.* London: Routledge.

Panoff, M. (1969). The notion of time among the Maenge people of New Britain. *Ethnology, 8*, 153–166.

Piaget, J. (1932). *The moral judgment of the child.* London: Routledge & Kegan Paul.

Pollock, F., & Maitland, F. W. (1923). *The history of English law before the time of Edward I.* Cambridge: Cambridge University Press.

Read, K. E. (1955). Morality and the conception of the person among the Gahuku-Gama. *Oceania, 25*, 233–282.

Read, K. E. (1966). *The high valley.* London: Allen & Unwin.

Reichard, G. A. (1963). *Navaho religion: A study of symbolism* (2nd ed.). Princeton, NJ: Bollingen Foundation.

Scribner, S., & Cole, M. (1981). *The psychology of literacy.* Cambridge, MA: Harvard University Press.

Snarey, J. R. (1985). Cross-cultural universality of social-moral development: A critical review of Kohlbergian research. *Psychological Bulletin, 97*, 202–232.

Woodburn, J. (1968). Discussion. In R. B. Lee & I. De Vore (Eds.), *Man the Hunter* (p. 91). Chicago: Aldine.

12

Social Decisions, Social Interactions, and the Coordination of Diverse Judgments

Elliot Turiel

Samuel Beckett began his much-acclaimed novel, *Murphy* (1938/1970), with: "The sun shone, having no alternative, on the nothing new." The compulsion so starkly and eloquently portrayed by Beckett with regard to the physical cosmos, is deeply rooted in psychological explanations starting, at least, with two very influential theoretical orientations in the first part of the 20th century—psychoanalytic and behaviorist theories. Both theoretical approaches presumed that there is an absence of choice on the part of human beings. The compulsion in Freud's conception of human functioning was due to rather complicated dynamics of conflicts and the unknown in the depths of the psyche involving equally complicated biological and learned dispositions. Although an element of choice was ultimately and painstakingly attainable in Freud's vision, it is irrelevant in behaviorist conceptions of the mechanisms of learning and the control over behavior by environmental conditions. Most notably in his *Beyond Freedom and Dignity,* B. F. Skinner (1971) maintained that many of our notions pertaining to freedom, choice, and autonomy are illusory so far as psychological functioning is concerned. According to Skinner, we refer to autonomy (which he sees as akin to saying individuals are miraculous) only because we do not know how to adequately explain behavior. The freedom attributed to individuals by the concept of autonomy needs to be replaced by analyses of the control of behavior.

Most contemporary approaches hold psychoanalytic and behaviorist theories at a distance, regarding each as outdated. I dredge up theories often considered ancient history in our relatively young field because many contemporary approaches also hold in common with those theories the psychological idea of compulsion; of an absence of freedom or choice on the part of human beings. Whether contemporary assumptions are a legacy of the earlier theories or reflect independently held similar assumptions, or both, are historical questions that are difficult to answer. Either way, I argue that these assumptions are fundamentally flawed and that in certain quarters of psychology there is a failure to recognize the types of reasoning that allow for what can be considered aspects of freedom, choice, and autonomy.

The aim of this chapter is to present an approach to moral and social development based on the propositions that individuals form systematic types of rationality in different domains, exercise autonomy and choice, and coordinate varying concepts in their social decisions. First, I describe research in social and cognitive psychology that has focused on the irrational or non-rational in decision-making. After a brief consideration of the historical roots of such approaches in the theory of cognitive dissonance, I consider theory and research into heuristics and intuitions in decision-making about economics and probabilities. I present an alternative view as to how decision-making involves a weighing and balancing of judgments about multiple goals and considerations that include processes of reasoning that go beyond heuristics or intuitions. I then apply a similar perspective to presumptions regarding moral heuristics. This is followed by discussion of traditions in philosophy and psychology based on propositions regarding the centrality of rationality and autonomy in moral and social judgments. Research is examined documenting that individuals do not rely on heuristics but instead make complex judgments about moral issues and discriminate among different social domains. I argue that the heterogeneity of individuals' thought stems from multifaceted social experiences and makes for non-homogeneous orientations within cultures. I also maintain that individuals' moral development is not constrained by the types of homogeneous cultural orientations presumed in conceptions of cultures as cohesive or as ordered on developmental or evolutionary scales. Finally, I explicate through discussion of research on rights and honesty the ways social decisions involve coordination within the moral domain or among different domains of judgment. The best evidence from research provides support for the view that individuals reason about social and moral issues and exercise choice and autonomy.

UNDER THE CONTROL OF COGNITIVE LIMITATIONS

One manifestation, for example, of the assumption of an absence of choice in psychological functioning is the long-standing social psychological approaches to social decisions and attitudes in general. The focus of a good deal of that sub-discipline during the 1950s and 1960s on "cognitive dissonance" exemplifies the assumption of nonrationality and irrationality in decision making. The major architect of the theory of cognitive dissonance, Leon Festinger (1957), closely linked decision making to basic needs to avoid and reduce psychological discomfort. The main problem addressed by the theory is how people react to internal inconsistencies—such as between different preferences, between different choices, and between beliefs and actions. Inconsistencies produce dissonance, and since dissonance entails discomfort, the individual is motivated to reduce the dissonance.

The idea that individuals are motivated to reduce cognitive dissonance does not, in itself, imply nonrationality or an absence of choice. The way the theory of cognitive dissonance was formulated and developed over the years, however, does show a distinct affinity for the nonrational. In the first place, Festinger maintained that dissonance is motivating in ways analogous to physiological drives: "cognitive dissonance...leads to activity oriented toward dissonance reduction just as hunger leads to activity oriented toward hunger reduction" (1957, p. 3). Festinger explicitly stated, "dissonance acts in the same way as a state of drive or need or tension" (p. 18). The main motivation, then, is that one is compelled to reduce the need or tension—which typically occurs through a number of mental and emotional gyrations, including avoidance of information, distortions of reality, and rationalizations that alter beliefs or knowledge in whatever ways the tension is most easily and effectively reduced. In this perspective, individuals do not deal with conflicts by seeking ways of better understanding their environments or themselves. They do not attempt to better understand beliefs, opinions, or problems so as to come to more adequate solutions to conflicts. Indeed, the motivation is one of avoidance rather than exploration or experimentation since according to Festinger (1957): "the greater the dissonance, the greater will be the intensity of the action to reduce the dissonance and the greater the avoidance of situations that would increase the dissonance" (p. 18).

Social psychologists in particular have frequently focused on psychological mechanisms by which individuals fool themselves (shades of Freud?) to avoid problems or tensions and to make themselves feel better. A consistent theme in these social psychological formulations—and in some formulations in cognitive psychology—is that flaws, mistakes, and errors are hallmarks of human thought. Mistakes and errors are regarded as both characteristic of human thought and evidence of the prevalence of nonrationality. It has been maintained, for instance, that decision making is not based on rational scrutiny or reflective analyses, but on the use of "heuristics," biases, and by the way an issue is framed (Kahneman, Slovic, & Tversky, 1982).

The work on heuristics and framing has influenced long-standing assumptions about what economists and psychologists considered central in rational decision making: maximizing the interests of the self. In these views the rational actor makes self-interested decisions that involve considerations of costs and benefits to the self. When evidence accumulated that people often make decisions that do not lead to maximizing benefits to self, it was argued that decision making is not commonly rational. It has been said that people not only make misjudgments, but also that their decisions and actions are often irrational since they go against their self-interest by not maximizing material gains.

The validity of this line of reasoning rests on the definition of rationality in economic decisions—a definition that reduces rationality to self-interest and to one type of self-interest at that. Implicitly, it is assumed that if individuals acted rationally, maximizing financial gains in economically related situations would prevail over other considerations. However, if individuals can be shown to hold a variety of goals in addition to maximizing self-interest, it becomes apparent that referring to decisions that do not maximize material gains as nonrational is incorrect. For example, a person may hold moral beliefs pertaining to equality and respect for persons that may be connected to their conceptions of the importance of promoting justice, insuring the rights of individuals, and maintaining the welfare of self and others. These moral ideas and goals may well involve reasoning and understandings about how one wants social interactions to take place (Rawls, 1971). In that case, decision making would involve weighing and balancing moral and personal considerations (including self-interest), as well as other social and prudential considerations. Decision making entails a process of coordinating different domains of judgment, such that multiple goals and considerations are taken into account in most situations—including situations involving economic decisions.

The ways in which decisions involve multiple goals and considerations can be illustrated through some simple examples. First, suppose that a person places a good deal of importance on the happiness and well-being of his or her children. Also suppose that the parent makes decisions that involve forsaking the maximization of benefits to the self in order to help increase the future happiness and well-being of the children. Is that a nonrational decision? Is it a decision that goes against maximizing benefits? Another example: Suppose an individual is offered two jobs in his or her area of expertise, with one paying substantially more than the other. And suppose that in the lower paying position the person would be working with others with similar religious and ethnic identities, whereas in the higher position she would be working with others who do not share those identities. Is it nonrational to choose the lower paying position?

In a simple way, these examples illustrate how people might weigh and balance different goals in decisions involving self-interest, benefits, and economics. Some analysts have a tendency to take realms of decision making in isolation and assume that rationality can be computed within such narrow domains. Thus, in the domain of economics, maximizing gains and profits are treated as rational decisions and decisions that appear to go against self-interest are deemed nonrational or irrational. Many economic decisions are even more complicated than the examples I have given, involving multiple dimensions about life choices that need to be coordinated with each other.

THE CONCEPT OF HEURISTICS: A SOURCE OF MANY ERRORS

In addition to studies of judgments about economic outcomes, research on heuristics has often examined judgments involving probabilities and predictions of outcomes of various types. In that research, respondents typically are asked for predictions of a future outcome or estimations of the likelihood that persons described in particular ways fit a category such as a political affiliation or occupational group. I present two examples from work by Tversky and Kahneman (1983) to illustrate the approach and how decisions seen as entailing heuristics might involve deeper cognitive processes. In one example, respondents were presented with a personality sketch of a woman (Linda) and a set of occupations and avocations associated with it. The sketch is as follows (from Tversky & Khaneman, 1983):

> Linda is 31 years old, single, outspoken and very bright. She majored in philosophy. As a student, she was deeply concerned with issues of discrimination and social justice, and also participated in anti-nuclear demonstrations. (p. 297)

For our purposes, the most relevant occupations/avocations listed for respondents were:

> Linda is active in the feminist movement. (designated F)
> Linda is a bank teller. (T)
> Linda is a bank teller and is active in the feminist movement (T & F).
> (p. 297)

It was found that the large majority ranked as more probable that Linda is a bank teller and active in the feminist movement (the conjunction of T & F) than that she is a bank teller (T). From the viewpoint of probabilistic thinking, this is in error since it is a violation of what Tversky and Kahneman (1983) refer to as the conjunction rule (that the likelihood of both occurring is less than one of the elements). The finding was taken to mean that a heuristic was being used (representativeness) and as demonstrating that intuition is at work rather than logic.

This type of research has demonstrated that errors do occur in judgments requiring probabilistic assessments. Probabilistic thinking may in some ways develop spontaneously (that is, out of experience without formal training), but in other ways does involve the acquisition of specialized knowledge. This line of research has documented that a lack of knowledge in a given domain may result in many errors and misattributions in people's judgments. This does not mean, however, that intuitions and heuristics are used in decisions like the one regarding the greater likelihood that Linda is a bank teller and active in the feminist movement. Missing in the propositions regarding heuristics are analyses of how people might be responding at levels deeper and more extensive than intuitions. Errors in judgment do not equate with use of heuristics or intuitions (versus logic).

What type of reasoning might be involved that leads to errors in the application of principles of probability? The most obvious in the example of Linda the bank teller is reasoning about the psychology of choices of occupations and activities. Respondents may have been drawing the psychological inference that a 31-year-old bright woman with an education in philosophy and interests in social justice will not feel satisfied or fulfilled as a bank teller and be highly motivated to engage in political activism of one kind or another. If it were correct that respondents reasoned this way, regardless of the accuracy of their predictions, it would have to be said that they were engaging in complex reasoning in the psychological domain with regard to people's occupations and avocations. Indeed, in conditions solely identifying Linda as a "31-year-old woman" the large majority thought is was less likely that she would be a bank teller and active feminist than a bank teller.

Another one of the conditions used by Tversky and Kahneman (1983, p. 307) illustrates the point that decisions involving probability judgments can also include other considerations involving logical inferences. In 1982, professionals involved in forecasting were asked to evaluate the probability of two forecasts: (1) A complete suspension of diplomatic relations between the United States and the Soviet Union, sometime in 1983; and (2) a Russian invasion of Poland, and a complete suspension of diplomatic relations between the United States and the Soviet Union, sometime in 1983. The conjunction of invasion and suspension of relations in (2) is less likely than suspension of relations in (1), particularly since the suspension in (1) could have come about for a variety of reasons. Nevertheless, the estimates of probability were higher for the invasion and suspension item. Whereas respondents may have ignored features that would lead them to a more accurate answer, they were likely looking for a plausible cause to suspension of diplomatic relations in order to make sense of the situation. Again, the issue is not whether the reasoning results in error, but whether individuals were using a heuristic or engaging in a process of reasoning.

There have been attempts to attribute intuitions (Haidt, 2001) and to generalize the idea of heuristics to the moral realm as well. Sunstein (2004), for instance, has argued that people sometimes (often?) employ moral heuristics, which can produce serious mistakes. In Sunstein's view, moral heuristics are generalizations that usually work well, but will sometimes result in moral errors. Sunstein used the following two examples of positions presumably voiced by many in the American media in 2003 to illustrate how heuristics result in moral errors (Sunstein, 2004):

> A. When you have been a fan of a sports team, you have a moral obligation to continue to be a fan even if the team is now terrible. It is disloyal to cease being a fan merely because the team keeps losing. "Once you are a fan, you're a fan for life."

> B. In opposing military action to topple Saddam Hussein, France violated its moral obligations. The United States liberated France from Hitler's Germany, and if the United States favored military action to topple Saddam Hussein, France was under a moral obligation to support the United States. (p. 1556)

These are presented as examples of heuristics that have a structure rendering them recognizable by generalizing moral intuitions and rules of thumb (which may often work well) from one context (relationships between friends) to superficially similar contexts. According to Sunstein, the idea that you should not abandon a friend who has fallen on hard times is applied to a sports team, and the idea that you should not stab your benefactors in the back when they are at risk is applied to different times and circumstances. Friends are not like a sports team and a nation is not obligated to accept another nation's position if the latter's position is considered unjust.

Sunstein makes questionable assumptions about each example, which differ from each other in important ways. In the first place, I would question his assertion that both positions have been "voiced by many people in the American media in 2003." Whereas the second position pertaining to France may have been often voiced in one form or another, the first position regarding a sports team is unfamiliar (except perhaps as a light or jestful comment). Starting in childhood, sports and games are recognized to be different from moral issues pertaining to welfare, justice, and rights (Turiel, 1983). Obligations to friends are not confused with allegiances to sports teams. It is highly questionable that people think about being a fan as a lifelong activity entailing a moral obligation. This is one of the reasons people so often change allegiances (as players change sports teams) and can be so critical of their team when it does not perform well.

It is, therefore, important to recognize that the two supposed examples of heuristics are very different from each other. People's judgments about games differ in fundamental ways from their judgments about nations at war and the issues of life and death involved. Is the second position, then, an example of a moral heuristic? It appears to be so if we consider only the assertion that France has a moral obligation to support the United States without also considering how people might be thinking about the situation. To understand why many people stated the position, it would be necessary to ascertain their understandings of the situation leading to such a position. Like Sunstein, I have no empirical data as to how people understood the situation. I propose, however, that a line of reasoning was involved that went beyond the overgeneralization of otherwise useful intuitions and rules of thumb.

We can best construe how people might have been led to the position that France should have supported the United States in Iraq by placing it into a broader context of their assumptions (not necessarily correct ones) about what was occurring in the world and in their lives. Given the events of September 11, 2001 and communications from President Bush and others, many people believed that the United States was in a type of confrontation and danger analogous to what existed for France in World War II. A common view was that the United States and other parts of the Western world were in the type of danger that could threaten their ways of life and the lives of people. The perceived willingness of terrorists to launch attacks like the ones of September 11 was seen as a great danger. In that context, people thought that France should have recognized that the United States was in a position with similarities to the situation France confronted during World War II and was, therefore, obligated to help for the reasons the United

States helped France and because the United States did help France in circumstances considered to have enough similarities to the current situation.

There is much with which to disagree in these positions regarding the current situation, the analogies with World War II, and the reasons for military action in Iraq. My point is that people were not simply employing moral heuristics or applying rules of thumb with an absence of thought about the situation. They maintained a set of assumptions about the motives of others, the vulnerabilities of their country, and the dire consequences likely to occur. People held conceptions about the psychological dispositions of others (e.g., terrorists, Saddam Hussein) and aspects of reality. (Most likely, it is because people held assumptions about the state of the world that President Bush was able to convince many of his falsehoods regarding the presence of weapons of mass destruction in Iraq, the connections of Al Queda to Iraq, and to use fear to garner votes in the presidential election of 2004.)

Individuals do employ shorthand ways of communicating the complex judgments they make—especially when publicly advocating political and controversial positions like France has a moral obligation to support the United States in Iraq. Some examples of the types of positions Sunstein might consider to be intuitions or heuristics have been researched. One issue, not mentioned by Sunstein, is abortion. It is well known that people will signal their positions on abortion as "prolife" or "prochoice." These shorthand ways of communicating reflect complex sets of judgments that entail assumptions about the status of the fetus as a life (Turiel, Hildebrandt, & Wainryb, 1991). It has been shown that those who believe abortion is acceptable value the sacredness of life in the same ways as those who judge abortion to be wrong. They disagree on whether the fetus prior to a certain point in a pregnancy constitutes a life. Similarly, those judging abortion to be wrong accept the validity of freedom of choice in many realms. Judgments about life, laws, and abortion are by no means limited to intuitions about the value of life or the value of freedom of choice.

Another issue is that of lying, which was used by Sunstein to illustrate how everyday morality consists of "simple rules." Sunstein claims that the rule, it is wrong to lie, is a "heuristic" that misfires when a lie would save a human life. It is true that when asked most children and adults say that lying is wrong (Perkins & Turiel, 2007). However, most individuals say lying is acceptable under many circumstances, including situations in which perceived benefits are to save lives and even to prevent lesser harms. Studies have shown that adults and adolescents accept that a lie is not wrong when it is aimed at preventing harm, promoting the welfare of others, preventing injustices, and preserving their realms of personal choice (Freeman, Rathore, Weinfurt, Schulman, & Sulmasy, 1999; Perkins & Turiel, 2007). All these findings demonstrated that "it is wrong to lie" is far from a heuristic or a rule of thumb for most people since they make nuanced judgments about circumstances in which lying is acceptable and ones in which it is not. Parallel findings were obtained regarding another "heuristic" mentioned by Sunstein—the endorsement of freedom of speech as absolute. Most adolescents and adults endorse rights like freedom of speech when asked in abstract terms (Helwig, 1995; McClosky & Brill, 1983; Turiel & Wainryb, 1998), but most do not treat rights as absolute since they subordinate rights to other social and moral considerations in a variety of situations (more about honesty and rights below).

GOING A LITTLE DEEPER: SEEMING STRUCTURES OF MORAL THOUGHT

The work on heuristics can be seen as a revisiting of the assumption that reason, autonomy, and choice do not explain human decision making. I have provided counterexamples to illustrate that reasoning goes deeper than the presumed application of heuristics in economic choices, probabilistic judgments, and moral decisions. I have also attempted to show that the reasoning involved in such decisions includes considerations from more than one domain. In the domain of morality, even when processes of reasoning are analyzed, there is a tendency to view decisions only within the confines of the domain—and even one type of judgment within the moral domain—without taking into account the coordination of other domains with the moral or the coordination of different moral considerations. This "bounded" approach to moral decisions takes various forms. These include attribution of moral decisions and actions to cultural orientations and emotional dispositions. A commentary by Appiah (2005) with regard to the overuse of culture in certain quarters would seem to apply to some approaches to the development of morality: "It hasn't escaped notice that 'culture'—the word—has been getting a hefty workout in recent years. The notion seems to be that everything from anorexia to zydeco is illuminated by being displayed as the product of some group's culture" (p. 114). Emotion—and as tied to so-called intuitions—has also started to get a hefty workout in recent years. In this case, the notion seems to be that all moral decisions are explained by being displayed as the product of immediate, unreflective, nonrational reactions of an aversive kind (Haidt, 2001).

Issues of reason, autonomy, and choice are very much part of some traditions of research in psychology and in philosophical analyses. Among philosophers, Appiah's thinking is within one of those traditions in philosophy. Along with some psychologists concerned with culture, he does not discount culture but places it into the context of individual participants who engage in self-development through faculties of observation, reasoning, and judgment. Following John Stuart Mill, Appiah regards autonomy as necessary for human functioning. Rawls's (1971) widely known theory of justice was also based on the plausibility of rational choice with deliberation and reflection upon facts, situations, and consequences (see Appiah, 2005, p. 7). Individuality and autonomy are central to the formation of identities that do entail collective affiliations. However, identity is not determined by a collective affiliation or participation in a culture:

> I don't say the word "culture" should be banned from our lexicon; I do not claim it is always entirely without utility. But, as we have seen, its weed

like profusion can sometimes crowd out analysis. Treating international difference, between what Rorty calls "the West" and the "non-West," as an especially profound kind of something called "cultural difference" is, in my view, a characteristically modern mistake. (Appiah, 2005, p. 254; for similar critiques, see Abu-Lughod, 1993; Nussbaum, 1999; Turiel, 2002; Wikan, 2002)

Appiah (2005) further argues that the use of culture as reflecting differences between groups can be a product of a disciplinary artifact because the field of anthropology has a professional bias toward difference: "Who would want to go out for a year of fieldwork 'in the bush' in order to return with the news that 'they' do so many things just as we do?" (p. 254). Appiah also points out that difficulties in cross-cultural dialogue are no more substantial than difficulties of dialogues within societies. Difficulties of dialogues within societies exist not only because there are varying groups within societies, but also more importantly because individuals do not hold one type of perspective on the world determined by a homogenous cultural orientation, an adaptation, or a singular identity. Sen (2006) forcefully argued that individuals always belong to several groups and that they maintain the freedom to determine loyalties and priorities among these different groups. With abilities to make choices and use their powers of reasoning, individuals maintain multiple identities involving social class, nationality, gender, occupation, language, morality, politics, and more. Sen, too, emphasized the importance of diversity within groups or cultures and within individuals: "a person has to make choices—explicitly or by implication—about what relative importance to attach, in a particular context, to the divergent loyalties and priorities that may compete for precedence" (Sen, 2006, p. 19).

According to Sen, reasoning is influenced by culture, with its internal variations, but not determined by it. Moreover, human beings can question and challenge what they are taught. Sen's ideas about multiple identities and variations (nonhomogeneity) within groups are intricately connected to the power of reasoning and the freedoms of choice it affords. Unlike many of the traditional psychological approaches I have mentioned, philosophers like Sen, Appiah, and Rawls work on the assumption that, like scholars in philosophy, psychology, and other disciplines, laypersons engage in reasoning and attempt to act rationally. Characterizing a tradition that can be traced to Kant and Mill and which would include Appiah and Sen, Nussbaum (1999) stated that "human beings …, just by being human, are of equal dignity and worth…and the primary source of this worth is a power of choice within them" (p. 57). Moral choice exists because "human beings are above all reasoning beings" (p. 71).

Sen made this point, too, quoting the Muslim Indian Emperor of the 1590s: "The pursuit of reason and rejection of traditionalism are so brilliantly patent as to be above the need of argument. If traditionalism were proper, the prophets would merely have followed their own elders (and not come with new messages)" (as quoted by Sen, 2006, p. 161). Sen goes on to explain: "reason had to be supreme, since even in disputing reason, we would have to give reasons." Indeed, all those psychologists, including Skinner, who propose that human beings do not engage in reasoning themselves use reason, argumentation, and evidence to put forth those claims (see Turiel, 2006 for further discussion).

There is, of course, a tradition in psychological research that takes reason and autonomy seriously. Within that tradition, Piaget (1932) focused on autonomy in the development of moral reasoning, and Kohlberg (1969) continued that line of thinking. However, those analyses of morality did not go far enough in examining the choices people make by coordinating different types of considerations and goals in social and moral decision making.

I can illustrate how those approaches do not sufficiently recognize the importance of processes of coordination through another set of examples of shorthand communications in political contexts regarding the issues of public concern. These examples also illustrate the heterogeneity of societies and difficulties of dialogues within societies that Appiah and Sen discussed. One example comes from debates in the United States about the rights, benefits, and reactions to an influx of immigrants who are in the country without legal documentation. Proposals of legislation in Congress to address the status of immigrants with regard to matters like schooling, health care, and employment have produced debates with two sides that seems to divide by proponents of "law and order" (illegal immigrants must not be given benefits, jobs, or amnesty because they have broken the law) and proponents of compassion and flexibility (illegal immigrants are fellow human beings who should be respected and whose welfare should be protected). At the level of the shorthand characterizations it may be thought that the "law and order" approach to immigrants constitutes use of a heuristic that it is wrong to violate the law, without taking other issues into consideration. Those who invoke violations of law to support their opposition to undocumented immigrants and oppose new legislation to provide them with benefits and services probably maintain ideas that go beyond assertions about the need to obey laws (as in the examples already discussed). Their shorthand position likely reflects additional judgments about maintaining national identities or community interests, preserving perceived limited resources in areas like health care, schooling, and employment, and concerns with equal application of the law.

The distinction between a law and order orientation and an orientation to respect and welfare seems to fit Kohlberg's (1969, 1971) analyses of the moral structures of thought that go beyond heuristics and intuitions. Kohlberg identified six stages of development, including a stage (Stage 4) represented by an orientation to maintaining laws as the basis for moral judgment. Is it that opponents of undocumented immigrants, who generally are on the politically conservative side of things, are functioning at Stage 4 and, thereby, judge on the basis of whether laws are violated or followed? Is it that those concerning themselves with respect for the welfare of individuals, who generally are on the politically liberal side of things, are functioning at other stages (e.g., Stages 5 and 6)?

From the perspective of Kohlberg's formulations, it is expected that a stage of thinking would be applied across issues. This expectation does not appear to hold in other shorthand communications about other public issues. Positions regarding the need to uphold laws seem to be reversed with regard to issues that have been in the public eye since the terrorist attacks of September 11: wiretapping, secret surveillance of financial transactions, imprisonment and interrogation of suspected terrorists, and the use of evidence in trials. It is the politically liberal, espousing flexibility of law regarding immigrants, who have stressed the need to heed the rule of law on these matters. They argue that the government, under the administration of President Bush, is wrong to undertake these types of activities because they violate laws. The politically liberal have continually stressed the importance of following the rules of the Geneva Conventions in the treatment of prisoners taken in the "war on terror" and in the Iraqi war. By contrast, it is the politically conservative, espousing the need to follow the law regarding immigrants, who have stressed the need for flexibility on these matters. They argue, for instance, that in order to protect lives from the actions of terrorists it is necessary to engage in activities like wiretapping, and to bend the rules of the Geneva Conventions.

The inconsistencies in people's use of the need to adhere to the rule of law in these different situations is not itself inconsistent with ideas about heuristics—although the inconsistencies may be discrepant with expectations about stages or structures of moral thought. It may be that moral decisions do vary by situational contexts and political affiliations in ways that result in the use of moral heuristics in some situations and not in others. It may also be that the same individuals employ different heuristics in different situations. Hence the law and order heuristic is used by some people in situations involving issues of immigration but not with regard to combating terrorism (and the reverse for other people). I am proposing an alternative view to the idea of heuristics, as well as to the particular stages of moral thought in Kohlberg's formulation. I have already discussed how economic decisions and the examples used by Sunstein entail the coordination of different considerations, purposes, and goals. It is also likely that those who seem to invoke the rule of law regarding issues like electronic surveillance and interrogation of prisoners are also concerned with individual rights, due process, the welfare of individuals, and the identity of the nation (as those calling for flexibility in the application of laws on these matters are concerned with the importance of maintaining laws). All these judgments coexist in ways that go deeper than the use of heuristics.

We do not have good explanations as to why people come to different conclusions on these matters. If, however, we are to come closer to such explanations, it is necessary to understand the different types of judgments, considerations, goals, and purposes formed in the process of development. In my view, a key to doing so is in the recognition that individuals form different domains of social thinking and that they draw priorities among different considerations faced in a situation—which has been the recurring theme in the way I have discussed the various examples. Part of that theme is that individuals' moral judgments go beyond the application of rules of thumb or surface intuitions—a proposition that is consistent with efforts like those of Kohlberg (1969), and Piaget (1932) before him, to explain the structures of moral thinking as they change with age. Another part of the theme is that in coming to social decisions, individuals apply and coordinate multiple judgments—a proposition that is discrepant with the particular models of moral development proposed by Piaget and Kohlberg.

Both Piaget and Kohlberg proposed what can be referred to as differentiation models of the development of moral judgments. As is well known, Piaget maintained that young children's initial sense of morality entailed judgments of obligation based on a heteronomous orientation to authority and rules in which their understandings of physical, psychological, and moral rules were undifferentiated. He proposed that at later ages children form distinct moral understandings of justice in an autonomous orientation that entails differentiating the moral from the nonmoral. One of the salient confusions resolved with development from heteronomy to autonomy is the differentiation of "what ought to be from what is" (p. 350). Heteronomous thought identifies "what is with what ought to be" (p. 347).

As is also well known, Kohlberg extended and refined Piaget's formulation into a six-stage sequence. The six-stage sequence, though different in details from Piaget's conceptions of heteronomy and autonomy, also entails progressive differentiations of what ought to be from what exists. In this formulation, too, distinct moral understandings do not emerge until the highest stages of thinking. Development is explained as a process of increasing differentiations of moral judgments from other realms. As put by Kohlberg (1971):

> The individual whose judgments are at stage 6 asks "Is it morally right?" and means by morally right something different from punishment (stage 1), prudence (stage 2), conformity to authority (stages 3 and 4) etc. Thus, the responses of lower-stage subjects are not moral for the same reasons that responses of higher-stage subjects to aesthetic or other morally neutral matters fail to be moral…. This is what we had in mind earlier when we spoke of our stages as representing an increased differentiation of moral values and judgments from other types of values and judgments. (p. 216)

In this type of differentiation model, distinct moral judgments emerge through a lengthy process of distinguishing issues of welfare, justice, and rights from other judgments (punishment and prudence at first, and then authority, rules, and conventions). It is not until the highest stages (in terms of age, late adolescence at the earliest) that understandings of morality are distinguished from understandings based on commitments to following rules, adherence to authority dictates, and respect for society (that is, in the shift from Stage 4 to Stages 5 and 6). Moreover, in these formulations it is implicitly assumed that decisions are bounded within the moral domain, without consideration of how domains are coordinated. This is because embedded in the idea of progressive differentiations of domains is the idea that moral judgments *displace* other and developmentally lower types of judgments. The types of moral understandings that characterize the highest stages involve overarching principles that serve to organize priorities in decisions. At the highest stages, moral principles are given priority over other domains because the process of development involves the formation of judgments out of prior confusions. Since development entails a disentanglement of morality from other social considerations, it is presumed that morality will then be given priority over the "less adequate" forms of judgment represented in the lower stages.

As I have stressed, decision making involves weighing and balancing different considerations and goals in particular situations. The decision-making process is not bounded within a domain, but includes a coordination of different domains like morality, prudence, convention, and personal jurisdiction. A variety of judgments, which coexist across ages, are brought to bear in making decisions. An extensive program of research (e.g., Turiel, 2006) shows that development is not a process in which one type of judgment displaces another. Children begin to form distinct domains of moral, social, prudential, and personal reasoning at a relatively young age (by 5 or 6 years).

Since the research on these domains is extensively discussed in many places (Nucci, 2001; Turiel, 1983, 1998, 2002, 2006), I only briefly summarize some of the features of children's moral and social conventional thought. It is evident from that large body of research that young children do not make moral judgments on the basis of the punishment involved, power and status, personal inclinations, reverence for those in authority, or rigid adherence to rules or laws. All of these considerations are part of people's judgments, but are understood differently from moral considerations of welfare, justice, and rights. Since young children make judgments about social conventions that differ from their moral judgments, it cannot be said that the development of a distinct moral domain stems from its differentiation at later ages from convention.

Both the moral and conventional domains involve understandings of different types of norms and social relationships, and their distinction does not solely involve a simple discrimination between categories. A complex configuration is connected to each domain, including what has been referred to as criterion judgments and justifications. The criterion judgments, which are not age-related, refer to whether morality or convention is seen as contingent on rules, dependent on authority dictates, or based on common practice or existing social arrangements. Many studies show that moral norms are judged to be obligatory and non contingent on rules, authority, or existing practices and agreements. By contrast, conventional norms are judged to be contingent on rules, authority, common practice, and are based on social agreements. Justifications—or reasons for evaluations and criterion judgments—also differ by domain and do involve age-related changes. Justifications in the moral domain are based on concepts of welfare, justice, and rights, whereas in the conventional domain they are based on tradition, social agreement, and social coordinations. Levels of development have been identified for the domain of social convention (Turiel, 1983). Although less is known about development in the moral domain, shifts occur from a focus on harm among younger children to concerns with welfare and justice in later childhood (David-son, Turiel, & Black, 1983; Nucci, 2001; Turiel, 1998). There are different strands of developmental transformations within individuals—in the context of the main-tenance of the domain distinctions across ages.

Another difference between the two approaches is in their respective per-spectives on the influences of children's social experiences. In the differentiation models distinctions are not drawn between types of social experiences associated with moral judgments and other social judgments. For instance, Kohlberg did not specify, except in general terms, experiences that serve to stimulate develop-ment to the highest stages. He referred to increased role-taking opportunities, dis-cussion or argumentation, and conflicts that allow for increased differentiations. Kohlberg (1971) theorized that there would be experienced-based constraints on the level of development attained by individuals due to the equilibration of their thinking with levels of complexity in the social environment (see also Hallpike, this volume). Relying on analyses of a hierarchy of societies provided by the sociologist Hobhouse (1906), Kohlberg attempted to map his stages of individual development onto societal levels.

From the perspective of the development of distinct domains there are sev-eral shortcomings in the characterizations of social experiences and constraints in the differentiation models. One is that social experiences that would be associ-ated with domains other than the moral are left out of the analyses. Therefore, the variety or multitude of social experiences is left unanalyzed. A number of studies have shown that children's social experiences differ in type with regard to social conventional and moral issues (Nucci & Nucci, 1982a, 1982b; Turiel, in press). Interactions and communications about moral issues revolve around the effects of acts on people, the perspectives of others, the need to avoid harm, and the pain and emotions experienced, whereas with regard to conventional events, they revolve around adherence to rules, commands from those in authority, and an emphasis on social order.

A second shortcoming stemming from the first is that the characterizations of experiences are at a general level (e.g., role-taking opportunities, discussion, and argumentation), rather than in the ways children might attend to the substance of particular types of events, interactions, and relationships. Observational and other studies (Wainryb, Brehl, & Matwin, 2005) indicate that substantive features of events and social interactions experienced by children do influence their develop-ment. By this I mean that it is not solely or mainly general features like role-taking opportunities, or cultural practices, or structural complexity that are implicated in development; rather, it is children's continual participation in and observations of events of many types that are closely related to the formation of moral judgments. Children participate in events that involve, as examples, people harming or help-ing each other, sharing or failing to share, excluding or including others, treating people equally or unequally. Children's observations and reflections on events are major sources of formation and changes of moral and social judgments. Therefore, children are in reciprocal interaction with other people and form judgments of fairness about those interactions by an early age.

The findings on domain distinctions, which were obtained in many Western and non-Western cultures (including traditional societies in Africa, Asia, the Middle East, and South America), have implications for how cultures are to be characterized. There is a tendency to characterize cultures in homogeneous terms. For instance, many analyses of culture and individual moral development and the development of self (e.g., Markus & Kitayama, 1991; Shweder, Mahapatra, & Miller, 1987) begin with the premises, rejected by Appiah and Sen, that cultures are organized homogeneously either by individualist or collectivist orientations and that through their participation in such cultures individuals acquire moral judgments and conceptions of self and others that are in accord with those orientations. Briefly put, morality in collectivist cultures is based on duties, adhering to social roles, and subsuming self to a broader conception of the group. Since in collectivist societies persons are seen as part of interconnection and interdependence, a sense of autonomy or individuality is minimized. Morality in individualist societies is based on the centrality accorded to the individual and, therefore, it is oriented to individual rights rather than duties, and emphasis is given to independence and autonomy.

There is a sense in which the stages of moral judgments proposed by Kohlberg match the proposed dichotomy of individualism and collectivism. The earliest stages (based on prudence and personal interest) and the latest stages (based on rights and justice) are more or less in accord with the idea of individualism. The middle stages (based on conventions, social order, and authority) are more or less in accord with the idea of collectivism. As stages of development, these are supposed to characterize, across cultures, individual reasoning on an ordering of development. Nevertheless, it has been proposed that the level of social structural complexity of the society or culture places constraints on the stage of attainment of individuals (Kohlberg, 1971; Hallpike, this volume). This proposition represents a third shortcoming in the differentiation models. In the first place, the body of research on the domains of morality, social convention, and the personal indicates that cultures cannot be characterized as mainly oriented to collectivism or individualism—see Turiel and Wainryb (1994), and Turiel (2002) for more extensive discussion), and that the heterogeneity in cultures and in the reasoning of individuals precludes placing constraints on individual development in accord with societal complexity. In all the cultures we have studied, individuals make judgments about morality, conventions, and persons that do not fit characterizations of societies as oriented to personal needs, power, prudence, authority, or the conventionally constituted system, including social duties and roles.

Perhaps most to the point is that research has shown that social opposition is regularly engaged in by children and that moral opposition to societal arrangements and resistance is displayed in everyday lives, by at least adolescence and into adulthood, by those subjected to inequalities and injustices embedded in cultural practices and the structure of social systems. Both psychological and anthropological research has examined how individuals think about and react to inequalities and restrictions placed on groups lower (e.g., females) in the social hierarchy by groups with greater power (e.g., males). The findings show, first, that those lower in the social hierarchy critically judge as unfair the restrictive acts of those of greater power and status (Conry-Murray, 2006; Mensing, 2002; Neff, 2001; Wainryb & Turiel, 1994). Therefore, judgments about avoiding harm, promoting rights, and fairness are applied, for example, to those who are in positions of power and who are accorded many entitlements. This is the case in close relationships in that women are critical of their husbands when they are perceived to act unfairly. This is also the case with regard to the social system in that individuals are critical of social norms and cultural practices that institutionalize inequalities and power differences. Anthropological research (Abu-Lughod, 1993; Wikan, 1996, 2006) provides evidence that females act on those judgments by opposing and resisting certain norms. They also attempt, through acts of subversion, to change cultural practices of unequal power.

COORDINATION OF DIFFERENT JUDGMENTS
IN SOCIAL DECISION MAKING

Social and moral opposition, resistance, and subversion are all activities demonstrating that human beings possess the power of moral choice. These activities, which are displayed by most people in many circumstances, involve reasoning about existing practices, the structure of the social system, and interpersonal relationships. The reasoning of individuals also involves abilities to perceive different components of situations and make multiple judgments about varying facets of life. Therefore, reasoning cannot be defined in unitary terms, such as in the idea that rational decisions are ones that maximize economic benefits and minimize losses.

Discussions regarding rights, an issue I have already mentioned, among political scientists and philosophers are informative in this regard. Over the years, large-scale public opinion surveys of adult Americans have shown that they endorse rights in some situations and do not in other situations (Hyman & Sheatsley, 1953; McClosky & Brill, 1983; Stouffer, 1955). To some political scientists (e.g., Protho & Grigg, 1960; Sarat, 1975), the findings mean that most Americans do not adequately understand the concept of rights. In their view, an adequate understanding of rights would result in consistently upholding rights across situations. Such a view of the concept of rights is in accord with the idea in the differentiation models that attainment of the highest stages (as in Kohlberg's framework) results in true moral understandings and consistently giving priority to a moral concept, like rights, over other considerations.

However, some philosophers have put forth the alternative view that rights constitute one type of moral norm that is weighed and balanced against other competing moral and social norms in particular situations (Dworkin, 1977; Gewirth, 1982). Adequate understandings of rights can lead to sometimes subordinating rights to other goals. For example, a right to free speech may be judged in relation to the harm to persons' physical welfare that might result from its exercise (Helwig, 1995). Along those lines, the findings from the public opinion surveys can be interpreted to mean that individuals, though endorsing rights in the abstract, will evaluate the application of rights and freedoms in comparison with other moral and social goals (Turiel, Killen, & Helwig, 1987). By making choices among different goals, individuals sometimes uphold rights and at other times subordinate rights in order to, for instance, prevent harm or promote community interests. This involves coordinating different considerations.

In contrast with the survey method of solely assessing whether individuals state that they do or do not uphold rights, other research has examined the judgments children, adolescents, and adults make about rights. Studies conducted in several countries (see Helwig & Turiel, 2002 for a summary) have found that at all ages rights pertaining to such matters as freedom of speech and religion were upheld in the abstract, regarded as an obligatory norm in that they were judged to generalize across groups or cultures, and seen as serving needs for self-expression and autonomy. As found in the surveys, in some contexts rights were subordinated to preventing psychological harm (e.g., a public speech with racial slurs), physical harm (a speech advocating violence), and inequality (advocating exclusion). At all ages, individuals took into account the different considerations posed in a given situation and drew priorities between conflicting norms or goals.

The coordination of judgments between different domains or between different judgments in a domain (e.g., rights and preventing physical harm) involves making choices. Research on concepts of rights provides one example of how what might appear to be a readily known intuitive notion is not that. People do not use rights as a heuristic—even though people readily claim, in a rule of thumb way, that rights should not be violated. Much more is at work when individuals respond to situations implicating rights. Similarly, the "rule of thumb" mentioned by Sunstein (2004), that it is wrong to lie involves more complex judgments and processes of decision making. A number of studies show that children, adolescents, and adults judge that honesty is important but that in many situations lying is also acceptable.

The situations in which lying is seen as acceptable range from those involving the need to spare the feelings of others (so-called white lies), to protecting people from physical harm and maintaining their welfare, to circumventing injustices, to promoting perceived legitimate personal ends in the face of relationships of unequal power (Turiel, 2002; Turiel & Perkins, 2004). Consider three types of studies. One is research on physicians' judgments of deception as a means of obtaining a necessary treatment for patients (Freeman et al., 1999). It was found that the majority of physicians judged deception of an insurance company acceptable if it were the only means to obtain treatment for a seriously ill patient (but not for an elective treatment like cosmetic surgery). The physicians judged that protecting the welfare of patients has priority over maintaining honesty.

The second type of study shows that judgments about the value of honesty and the legitimacy of deception are connected to the domain of the issue and types of relationships in ways that involve coordination among several features. In one study (Perkins & Turiel, 2007), it was found that adolescents state, in the abstract, that lying is wrong and judge lying for self-interested goals (e.g., to cover up a misdeed) as wrong. However, they judged that it was not wrong for an adolescent to lie to parents when parents attempt to get them to act in ways considered morally wrong or when parents impose restrictions on areas of personal jurisdiction. Lying is seen as justified to avoid unfairness or harm, or as a way of circumventing undue control in relationships of inequality of power. However, lying to parents was judged to be wrong in the context of directives considered by the adolescents within legitimate parental authority (e.g., prudential matters involving the adolescent's physical safety). In addition, the adolescents judged as wrong the same acts of deception in relationships of more or less equality (with friends). Similar results have been obtained in a study of the judgments of college students and married adults regarding the use of deception in the context of inequalities in marital relationships (Turiel & Perkins, 2004).

A third type of research is the anthropological investigations of acts of opposition and resistance (Abu-Lughod, 1993; Wikan, 1996). Those studies included observations of women who engaged in acts of deception to get around restrictions imposed upon their leisure activities, as well as opportunities for education and employment. In these cases, it would be expected that the heuristic that it is wrong to lie would be reinforced by heuristics associated with strongly sanctioned cultural practices in patriarchal societies pertaining to relationships between males and females. Yet, women acted deceptively when they judged inequalities and power differences as unjust.

CONCLUSION

The research showing that decision making in social situations frequently involves the coordination of different considerations and goals provides an alternative to the idea that people often fall prey to errors because of their reliance on heuristics. What appear to be errors due to the use of rules of thumb reflect the difficulties of applying different judgments to multifaceted social situations. The coordination required in such situations may be between different considerations within a domain or between domains of judgment. That individuals begin to distinguish social domains at early ages means that they construct forms of reasoning through reciprocal interactions in a multifaceted social environment. That individuals apply those judgments in different situations means that they are able to make reasoned choices on the basis of a recognition of varying components and attempt to draw priorities. Part of the process of making such choices involves a commitment to culture that is combined with scrutiny and critique of cultural practices and societal arrangements. In turn, critique and opposition means that the social system does not limit the moral judgments of individuals. Perhaps the sun may shine on the nothing new, having no alternative. Human beings, by contrast, do create alternatives and construct much that is new.

References

Abu-Lughod, L. (1993). *Writing women's worlds: Bedouin stories.* Berkeley: University of California Press.

Appiah, K. A. (2005). *The ethics of identity.* Princeton, NJ: Princeton University Press.

Beckett, S. (1970). *Murphy.* New York: Grove Press. (Original work published 1938)

Conry-Murray, C. (2006). *Reasoning about gender hierarchy in Benin, West Africa: The Role of informational assumptions and pragmatic concerns.* Unpublished doctoral dissertation, University of California, Berkeley.

Davidson, P., Turiel, E., & Black, A. (1983). The effect of stimulus familiarity on the use of criteria and justifications in children's social reasoning. *British Journal of Developmental Psychology, 1,* 49–65.

Dworkin, R. (1977). *Taking rights seriously.* Cambridge, MA: Harvard University Press.

Festinger, L. (1957). *A theory of cognitive dissonance.* Stanford, CA: Stanford University Press.

Freeman, V. G., Rathore, S. S., Weinfurt, K. P., Schulman, K. A., & Sulmasy, D. P. (1999). Lying for patients: Physician deception of third-party payers. *Archives of Internal Medicine, 159,* 2263–2270.

Gewirth, A. (1982). *Human rights: Essays on justification and applications.* Chicago: University of Chicago Press.

Haidt, J. (2001). The emotional dog and its rational tail: A social intuitionist approach to moral judgment. *Psychological Review, 108,* 814–834.

Helwig, C. C. (1995). Adolescents' and young adults' conceptions of civil liberties: Freedom of speech and religion. *Child Development, 66,* 152–166.

Helwig, C. C., & Turiel, E. (2002). Civil liberties, autonomy, and democracy: Children's perspectives. *Journal of Law and Psychiatry, 25,* 253–270.

Hobhouse, L. Y. (1906). *Morals in evolution.* London: Chapman & Hall.

Hyman, H. H., & Sheatsley, P. B. (1953). Trends in public opinion on civil liberties. *Journal of Social Issues, 9,* 6–16.

Kahneman, D., Slovic, P., & Teversky, A. (Eds.). (1982). *Judgment under uncertainty: Heuristics and biases.* Cambridge: Cambridge University Press.

Kohlberg, L. (1969). Stage and sequence: The cognitive-developmental approach to socialization. In D. Goslin (Ed.), *Handbook of socialization theory and research* (pp. 347–480). Chicago: Rand McNally.

Kohlberg, L. (1971). From is to ought: How to commit the naturalistic fallacy and get away with it in the study of moral development. In T. Mischel (Ed.), *Psychology and genetic epistemology* (pp. 151–235). New York: Academic Press.

Markus, H. R., & Kitayama, S. (1991). Culture and the self: Implications for cognition, emotion, and motivation. *Psychological Review, 98,* 224–253.

McClosky, M., & Brill, A. (1983). *Dimensions of tolerance: What Americans believe about civil liberties.* New York: Russell Sage.

Mensing, J. F. (2002). *Collectivism, individualism, and interpersonal responsibilities in families: Differences and similarities in social reasoning between individuals in poor, urban families in Colombia and the United States.* Unpublished doctoral dissertation, University of California, Berkeley.

Neff, K. D. (2001). Judgments of personal autonomy and interpersonal responsibility in the context of Indian spousal relationships: An examination of young people's reasoning in Mysore, India. *British Journal of Developmental Psychology, 19,* 233–257.

Nucci, L. P. (2001). *Education in the moral domain.* Cambridge: Cambridge University Press.

Nucci, L. P., & Nucci, M. S. (1982a). Children's reponses to moral and social conventional transgressions in free-play settings. *Child Development, 53,* 1337–1342.

Nucci, L. P., & Nucci, M. S. (1982b). Children's social interactions in the context of moral and conventional transgressions. *Child Development, 53,* 403–412.

Nussbaum, M.C. (1999). *Sex and social justice.* New York: Oxford University Press.

Perkins, S. A. & Turiel, E. (2007). To lie or not to lie: To whom and under what circumstances. *Child Development, 78,* 609–621.

Piaget, J. (1932). *The moral judgment of the child.* London: Routledge & Kegan Paul.

Protho, J. W., & Grigg, C. M. (1960). Fundamental principles of democracy: Bases of agreement and disagreement. *Journal of Politics, 22,* 276–294.

Rawls, J. (1971). *A theory of justice.* Cambridge, MA: Harvard University Press.

Sarat, A. (1975). Reasoning in politics: The social, political, and psychological bases of principled thought. *American Journal of Political Science, 19,* 247–261.

Sen, A. (2006). *Identity and violence: The illusion of destiny.* New York: Norton.

Shweder, R. A., Mahapatra, M., & Miller, J. G. (1987). Culture and moral development. In J. Kagan & S. Lamb (Eds.), *The emergence of morality in young children* (pp. 1–83). Chicago: University of Chicago Press.

Skinner, B. F. (1971). *Beyond freedom and dignity.* New York: Knopf.

Stouffer, S. (1955). *Communism, conformity and civil liberties.* Garden City, NY: Doubleday.

Sunstein, C. (2004). Moral heuristics and moral framing. *Minnesota Law Review, 88,* 1556–1597.

Turiel, E. (1983). *The development of social knowledge: Morality and convention.* Cambridge: Cambridge University Press.

Turiel, E. (1998). The development of morality. In W. Damon (Series Ed.) & N. Eisenberg (Vol. Ed.), *Handbook of child psychology: Vol. 3. Social, emotional, and personality development* (5th ed., pp. 863–932). New York: Wiley.

Turiel, E. (2002). *The culture of morality: Social development, context, and conflict.* Cambridge: Cambridge University Press.

Turiel, E. (2006). Thought, emotions, and social interactional processes in moral development. In M. Killen & J. G. Smetana (Eds.), *Handbook of moral development* (pp. 7–35). Mahwah, NJ: Lawrence Erlbaum.

Turiel, E. (in press). Thought about actions in social domains: Morality, social conventions, and social interactions. *Cognitive Development.*

Turiel, E., Hildebrandt, C., & Wainryb, C. (1991). Judging social issues: Difficulties, inconsistencies, and consistencies. *Monographs of the Society for Research in Child Development, 56* (2, Serial No. 224).

Turiel, E., Killen, M., & Helwig, C. C. (1987). Morality: Its structure, functions and vagaries. In J. Kagan & S. Lamb (Eds.), *The emergence of moral concepts in young children* (pp. 155–244). Chicago: University of Chicago Press.

Turiel, E., & Perkins, S. A. (2004). Flexibilities of mind: Conflict and Culture. *Human Development, 47,* 158–178.

Turiel, E., & Wainryb, C. (1994). Social reasoning and the varieties of social experiences in cultural contexts. In H. W. Reese (Ed.), *Advances in child development and behavior* (Vol. 25, pp. 289–326). New York: Academic Press.

Turiel, E., & Wainryb, C. (1998). Concepts of freedoms and rights in a traditional hierarchically organized society. *British Journal of Developmental Psychology.*

Tversky, A., & Kahneman, D. (1983). Extensional versus intuitive reasoning: The conjunction fallacy in probability judgment. *Psychological Review, 90,* 293–315.

Wainryb, C., Brehl, B. A., & Matwin, S. (2005). Being hurt and hurting others: Children's narrative accounts and moral judgments of their own interpersonal conflicts. *Monographs of the Society for Research in Child Development, 70* (3, Serial No. 281).

Wainryb, C., & Turiel, E. (1994). Dominance, subordination, and concepts of personal entitlements in cultural contexts. *Child Development, 65,* 1701–1722.

Wikan, U. (1996). *Tomorrow, God willing: Self-made destinies in Cairo.* Chicago: University of Chicago Press.

Wikan, U. (2002). *Generous betrayal: Politics of culture in the new Europe.* Chicago: University of Chicago Press.

Author Index

Subject Index